Bruce Songs

BRUCE
SONGS

The Music of
BRUCE SPRINGSTEEN,
Album-by-Album, Song-by-Song

KENNETH WOMACK & KENNETH L. CAMPBELL

Rutgers University Press
New Brunswick, Camden, and Newark, New Jersey
London and Oxford

Rutgers University Press is a department of Rutgers, The State University of New Jersey, one of the leading public research universities in the nation. By publishing worldwide, it furthers the University's mission of dedication to excellence in teaching, scholarship, research, and clinical care.

Library of Congress Cataloging-in-Publication Data

Names: Womack, Kenneth, author. | Campbell, Kenneth L., author.
Title: Bruce songs : the music of Bruce Springsteen, album-by-album, song-by-song / Kenneth Womack and Kenneth L. Campbell.
Description: [1.] | New Brunswick : Rutgers University Press, 2024. | Includes bibliographical references and index.
Identifiers: LCCN 2024005133 | ISBN 9781978830714 (hardcover) | ISBN 9781978830738 (epub) | ISBN 9781978830745 (pdf)
Subjects: LCSH: Springsteen, Bruce—Criticism and interpretation. | Springsteen, Bruce—Analysis, appreciation. | Springsteen, Bruce—Discography. | Rock music—United States—History and criticism. | LCGFT: Discographies.
Classification: LCC ML420.S77 B777 2024 | DDC 782.42166092—dc23/eng/20240202
LC record available at https://lccn.loc.gov/2024005133

A British Cataloging-in-Publication record for this book is available from the British Library.

∞ The paper used in this publication meets the requirements of the American National Standard for Information Sciences—Permanence of Paper for Printed Library Materials, ANSI Z39.48-1992.

rutgersuniversitypress.org

For Adele Zerilli Springsteen (1925–2024)

Contents

Preface

The life and work of Bruce Springsteen have enjoyed increasing critical attention since the 1970s. His distinctive achievements as a musician and time-eclipsing songwriter clearly merit this level of scholarship. For the purposes of this book, we have drawn William J. Dowlding's *Beatlesongs* (1989) as our model. Along with Mark Lewisohn's groundbreaking *The Beatles Recording Sessions* (1988), Dowlding's work provided scholars with a vital starting place for exploring the Beatles' corpus. In terms of Springsteen's corpus, we hope that readers will enjoy a similar vantage point with *Bruce Songs*.

Our book is divided into three principal sections, including discussion of the studio albums, a discography, and a bibliography and sources for further reading. Given that Springsteen's primary achievement involves his twenty-one landmark album releases, we have devoted particular attention to providing a detailed study of each album's composition and production, as well as its commercial release and public reception. Additionally, each album entry includes comprehensive information about the musicians and production personnel. In order to trace Springsteen's musical and commercial growth, we have also compiled vital information, commentary, and statistics from authoritative sources. Each entry features a series of contemporaneous reviews and, whenever possible, insider accounts about the album's origins and recording. Considerable attention is devoted to examining each song within the context of the album in which it was originally released. Finally, the book brings the artist's work into greater relief through the inclusion of several sidebars devoted to key moments in Springsteen's life and times.

In this way, *Bruce Songs* provides music fans, students, and teachers with an introductory guide to Springsteen's recordings. It is our sincere hope that readers will not only learn more about each album but find themselves returning to the recordings themselves in order to put their knowledge into practice and to glean even more enjoyment from Springsteen's timeless creations.

Bruce Songs

THE
STUDIO
ALBUMS

GREETINGS FROM ASBURY PARK, N.J.

Released in January 1973, Springsteen's debut album found the nascent recording artist already at a creative crossroads. On the one hand, he was being touted as the second incarnation of Bob Dylan; industry stalwart John Hammond famously signed both artists with Columbia Records, in 1961 and 1972, respectively. With his acoustic guitar in hand and freewheeling penchant for sticking a rhyme, Springsteen seemed to fit the bill. But, on the other hand, Springsteen had spent the past several years plying his trade as a bandleader of groups such as Steel Mill and the Bruce Springsteen Band, both of which had a proclivity for electric guitar rock. Which Springsteen persona would win out—the folkster or the metal head?

Springsteen would never forget the moment he and his manager crossed the threshold into Hammond's office. "Immediately, as the door opened, my representative, Mike Appel, showed a personal tendency for unnecessary confrontation that would weigh on us as time passed," Springsteen later wrote. "I figure once the door is open you can stop kicking at it. Not Mike;

he walked in swinging. Straightaway, with no discernible self-consciousness and before I'd played a note, he told John Hammond of Columbia Records I was perhaps the second coming of Jesus, Muhammad, and Buddha and he'd brought me there to see if Hammond's discovery of Dylan was a fluke or if he really had ears. I found this an interesting way of introducing and ingratiating ourselves to the man who held our future in his hands" (Springsteen, *Born to Run*, 2016).

Appel's gambit clearly succeeded. *Greetings from Asbury Park, N.J.* was produced by Appel and his partner, songwriter Jim Cretecos, at low-budget 914 Sound Studios, a former filling station in Blauvelt, New York. The album was recorded between June and October 1972, with the lion's share of the work being carried out in the last week of June. Things came to a head when Appel submitted the LP to Columbia Records president Clive Davis in August 1972. The draft version of *Greetings* represented both halves of Springsteen's artistic persona. Appel and Hammond preferred the solo acoustic songs that had succeeded in getting Bruce's foot in the door, while Springsteen favored the band numbers. They effected a compromise by including five solo acoustic numbers and five band recordings.

But Davis wasn't having it. While he enjoyed the recordings, the label head didn't hear a potential hit single among its contents, sending Springsteen back to the drawing board. In short order, Springsteen composed "Blinded by the Light" and "Spirit in the Night," both of which he recorded on September 11, 1972, with a three-person lineup that included Springsteen on guitar, bass, and piano, backed by Vini "Mad Dog" Lopez on drums and Clarence Clemons, who had been unavailable during the earlier sessions, on saxophone. With the addition of "Blinded by the Light" and "Spirit in the Night," Davis duly approved *Greetings* for release, making special note of Springsteen's enthusiastic response to his concerns. And with that, an exciting new career was underway.

HISTORICAL CONTEXT

"The sixties are over, so set him free," the folk singer Joan Baez sang in a song devoted to Bob Dylan called "Winds of the Old Days," which appeared on her 1975 album, *Diamonds and Rust*. Dylan, along with Elvis Presley and the Beatles, was one of the major musical influences on a young Bruce Springsteen. Dylan especially influenced his first studio album, *Greetings from Asbury Park, N.J.*, released on January 5, 1973. When Baez referred to the end of the "sixties," she no more referred merely to the chronological end of a ten-year period than anyone else who used that term practically from 1970 forward. The sixties had come to represent a period of civil rights marches; protests against the Vietnam War; sexual liberation; a youth counterculture that emphasized personal freedom, including the use of drugs, changing dress codes, and lifestyle; a nascent women's liberation movement; and, more or less uniting all of these developments, rock and roll music.

In fact, popular music itself had seen a plethora of new and interesting developments, and rock and roll music, which had always incorporated a blend of diverse musical genres, enveloping a wide range of subgenres, became increasingly known simply as rock music. Rock contained pop rock, acid rock, psychedelic rock, folk rock, country rock, and hard rock, among other variations, but importantly included soul, rhythm and blues, funk, and a number of additional subgenres of pop music. These variations were designed to appeal to the outsized

Springsteen's "Mutt"

Perhaps second only to Paul McCartney's iconic Höfner violin bass, Bruce Springsteen's Fender Esquire is one of the most recognizable instruments in music history. Springsteen purchased the instrument in 1972 after landing his first recording contract with Columbia Records. The hybrid Fender guitar featured a Telecaster body and an Esquire neck. Springsteen later recalled that he bought the guitar from Phil Petillo's Belmar, New Jersey, guitar shop for the modest sum of $185. "With its wood body worn in like the piece of the cross it was," Springsteen later wrote, "it became the guitar I'd play for the next 40 years. It was the best deal of my life" (St. John, "Springsteen's Favorite Guitar," 2016).

The guitar had a familiar butterscotch-blonde finish and jet-black pick guard, and Springsteen simply couldn't resist making the purchase. "I wanted a Telecaster because I had played a Telecaster when I was younger," he recalled during an interview with the Rock and Roll Hall of Fame. "It was a versatile instrument. It was a light instrument. I wasn't playing heavy rock and roll anymore. I was playing something that was tilting more to soul music, and so I wanted a guitar that could handle the funk and that feeling." According to Springsteen's guitar techs, the legendary guitar was likely manufactured in 1953 or 1954. After making the sale to Springsteen, Petillo added several modifications, including adding hot-wound single-coil pickups and installing his own Petillo Precision Frets, with their distinctive triangular cross-section.

His "mutt" guitar is "unique amongst all my guitars the way it sounds," Springsteen remarked in his interview with the Rock and Roll Hall of Fame. "For me, when I put it on, I don't feel like I have a guitar on. It's such an integral part of me. I've held it aloft to the audience on thousands and thousands and thousands of nights, I suppose with the idea that it says something about the power of rock and roll, and the power of us."

Springsteen's "Mutt" (Kenneth Womack) [Fender Telecaster]

baby-boom generation, comprising those born between 1946 and 1964, which exercised an enormous influence on the culture, as well as the music and entertainment industries.

Bruce Springsteen, born in 1949, was part of the baby boom that came of age during this turbulent period and provided a new generation of artists who emerged in the 1970s, by which time much of the rebellious spirit and many of the radical hopes for change associated with the 1960s had died or ended in profound disappointment and alienation. All of Springsteen's heroes predated the baby boom: Elvis Presley was born in 1935; Bob Dylan in 1941; George Harrison,

Tex and Marion Vinyard

One of the premises of Malcolm Gladwell's 2008 book *Outliers*, which dealt with the conditions and reasons for success, was the support successful individuals receive from others along the way. (The book is probably best known for its emphasis on the so-called 10,000-hour rule, which describes the amount of time supposedly necessary for one to become a master practitioner of a craft, a condition that Springsteen certainly must have met by the time he released his first album in 1973.) Springsteen could give, and graciously and often has given, others credit for their assistance and inspiration on his road to stardom. Perhaps no people played bigger roles in instilling confidence and alleviating the doubts of an insecure teenage musician than Gordon "Tex" and Marion Vinyard. Bruce was first introduced to Tex, a thirty-two-year-old laborer out on strike from his factory job, and his wife, Marion, by George Theiss, who had invited Bruce to audition as lead guitarist for his garage rock band, the Castiles. The Castiles had taken to practicing in the Vinyards' apartment, and Tex became a manager, mentor, and surrogate father for the boys in the band. The Vinyards had no children of their own, and Marion developed a fondness for the young musicians, detecting an innocence in them that belied the false bravado required of anyone willing to put their skills on display on a stage. It was the foresightful Tex, however, who saw something special about the young guitarist who had come to his house for that audition. At first, he encouraged Springsteen to learn more songs before he would consider admitting him to the band, but when Springsteen showed up the next night having mastered five new ones, Tex could hardly contain his excitement and admitted the future Rock and Roll Hall of Famer to the Castiles. In his 2016 memoir, *Born to Run*, Springsteen recalled the role of the Vinyards not only fondly but lovingly, and gave them credit not only for accepting him and his bandmates but for passionately encouraging their hopes, dreams, and aspirations—exactly what the young Springsteen needed at that stage of his life.

the youngest of the Beatles, in 1943. Therefore, when Springsteen released his first album in 1973, it appeared in a different time and historical context than theirs: these earlier artists had shaped the Sixties; Bruce Springsteen was shaped by them. He had gotten his start playing in a series of bands around the New Jersey shore town of Asbury Park, which he significantly referenced in the title of his debut album. Several of his early songs with these bands provided a critique of the Vietnam War and the effect it had on soldiers and on American society.

But no one who had heard the Castiles, Steel Mill, Child, or any of the other iterations of Springsteen's early bands had heard anything like the songs he introduced on *Greetings*. They had impressed John Hammond at Columbia Records enough to give him a recording contract and Springsteen used that to create a first album of entirely original material intended to display his skills as a singer-songwriter. The record label promoted Springsteen as the next Bob Dylan and tried to capitalize on the growing popularity of singer-songwriters like Jackson Browne, Carole King, and James Taylor, but Springsteen was doing something unique that reflected the changing times. The conservative president Richard Nixon had won reelection in 1972 and had authorized an intensified bombing campaign in the week that saw the appearance of *Greetings*, an album that looked at the end of youthful innocence exactly when the country had lost its own and there was no clear direction forward for Springsteen's generation or the country at large.

PRODUCTION

Released on January 5, 1973, Columbia Records
Produced by Mike Appel and Jim Cretecos
Engineered by Louis Lahav
Recorded at 914 Sound Studios, Blauvelt, NY, June to October 1972
Mixed by Jack Ashkinazy at Columbia Sound Studios

PERSONNEL

Bruce Springsteen: vocals, electric guitar, electric bass, acoustic guitar, piano, keyboards, harmonica
Clarence Clemons: tenor saxophone, backing vocals
Vini "Mad Dog" Lopez: drums, backing vocals
David Sancious: piano, organ, keyboards
Garry Tallent: electric bass
Richard Davis: upright double bass
Harold Wheeler: piano

COVER ART AND PACKAGING

Cover design: John Berg
Front cover postcard photograph courtesy of Tichnor Brothers
Back cover photography: Fred Lombardi

Bruce Springsteen: "When I was recording my first album, the record company spent a lot of money taking pictures of me in New York City. But . . . something didn't feel quite right. So I was walking down the boardwalk one day, stopped at a souvenir stand and bought a postcard that said 'Greetings from Asbury Park.' I remember thinking, 'Yeah, that's me'" (New Jersey Hall of Fame induction acceptance speech, April 10, 2014).

TRACK LISTING

All songs composed by Bruce Springsteen

Side one
1. "Blinded by the Light"
2. "Growin' Up"
3. "Mary Queen of Arkansas"
4. "Does This Bus Stop at 82nd Street?"
5. "Lost in the Flood"
Side two
1. "The Angel"
2. "For You"
3. "Spirit in the Night"
4. "It's Hard to Be a Saint in the City"

CONTEMPORARY REVIEWS

Richard Williams (*The Times*, April 14, 1973): "Since the beginning of the 1970s, pop music's primary search has been for the current equivalents of those major revolutionaries of the previous decade, the Beatles and Bob Dylan. Both, of course, are inimitable and irreplaceable, but pop is badly in need of figures of similar stature. A 22-year-old American named Bruce Springsteen will, within the next few weeks, be dubbed 'the new Dylan.' . . . Springsteen is special because he's mastered Dylan's Joycean use of imagery. He spits out his rapid-fire verses with a raging intensity and, further, he makes more consistent sense than his predecessor did. Dylan's scattershot effect is more tightly focused in Springsteen's work, the words rarely straying from their target-area. Over an imaginative, hard-edged small band, he sings in a tired, abrasive drawl which sometimes switches to a shout of pure youthful arrogance. His stories are riveting, told through vivid description and freewheeling internal rhymes."

Dave Marsh (*Creem*, May 1973): "Well, bullshit, because Bruce Springsteen is really a throwback all the way to the '50s. Springsteen is like Bo Diddley, like Elvis, like Jerry Lee. His entire career is based upon a total disregard for taste and control on the most fundamental level. . . . If Elvis is the Pope of Pop with the ultimate secular call-and-response gospel show at his fingertips, Bruce Springsteen is like a Gnostic who spent three and a half years just slightly A.D. sitting on a rock in the middle of the desert, without eating so much as a breadcrust and came down jibjabbering, having not only seen the Lord but become him, if only for a Warholian quarter-hour. He spews it on out."

Lester Bangs (*Rolling Stone*, July 5, 1973): "Because what makes Bruce totally unique and cosmically surfeiting is his words. Hot damn, what a passel o' verbiage! He's got more of them crammed into this album than any other record released this year, but it's all right because they all fit snug, it ain't like Harry Chapin tearing right-angle malapropisms out of his larynx.

What's more, each and every one of 'em has at least one other one here that it rhymes with. Some of 'em can mean something socially or otherwise, but there's plenty of 'em that don't even pretend to, reveling in the joy of utter crass showoff talent run amuck and totally out of control: 'Madman drummers bummers and Indians in the summer with a teenage diplomat / In the dumps with the mumps as the adolescent pumps his way into his hat' begins the very first song, and after that things just keep getting more breathtakingly complicated. You might think it's some kinda throwback, but it's really bracing as hell because it's obvious that B.S. don't give a shit. He slingshoots his random rivets at you and you can catch as many as you want or let 'em all clatter right off the wall which maybe's where they belong anyway. Bruce Springsteen is a bold new talent with more than a mouthful to say, and one look at the pic on the back will tell you he's got the glam to go places in this Gollywoodlawn world to boot. Watch for him; he's not the new John Prine."

PROMOTION

The ad campaign for *Greetings from Asbury Park, N.J.* concentrated on promoting Springsteen as the "New Dylan" in regional, national, and international markets.

CHART ACTION

Billboard Top LPs and Tape: did not chart during its initial release.

Billboard Top LPs and Tape (October 18, 1975): number sixty.

With the success of *Born to Run, Greetings from Asbury Park, N.J.* debuted on the

Billboard charts at number 184 on July 26, 1975. The number-one album that week was the Eagles' *One of These Nights*. The album peaked at number sixty on October 18, 1975. The number-one album that week was John Denver's *Windsong*.

Greetings from Asbury Park, N.J. spent forty-three weeks on the *Billboard* charts.

COMMENTS FROM SPRINGSTEEN AND HIS CIRCLE

Bruce Springsteen: "'I see these situations happening when I sing them, and I know the characters well. I use them in different songs and see them in shadows. They're probably based on people I know or else they are flashes that just appear there. There's a lot of activity, a whole mess of people. It's like if you're walking down the street, my songs are just what you see, only distorted. A lot of songs were written without any music at all. It's just that I do like to sing the words.' . . . 'My songs are supposed to be bigger than life' he claims, but he insists he has not been blessed with any greater powers of insight than the next person. 'Jersey was so intense you couldn't even walk down the street, so I used to go to New York and hang out in the village mostly but also uptown a bit I was mostly by myself with no particular place to go'" (*Zig Zag* magazine, 1978).

Vini Lopez: "I was working in a boatyard, and he called me up, and said, 'Listen, I'm going to be doing an album, you wanna play on it?' I said sure. We started rehearsing down in Point Pleasant and got the first album together in about a week, actually . . . it only took one day to do all the basic tracks!" (*Thunder Road* magazine, 1979).

Clive Davis: "When Bruce finished the first album, I listened for a breakthrough radio cut and didn't hear one, so I called him. I said, 'you know, everybody needs a breakthrough cut. Have you thought which could be yours? Because I'm not sure if you have one.' Most artists, if you discuss that get very defensive, but he said, 'you know, you're right. Let me spend some time with this.' And he went back and wrote 'Blinded by the Light' and 'Spirit in the Night'" (*Backstreets* magazine, 1998).

Mike Appel: "I thought Bruce and an acoustic guitar was going to be enough. And so did Hammond. There was a purity about Bruce and his music we were all entertaining. . . . [It] was the most screwed-up audition. Guys didn't know the songs, they weren't together, they weren't adding anything, and I told Bruce. 'No,' he said, 'I need the band'" (Eliot and Appel, *Down Thunder Road*, 1992).

MISCELLANEOUS

Mike Appel estimated the production costs for *Greetings from Asbury Park, N.J.* at $11,000. With a budget of $40,000, the differential afforded Springsteen and Appel a rare profit during his early years as a professional musician (Eliot and Appel, *Down Thunder Road*, 1992).

During his 1974 audition to join the E Street Band, Max Weinberg performed the drum parts for "Blinded by the Light" and "4th of July, Asbury Park (Sandy)" (*Thunder Road* magazine, 1979).

In 2003, *Rolling Stone* ranked the album at number 379 among its 500 Greatest Albums of All Time. In 2013, the magazine listed the

LP among the 100 Greatest Debut Albums of All Time.

On November 22, 2009, Springsteen and the E Street Band performed *Greetings from Asbury Park, N.J.* in its entirety at Buffalo, New York's HSBC Arena.

SONG ANALYSES

SIDE ONE

"Blinded by the Light"
Bruce Springsteen: vocals, electric guitar, electric bass, keyboards
Clarence Clemons: saxophone, backing vocals
Vini "Mad Dog" Lopez: drums, backing vocals
Harold Wheeler: piano

Written with the aid of his rhyming dictionary, "Blinded by the Light" is a fusillade of words and imagery. In *VH1 Storytellers*, Springsteen claimed that "Blinded by the Light" was the lyrical embodiment of why he never took drugs. The song contains clear references to the composer's own life, including "madman drummers" (Vini Lopez) and "Indians in the summer," the name of his Little League baseball team. For the song's guitar introduction, Springsteen drew on the rhythm part from the Doobie Brothers' "Listen to the Music," the band's breakthrough 1972 hit. In its *Bruce Springsteen Collector's Edition* (2022), *Rolling Stone* listed "Blinded by the Light" as number eighty-nine among the artist's top 100 songs.

CHART ACTION
"Blinded by the Light," *Billboard* Hot 100: did not chart.

"Blinded by the Light" b/w "The Angel" was released in February 1973. The number-one song that week was Elton John's "Crocodile Rock."

With the conspicuous addition of the piano melody from "Chopsticks," Manfred Mann's Earth Band featured a cover version of "Blinded by the Light" on *The Roaring Silence* (1976). The group's take on "Blinded by the Light" registered a number-one hit on the *Billboard* charts, marking Springsteen's only career chart-topper as a songwriter on the *Billboard* Hot 100.

"Growin' Up"
Bruce Springsteen: vocals, acoustic guitar
Vini "Mad Dog" Lopez: drums
David Sancious: piano, keyboards
Garry Tallent: electric bass

An autobiographical tune about his adolescent experiences in Freehold, New Jersey, "Growin' Up" was included as part of Springsteen's 1972 audition for Columbia Records' John Hammond. The song underscores the nature of his rebellious teenage years, with Springsteen singing, "When they said, 'sit down,' I stood up." Springsteen's long-running references to automobiles is represented in the song when he refers to finding "the key to the universe" in "the engine of an old parked car." In addition to being featured on future compilation albums, his acoustic performance was included on *Chapter and Verse*, the companion recording for *Born to Run*, his 2016 autobiography. In its *Bruce Springsteen Collector's Edition* (2022), *Rolling Stone* listed "Growin' Up" as number forty-eight among the artist's top 100 songs.

David Bowie recorded a cover version of "Growin' Up" during the sessions for *Diamond Dogs* (1974). As *Rolling Stone*'s Andy Greene observed, "Shortly after *Pin Ups* was finished, he came across Bruce Springsteen's debut LP *Greetings from Asbury Park, NJ*. The album tanked in America despite a promotional campaign that called Springsteen the 'New Dylan,' but Bowie loved what he heard and covered

'Growin' Up' during the early sessions for *Diamond Dogs* with Ronnie Wood on guitar" (*Rolling Stone*, 2021). In 1990, Bowie's version was included as a bonus track on the rerelease of *Diamond Dogs*.

"Mary Queen of Arkansas"
Bruce Springsteen: vocals, acoustic guitar, harmonica

As with "Growin' Up," "Mary Queen of Arkansas" was performed by Springsteen during his May 1972 audition for John Hammond. The song originally found its inspiration in *Mary, Queen of Scots*, a 1971 biopic devoted to the life of Mary Stuart, queen of Scotland, which starred Vanessa Redgrave in the title role. For "Mary Queen of Arkansas," Springsteen creates a literary burlesque by taking its high subject (Mary, Queen of Scots) and rendering it in a lower or debased form (Mary, Queen of Arkansas), a point that Springsteen makes when he sings his doubts about the Arkansas queen's purity: "your white skin is deceivin'." A burlesque is understood to be an absurd or comically exaggerated imitation of something, especially in a literary or dramatic work. Springsteen would adopt a similar storytelling technique in *Born to Run*'s "Jungleland."

"Does This Bus Stop at 82nd Street?"
Bruce Springsteen: vocals, acoustic guitar
Vini "Mad Dog" Lopez: drums
David Sancious: piano
Garry Tallent: electric bass

Originally recorded as part of Springsteen's Columbia Records demo in May 1972, "Does This Bus Stop at 82nd Street?" finds its roots in a bus trip that Springsteen took from New Jersey into Manhattan to visit his girlfriend in Spanish Harlem. Along the way, he provides a narration of the city streets, as well as non sequitur references to "Broadway Mary" and

Academy Award–winning actress Joan Fontaine. Lacking a chorus, the song exists as an anomaly among Springsteen's corpus.

"Lost in the Flood"
Bruce Springsteen: vocals, piano (uncredited)
Vini "Mad Dog" Lopez: drums
David Sancious: piano, organ
Garry Tallent: electric bass
Steven Van Zandt: sound effects (uncredited)

Drawing upon biblical imagery, "Lost in the Flood" explores the death of Springsteen's friend Walter Cichon during the Vietnam War, as well as issues associated with the harsh treatment of veterans in the United States. Springsteen later remarked that "Walter Cichon was the greatest rock-and-roll front man on the Jersey Shore in the bar-band '60s. He was in a group called the Motifs. He was the first real rock star I ever laid my eyes on. He had it in his bones and in his blood and in the way he dressed and carried himself. . . . In our little area, he showed us by the way that he lived. That you could live your life the way you chose. You could look the way you wanted to look. If you had the courage, you could play the music that was in your heart that you wanted and needed to play" (*Springsteen on Broadway*, 2017). In its *Bruce Springsteen Collector's Edition* (2022), *Rolling Stone* listed "Lost in the Flood" as number forty-seven among the artist's top 100 songs.

SIDE TWO

"The Angel"
Bruce Springsteen: vocals
David Sancious: piano
Richard Davis: upright double bass

With "The Angel," Springsteen traces the imagery of combustion engines and highways that characterizes much of his early songwriting. "The Angel" refers to a motorcycle-borne outlaw who traverses "hubcap heaven," the simultaneously lonely and dangerous thoroughfares. In a key line from "The Angel" that presages "Born to Run" and its "highways jammed with broken heroes," Springsteen sings about life on the interstate, which is "choked with nomadic hordes in Volkswagen vans with full running boards."

"For You"
Bruce Springsteen: guitar, vocals
Vini "Mad Dog" Lopez: drums
David Sancious: piano, keyboards
Garry Tallent: electric bass

In "For You," Springsteen explores a woman's suicidal intentions and her lover's desperate intentions to save her despite the fact that her life's been "one long emergency." In its *Bruce Springsteen Collector's Edition* (2022), *Rolling Stone* listed "For You" as number thirty-eight among the artist's top 100 songs. Greg Kihn recorded a cover version of the song for *Greg Kihn Again* (1975). Manfred Mann's Earth Band recorded a cover version of "For You" for *Chance* (1980). The band's "For You" single failed to enjoy the same level of success as its versions of "Blinded by the Light" and "Spirit in the Night."

"Spirit in the Night"
Bruce Springsteen: piano, electric bass, clapping, vocals
Clarence Clemons: saxophone, clapping, backing vocals
Vini "Mad Dog" Lopez: drums, clapping, backing vocals
Harold Wheeler: piano

With Clemons's atmospheric saxophone performance, "Spirit in the Night" traces the story of a group of teenagers hanging out at Greasy Lake, where a motley array of characters such as

Wild Billy, Hazy Davy, Crazy Janey, Killer Joe, G-Man, and the Mission Man pursue a night of drinking and sexual high jinks. Greasy Lake likely refers to Ocean County, New Jersey's Lake Shenandoah Park. The character Crazy Jane may exist as a reference to Irish poet William Butler Yeats's series of poems about a lascivious character of the same name. Likely a prostitute, Yeats's Crazy Jane acts as an earthly temptress who blurs notions of purity with sin, recognizing that our desires for attaining goodness are often trumped by humanity's inevitable imperfections. In its *Bruce Springsteen Collector's Edition* (2022), *Rolling Stone* listed "Spirit in the Night" as number thirty-three among the artist's top 100 songs.

CHART ACTION
"Spirit in the Night," *Billboard* Hot 100: did not chart.

"Spirit in the Night" b/w "For You" was released in May 1973. The number-one song that week was Tony Orlando and Dawn's "Tie a Yellow Ribbon Round the Ole Oak Tree."

Manfred Mann's Earth Band recorded a cover version of the song as "Spirits in the Night" for *Nightingales and Bombers* (1975). "Spirits in the Night" notched a number ninety-seven showing on the *Billboard* Hot 100.

"It's Hard to Be a Saint in the City"
Bruce Springsteen: vocals, guitar
Vini "Mad Dog" Lopez: drums
David Sancious: piano
Garry Tallent: electric bass

A classic Springsteen composition about a young man's desire to maintain his goodness in spite of the city's manifold temptations, "It's Hard to Be a Saint in the City" finds its main character wrestling with urban demons involving greed and sinfulness. The song reportedly inspired Mike Appel to become Springsteen's manager. As with "Growin' Up" and "Mary Queen of Arkansas," "It's Hard to Be a Saint in the City" was performed by Springsteen during his May 1972 audition for John Hammond. As with several songs on the album, Springsteen composed the song in 1971, when he was twenty-two. David Bowie recorded a cover version during the sessions for *Young Americans* (1975). In 1989, Bowie's version of the song was released as part of his *Sound + Vision* box set.

THE WILD, THE INNOCENT AND THE E STREET SHUFFLE

Released in November 1973, Springsteen's sophomore album made for a starkly different production than *Greetings from Asbury Park, N.J.* While the previous record featured both solo and full-band efforts behind his songs, *The Wild, the Innocent and the E Street Shuffle* was a group-oriented tour-de-force. As producers, Mike Appel and Jim Cretecos felt more sure-handed in the control booth, creating a more cohesive and exciting album than its predecessor. For his part, Springsteen was heartily satisfied with the results, later writing

that "this record gave me much greater satisfaction than *Greetings*. I felt it was a true example of what I could do with the recording, playing, and arranging of my band. With 'Kitty's Back,' 'Rosalita,' 'New York City Serenade' and the semiautobio of 'Sandy,' I was confident we showed the kind of depth, fun, and excitement we could stir on records" (*Born to Run*, 2016).

Working at 914 Sound Studios, Springsteen recorded the album between May and September 1973, with many of the basic tracking sessions taking place during the later weeks of June. Springsteen's backing band featured Clarence Clemons on saxophone, Danny Federici on organ and accordion, David Sancious on piano, Garry Tallent on bass, and Vini "Mad Dog" Lopez on drums. For Springsteen, having both Federici and Sancious afforded the band a powerful "double keyboard attack." Living in New Jersey meant braving the traffic of Greater New York City to make the trek up to 914 Sound Studios. "We drove every day to Blauvelt up from the Shore and back again every night," Springsteen recalled. "In the end we held marathon sessions around the clock. Clarence and I pitched a tent out back in a small yard and slept there for days while finishing our final overdubs. Toward the end of the mixing process I'd been up for three days with no stimulants. I couldn't stay awake for one complete playback of a song; I kept nodding off a minute or two into each cut until someone would rustle me awake to approve the rest of the mix" (Springsteen, *Born to Run*, 2016).

Drawing inspiration from *The Wild and the Innocent*, the 1959 Audie Murphy Western, Springsteen titled his new LP *The Wild, the Innocent and the E Street Shuffle*. On the eve of the album's release, Springsteen discovered that the landscape at Columbia Records had changed dramatically; John Hammond had drifted into retirement and Clive Davis had shifted into new pastures by founding Arista Records. "The great record men, my great supporters, the men who brought me into the company, were vanishing," Springsteen wrote. "There was a power void and a variety of new people stepped in to fill the gap. I was called in to see Charles Koppelman, then head of A&R, to review the album. We played a good piece of the first side, and I was immediately informed the album was unreleasable" (Springsteen, *Born to Run*, 2016).

Proud and confident about the state of *The Wild, the Innocent and the E Street Shuffle*, Springsteen refused to budge. At that, Koppelman delivered a stinging retort. "If I insisted on the recording being released as it was it would most likely go in the trash heap, receive little promotion and, along with me, disappear," Springsteen recalled. "What could I do? I liked it the way it was, so I fiercely insisted it remain unmeddled with, and what Mr. Koppelman promised was exactly what happened" (Springsteen, *Born to Run*, 2016).

HISTORICAL CONTEXT

The Wild, the Innocent and the E Street Shuffle did not have perhaps the direct connection to history that some of Springsteen's later albums would, nor did it address contemporary issues to the extent that his first album, *Greetings from Asbury Park, N.J.*, did. But every album, book, film, television series, or work of art is created at a particular moment, in a particular place and time. In this case, Bruce Springsteen's second album still very much reflected his concern with the local perspective from Asbury Park, where Springsteen had lived in the three years preceding its 1973 release.

Asbury Park had suffered more than most towns from the race riots and urban blight that had characterized many parts of the country in the late 1960s and early 1970s. Springsteen's beloved boardwalk was still there but, compared to its heyday, it drew fewer people, while the painted signs and buildings seemed faded, the place more run down, lacking the ostentation of years past. The lyrics came out of the changes, frustrations, and aspirations of Springsteen's own life, but they still reflected a sense of disillusionment that afflicted society at large and especially the younger generation who had

The Next Bob Dylan

Once they started to discover Bruce Spring-steen's mastery of songwriting and live performance, audiences, including executives at his record label at Columbia and rock journalists, began to situate him within the industry, frequently by comparing him to Bob Dylan and promoting him as "the new Bob Dylan." Springsteen bristled at the label and the hype associated with it, partly because he knew how hard it would be to live up to the folk legend and partly because he wanted to be judged on his own merits and had enough creative pride to not want others to consider him a clone of someone else.

Even so, Dylan was, by Springsteen's own admission, an important (if often exaggerated) influence and enough similarities existed between the dense and complex lyrics of Springsteen's early albums and Dylan compositions like "Desolation Row" and "Like a Rolling Stone" that perhaps such comparisons, however unfair, were inevitable. It also did not help that John Hammond, who signed Springsteen to Columbia, had also discovered Bob Dylan and signed him to the same label in 1961. Chris Charlesworth noted the similarities between Springsteen and Dylan in the British music publication *Melody Maker* in February 1974, even comparing their appearance, although he acknowledged that Bruce looked "more like Dylan of 1965 than Dylan of 1974." In a March 1974 review of a live performance at Georgetown University, *Sounds* writer Jerry Gilbert wrote that "he came on like Bob Dylan—a frail city urchin with a scrubby beard and tousled hair and clothes that he might have been living in for the past six months."

Critics largely panned *Greetings from Asbury Park, N.J.*, and apart from a few stations in New Jersey and Philadelphia the album got very little airplay. "The next Bob Dylan indeed!" they seemed to scoff. But as he started to become better known and critics started listening to Springsteen's second album, *The Wild, the Innocent and the E Street Shuffle*, they began to change their tune. It helped that respected critic Jon Landau gave him such a glowing review and called him "the future of rock and roll." In November 1974, Michael Watts wrote a review in *Melody Maker* that addressed the comparisons between Springsteen and Dylan and suggested that perhaps it was time to move past them. Noting that it was no insult to say someone has been influenced by Dylan ("if you were healthy at all . . . you'd better be influenced by him!"), Watts gave a glowing review of a series of now-renowned Springsteen performances in Texas, noting how Springsteen's appeal had now outgrown the Jersey Shore and New York City areas. One of the themes of the article was that, by remaining true to himself, Bruce Springsteen was starting to be recognized as a unique and creative artist in his own right. By the time of his third album, *Born to Run*, no one was talking about the next Bob Dylan—they were talking about the new Bruce Springsteen.

come of age during the previous decade and who had hoped for better.

Springsteen biographer Dave Marsh wrote, "The Band sings about an America most of us have felt, but have never seen. Springsteen sings about a version of the nation most of us have seen without feeling" (*Two Hearts*, 2004).

In the country, the televised Senate Watergate hearings had just ended in August, having preoccupied the American viewing public for much of the summer. Negotiations for settling the Vietnam War and bringing American troops home were ongoing. An embargo on oil exports from Arab countries in the Middle East that October in retaliation for US support for Israel in the Yom Kippur War would call attention to the fragility of the American economy and its dependence on foreign oil. When he sang his goodbye to Sandy in "4th of July, Asbury Park," Springsteen was capturing both an end to one phase of his life and a metaphorical end to an era, both singer and country unsure of what would come next. As Peter Ames Carlin put it, "Eyes wide open mile after mile, Bruce traced a vision of modern American life as viewed by the perpetual passerby. All of it reminded him of his own life" (*Bruce*, 2012).

When he recorded *The Wild, the Innocent and the E Street Shuffle*, Springsteen had just come off a disappointing tour as the opening act for the popular jazz rock band Chicago. After a particularly disheartening reception in Philadelphia, Springsteen vowed never to perform an opening act again. Like the singer in "Rosalita," who had just received "a big advance,"

Springsteen had much larger aspirations for himself and his band.

PRODUCTION

Released on November 5, 1973, Columbia Records
Produced by Mike Appel and Jim Cretecos
Engineered by Louis Lahav
Recorded at 914 Sound Studios, Blauvelt, NY, May to September 1973

Vini Lopez recalled that during the production of *The Wild, the Innocent and the E Street Shuffle*, he and bandmate Clarence Clemons "used to camp out in army tents behind the record studio when we weren't needed" (*Tuesday Night Record Club*, 2022).

PERSONNEL

Bruce Springsteen: vocals, electric and acoustic guitars, harmonica, mandolin, recorder, maracas
Clarence Clemons: tenor saxophone, backing vocals
Danny Federici: piano, organ, accordion, backing vocals
Vini "Mad Dog" Lopez: drums, conga, triangle, tambourine, clapping, backing vocals
David Sancious: piano, mellotron, organ, clavinet, soprano saxophone, backing vocals
Garry Tallent: electric bass, backing vocals, tuba
Richard Blackwell: congas, percussion
Suki Lahav: backing vocals
Albee "Albany Al" Tellone: baritone saxophone

COVER ART AND PACKAGING

Cover design: Teresa Alfieri and John Berg
Front and back cover photography: David Gahr

For the LP's back cover, Gahr photographed Springsteen and his band in the doorway of a Long Branch, New Jersey, antique store. As for the cover photo, Vini Lopez commented that Gahr photographed Springsteen in a pizza restaurant: "Everybody thinks Bruce is so studious here," Lopez recalled. "He's actually wiping a piece of salami off; we were eating lunch at Roselli's pizza place" (*Tuesday Night Record Club*, 2022).

TRACK LISTING

All songs composed by Bruce Springsteen.

Side one
1. "The E Street Shuffle"
2. "4th of July, Asbury Park (Sandy)"
3. "Kitty's Back"
4. "Wild Billy's Circus Story"
Side two
1. "Incident on 57th Street"
2. "Rosalita (Come Out Tonight)"
3. "New York City Serenade"

UNRELEASED OUTTAKES

"The Fever": released on *18 Tracks* (1999)
"Seaside Bar Song": released on *Tracks* (1998)
"Santa Ana": released on *Tracks* (1998)
"Thundercrack": released on *Tracks* (1998)
"Zero and Blind Terry"

CONTEMPORARY REVIEWS

Nick Kent (*New Musical Express*, February 2, 1974): "Springsteen's new album is marginally better than the first if only because his band is more together, and the arrangements are often pretty neat. I really liked the track '4th July, Asbury Park (Sandy)' simply because it had an accordion featured on it—until Springsteen goes and ruins it all by growling a self-conscious 'Sandy, that waitress I was seeing, lost her desire for me.' No two ways about it, the boy just cannot step back to avoid that kind of greasy rococo overkill—he thrusts as much imagery as he can into one song until it all gets so bloated you don't even want to know what's going on. Sad really, because under it all you figure the guy might just have something to say. Oh, yeah, and that cover of him staring pensively into space? Betcha he's contemplating a wet-dream he had the night before about Rita Moreno. . . . Last year's Bob Dylan? Maybe Leonard Cohen'll write a song about him."

Bruce Pollock (*New York Times*, December 16, 1973): "Now, after five solid months of dedicated labor, that second piece of work is here . . . and in an era of diminishing returns, false prophets and false bottoms, where the best of our instant pop-up superstars are either choked-off, laid-back, lame or laid out flat, it is with a great sense of relief that I announce to the disbelievers that Bruce Springsteen has delivered another stone, howling, joyous monster of a record. Of course, the fanatics knew the issue was never really in doubt. Springsteen is a word virtuoso who uses language the way his bandmate Clarence Clemons plays the sax: tough, fast and funky, sometimes frivolous, often devastating. His lyrics are intuitive, emotional, a mass of flung images that spin toward you from all directions and somehow hang on a canvas—great swatches of local color that blend into a landscape of remembered adolescent scenes and dreams in the swamps and seasides of Jersey, in the slums of New York."

Ken Emerson (*Rolling Stone*, January 31, 1974): "Like *Greetings*, the new album is about the streets of New York and the tacky Jersey Shore,

but the lyrics are no longer merely zany cut-ups. They're striking amalgams of romance and gritty realism: 'And the boys from the casino dance with their shirts open like Latin lovers on the shore, / Chasin' all those silly New York virgins by the score.' The loveliness of the first line, the punk savvy of the second, and the humor of the ensemble add up to Springsteen's characteristic ambivalence and a complex appeal reminiscent of the Shangri-Las. In the midst of a raucous celebration of desire, 'Rosalita,' he can suddenly turn around and sing, 'Someday we'll look back on this and it will all seem funny.' But none of this would matter if the music were humdrum—it isn't. The band, especially David L. Sancious on keyboards and Clarence Clemons on saxes, cook with power and precision, particularly on 'Rosalita' and 'Kitty's Back,' the album's outstanding rockers. They're essentially an R&B outfit—funkybutt is Springsteen's musical pied-a-terre—but they can play anything thrown at them, be it jazz or *Highway 61 Revisited*. Springsteen himself is an undistinguished but extremely versatile guitarist, which he needs to be to follow his own changes."

Ed Ward (*Creem*, April 1974): "Well, talk about outa nowhere. Not completely out of thin air, maybe, but I woulda never thunk. . . . Listen, this album is great! I know, I know. You think Springsteen is some kinda wind-up wordmill, and that's pretty much what his first album sounded like to me, too, but this here is something else. It's either a flawed work of genius or else a work of flawed genius. It's irregular as hell, inconsistent, annoying sometimes, but once you've listened to it a couple times and start to see what's going on, you forgive all that and just Get Off. I do all the time, In fact, I haven't been so mystified and entranced by an album since *Astral Weeks*, and there's more than a couple parallels there. . . . He sounds like Van Morrison, for one thing. But he also sounds a lot like Mick Jagger, and Bob Dylan and Lou Reed. A lot of the time he sounds like Bruce Springsteen, too. The lyrics are . . . maddening. Thoroughly frustrating because a lot of the threads of storyline that get thrown out are never gathered together; a lot of the same words and images appear through the songs, and more than once he blows a powerful line by putting too many words in it, which makes me think he needs an editor. But Jesus, when the words and music jell, there is something there that'll make your hair stand on end."

Jon Landau (*Real Paper*, April 10, 1974): "Bruce Springsteen's *The Wild, the Innocent, and the E Street Shuffle* is the most underrated album so far this year. An impassioned and inspired Street fantasy that's as much fun as it is deep. Like so many special rock albums. *The E Street Shuffle* defines not only a persona but a sensibility. With *The Band*, that group began making music that seems synonymous with americana—it was rooted in a mythic concept of the past but about the relationship between the past and the way we live now. With his solo albums Van Morrison became a Belfast cowboy, the European tough re-experiencing his loss of innocence as he passes through an alien culture, and explorer confronting New Horizon's head on. And with his second record Springsteen proves so skilled a chronicler of urban fantasies that he may become a symbol of them—if he ever attained the stardom that seemed imminent since the release of his first album *Greetings from Asbury Park, NJ*. . . . I hope Springsteen persists despite this album's lack of acceptance. He's the most impressive new song-writer since James Taylor (and far superior to Elliot Murphy, in my opinion). Next time around, he ought to work a little harder on matching the

production to the material, round out a few rough edges and then just throw some more hot ones on the vinyl. The subway he sings so much about keeps rolling all night long and the way this boy rocks it's just a matter of time before he starts picking up passengers."

PROMOTION

Given the senior-level shifts in the label's man-agement, Columbia Records did not engage an ad campaign in support of *The Wild, the Inno-cent and the E Street Shuffle.*

CHART ACTION

Billboard Top LPs and Tape: did not chart dur-ing its initial release.

Billboard Top LPs and Tape (October 18, 1975): number fifty-nine. With the attendant success of *Born to Run, The Wild, the Innocent and the E Street Shuffle* debuted on the *Billboard* charts at number 181 on July 26, 1975. The number-one album that week was the Eagles' *One of These Nights.* The album peaked at number fifty-nine on October 18, 1975. The number-one album that week was John Denver's *Windsong.*

The Wild, the Innocent and the E Street Shuffle spent thirty-four weeks on the *Billboard* charts.

COMMENTS FROM SPRINGSTEEN AND HIS CIRCLE

Bruce Springsteen: "There was a moment dur-ing the [recording of] *The Wild, the Innocent and the E Street Shuffle* when the band was having a kind of breakdown—we couldn't make the rec-ord, the sessions weren't going well. I happened to bump into Jon Landau outside a club I was playing in Boston. . . . So he came in, he had some ideas about how the band should sound, about how the band should be arranged. We listened to the records together, and we said we like this drum sound, that guitar sound. And it became clear to me what he was doing was assisting me in doing what I wanted to do. . . . And I felt comfortable" (*Entertainment Weekly*, 2003).

Mike Appel: "I would say that [Bruce] performed more [as a producer] on the second [album], took a more active role on the creative side than he had previously. . . . As for its commercial success, it was more successful that the first. . . . I was happy with the progress, not with the exact units sold" (Eliot and Appel, *Down Thunder Road*, 1992).

David Sancious: "*The Wild, the Innocent and the E Street Shuffle*—that was fun. The only arranging I did was the strings. There were a couple of keyboard ideas I came up with, but I don't think they constituted the arrangement of the songs. Bruce works in such a way that whenever he writes a song, he knows exactly how we wants it to sound. . . . He'll verbally tell you what kind of thing he wants, and then it's up to you. When I first came in, they had a bunch of tracks together, and Danny had played some parts, but there were holes. Like 'Kitty's Back,' they had the basic thing. I did the organ solo, electric piano. Then we recorded some things together. I was ill with tonsilitis for almost all the sessions and didn't know it. They were great sessions" (*Thunder Road* magazine, 1979).

Vini Lopez: "The songs went through a lot of changes before they became what it is on the record. Mike Appel always gave me where to put them drum licks" (*Tuesday Night Record Club*, 2022).

MISCELLANEOUS

Springsteen drew the album's title from the 1959 Audie Murphy vehicle *The Wild and the Innocent*. The Western film was set in Wyoming, where "mountain trapper Yancey (Murphy) goes to the nearest town to trade his pelts, but gets into trouble when he tries to save runaway dance-hall girl Rosalie (Sandra Dee) from her shameful job" (*Internet Movie Database*).

The release of *The Wild, the Innocent and the E Street Shuffle* enjoyed less fanfare than Springsteen's debut album. By this time, Clive Davis had left Columbia to found Arista Records, and John Hammond, the man who originally signed the singer-songwriter to a recording contract, had retired. Davis's and Hammond's successors—particularly A&R head Charles Koppelman—refused to promote the album. Vini Lopez recalled that "a few times, Me, Danny, Clarence—we'd all go up to New York City to Mike Appel's office and we'd stuff envelopes with albums and promo stuff, and Mike would send them to every college radio station and radio station in America" (*Tuesday Night Record Club*, 2022).

While the album received very little in the way of promotion from Columbia Records, it enjoyed a grass-roots reputation among deejays. WNEW FM's Richard Neer became enamored of the record, often playing side two of the album without interruption during his overnight shifts (Dolan, *Bruce Springsteen and the Promise of Rock 'n' Roll*, 2012).

Drummer Vini Lopez would be dismissed by Springsteen in February 1974 prior to beginning the recording sessions for *Born to Run*. As Springsteen later recalled, "Discussions were held, grievances aired. The fellows had had enough trouble, Mike too. Vini always felt he was let go because he'd been too outspoken about the way our business was being handled. He may have been right about that, but everyone had their own reasons for wanting Vini to depart. For me, it all came down to the fact that my music was changing, and I needed someone with a more sophisticated palate, with clearer and better time, for the new music I was writing" (Springsteen, *Born to Run*, 2016). The two men maintained a cordial relationship. That September, Springsteen invited Lopez to join him, along with Garry Tallent and Southside Johnny, for a brief set at the Stone Pony, including a performance of "Twist and Shout."

In 1976, Springsteen's fellow Jersey Shore artists Southside Johnny and the Asbury Jukes recorded "The Fever," one of the outtakes from *The Wild, the Innocent and the E Street Shuffle* sessions, for their debut LP *I Don't Want to Go Home*. Produced by Steven Van Zandt, the album also featured Springsteen's composition "You Mean So Much to Me." Springsteen also penned the liner notes for *I Don't Want to Go Home*.

On November 7, 2009, Springsteen and the E Street Band performed *The Wild, the Innocent and the E Street Shuffle* in its entirety at New York City's Madison Square Garden.

In 2020, *Rolling Stone* ranked *The Wild, the Innocent and the E Street Shuffle* at number 345 among its 500 Greatest Albums of All Time.

SONG ANALYSES

SIDE ONE

"The E Street Shuffle"
Bruce Springsteen: vocals, electric guitar, recorder, maracas

Clarence Clemons: tenor saxophone, backing vocals
Danny Federici: backing vocals
Vini "Mad Dog" Lopez: drums, cornet
David Sancious: piano, soprano saxophone, clavinet
Garry Tallent: electric bass, tuba
Richard Blackwell: percussion
Albee Tellone: baritone saxophone

Inspired by Major Lance's 1963 hit "The Monkey Time," "The E Street Shuffle" showcases Springsteen's group, which would soon rechristen themselves as the E Street Band. "I put my band together as soon as I had a little money, the ability to do it," he remarked during a 1974 interview. "If I had guys behind me. I want each guy to be happening. It makes the whole different. I got guys that play great—let 'em play!" (Hiatt, *Bruce Springsteen: The Stories Behind the Songs*, 2019). In its *Bruce Springsteen Collector's Edition* (2022), *Rolling Stone* listed "The E Street Shuffle" as number ninety-three among the artist's top 100 songs.

"4th of July, Asbury Park (Sandy)"
Bruce Springsteen: vocals, acoustic guitar, electric guitar
Clarence Clemons: tenor saxophone, backing vocals
Danny Federici: accordion, backing vocals
Vini "Mad Dog" Lopez: drums
David Sancious: piano
Garry Tallent: electric bass
Suki Lahav: backing vocals

Northern Irish musician Van Morrison's album *Astral Weeks* (1968) was a key influence for Springsteen in terms of drawing on real people and places in his compositions. "4th of July, Asbury Park (Sandy)" explores Jersey Shore beach culture, referencing in particular Madame Marie, a boardwalk fixture. As Springsteen later recalled, "I'd lived in Asbury Park for the past three years. I watched the town suffer some pretty serious race rioting and slowly begin to close down. The Upstage Club, where I met most of the members of the E Street Band, had long ago shut its doors. The boardwalk was still operating, Madam Marie was still there, but the crowds were sparse. Many of the usual summer vacationers were now passing Asbury Park by for less troubled locations further south along the coast" (Springsteen, *Born to Run*, 2016).

The Hollies recorded a cover version of "4th of July, Asbury Park (Sandy)," which they included on *Another Night* (1975) and for which they enjoyed a minor hit on the *Billboard* charts. Soft rockers Air Supply would later include a cover version of the song on their eponymous 1985 album. Singer-songwriter Richard Shindell often performs the song live and included it on his live 2002 album, *Courier*, introducing it by saying "this is not going on the album." The song would take on even greater poignancy when Danny Federici played his accordion part during his final appearance with Springsteen and the E Street Band on March 20, 2008, at Indianapolis's Conseco Fieldhouse. He died that April at age fifty-eight after suffering from melanoma. In its *Bruce Springsteen Collector's Edition* (2022), *Rolling Stone* listed "4th of July, Asbury Park (Sandy)" as number fifteen among the artist's top 100 songs.

"Kitty's Back"
Bruce Springsteen: vocals, electric guitar
Clarence Clemons: tenor saxophone, backing vocals
Danny Federici: organ, backing vocals
Vini "Mad Dog" Lopez: drums, backing vocals
David Sancious: piano, organ solo, backing vocals
Garry Tallent: electric bass, backing vocals

Inspired by the music of Van Morrison, with a nod to David Rose and His Orchestra's "The Stripper," "Kitty's Back" was one of the last songs completed for the album. The germ of the song first came to Springsteen after he spotted the title on a neon sign affixed to a strip club on the Jersey Shore. As he later wrote, "Kitty's Back" was "a remnant of some of the jazz-tinged rock I occasionally played with a few of my earlier bands. It was a twisted swing tune, a shuffle, a distorted piece of big band music. In '73 I had to have songs that could capture audiences who had no idea who I was. As an opening act, I didn't have much time to make an impact. I wrote several wild, long pieces—'Thundercrack,' 'Kitty's Back,' 'Rosalita'—that were the soul children of the lengthy prog pieces I'd written for Steel Mill and were arranged to leave the band and the audience exhausted and gasping for breath" (Springsteen, *Born to Run*, 2016).

"Wild Billy's Circus Story"
Bruce Springsteen: vocals, acoustic guitar, harmonica, mandolin
Danny Federici: accordion
Vini "Mad Dog" Lopez: snare roll
Garry Tallent: tuba

Described by Springsteen as a "black comedy," "Wild Billy's Circus Story" finds its roots in the composer's memories of the Clyde Beatty–Cole Bros. Circus that visited Freehold during his boyhood summers. Located in a field near the local racetrack, the circus seemed like the gateway to a forbidden world. "I was always curious about what was going on in the dim alleys off the midway," he later wrote. "As I walked by, my hand safely enclosed in my mother's, I felt the musky underbelly to the shining lights and life I'd just seen in the center ring. It all felt frightening, uneasy and secretly sexual. I was happy with my Kewpie doll and cotton candy but that wasn't what I wanted to see." For Springsteen, "Wild Billy" was ultimately "about the seduction and loneliness of a life outside the margins" (Springsteen, *Born to Run*, 2016).

The Geography of Bruce Springsteen

The very title of Bruce Springsteen's first album, *Greetings from Asbury Park, N.J.*, presaged how important a role geography and place would play in his songwriting. If we were to trace in a longer study devoted to this topic a particular pattern or narrative arc along these lines, we could point to a gradual broadening of the writer's horizons, starting locally, then expanding to take in a much wider range or perspectives and locations across the breadth of America in the late twentieth and early twenty-first centuries. But even a cursory glance predicated on this premise would reveal how important the region of the central Jersey Shore and the geography of Monmouth County, New Jersey, and his hometown of Freehold would play in Springsteen's early songs. For example, on *Greetings*, the song "Spirit in the Night" is set along Route 88, a state highway that runs from the shore town of Point Pleasant ten miles inland to Lakewood, where a county park on Lake Shenandoah may have served as the inspiration for the idealized "Greasy Lake," which Springsteen immortalized in the song.

Springsteen followed up *Greetings from Asbury Park* with one of his best early songs, "4th of July, Asbury Park (Sandy)," which included many specific references to the shore town where Springsteen spent so much time hanging out as a youth, including the real-life fortune teller, Madame Marie, who, despite Springsteen having her "finally busted" in the song, continued prognosticating for her customers until her retirement in 1997. "4th of July" appeared on Springsteen's second album, *The Wild, the Innocent and the E Street Shuffle*, as did "Rosalita (Come Out Tonight)," which encompassed the swamplands of northern New Jersey, on which the Meadowlands were built), but saw Springsteen expanding his geographical horizons ever further to "a little place" he knew "down San Diego way," which was perhaps inspired by his parents' move to California and presaged Bruce's own preoccupation and eventual move to the West Coast.

Local references would continue to show up in Springsteen's songs throughout his career, from Highway 9 in "Born to Run" to South Street and other specific references to the sights of Freehold in 1984's "My Hometown." From a relatively young age, Springsteen also spent a great deal of time in New York City, which features so prominently in songs like "Jungleland," "New York City Serenade," and "Incident on 57th Street."

The Geography of Bruce Springsteen (Shutterstock) [Madame Marie's]

Songs from 1980's *The River* see a blend of geographical references to specific Jersey locations (St. Mary's Church in "Independence Day," "Eldridge Avenue" in "Stolen Car," and the town of Riverside in "Wreck on the Highway"), to those a little further afield (Baltimore in "Hungry Heart" and "Johnstown, Pennsylvania, in "The River"), while "Cadillac Ranch" was inspired by an actual place in Amarillo, Texas. This pattern would continue on subsequent albums and the inclusion of so many specific place names, only a few of which we have referenced here, help to give Springsteen's songs a feeling of concrete reality and their relatability. They help us to situate his songs in space, as well as in time, as Springsteen seemed to have an innate ability to find the universal in the specific and to make his listeners feel like his hometown was their hometown.

SIDE TWO

"Incident on 57th Street"
Bruce Springsteen: vocals, electric guitar
Danny Federici: organ
Vini "Mad Dog" Lopez: drums
David Sancious: piano
Garry Tallent: electric bass
Suki Lahav: backing vocals

Inspired by the star-crossed lovers in Leonard Bernstein and Stephen Sondheim's 1957 Broadway hit *West Side Story*, "Incident on 57th Street" traces the gangland relationship between streetwise "Spanish Johnny" and "Puerto Rican Jane." For Springsteen, the turbulent story of Johnny, a male prostitute, and Jane held the opportunity for the lovers to find a sense of redemption despite the gritty nature of their circumstances. "Incident on 57th Street" marks one of Springsteen's earliest attempts at extended storytelling. In its *Bruce Springsteen Collector's Edition* (2022), *Rolling Stone* listed "Incident on 57th Street" as number eighteen among the artist's top 100 songs.

"Rosalita (Come Out Tonight)"
Bruce Springsteen: vocals, electric guitar
Clarence Clemons: tenor saxophone, backing vocals
Danny Federici: backing vocals
Vini "Mad Dog" Lopez: drums
David Sancious: piano
Garry Tallent: electric bass

Legend has it that Springsteen composed "Rosalita (Come Out Tonight)" after meeting his girlfriend Diane Lozito's grandmother Rose, who, like Diane's father, objected to her relationship with an itinerant musician. For Springsteen, the incident with Lozito was the latest in a long line of romantic dalliances in which his intended's family took issue with him. "As a teenager, I'd had a girlfriend whose mother had threatened to get a court injunction against me to keep me away from her daughter due to my low-rent beginnings and defiant (for my little town) appearance," he later wrote. "The daughter was a sweet blonde who I believe was the first gal I had successful intercourse with, one fumbling afternoon at chez mama (though, due to the fog of war, I can't be absolutely sure)." To Springsteen's mind, "I wrote 'Rosalita' as a kiss-off to everybody who counted you out, put you down or decided you weren't good enough. It was a tall tale from my past that also celebrated my present ('the record company, Rosie, just gave me a big advance') and took a peek into the future ('Someday we'll look back on this and it will all seem funny'). Not that it would all BE funny, but that it would all SEEM funny. Probably one of the most useful lines I've ever written" (Springsteen, *Born to Run*, 2016).

Springsteen performed an early, solo acoustic version of the song, which went under the title of "Henry's Boy," at the famed New York City nightclub Max's Kansas City. As with "Vibes Man," the precursor for "New York City Seranade," "Henry Boy" was included on the cassette tape—the "London Publishing Demos"—that Springsteen recorded in 1972. A masterpiece of epic storytelling and rock 'n' roll panaches, "Rosalita (Come Out Tonight)" would emerge as one of Springsteen's most iconic concert staples. In 2010, the Rock and Roll Hall of Fame ranked "Rosalita (Come Out Tonight)" among the 500 Songs that Shaped Rock. In its *Bruce Springsteen Collector's Edition* (2022), *Rolling Stone* listed "Rosalita (Come Out Tonight)" as number eleven among the artist's top 100 songs.

"New York City Serenade"
Bruce Springsteen: vocals, acoustic guitar
Clarence Clemons: tenor saxophone, backing vocals

Danny Federici: backing vocals
Vini "Mad Dog" Lopez: conga, triangle, tambourine, clapping, backing vocals
David Sancious: piano, mellotron
Garry Tallent: electric bass
Richard Blackwell: congas

"New York City Serenade" finds its origins in "Vibes Man," a demo that he recorded with a solo piano accompaniment. As with "Henry Boy," "Vibes Man" was included on the cassette tape—the "London Publishing Demos"—that Springsteen recorded in 1972. The composer cites "New York City Serenade" as being among "my romantic stories of New York City, a place that had been my getaway from small-town New Jersey since I was sixteen." He also attributes the song's influence to Van Morrison, who "has always been one of my great, great heroes and an enormous source of inspiration for everything I've done. Van put the white soul into our early E Street records. Without Van, there is no 'New York City Serenade' or jazz soul of 'Kitty's Back'" (Springsteen, *Born to Run*, 2016). In its *Bruce Springsteen Collector's Edition* (2022), *Rolling Stone* listed "New York City Serenade" as number thirty-one among the artist's top 100 songs.

Born to Run (Alamy) [LP cover]

BORN TO RUN

Released in 1975, Springsteen's third album transformed his artistic reputation, elevating him from a regional Northeast sensation into a musician and songwriter of global renown. With hit singles releases in the form of "Born to Run" and "Tenth Avenue Freeze-Out," the album catapulted his emergence as a mainstream artist that continues into the present day. In contrast with his previous two LPs, *Born to Run* enjoyed considerable radio airplay, with virtually all of the album's tracks becoming FM radio staples. Meanwhile, album cuts such as "Thunder Road"

and "Jungleland" would become vaunted entries in Springsteen's setlists across his career.

Born to Run also marked the first formal release associated with the E Street Band. Although the group had been in existence since October 1972, the musicians did not assume the name until September 1974, during *Born to Run*'s production. The E Street Band took its name from E Street in Belmar, New Jersey, where keyboard player David Sancious's mother, Stelma, lived. She often allowed the band to rehearse in her garage. The song

"Tenth Avenue Freeze-Out" commemorated the band's origins, although Springsteen mistakenly located Stelma Sancious's home on Tenth Avenue, when in fact her residence was located at 1107 E Street. In the ensuing years, the corner of E Street and Tenth Avenue has emerged as a popular tourist attraction on the Jersey Shore.

For the recording sessions associated with *Born to Run*, the E Street Band experienced several personnel changes. In February 1974, Springsteen had asked drummer Vini "Mad Dog" Lopez to resign from the band. He was replaced in the band by Ernest "Boom" Carter, though Carter and Sancious then left the E Street Band to form the jazz fusion group Tone. Sancious and Carter were replaced, respectively, by keyboard player Roy Bittan and drummer Max Weinberg, who joined original members Clarence Clemons on saxophone, Garry Tallent on bass, and Danny Federici on keyboards and accordion. In 1975, guitarist "Miami Steve" Van Zandt, who had known and played with Springsteen intermittently since 1966, joined the E Street Band. Violinist Suki Lahav would briefly join the lineup during the *Born to Run* sessions before emigrating to Israel in March 1975.

HISTORICAL CONTEXT

Bruce Springsteen would later note in his book *Songs* that *Born to Run* was his first post-Vietnam album. Saigon had fallen on April 29, about four months before the release of Springsteen's third album. The United States had failed to halt the spread of communism and the domination of Vietnam by Ho Chi Minh's Viet Minh party. Although Springsteen would later deny any overt political content existed on the album, he acknowledged that the antiwar movement and the counterculture of the sixties

had influenced him, as it did virtually every American of his generation. America's failure in Vietnam, the political corruption exposed in the Watergate scandal, and the frailty of the American economy caused by its dependence on foreign oil left many people of Springsteen's baby-boom generation yearning for simpler times or a recovery of the lost innocence of their youth. Whatever the artist's intentions or degree of political consciousness, this was the historical context *Born to Run* entered when released shortly before Labor Day as the summer of 1975 neared its end. It was the summer of Steven Spielberg's blockbuster *Jaws* (based on the novel by Peter Benchley), the near bankruptcy of New York City, and a new dance craze called the Hustle, based on a disco song of that name by Van McCoy and the Soul City Symphony.

Springsteen acknowledged that "the dread that I managed to keep out of 'Rosalita' squeezed its way into the lives of the people on *Born to Run*" (Springsteen, *Songs*, 1998). Yet when people heard the album, they encountered a furious blend of exhilarating rock and roll and soulful ballads that sounded old and new at the same time. Jon Landau, who would help produce the album and soon become Springsteen's manager, had famously identified Bruce as the future of rock and roll after seeing him live at the Harvard Square Theater in Cambridge, Massachusetts, in 1974. But Landau had also written in that same review he had seen his "rock 'n' roll past flash before my eyes." Landau spoke for a generation that had become cynical, not only in the face of the failed dream of the 1960s and the troubled political and economic and landscape of the mid-1970s but also because of the dissatisfaction many rock fans felt with the musical directions of the time. With the caveat that broad generalizations are unfair to the creativity and talent of specific individuals or groups (Steely Dan and Queen come to mind), to many music fans AM radio had become a vapid wasteland of saccharine and escapist pop tunes, while FM radio favored progressive rock bands whose esoteric music deliberately distorted the elementary nature of early rock and roll. *Born to Run* eschewed these destructive tendencies and, at the same time that it revived the spirit of early rock and roll, it infused it with new energy and reinvigorated the art form, making Landau's 1974 review seem prophetic. It allowed listeners to escape to an earlier time, while recognizing the complexities of life for the struggling but hopeful characters that populate the album.

PRODUCTION

Released on August 25, 1975, Columbia Records

Produced by Bruce Springsteen, Mike Appel, and Jon Landau

Engineered by Jimmy Iovine; "Born to Run" engineered by Louis Lahav

Mixed by Iovine, assisted by Thom Panunzio, Corky Stasiak, Dave Thoener, Ricke Delena, Angie Arcuri, and Andy Abrams

Mastered by Greg Calbi at the Record Plant, with Paul Prestopino serving as maintenance engineer

Recorded at 914 Sound Studios, Blauvelt, NY, May 1974 to April 1975; the Record Plant, New York City, April to July 1975

Jon Landau: "I said to Bruce, 'You are a first-class artist. You belong in a first-class recording studio.' So we moved to a popular recording studio at the time, the Record Plant" (*Wings for Wheels*, 2005).

Bruce Springsteen: "On our first evening [at the Record Plant] there, a skinny Italian kid was operating the tape machine. His job was to change the tape reels and turn the player off and on upon the engineer's command. He was a classic New York character, quirky, funny, with attitude to spare. When I came in the next night, he was sitting at the center of the long recording board, replacing Louis Lahav. Jon felt we needed a new engineer, and he and Mike decided to take action. I asked Jon if he thought this kid could pull it off. He said, 'I think he can.' So Jimmy Iovine, brilliant impostor, young studio dog with the fastest learning curve I've ever seen (and soon to be one of the world's biggest music moguls and star of *American Idol*?!), became the engineer on the most important record of my life" (Springsteen, *Born to Run*, 2016).

PERSONNEL

Bruce Springsteen: lead vocals, electric and acoustic guitars, harmonica, and horn arrangement

Roy Bittan: piano, glockenspiel, harpsichord, organ, Fender Rhodes electric piano, and background vocals

Clarence Clemons: saxophones

Garry Tallent: electric bass guitar

Max Weinberg: drums

Ernest "Boom" Carter: drums

David Sancious: organ

Steven Van Zandt: background vocals and horn arrangement

Mike Appel: background vocals

Randy Brecker: trumpet and flugelhorn

Michael Brecker: tenor saxophone

David Sanborn: baritone saxophone

Wayne Andre: trombone

Richard Davis: bass guitar

Suki Lahav: violin

Charles Calello: string arrangement and conductor

COVER ART AND PACKAGING

Cover design: John Berg and Andy Engel
Cover photography: Eric Meola

The album's iconic album cover was shot by Eric Meola on June 20, 1975. One of some 900 photographs taken during the three-hour session, the cover art depicted Springsteen leaning against Clemons, with both musicians cradling their respective instruments—Springsteen's legendary Fender Telecaster and Clemons's tenor saxophone. Meola recalled being influenced by "Dan Kramer's images of Bob Dylan and by Bruce's on-stage moves. I kept reading over and over about how there was such a disparity between the stage shows and the albums." The photographer wanted to capture "the interplay between him and Clarence, the sense of a brooding, street-wise poet who held an audience in the palm of his hands, and kept them spellbound with his music. So I planned to shoot in black-and-white, because I thought it would help to simplify the images and to me, that's what rock 'n' roll was always about—the contrast, the shadows, black leather, white light" (*Popular Photography*, 2008).

For Springsteen, Meola's *Born to Run* photograph was a revelation: "I brought Clarence to the Eric Meola session because I wanted to be photographed with him. Instinctively, I knew there was something about the two of us standing side by side that I wanted to say. It was dramatic, exciting and a little bit more. It captured what I'd felt the first night Clarence stepped on the stage to jam at the Student Prince. That night a real story, one you can't contrive, only discover, was born." In his autobiography, Springsteen describes the cover as being "filled with the subtle mystery of race and a mischievous sense of fun and power promising to be unleashed, It's a photo that makes you wonder, 'Who are these guys, what's the joke they're sharing, what's their story?' That image grew naturally out of the strength and deep feeling between the two of us" (Springsteen, *Born to Run*, 2016).

John Berg and Andy Engel designed the album's packaging. With Meola's photograph as its central image, *Born to Run* has emerged as one of popular culture's most salient and recognizable images. Over the years, the album has been parodied by a diversity of artists and cultural figures, including Cheap Trick's *Next Position Please* (1983), radio commentators Tom and Ray Magliozzi's *Born Not to Run: More Disrespectful Car Songs* (2004), Los Secretos's *Algo Prestado* (2015), and even Sesame Street's *Born to Add* (1983), which depicted Bert and the Cookie Monster mimicking Springsteen and Clemons's famous pose.

TRACK LISTING

All songs composed by Bruce Springsteen.

Side one
1. "Thunder Road"
2. "Tenth Avenue Freeze-Out"
3. "Night"
4. "Backstreets"

Side two
1. "Born to Run"
2. "She's the One"
3. "Meeting across the River"
4. "Jungleland"

UNRELEASED OUTTAKES

"Janey Needs a Shooter"
"Linda, Let Me Be the One": released on *Tracks* (1998)

"Lonely Night in the Park"

"A Love So Fine"

"Lovers in the Cold"

"A Night Like This"

"So Young and in Love": released on *Tracks*
    (1998)

CONTEMPORARY REVIEWS

Unsigned review (*Co-Ed*, February 1975): *Born to Run* "may just be the most important album since *Sgt. Pepper*."

Unsigned review (*Billboard*, September 6, 1975): "Sounds like the third LP from the Asbury Park kid is going to be the magic one that lifts him into the national spotlight. This effort reflects Springsteen at his best. . . . Songs used vary nicely tempo-wise, but overall fare comes down to putting poetic imagery of the '70s together with some good ol' rock 'n' roll. Good Spector-like sound on several cuts."

Jerry Gilbert (*Sounds*, September 13, 1975): "Comparisons with Dylan seem to move further into the distance. Bruce's self-portraits show him to be a James Dean figure but then Dylan was a product of the same ethos—yet there are times when you could be listening to Wilson Pickett! Three tracks, 'Night,' 'Jungleland,' and the beautiful reflective 'Meeting across the River,' are a model of structure composition. But elsewhere the band fails to convey the variation of mood that Springsteen's songs demand. They don't all require the urgency that accompanies city paranoia and Mike Appel and Jon Landau aren't able to provide the necessary dispassionate ears to detect studio foibles. This is not an essential album to have in the way that the previous two were, and yet my initial mixed feelings of surprise and slight disappointment have abated. Springsteen's new musicians have got

the chops alright while his own brilliance is now contained rather than allowed to run free. But the point is that it's still there and it's the distinction from the two previous efforts that makes this album so interesting. I have grown to love it but newcomers to Bruce's music would be better advised to check out what the critics have been raving about in the past. Old fans will need to persevere."

Robert Christgau (*Village Voice*, September 22, 1975): "Just how much American myth can be crammed into one song, or a dozen, about asking your girl to come take a ride? A lot, but not as much as romanticists of the doomed outsider believe. Springsteen needs to learn that operatic pomposity insults the Ronettes and that pseudo-tragic beautiful loser fatalism insults us all. And around now I'd better add that the man avoids these quibbles at his best and simply runs them over the rest of the time. If 'She's the One' fails the memory of Phil Spector's innocent grandeur, well, the title cut is the fulfillment of everything 'Be My Baby' was about and lots more. Springsteen may well turn out to be one of those rare self-conscious primitives who gets away with it."

Greil Marcus (*Rolling Stone*, October 9, 1975): Springsteen's *Born to Run* "is a magnificent album that pays off on every bet ever placed on him—a '57 Chevy running on melted down Crystals records that shuts down every claim that has been made. And it should crack his future wide open. The song titles by themselves— 'Thunder Road,' 'Night,' 'Backstreets,' 'Born to Run,' 'Jungleland'—suggest the extraordinary dramatic authority that is at the heart of Springsteen's new music. It is the drama that counts; the stories Springsteen is telling are nothing new, though no one has ever told them better or made them matter more. Their familiar romance is half their power: the promise and the threat of the night; the lure of the road; the quest for a chance worth taking and the lust to pay its price; girls glimpsed once at 80 miles an hour and never forgotten; the city streets as the last, permanent American frontier. We know the story: one thousand and one American nights, one long night of fear and love."

John Rockwell (*New York Times*, October 24, 1975): "At this point, the enthusiasm for Mr. Springsteen has reached such a point that one does have to worry about a backlash. But ultimately, Mr. Springsteen's future depends on what it has always depended on: his own ability to withstand the pressures of success and his own ability to keep on writing songs of the same quality he's written so far. . . . Sometimes his lyrics still lapse too close to self-conscious myth-making but generally they epitomize urban folk poetry at its best—overflowing with pungent detail and evocative metaphors, but never tied to their sources in a way that is binding. This is poetry that contains universality through the very sureness of its concrete imagery. . . . Hearing these songs is like hearing your own life in music, even if you never lived in New Jersey or made love under the boardwalk in Asbury Park."

Lester Bangs (*Creem*, November 1975): "As if we weren't suspicious enough already of all run-on rhapsodic juvenile delinquents, we have another cabal of rock critics . . . making extravagant claims for [Springsteen], backed up by one of the biggest hypes in recent memory. . . . Springsteen can withstand the reactionaries, though, because once they hear this album, even they are gonna be ready to ride out all cynicism with him. Because, street-punk image, bardic posture, and all, Bruce Springsteen is an American archetype, and *Born to Run* will probably be the finest record released this year."

Mike Jahn (*High Fidelity*, 1975): "Springsteen stands in immediate danger of becoming typecast—if you will, becoming a character composer. Midnight Cowboys, losers seeking to ride hot Chevies off into the sunset, sweaty greasers combing their hair in the reflections of store windows appear and reappear in his songs. He has created a host of contemporary Damon Runyon figures but, in the course of three LPs has said more than needs to be said about them. Sweat is sweat no matter how many different ways you try to depict it. The title song 'Born to Run,' a semi-literary version of Steppenwolf's 'Born to Be Wild,' is the album's best, mainly because the 'tramps like us' words are backed with exciting rock. Another car song, 'Thunder Road,' is enjoyable, and 'Meeting across the River' contains a fine lyric about a desperado trying to 'score' in order to impress his girl. It's heartening to recognize the existence of a rock composer thoughtful enough to want to create his own Stanley Kowalski. Now if Bruce Springsteen were only Tennessee Williams, he might produce rock works of true and varied literary value. But he isn't."

PROMOTION

Following the lackluster sales of Springsteen's first two albums, manager Jon Landau succeeded in negotiating a $150,000 advertising budget from Columbia in order to promote the album. During the week of October 27, 1975, Springsteen was featured on the covers of *Time* and *Newsweek* magazines, underscoring his sudden and massive emergence on the national music scene. Writing in *Time*, critic Jay Cocks hailed the songwriter as the "next Dylan."

As part of the promotional campaign, Columbia deployed Landau's famous "I saw rock and roll future and its name is Bruce Springsteen" quote during the PR campaign. The campaign raised the ire of Springsteen, who felt that such boastfulness was in bad form, later remarking that "I would like to strangle the guy who thought that up." Later that year, when Springsteen and the E Street Band made their UK debut at London's Hammersmith Odeon in November, he objected vehemently to the "Finally, the World Is Ready for Bruce Springsteen" posters displayed in the venue's lobby, along with buttons saying, "I have seen the future of rock 'n' roll at the Hammersmith Odeon." After tearing the poster down, Springsteen refused to allow the buttons to be distributed.

The *Born to Run* tour ran from July 1975 through May 1976. During the tour, Springsteen famously began including "The Detroit Medley" among his sets. A revue of old rock and roll standards such as Shorty Long's "Devil with a Blue Dress On" and Little Richard's "Good Golly Miss Molly," the medley has emerged as a perennial concert staple for Springsteen and the E Street Band.

CHART ACTION

Billboard Top LPs and Tape: number three.

Released on August 25, 1975, *Born to Run* peaked at number three, achieving sales of more than six million copies, earning platinum status from the Recording Industry Association of America (RIAA). The album debuted on the album charts at number eighty-four on September 13, when the number-one album was the Isley Brothers' *The Heat Is On*. During the following week, *Born to Run* entered the *Billboard* top ten at number eight. By mid-October, the album would reach its peak position at number three, with Pink Floyd's *Wish You Were Here*

holding down the top spot. In later years, *Born to Run* would return to the album charts in 1980 after the release of *The River* and for much of 1985 in the wake of the mega success of *Born in the U.S.A.*

Born to Run spent 110 weeks on the *Billboard* charts.

COMMENTS FROM SPRINGSTEEN AND HIS CIRCLE

Bruce Springsteen: "My first challenge was *Time* and *Newsweek* calling to put me on the cover of their magazines. I hesitated, because, back then, popular entertainers, particularly rock 'n' rollers, were not on the covers of what were considered serious news publications. I had a choice. No interview, no cover. Interview, cover . . . two of 'em. Though I was young, I'd had my season in obscurity. I knew well the near misses, the disappointments, the many miles covered and the small tastes of near discovery that went sour. THIS WAS NO TIME TO BUCKLE! I was reticent and would remain so, but I needed to find out what I had. Forty years later I did not want to be sitting in my rocking chair on a sunny afternoon with the woulda, shoulda, coulda blues. . . . *Born to Run* lifted us into another league. We were a new young force to be reckoned with and were removed financially from the red column and placed firmly in the black (hypothetically)" (Springsteen, *Born to Run*, 2016).

Mike Appel: "There really was no plan in 1974. The plan was for Bruce to write hit songs, and for me to get promotion and to make money. . . . Bruce had told me he had an idea for the next album: he wanted a Phil Spector sound. [But] 'Born to Run' had adult lyrics, not Phil Spector-type lyrics" (*Backstreets*, 2019).

Hammersmith Odeon, London, 1975

Building on the success of *Born to Run* and the publicity generated by his appearance on the covers of both *Time* and *Newsweek*, Bruce Springsteen and the E Street Band made plans for a European tour starting with a performance at London's Hammersmith Odeon theater on November 18, 1975. Springsteen arrived in London in a less-than-confident mood, a little intimidated by the prospect of performing in the homeland of so many of his own rock icons—the Beatles, the Rolling Stones, the Animals, the Kinks, and many more representatives of the British invasion that had so shaped his own musical evolution.

Hailed as a rock and roll genius, the future of rock and roll, in Jon Landau's famous review, astonished by the hype his appearance was receiving and a little afraid of his—or anyone's ability—to live up to such heightened expectations. To make matters worse, when he arrived at the theater he saw emblazoned on the marquee the words, "Finally!! London Is Ready for Bruce Springsteen." He unhesitatingly set about removing every promotional poster or flyer he could get his hands on, determined, as always, to let his music speak for itself instead of having a public relations campaign proclaim his greatness before he even took the stage.

Hammersmith Odeon, London, 1975 (Getty) [with Clemons and Van Zandt]

As the concert began, Springsteen opening with "Thunder Road," London critics looked askance at this rock parvenu bestriding the darkened stage and ended up giving the concert mixed reviews. British fans, however, were hypnotized by the ebullient performance and the inexhaustible Springsteen who cast his spell of enchantment over the crowd and seemed to embody the fulfillment of Landau's prognostication. The fans marveled at his energy and how transcendently he had transformed rock and roll into something that sounded at the same time familiar and new. He arrived in London a twenty-five-year-old "provincial young man," in his own words. He ended the show concerned that he had tried too hard, that he had allowed his own insecurities and conflicted feelings about his newfound superstardom to affect his performance. But perform he did, and in such a way that the concert left him a little more worldly, better prepared for the rest of his European tour, and, in some ways, better equipped for a career in which the expectations he had for himself would frequently conflict with those others would place upon him.

SET LIST:

"Thunder Road"	"Backstreets"
"Tenth Avenue Freeze-Out"	"Kitty's Back"
"Spirit in the Night"	"Jungleland"
"Lost in the Flood"	"Rosalita (Come Out Tonight)"
"She's the One"	"4th of July, Asbury Park (Sandy)"
"Born to Run"	
"The E Street Shuffle"	"Detroit Medley"
"It's Hard to Be a Saint in the City"	"For You"
	"Quarter to Three"

Jon Landau: "Bruce works instinctively. He is incredibly intense, and he concentrates deeply. Underneath his shyness is the strongest will I've ever encountered. If there's something he doesn't want to do, he won't. . . . Bruce made every important artistic decision on the LP. The biggest thing I learned from him was the ability to concentrate on the big picture. 'Hey, wait a minute,' he'd say, 'the release date is just one day. The record is forever'" (*Time*, 1975).

Steven Van Zandt: "He [Bruce] really thought it was over. He'd sold, like, 10,000 records. He was philosophical about it. He wasn't like it was the end of his life, he thought he'd come back and try again. So he decided to put everything he had into this one song, 'Born to Run.' I think I probably heard it the first time at a rehearsal—I'd just go to the studio to hang around. It was around in various forms for around six months before it was recorded. It was a tough time. There was a lot of pressure; he was feeling it. All I did on *Born to Run* were the horns on 'Tenth Avenue Freeze-Out.' I was just in the studio, hanging around. [Springsteen] said, 'What do you think?' and I said, 'I think it sucks.' And he said, 'Well, go f-cking fix it, then.' So I went and fixed it. People came to the Bottom Line basically to laugh at us. And a funny thing happened: [after *Born to Run*] we f-cking blew their minds" (*NME*, 2010).

Roy Bittan: "We worked in a garage for a month. Bruce had the songs—some were sketchier than others—and we would sit down and create parts. He was very in tune to listening to what I had to say musically. We recorded that album piano, bass and drums and added everything else later. So what I laid down on those basic tracks was really the foundation for the rest of the album. . . . Sometimes Bruce would say, 'That's pretty good, but let's change it like this.' It was a terrific give and take. I almost felt like he was subconsciously giving me the opportunity to assert myself, being the new member of the band" (*Thunder Road* magazine, 1982).

Clarence Clemons: "The first two albums tanked, so the feeling was that this was our last shot. There was tremendous pressure on Bruce to deliver not just a hit, but a masterpiece. And the more time we spend in the studio, the greater the pressure got" (Clemons and Deo, *Big Man*, 2009).

Max Weinberg: "*Born to Run* was very arranged. Every single note that was played was well thought out. . . . I don't look at *Born to Run* as a 'band' record. It was definitely a Bruce Springsteen LP. . . . During *Born to Run*, we were a new band. I view that time as an intense learning period. A new alive time. It was pre-success, *Born to Run* hysteria" (*Thunder Road* magazine, 1979).

Martin Scorsese: "There was a time in 1975 when you could hear those songs blaring from car radios and apartment windows, and no matter how many times you listened to them, they never lost their edge. . . . Springsteen had already made two beautiful albums before *Born to Run*, but that was the one that put him on the map, and it still has the same wild grandeur it had when it first hit the airwaves" (Sawyers, *Racing in the Street*, 2004).

Dave Marsh: "*Born to Run* is as locked into an America of screen doors, fast cars, and casual violence as the Beatles' 'Penny Lane' is locked into the English everyday. To miss the point is to miss the reason why Bruce Springsteen is such a powerful influence on his fans. As the American Incarnate, he has become the first American hard rock hero since . . . well, I'll argue, since Elvis himself" (Marsh, *Born to Run*, 1981).

MISCELLANEOUS

Springsteen composed much of *Born to Run* on a piano at a rented house at 7½ West End Court in Long Branch, New Jersey. The working title of the album, *Wings for Wheels*, was based on the song "Thunder Road."

The initial pressings of *Born to Run* included a misspelling of Landau's name as "John Landau." The rare versions featuring the misprint have become highly sought after by collectors and audiophiles.

In 1980, Springsteen would revamp "Janey Needs a Shooter" with Warren Zevon for release as "Jeannie Needs a Shooter" on Zevon's *Bad Luck Streak in Dancing School* album. In 2020, Springsteen would release a version of "Janey Needs a Shooter," recorded with the E Street Band in 2020, on his *Letter to You* album.

In 1987, *Born to Run* earned a number eight ranking on *Rolling Stone*'s 100 Best Albums of the Last Twenty Years.

In 2003, *Rolling Stone* ranked *Born to Run* at number eighteen among its 500 Greatest Albums of All Time.

Born to Run has also been packaged as a box set—most notably, in a November 2005 thirtieth-anniversary edition, remastered by Bob Ludwig. "*Born to Run* is the one I've remastered several times," Ludwig observed. The 2005 version is "the one that Bruce told me sounded closest to the way he'd imagined it in his head, which is the ultimate compliment." The box set also featured the documentary *Wings for Wheels: The Making of Born to Run* (2005), directed by Thom Zimny, which narrated the album's original production and earned a 2007 Grammy Award for Best Long Form Music Video.

In December 2005, US Representative Frank Pallone—a New Jersey Democrat hailing from Asbury Park—cosponsored a bill commemorating the anniversary of *Born to Run*: "Congratulating Bruce Springsteen of New Jersey on the 30th anniversary of his masterpiece record album *Born to Run* and commending him on a career that has touched the lives of millions of Americans."

Springsteen and the E Street Band have performed *Born to Run* in its entirety on several occasions, beginning with a benefit performance at the Count Basie Theatre in Red Bank, New Jersey, in May 2008. They would later play the album as a complete work during shows on the 2009 *Working on a Dream* tour and the 2013 *Wrecking Ball* tour. On June 20, 2013, Springsteen and the E Street Band performed the album in memory of actor James Gandolfini, who had died the previous day.

In 2014, *Born to Run* was included among Columbia's Legacy Recordings compilation entitled *The Album Collection, Volume 1: 1973–1984*. *Born to Run* is also listed among the Library of Congress's National Recording Registry of historic recordings.

SONG ANALYSES

SIDE ONE

"Thunder Road"
Bruce Springsteen: vocals, electric guitar, harmonica
Roy Bittan: Fender Rhodes, glockenspiel

Clarence Clemons: saxophone, backing vocals
Garry Tallent: electric bass
Steven Van Zandt: backing vocals
Max Weinberg: drums
Mike Appel: backing vocals

Originally composed under the working title of "Wings for Wheels," "Thunder Road" earned its name after Springsteen spotted the movie poster for *Thunder Road*, a 1958 Robert Mitchum vehicle. As the song developed, Springsteen considered several names for his central female character, including Angelina, Chrissie, and Christina before settling on Mary. In his autobiography, the composer noted that "Mary can be many people: A mother Mary, Jesus' Mary, a fictional Mary—pretty much whoever you want her to be" (Springsteen, *Born to Run*, 2016).

Springsteen selected "Thunder Road" to open the album because it represented *Born to Run*'s "central proposition: Do you want to take a chance? On us? On life?" (Springsteen, *Songs*, 1998). The song also addressed Springsteen's own predicament during the album's production. The lyrics connote the musician's key challenge: "We got one last chance to make it real. / To trade in these wings on some wheels." With his first two albums having sold fewer than 90,000 copies, Springsteen was determined to ensure that *Born to Run* was a success or risk losing his Columbia Records contract. "Thunder Road" owes a musical debt to Roy Orbison's 1960 hit "Only the Lonely," which Springsteen name-checks in the song's lyrics. In a 1995 interview, the songwriter observed that he "tried to sing really full voiced and out of my chest because I was fanatically listening to Roy Orbison at the time, and his vocal power, there will never be a voice like that" (Australian TV interview, 1995).

"Thunder Road" also marked one of Landau's earliest contributions to shaping Springsteen's music and the direction of his career. In particular, Landau suggested that Springsteen consider shifting Clarence Clemons's tenor saxophone solo to the end of the song in order to afford it a triumphant ending. As Nick Hasted later observed, "Landau fixed an edit of an early 'Thunder Road.' By April, he was co-producer, and signed up for two percent of whatever the record made" (*Uncut* magazine, 2005). Over the years, "Thunder Road" has emerged as a concert staple, with Springsteen often redeploying the song as a solo acoustic number or a plaintive piano rendition. In its *Bruce Springsteen Collector's Edition* (2022), *Rolling Stone* listed "Thunder Road" as number three among the artist's top 100 songs.

"Tenth Avenue Freeze-Out"

Bruce Springsteen: vocals, electric guitar
Roy Bittan: piano
Clarence Clemons: tenor saxophone, backing vocals
David Sanborn: baritone saxophone
Garry Tallent: electric bass
Steven Van Zandt: horn arrangement
Max Weinberg: drums
Wayne Andre: trombone
Michael Brecker: tenor saxophone
Randy Brecker: trumpet

As the last song recorded for the album, "Tenth Avenue Freeze-Out" traces the story of the E Street Band's formation. In the song, "Bad Scooter" refers to Springsteen, while the "Big Man" connotes Clemons, affording their relationship with a mythic quality. "Tenth Avenue Freeze-Out" would prove to be especially significant to Van Zandt, who stepped in to help out with the horn arrangement. As Landau later recalled, "Van Zandt said, 'Just listen to me. I'm gonna tell you what to do'" (*Wings for Wheels* documentary, 2005).

As Springsteen remembered, Van Zandt "spontaneously arranged, badgered, and befuddled the jazz players of a prize New York City horn section, amongst whom were the Brecker Brothers and David Sanborn (all of whom must've been thinking, 'Who is this crazy f-cker in the wife-beater tee and straw fedora?'), into honking out some primitive boardwalk soul" (Springsteen, *Born to Run*, 2016). That same night, Landau recommended to Springsteen, "It was time to get Steve in the band" (*Wings for Wheels* documentary, 2005). Van Zandt officially joined the E Street ranks for the *Born to Run* tour.

Listeners often associate the song with Tenth Avenue in Belmar, New Jersey, which serves as a cross street with E Street, not far from the garage where the band rehearsed during that era. Music historian Stan Goldstein suggests that Tenth Avenue may, in fact, refer to the trucking route that exists on Manhattan's West Side, making a southern route from Hell's Kitchen to the West Village, where Springsteen often performed in the city's nightclubs. During its pregentrified days, the West Village presented a gritty setting much like the atmosphere that Springsteen depicts in "Tenth Avenue Freeze-Out" (Goldstein, *Rock 'n' Roll Tour of the Jersey Shore*, 2014). In its *Bruce Springsteen Collector's Edition* (2022), *Rolling Stone* listed "Tenth Avenue Freeze-Out" as number twenty among the artist's top 100 songs.

CHART ACTION

Billboard Hot 100: number eighty-three.

"Tenth Avenue Freeze-Out" b/w "She's the One" was released in December 1975. The number-one song that week was Silver Convention's "Fly, Robin, Fly."

"Night"

Bruce Springsteen: vocals, electric guitar
Roy Bittan: piano, Baldwin electric harpsichord,
  glockenspiel
Clarence Clemons: saxophone
Garry Tallent: electric bass
Max Weinberg: drums

"Night" epitomizes Springsteen's storytelling fascination with the freedom associated with automobile and youth culture, a nocturnal world in which his blue-collar characters blow off steam via drag-racing and an ongoing search for romantic and erotic love. In his own youth, Springsteen cited the Animals' 1965 hit "We Gotta Get Out of This Place" as a key aspect of his teenage philosophy, a primal need for self-liberation. As with such songs as "Growin' Up" and "Born to Run," the combustible engine represents a central means of escape for Springsteen's characters.

For songs like "Night," "Backstreets," and "Born to Run," Springsteen wanted to simulate the Wall of Sound recording technique as popularized by producer Phil Spector. With the Wall of Sound, Spector would imbue his orchestral arrangements with a more potent and expansive sound by feeding the signal from the studio into an echo chamber during the recording process. To emulate this production style, Springsteen and his coproducers established a dense mix of instrumentation and, in so doing, a massive rock and roll sound. In its *Bruce Springsteen Collector's Edition* (2022), *Rolling Stone* listed "Night" as number eighty-one among the artist's top 100 songs.

"Backstreets"

Bruce Springsteen: vocals, electric guitar
Roy Bittan: piano, organ
Garry Tallent: electric bass
Max Weinberg: drums

At one point in 1974, "Backstreets" was a contender to be the title track of Springsteen's third album. As with "Night," the song simulated Phil Spector's Wall of Sound production technique. For Springsteen, "Backstreets" attempted to capture the "broken friendships" of the past through the powerful swell of the song's piano and organ introduction. In its *Bruce Springsteen Collector's Edition* (2022), *Rolling Stone* listed "Backstreets" as number six among the artist's top 100 songs, noting in particular the melody's similarities to Bob Dylan's "Positively 4th Street" and the folk artist's mid-1960s sound. In his original *Rolling Stone* review, Greil Marcus contends that "Backstreets" "begins with music so stately, so heartbreaking, that it might be the prelude to a rock 'n' roll version of *The Iliad*." With Roy Bittan's minute-long keyboard introduction as its bedrock, the song establishes its dramatic atmospherics as a metaphor for the danger and possibility lurking in the shadows of Springsteen's backstreet netherworld.

SIDE TWO

"Born to Run"

Bruce Springsteen: vocals, electric guitar
Ernest "Boom" Carter: drums
Clarence Clemons: tenor saxophone
Danny Federici: organ, glockenspiel
David Sancious: keyboards
Garry Tallent: electric bass

In his autobiography, Springsteen recalled sequencing the "wide-screen rumble" of "Born to Run" "dead in the middle of the record, anchoring all that comes before and after" (Springsteen, *Born to Run*, 2016). The song had been roiling around the composer's mind since the latter months of 1973, when he woke up on tour in Tennessee and wrote down the title. As "Born to Run" developed, Springsteen contrived the song's arresting opening riff on his guitar, clearly drawing on the influence of tunes from his youth like Little Eva's "The Loco-Motion" and Duane Eddy's "Because They're Young."

As for the lyrics, "Born to Run" traces the story of Wendy, patterned after J. M. Barrie's *Peter Pan*, a young woman with a thirst for adventure, yet stymied by her own hesitancy about taking chances on life and love. As with the Barrie character, who eventually joins Peter Pan on a wayward life of escape and exploration among the Lost Boys of Neverland, Springsteen's Wendy must be coaxed into accompanying his protagonist on a self-liberating journey. The central conduit in their escape exists in the mean streets of New Jersey's Highway 9, where they risk their lives and the possibilities of a romantic future in "suicide machines."

For Springsteen, "Born to Run" took on dramatic proportions when it came to furthering his career, given Columbia Records' insistence on a potential hit single. As he commented to the *Boston Globe* in April 1974, "The Columbia people won't let us cut the next album. At least not until we deliver a single. Imagine that! It's like a publisher demanding a middle chapter before agreeing to publish a novel." With a spine-tingling glockenspiel accompaniment and Springsteen's sizzling guitar work, "Born to Run" clearly fit the bill.

Springsteen and the E Street band began performing early versions of "Born to Run" later that year, including the song in their July 1974 set at the Bottom Line, New York City's legendary nightclub. By November 1974—more than a year before the LP's release—the song was in circulation on regional FM radio stations in New York City, Cleveland, and Boston. Mike Appel had originally shared an early version of "Born to Run" with Philadelphia DJ Ed Sciaky, who promptly shared it among his colleagues in New England. In so doing, Sciaky and other rock radio denizens created a sense of anticipation among their listeners for the eventual album.

During the autumn months of 1975, "Born to Run" would land a top thirty hit for Springsteen, catapulting the album to the upper echelons of the *Billboard* charts in the process. Since 1974, the song has enjoyed a vaunted place on Springsteen's setlist. In 2010, the Rock and Roll Hall of Fame ranked "Born to Run" among the 500 Songs that Shaped Rock. In its *Bruce Springsteen Collector's Edition* (2022), *Rolling Stone* listed "Born to Run" as number one among the artist's top 100 songs.

CHART ACTION
Billboard Hot 100: number twenty-three.

"Born to Run" b/w "Meeting across the River" was released on August 25, 1975. The number-one song that week was KC and the Sunshine Band's "Get Down Tonight."

"She's the One"
Bruce Springsteen: vocals, electric guitar
Roy Bittan: piano, harpsichord, organ
Clarence Clemons: saxophone, percussion, backing vocals
Garry Tallent: electric bass
Max Weinberg: drums

With its driving beat borrowed courtesy of Bo Diddley's 1957 R&B classic "Hey! Bo Diddley," "She's the One" explores its protagonist's infatuation with a beautiful woman who remains indifferent to his desires. Worse yet, he finds himself beset by emotional confusion, knowing that she has hard-heartedly betrayed their would-be love via her lies and deception. Critic Louis P. Masur contends that "'She's the One' finds its roots in an early draft of Springsteen's

'Virgin Summer Nights'" (Masur, *Runaway Dream*, 2009). The song is highlighted by Clemons's blistering tenor saxophone. In his autobiography, he fondly recalls "the Bo Diddley beat of 'She's the One' (written just so I could hear C blow that sax solo over the top of it)" (Springsteen, *Born to Run*, 2016). In its *Bruce Springsteen Collector's Edition* (2022), *Rolling Stone* listed "She's the One" as number sixty-three among the artist's top 100 songs.

"Meeting across the River"
Bruce Springsteen: vocals
Roy Bittan: piano
Randy Brecker: trumpet
Richard Davis: double bass

As with such songs as "Incident on 57th Street" and "Jungleland," "Meeting across the River" finds Springsteen exploring the terrors and possibilities of gangland. With Roy Bittan's foreboding piano and Randy Brecker's eerie jazz trumpet accompaniment, the song effects a film noir atmosphere, with its attendant elements of darkness, cynicism, and existential angst. "Meeting across the River" traces the story of a down-on-his-luck criminal's last-ditch chance for success in a hard-boiled world bent on destroying him. With the promise of a $2,000 payday, Springsteen's desperate narrator reasons that, with a little luck, he might not only get away with his life but preserve his tenuous relationship with his girlfriend in the bargain.

Early pressings of *Born to Run* identified the song's title as "The Heist," suggesting that the narrator might be caught up in a robbery or a drug deal, much like the Velvet Underground and Nico's 1967 song "I'm Waiting for the Man," which addresses the traumas associated with transacting a Harlem heroin deal. Several authors anthologized in *Meeting across the River: Stories Inspired by the Haunting Song by*

Bruce Springsteen (2005) draw attention to the *noir*-like influence of Springsteen's depiction of a host of characters and stories associated with pursuit of the American Dream. In its *Bruce Springsteen Collector's Edition* (2022), *Rolling Stone* listed "Meeting across the River" as number forty-two among the artist's top 100 songs.

"Jungleland"
Bruce Springsteen: vocals, electric guitar
Roy Bittan: piano, organ
Clarence Clemons: tenor saxophone
Garry Tallent: electric bass
Max Weinberg: drums

As with the title track, "Jungleland" finds its origins during the earliest *Born to Run* sessions. With "Backstreets," "Jungleland" was one of the first handful of songs under consideration for a potential third album. An early version of the song was captured in an extended synth-infused instrumental demo. As the song's narrative developed, Springsteen unfolded a desperate tale involving the Magic Rat, a low-level criminal bent on finding love, even a sense of sanctity and a possible future with the Barefoot Girl amid the underworld. As with so many of his 1970s-era compositions, "Jungleland" has a deeply rooted sense of place, with the couple meeting under the "giant Exxon sign" and disappearing into the allusive safety of Flamingo Lane. As the song makes its anthemic progress, the Magic Rat and his fellow gangsters come into bloody conflict with the police.

Springsteen symbolizes the fatalism inherent in the Magic Rat's final, fatal bout via an extended tenor saxophone solo courtesy of Clemons— quite possibly, the Big Man's finest moment ever committed to tape. The composer later recalled concocting the solo shoulder to shoulder and "phrase by phrase" with Clemons during their last "three-day, 72-hour sprint" to finish the album. Determined to capture his gritty vision involving "night, the city, and the spiritual battleground of 'Jungleland,'" Springsteen created some of his greatest poetry in the song's latter movements, singing, "The poets down here don't write nothing at all, / They just stand back and let it all be." In the end, he delivers a full-throated despairing cry with "the knife-in-the-back wail of my vocal outro, the last sound you hear, [which] finishes it all in bloody operatic glory" (Springsteen, *Born to Run*, 2016).

As with the burlesque intentions of "Mary Queen of Arkansas," "Jungleland" finds Springsteen identifying both the drama and the absurdity inherent in his characters' lowly plights. With Magic Rat and his dreams having been extinguished, Clemons's solo and Springsteen's vocal death-rattle bring "Jungleland" to a magnificent, heartbreaking close. Melissa Etheridge famously lauded the song in an interview with *Rolling Stone*, especially the song's powerful closing phrases: "When Bruce Springsteen does those wordless wails, like at the end of 'Jungleland,' that's the definition of rock 'n' roll to me. He uses his whole body when he sings, and he puts out this enormous amount of force and emotion and passion" (Luerrsen, *Springsteen FAQ*, 2012). In its *Bruce Springsteen Collector's Edition* (2022), *Rolling Stone* listed "Jungleland" as number thirteen among the artist's top 100 songs.

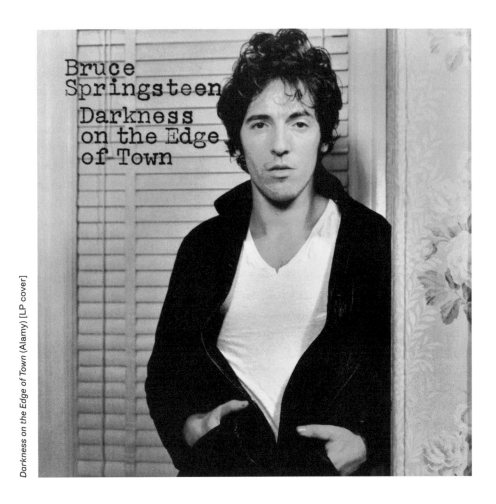

DARKNESS ON THE EDGE OF TOWN

Given the artist's protracted legal battle with estranged manager, Mike Appel, *Darkness on the Edge of Town* emerged some three years after the blockbuster success that Springsteen had enjoyed with *Born to Run*. Released in June 1978, Springsteen's latest album found the musician considering trenchant socioeconomic issues affecting the American cultural landscape.

By the time that recording sessions for his follow-up LP to *Born to Run* commenced in June 1977, Springsteen had amassed a slew of new material. "We cut forty, fifty, sixty songs of all genres," he later wrote. "Maybe after our two-year shutdown I was just hungry to record, to get all the songs and ideas out of my head, to clear a space for the record I really wanted to make. Very slowly . . . that's what happened. We were so rusty when we returned to the studio, weeks went by before a note of music was played" (Springsteen, *Born to Run,* 2016).

In contrast with those on *Born to Run*, the songs on *Darkness on the Edge of Town* were recorded live with the E Street Band in the studio, as opposed to being the product of numerous overdub sessions. Springsteen handled coproduction duties with Jon Landau, and Steven Van Zandt assumed a larger role in the control booth as assistant producer, a credit that he earned for his efforts at concocting arrangements for many of Springsteen's compositions.

In October 1977, Springsteen completed a first pass at the album, which he tentatively titled *Badlands*, a reference to the harsh world that he depicted on the new record, as well as the rugged national park located near the Black Hills of South Dakota. But he soon went back to the drawing board, believing that he had not fully captured the themes of cultural despair and interpersonal angst that were consuming him during this period. By January, the basic tracks for *Darkness at the Edge of Town* were complete, with Springsteen and his team turning to a spate of mixing sessions that concluded in March 1978.

Driven by the singles "Prove It All Night" and "Badlands," *Darkness on the Edge of Town* enjoyed rave critical reviews and became a top five American hit. While the triple-platinum LP came up short in terms of matching *Born to Run*'s blockbuster success, *Darkness on the Edge of Town* marked a spectacular return to the forefront of American music for Springsteen, who was only just getting started.

HISTORICAL CONTEXT

In the three years between *Born to Run* and the release of *Darkness on the Edge of Town* on June 2, 1978, a number of important changes had occurred, but the outlook for the country appeared no brighter than it had in 1975. Jimmy Carter had defeated Gerald Ford in the 1976 presidential election and came to Washington ostensibly as an outsider who would restore

morality and decency to government, but by 1978 the novelty had worn off, leaving people as disillusioned as before, if not more so. Carter had reduced the federal deficit, but at the expense of welfare programs, while still increasing defense spending. Elvis Presley, an American icon, had died of a drug overdose on August 16, 1977, at the age of forty-two. An American group, the Ramones, introduced the United States and Britain to punk rock, which aimed at unpretentiousness and sought to restore the original energy, rebelliousness, and primitive sound of early rock. Fans of punk rock looked down on the elite bands of the sixties and seventies like the Beatles, the Rolling Stones, the Who, and even Led Zeppelin for deviating from the early spirit of rock and roll. Somehow, the popularity of punk rock among anguished teenagers seemed fitting given the bleak and despairing nature of the times; this was even truer in Britain, where economic decline and stagnation were more severe and unemployment rates higher than in the United States and where Springsteen had started cultivating a following with his live performances at the Hammersmith Odeon in London in 1975.

In the meantime, Springsteen had undergone trials that tested his own faith in humanity and the fairness of the music industry. He fell out with his manager, Mike Appel, and became embroiled in legal suits and countersuits resulting from his own efforts to regain control over his creative output. His mindset began to shift from that of the rebellious and adventure-seeking youth who was "born to run" to one of a spokesperson for the blue-collar working class epitomized by his own father, Douglas Springsteen. Disturbed by the hype that had accompanied the release of *Born to Run* and his appearance (in the same week!) on the covers of both *Time* and *Newsweek*, Springsteen sought to tone down *Darkness on the Edge of Town* rather than try to duplicate the success and critical acclaim of its predecessor. His album would possess some of the grittiness of punk rock, even if, now approaching thirty, Springsteen took on more adult topics from a more mature perspective. The final title track on the album seemed especially to capture the spirit of the times, identifying a hidden darkness that threatened to engulf American society, even if people wanted to still believe in the American Dream or ignore its erosion.

In his autobiography, Springsteen wrote about what he attempted to achieve with this album: "I was searching for a tone somewhere between *Born to Run* and '70s cynicism. . . . I wanted my characters to feel weathered, older, but not beaten." He could have been perfectly describing himself at this stage of his career.

PRODUCTION

Released on June 2, 1978, Columbia Records
Produced by Bruce Springsteen and Jon Landau, assisted by Steven Van Zandt
Engineered by Jimmy Iovine, assisted by Thom Panunzio
Recording Assistants: Gray Russell and Jim Ball
Mixed by Iovine and Chuck Plotkin
Mastered by Mike Reese at the Mastering Lab, Los Angeles
Recorded at Atlantic Studios and the Record Plant, New York City, June 1977 to March 1978

PERSONNEL

Bruce Springsteen: vocals, electric and acoustic guitars, harmonica
Roy Bittan: piano, backing vocals
Clarence Clemons: tenor saxophone, percussion, backing vocals
Danny Federici: organ, glockenspiel
Garry Tallent: electric bass
Steven Van Zandt: electric guitar, backing vocals
Max Weinberg: drums

COVER ART AND PACKAGING

Cover design: Andrea Klein
Photography: Frank Stefanko

The cover photograph for *Darkness on the Edge of Town* was taken by Stefanko at Springsteen's home in Haddonfield, New Jersey.

Frank Stefanko: "That very first day, some of the test shots we did ended up being the cover for *Darkness*. . . . My concept was to shoot Bruce Springsteen as the young man that was standing in front of me" (*Entertainment Weekly*, 2018).

Springsteen: "When I saw the picture I said, 'That's the guy in the songs.' I wanted the part of me that's still that guy to be on the cover. Frank stripped away all your celebrity and left you with your essence. That's what that record was about." Stefanko felt the cover portrayed a sense of timelessness that resonated with listeners both on its release and in subsequent decades" (*Entertainment Weekly*, 2018).

TRACK LISTING

All songs composed by Bruce Springsteen.

Side one
1. "Badlands"
2. "Adam Raised a Cain"
3. "Something in the Night"
4. "Candy's Room"
5. "Racing in the Street"
Side two
1. "The Promised Land"
2. "Factory"

3. "Streets of Fire"
4. "Prove It All Night"
5. "Darkness on the Edge of Town"

UNRELEASED OUTTAKES

"Ain't Good Enough for You": released on
  The Promise (2010)
"Because the Night": released on *The Promise*
  (2010)
"Breakaway": released on *The Promise* (2010)
"The Brokenhearted": released on *The Promise*
  (2010)
"Candy's Boy": released on *The Promise* (2010)
"City of Night": released on *The Promise* (2010)
"Come on (Let's go Tonight)": released on
  The Promise (2010)
"Don't Look Back": released on *Tracks* (1998)
"Fire": released on *The Promise* (2010)
"Give the Girl a Kiss": released on *Tracks* (1998)
"Gotta Get That Feeling": released on
  The Promise (2010)
"Hearts of Stone": released on *The Promise*
  (2010)
"Iceman": released on *Tracks* (1998)
"It's a Shame": released on *The Promise* (2010)
"The Little Things (My Baby Does)": released
  on *The Promise* (2010)
"One Way Street": released on *The Promise*
  (2010)
"Outside Looking in": released on *The Promise*
  (2010)
"The Promise": released on *The Promise* (2010)
"Racing in the Street" ('78): released on *Tracks*
  (1998)
"Rendezvous": released on *The Promise* (2010)
"Save My Love": released on *The Promise* (2010)
"Someday (We'll Be Together)"
"Spanish Eyes": released on *The Promise* (2010)
"Talk to Me": released on *The Promise* (2010)
"The Way": released on *The Promise* (2010)

"Wrong Side of the Street": released on
  The Promise (2010)

CONTEMPORARY REVIEWS

Paul Rambali (*New Musical Express*, June 10,
1978): "So, *Darkness on the Edge of Town*
walks a fine line between the outrageous claims
made on Springsteen's behalf and his tendency
towards a grandiose, epic feel that encouraged
those claims in the first place. The 'blockbluster'
production techniques of *Born to Run* have been
studiously avoided, and the conquer-the-world
romantic of before sounds oddly disillusioned,
frustrated even."

Peter Silverton (*Sounds*, June 10, 1978): "Basically, Springsteen has grown up. Or more
accurately he's got older and moved on from the
adolescent concerns of his earlier work to the
trials and tribulations of adulthood. Gone are
the two-bit hoodlums, would-be hoodlums and
sidewalk hustlers down there on E Street. Now,
the action, like those kids has mostly got itself
a wife, two kids, a mortgage and a midnight
shift. . . . If, as many of those who should now
have said, Stallone's *Rocky* was the beginning
of a new dominance in American movies, blue-
collar rule, *Darkness* could well turn out to be
its rock and roll equivalent. Nearly every track
on it is Springsteen's vision of life as it's lived by
the inhabitants of (presumably) the industrial
sore that goes under the name of New Jersey. In
fact, this emphasis on blue-collar life is so nearly
obsessive that a more apt title for the album
would have been the key chorus of the second
track on side two, 'Factory': 'It's the working, the
working, just the working life.'"

Dave Marsh (*Rolling Stone*, July 27, 1978):
"Throughout the new album, Springsteen's lyrics are a departure from his early work, almost

its opposite, in fact: dense and compact, not scattershot. And if the scenes are the same—the highways, bars, cars and toil—they also represent facets of life that rock & roll has too often ignored or, what's worse, romanticized. *Darkness on the Edge of Town* faces everyday life whole, daring to see if something greater can be made of it. This is naïve perhaps, but also courageous. Who else but a brave innocent could believe so boldly in a promised land or write a song that not only quotes Martha and the Vandellas' 'Dancing in the Street' but paraphrases the Beach Boys' 'Don't Worry Baby'? . . . For many years, rock & roll has been splintered between the West Coast's monopoly on the genre's lyrical and pastoral characteristics and a British and Middle American stranglehold on toughness and raw power. Springsteen unites these aspects: he's the only artist I can think of who's simultaneously comparable to Jackson Browne *and* Pete Townshend. Just as the production of this record unifies certain technical trends, Springsteen's presentation makes rock itself whole again. This is true musically—he rocks as hard as a punk, but with the verbal grace of a singer/songwriter—and especially emotionally. If these songs are about experienced adulthood, they sacrifice none of rock & roll's adolescent innocence. Springsteen escapes the narrow dogmatism of both Old Wave and New, and the music's possibilities are once again limitless."

Mitchell Cohen (*Creem*, September 1978): "THIS AIN'T SALVATION. This ain't betrayal. *Darkness on the Edge of Town* is an artful, passionate, rigorous record that walks a slender line between defeat and defiance, and if it had considerably more of the go-for-broke recklessness that it celebrates, it might have also been a great record. But if frustration is its subject—the

walled-up sensation that pounds at your gut, the daytime monotony that leads to nighttime explosion—it's also its essence, its soul. The best of this music—'Badlands', 'Streets of Fire'—doesn't just describe the rage, it embodies it, and becomes apocalyptic sentimentality, the hero of these little dramas like a *film noir* fugitive (Dane Clark in *Moonrise*, Farley Granger in *They Live by Night*). Then the album is about as powerful as rock 'n' roll gets. As often, however, the songs sound mannered, overly solipsistic, and so serious. Doesn't this guy ever get in the car just to go get a pack of cigarettes? It's a major production every time he turns the ignition key."

PROMOTION

With Springsteen having rejected the PR campaign associated with *Born to Run*—namely, the "Finally, the World Is Ready for Bruce Springsteen" posters—Columbia Records intentionally took a minimalistic approach to promoting *Darkness on the Edge of Town*.

The *Darkness on the Edge of Town* tour ran from May 1978 through January 1979, featuring 100 concerts by Springsteen and the E Street Band.

CHART ACTION

Billboard Top LPs and Tape: number five.

Released on June 2, 1978, *Darkness on the Edge of Town* peaked at number five, achieving sales of more than three million copies, earning platinum status from RIAA. The album debuted on the album charts on June 17 at number thirty-nine. The number-one album was the *Saturday Night Fever* soundtrack. By late July, *Darkness on the Edge of Town* would reach its peak position of number five, with the *Grease* soundtrack holding down the top spot.

Darkness on the Edge of Town spent ninety-seven weeks on the *Billboard* charts.

COMMENTS FROM SPRINGSTEEN AND HIS CIRCLE

Bruce Springsteen: "*Darkness* came out of a place where I was afraid of losing myself. I'd had the first taste of success so you've realized it's possible for your talent to be co-opted and for your identity to be moved and shift in ways that you may not have been prepared for" (*Radio Times*, June 27, 2009).

Roy Bittan: "You realized after a while that the albums were made up of songs that had an emotional thread, not a collection of what the artist thought would do well on the radio" (*The Promise* documentary, 2010).

Clarence Clemons: Bruce "had different ideas about certain solos and certain songs he would direct me by telling me a story and then he would hum or sing it and then say, 'like this, Big Man.' . . . Bruce would write five songs to get one song" (*The Promise* documentary, 2010).

Danny Federici: "When you're first beginning and making a record, you think you need this big production and this big sound, so I think Bruce was a little futuristic in saying 'let's just be simple' . . . everyone put in their two cents about the music, and the production and maybe where something should be or shouldn't be and then there would be a lot of times when maybe Jon or Bruce or Steven would huddle up" (*The Promise* documentary, 2010).

Jimmy Iovine: "We recorded a lot of music, reels and reel and reels of tape for days and days and just recording songs and he was very prolific it was like he exploded. On *Born to Run*, there were only like nine songs, eight made the album; on *Darkness*, there were like 70 songs. That's a big difference if you think about it . . . somebody sculpting eight songs and then all of the sudden, the next album they're writing 70 songs. . . . Bruce was going for something and like he did on *Born to Run* he had something in his head and until he had that thing in his head on tape he would keep going and going and going" (*The Promise* documentary, 2010).

Jon Landau: "I had vaguely assumed that we'd pick up where we left off (from *Born to Run*). He wasn't planning to write the next 'Jungleland' or 'Backstreets'; I think that was one moment, and he was in another moment. . . . It was quite experimental that we didn't go into that record with an absolutely specific idea of what we wanted from it and how we were going to get there. I remember he really wanted to downsize the scale, that big sound, of *Born to Run*. . . . One phrase that we would use to discuss the sound of the record as it evolved was a 'sound picture.' What kind of picture was the sound that the record was suggesting? We did want a certain feeling of loneliness, a certain unglamorized mix—no sweetening, [not] a lot of overdubs, especially strings and horns; we wanted coffee black. . . . A lot of this album had a lot to do ultimately with Bruce's personal growth and trying to come to terms with his idea of what it meant to be a man" (*The Promise* documentary, 2010).

Chuck Plotkin: "I had never mixed anything before, I was not a mixer, I was a record producer. It had a certain rawness to it that I responded to as a listener. . . . I came back the next night, and he [Bruce] says, 'let me tell you something about this song'; he says, 'here's what I want you to do. I want you to imagine you're in a movie theatre; on the screen is the two lovers having a picnic, and then the camera shock-cuts to a dead body; every time this song comes up on the album, this song is that dead body. . . . He didn't tell me what to do with the music, he [Bruce] told me what he wanted the thing [the record] to feel like. . . . It captures the band in its leanest; you hear in the oral environment things struggling to make a place for themselves. It's not a grand, smooth open space; it's a harder and darker space. You hear the dynamic of the players fighting for space inside the music" (*The Promise* documentary, 2010).

Garry Tallent: "Everything was carpeted, everything was dead, nothing was allowed to breathe, and we wanted to capture the sound of the band live. . . . Nothing seemed to be working; we were just apes in the woods trying to figure out how to make a record that sounded like live, like in our heads, but not having the technology or the wisdom to figure it out" (*The Promise* documentary, 2010).

Patti Scialfa: "There were a lot of brilliant songs that didn't make the album, but they would have altered the picture. When you look at *Darkness* . . . there are no love songs on the record" (*The Promise* documentary, 2010).

Steven Van Zandt: "*Darkness On the Edge of Town* may still be his best collection of songs. That material really forms the depths of what we now know as Bruce Springsteen music, and maybe the circumstances of his life contributed to that. It's never completely autobiographical, and it's never completely not" (*Uncut*, June 2009).

Max Weinberg: "My sense of his reaction to this roadblock in his career was that determination, that will, that desire to do things his way became even greater, maybe his way of working

it all was to write songs. . . . The stakes were even higher in this respect; what is this guy going to do next? . . . We had these very, very set arrangements on *Born to Run*; *Darkness* was a little more freewheeling" (*The Promise* documentary, 2010).

MISCELLANEOUS

Springsteen's protracted legal struggle with former manager Mike Appel came to a conclusion on May 28, 1976, when they reached a settlement, the terms of which awarded Appel a lump sum as well as a percentage of the royalties associated with Springsteen's first three albums.

During this period, Springsteen shared his surfeit of new songs with other artists—most notably, "Fire," which enjoyed a respectable showing in the hands of rockabilly star Robert Gordon. With producer Richard Perry at the helm, the song was later recorded by the Pointer Sisters, who lodged a number-two smash hit with "Fire" in 1979. Fellow Jersey Shore rockers Southside Johnny and the Asbury Jukes featured Springsteen's "Hearts of Stone" and "Talk to Me" on their 1978 album *Hearts of Stone*, with Van Zandt sitting in on lead guitar with his former band for the title track.

In 1979, a cover version of Springsteen's "Because the Night" landed a top 20 hit in the hands of singer-songwriter Patti Smith. Meanwhile, the Greg Kihn Band recorded Springsteen's "Rendezvous" for their LP *With the Naked Eye*. That same year, the Knack recorded a version of "Don't Look Back" for their bestselling LP *Get the Knack* (1979), although Springsteen's composition didn't make the record's final cut. Other unused material from *Darkness at the Edge of Town* would be held over for his next album *The River*, including "Drive All Night," "Independence Day," "Ramrod," and "Sherry Darling."

In 2003, *Rolling Stone* ranked *Darkness on the Edge of Town* at number ninety-one among its 500 Greatest Albums of All Time.

SONG ANALYSES

SIDE ONE

"Badlands"
Bruce Springsteen: vocals, guitar
Roy Bittan: piano, backing vocals
Clarence Clemons: saxophone, percussion, backing vocals
Danny Federici: organ, glockenspiel
Garry Tallent: bass
Steven Van Zandt: guitar, backing vocals
Max Weinberg: drums

This initial song on the album might have led the listener to think that Springsteen's fourth studio album would be similar to *Born to Run*, which preceded it by three years. Musically, it has a similar rock vibe to "Born to Run," while the singer expresses a desire to escape "the same old played out scenes" and a desire for something more that will not come just by waiting around for it. However, the further into the song one gets, it becomes clear that escape will not come as easily as that which the singer promises his girl Mary in the iconic title song of the previous album. Instead, he realizes he has to accept the broken hearts as "the price you've gotta pay" and that the search for love continues in the hopes it will raise the singer above the badlands, or corrupt, grim, and competitive reality in which he finds himself and has to live every day.

Springsteen draws the central riff of "Badlands" from the Animals' 1965 hit "Don't Let Me Be

Misunderstood," which had originally been popularized by American singer-songwriter Nina Simone. During a 2012 speech at Austin's South by Southwest music festival, Springsteen acknowledged his debt to the Animals, particularly on the *Darkness* LP. During his keynote address, Springsteen played the opening riffs from "Don't Let Me Be Misunderstood" and "Badlands" in succession before announcing, "Listen up, youngsters! This is how successful theft is accomplished!"

"Badlands" also echoes the central theme of Elvis Presley's "King of the Whole Wide World." A selection from the soundtrack of Presley's 1962 film *Kid Galahad*, "King of the Whole Wide World" finds Elvis singing,

A poor man wants to be a rich man
A rich man wants to be a king
But the man who can sing when he hasn't got a thing
He's the king of the whole wide world.

In its *Bruce Springsteen Collector's Edition* (2022), *Rolling Stone* listed "Badlands" as number two among the artist's top 100 songs.

CHART ACTION
Billboard Hot 100: number forty-two.

"Badlands" b/w "Streets of Fire" was released in August 1978. The number-one song that week was the Rolling Stones' "Miss You."

"Adam Raised a Cain"
Bruce Springsteen: vocals, guitar
Roy Bittan: piano, backing vocals
Clarence Clemons: percussion, backing vocals
Danny Federici: organ, glockenspiel
Garry Tallent: bass
Steven Van Zandt: guitar, backing vocals
Max Weinberg: drums

Drawing on a biblical theme from the book of Genesis, Springsteen transforms the archetypal story of sibling rivalry into a song about his tortured relationship with his father, Douglas Springsteen. One of a number of songs in which the songwriter explores that relationship, "Adam Raised a Cain" finds Springsteen testifying here to the struggles of his father to achieve success, but which only leave him "with nothing but the pain" for his working-class jobs. Springsteen worries he will turn out like his father, that he will inherit the sins of the father and end up "paying for the sins of somebody else's past."

For the song's rock and roll bombast, Springsteen later admitted a debt to the punk band MC5, especially the raucous "Kick Out the Jams," which Springsteen later described as "a raging tribute to playing rock 'n' roll." In 1970, Landau had made his production debut with MC5's *Back in the USA*.

"Something in the Night"

Bruce Springsteen: vocals, guitar
Roy Bittan: piano, backing vocals
Clarence Clemons: percussion, backing vocals
Danny Federici: organ, glockenspiel
Garry Tallent: bass
Steven Van Zandt: guitar, backing vocals
Max Weinberg: drums

In a disheartening song that might have been one of several on the album influenced by Springsteen's legal struggles with former manager Mike Appel, the singer speaks of those who try to take something away as soon as you get it, after you come into this world with nothing. Like many in Springsteen's songs, the character is searching for something, but not quite sure of what that "something in the night" might be that will make the world seem right. Crushed and broken in spirit, the singer tries to "pick up the pieces and get away without getting hurt," to no avail as one last fight at the state line leaves him "burned and blind."

"Candy's Room"

Bruce Springsteen: vocals, guitar
Roy Bittan: piano, backing vocals
Clarence Clemons: percussion, backing vocals
Danny Federici: organ, glockenspiel
Garry Tallent: bass
Steven Van Zandt: guitar, backing vocals
Max Weinberg: drums

Another disheartening song—this time suggesting that the desolation belongs not to the singer but rather to the object of his affection, a girl named Candy with "a sadness all her own" that is "hidden in her pretty face." Thanks to the intensity of Weinberg's hi-hat introduction, the song has an insistent beat and cadence that propels the song forward and accelerates on the second verse. The singer wants to be part of Candy's world, in which something shines even in the darkness. The song echoes a common theme in popular music of the guy who thinks he can make a girl happy even though she has other men who buy her "fancy clothes and diamond rings" and "give her anything she wants."

For Springsteen, "Candy's Room" represented an early effort to countermand sexism and a pervasive male chauvinism. He later wrote that in "Candy's Room" he was critiquing "a misogyny grown from the fear of all the dangerous, beautiful, strong women in our lives crossed with the carrying of an underlying physical threat, a psychological bullying that is meant to frighten and communicate that the dark thing in you is barely restrained. You use it to intimidate those you love. . . . I can't lay it all at my pop's feet; plenty of it is my own weakness and inability at this late date to put it all away" (Springsteen, *Born to Run*, 2016). For the song's introduction, Springsteen adopts a spoken-word preamble in the style of Barry White. In its *Bruce Springsteen Collector's Edition* (2022), *Rolling Stone* listed

"Candy's Room" as number forty-five among the artist's top 100 songs.

"Racing in the Street"
Bruce Springsteen: vocals, guitar
Roy Bittan: piano, backing vocals
Clarence Clemons: percussion, backing vocals
Danny Federici: organ, glockenspiel
Garry Tallent: bass
Steven Van Zandt: guitar, backing vocals
Max Weinberg: drums

Springsteen always carefully selected the songs he wanted for each album, frequently eliminating those that others thought were better or would be more popular. Of no album is this truer than *Darkness on the Edge of Town*, which Springsteen described as being about sin and how we learn to carry our sins in this world. In this song, the protagonist wins a race that results in him stealing his opponent's girl. Here, racing cars is the singer's one outlet that lets him avoid the fate of those who "just give up living and start dying little by little." But whatever escape this provides for the singer, it fails to do this for his new girlfriend who ends up crying herself to sleep every night. In the penultimate verse, the singer says he and his girl are going to head down to the sea to "wash these sins off our hands," a very Christian image connoting baptism and rebirth, but the end of the song makes it clear the protagonist will soon be back to "racing in the street."

According to Springsteen, "Racing in the Street" existed as a "sequel" of sorts to the Beach Boys' 1964 hit "Don't Worry Baby," which told the story of shame and regret associated with a drag race. In its *Bruce Springsteen Collector's Edition* (2022), *Rolling Stone* listed "Racing in the Street" as number four among the artist's top 100 songs.

"The Promised Land"
Bruce Springsteen: vocals, guitar, harmonica
Roy Bittan: piano, backing vocals
Clarence Clemons: saxophone, percussion, backing vocals
Danny Federici: organ, glockenspiel
Garry Tallent: bass
Steven Van Zandt: guitar, backing vocals
Max Weinberg: drums

This song speaks to the importance of maintaining some kind of belief, faith, and hope for the future that is a central theme in Springsteen's songwriting. But it also speaks to the frustration and anger that life can sometimes shake one's faith and hope to its foundations. It is certainly possible that when Springsteen sings of the lies "that leave you nothing but lost and brokenhearted" at the end of the song, he is referencing his relationship with Mike Appel and the extent to which he felt deceived when he signed on with him without fully knowing what he was getting into.

If the song did partially arise out of Springsteen's specific situation, though, the lyrics remain universal enough, as usual, that anyone can relate to the disappointments and heartaches that can leave one disillusioned or worse, especially if you don't have "the faith to stand its ground." In its *Bruce Springsteen Collector's Edition* (2022), *Rolling Stone* listed "The Promised Land" as number ten among the artist's top 100 songs.

"Factory"
Bruce Springsteen: vocals, guitar
Roy Bittan: piano, backing vocals
Clarence Clemons: percussion, backing vocals
Danny Federici: organ, glockenspiel
Garry Tallent: bass
Steven Van Zandt: guitar, backing vocals
Max Weinberg: drums

This is another song inspired by the life of Springsteen's father, Douglas, and that speaks to the working-class life he endured throughout Springsteen's childhood. It is more literal than many of Springsteen's songs, describing the typical day in the life of a factory worker. The song does make clear, however, that the only mansions the factory worker will ever know will be "mansions of fear" and "mansions of pain." In this song, Springsteen views his father through a different lens than he did in a song such as "Adam Raised a Cain" and foreshadows his later treatment of his relationship with his father in 1984's "My Hometown."

"Streets of Fire"
Bruce Springsteen: vocals, guitar
Roy Bittan: piano, backing vocals
Clarence Clemons: percussion,
   backing vocals
Danny Federici: organ, glockenspiel
Garry Tallent: bass
Steven Van Zandt: guitar, backing vocals
Max Weinberg: drums

This song fits with the theme of darkness that hovers over the album and is reflected in its title. It is also another bitter song that emphasizes lies and the realization that "they tricked you this time," that again calls to mind Springsteen's legal struggle to regain control over his music and career in the years since his last album, 1975's *Born to Run*. The singer refers to himself as "a loser," but the song does not offer even the possibility of escape hinted at in "Badlands" and "The Promised Land." Instead, the singer just wanders through the "streets of fire, talking only with strangers and "angels who have no place." In its *Bruce Springsteen Collector's Edition* (2022), *Rolling Stone* listed "Streets of Fire" as number fifty-four among the artist's top 100 songs.

"Prove It All Night"
Bruce Springsteen: vocals, guitar
Roy Bittan: piano, backing vocals
Clarence Clemons: saxophone, percussion,
   backing vocals
Danny Federici: organ, glockenspiel
Garry Tallent: bass
Steven Van Zandt: guitar, backing vocals
Max Weinberg: drums

Perhaps in keeping with the song's up-tempo thematic about its taxi driver protagonist's efforts to find redemption, "Prove It All Night"—both musically and lyrically—is more upbeat than its predecessor on the album, falling more in line with "Badlands" and "The Promised Land." Here, the singer acknowledges that it would be nice if dreams came true, but he tells his lover they are not living through a dream and "you have to pay the price" to realize what you want out of life. The singer asks his lover to have faith in him, professing his willingness to "prove it all night." In its *Bruce Springsteen Collector's Edition* (2022), *Rolling Stone* listed "Prove It All Night" as number sixteen among the artist's top 100 songs.

CHART ACTION
Billboard Hot 100: number thirty-three.

"Prove It All Night" b/w "Factory" was released on May 23, 1978. The number-one song that week was Paul McCartney and Wings' "With a Little Luck."

"Darkness on the Edge of Town"
Bruce Springsteen: vocals, guitar
Roy Bittan: piano, backing vocals
Clarence Clemons: percussion,
   backing vocals
Danny Federici: organ, glockenspiel
Garry Tallent: bass
Steven Van Zandt: guitar, backing vocals
Max Weinberg: drums

In the final and title track of the album, the singer expresses a sense of deep resignation that life has not turned out the way he planned or wanted it to turn out, along with the theme of darkness that pervades the album. The song is reminiscent of those earlier on the album such as "Something in the Night" and "Streets of Fire" more than the upbeat rockers like "Badlands" and "The Promised Land," which at least offer a glimmer of hope, and much less than the joyous optimism and hopes for the future expressed in earlier songs like "Rosalita (Come Out Tonight)" or "Born to Run." Even in "Thunder Road," Springsteen proclaims in the last line that he's "pulling out of here to win."

But Springsteen's much more personal style of songwriting comes to the fore on this album, in this last song in particular. The singer's money and wife are gone, though he insists those things no longer matter to him. The rest of the lyrics belie that assertion, for in the beginning we learn that his wife now has "a house up in Fairview," alluding to a better neighborhood that contrasts with the edge of town, where he wants his wife to know that he is "easily found," amid the mysterious and pervasive darkness "where dreams are found and lost." In its *Bruce Springsteen Collector's Edition* (2022), *Rolling Stone* listed "Darkness on the Edge of Town" as number eight among the artist's top 100 songs.

The River (Alamy) [LP cover]

THE RIVER

The roots of the album that came to be known as *The River* when it was released in October 1980 were several tracks that were recorded in 1977, during the sessions associated with *Darkness on the Edge of Town*. Originally titled *The Ties That Bind*, Springsteen's latest project was intended to be a single record. Indeed, the title track was recorded more than a year prior to *The River*'s release and was debuted during the September 1979 Musicians United for Safe Energy (MUSE) concerts, which culminated in the documentary *No Nukes.*

Many of the eventual album's tracks were rehearsed at Telegraph Hill Studios, Springsteen's home recording facility, and later produced at the Power Station in New York City in time for a Christmas 1979 release. But after hearing the songs, Springsteen abruptly cancelled the upcoming release, commenting that "the songs lacked the kind of unity and conceptual intensity I liked my music to have." Jon Landau agreed, recommending that a double album would be a more appropriate vehicle for capturing the wide range and scope of Springsteen's vision. In the end, Springsteen and the E Street Band would record more than fifty songs, twenty of which would comprise *The River*.

In many ways, *The River* continued in the increasingly foreboding vein that he had introduced in *Darkness on the Edge of Town*. When they sequenced the LP, Springsteen and Landau intentionally juxtaposed the album's darker contents with its more upbeat numbers. In so doing, they established jarring contrasts that speak to life's multifaceted nature. "Rock 'n' roll has always been this joy, this certain happiness that is in its way the most beautiful thing in life. But rock is also about hardness and coldness and being alone," Springsteen commented at the time. "I finally got to the place where I realized life had paradoxes, a lot of them, and you've got to live with them."

The River's production values also marked a key transformation in Springsteen's and Landau's recording style. In Springsteen's memory, they intentionally shifted away from the warm studio ambience of late 1970s record production, especially evident in the music associated with Southern California, including artists such as the Eagles, Fleetwood Mac, and Linda Ronstadt. According to Springsteen, these soundscapes "didn't suit our East Coast sensibilities. We wanted open room mikes, smashing drums (the snare sound on Elvis's 'Hound Dog' was my Holy Grail), crashing cymbals, instruments bleeding into one another, and a voice sounding like it was fighting out from the middle of a brawling house party. We wanted the sound of less control. This was how many of our favorite records from the early days of rock 'n' roll had been recorded." In order to effect this kind of atmosphere at the Power Station, "we set mikes high above the band to capture as much ambient sound as we could, and we hoped to be able to dial in or out as much of it as we liked."

Ultimately, *The River* made for a deeply personal and reflective record that explores the themes of love, loss, and growing up. The album speaks to the complexity and contradictions of human relationships, while celebrating the resilience and strength of the human spirit in the face of adversity.

HISTORICAL CONTEXT

The September 22, 1980, issue of *Time* magazine featured a cover story on the "Poisoning of America," which detailed the dire threat posed by the 50,000 chemicals on the market in the United States, 35,000 of which the Environmental Protection Agency had identified as "definitely or potentially hazardous to human health." This must have come as dire news to people who a year earlier had become alert to the threat posed by reliance on nuclear energy because of a meltdown that had occurred at the Three Mile Island nuclear reactor in Pennsylvania. That event had inspired the formation of MUSE, which staged a series of concerts at Madison Square Garden to raise awareness for it. These environmental concerns added to a sense of individuals living under threat from larger forces that not only seemed beyond their personal control but threatened to overwhelm them with a sense of hopelessness.

At home, the economy was still in recession from the energy crisis, while abroad the Soviets had invaded Afghanistan and a revolution in Iran had removed a key American ally in the Middle East and introduced a resurgent wave of Islamist fundamentalism and anti-Americanism into the politics of the volatile region. In fact, when Springsteen released *The River* in October 1980, Iranian revolutionaries still held hostage fifty-two American citizens attached to the diplomatic corps in Tehran who had been held in captivity since November 4 of the previous year.

Springsteen was one of the artists who appeared at the "No Nukes" concerts at the Garden, although he alone refused to sign an antinuclear statement prepared by MUSE. He did, however, pen a song called "Roulette" in response to the Three Mile Island crisis that made clear his stand on the issue. His decision to leave the song off the new album, despite its doubled length, seemed to indicate his reticence at making too overt a political statement at the time, as did his disinclination to sign MUSE's statement a year earlier. Instead, *The River* spoke to a variety of concerns that reflected that sense of helplessness in the face of personal and historical fates that characterized the end of the 1970s and the early 1980s.

On the one hand, Springsteen sought to make the album more reflective of the energy fans experienced at his live shows, and the album contains several tracks that accomplish this purpose without delving too deeply into serious subjects. On the other hand, the double album includes a number of songs that show individuals struggling with forces or events that are outside of their control. Still others show Springsteen confronting issues with which he struggled personally, particularly in the areas of family, romantic relationships, and commitment. It is no wonder, then, that Springsteen opted for his first double album, as it was clear he could not accomplish everything he wanted with the limited number of tracks featured on his previous releases. In 1980, his life and the times were simply both too complex for that.

PRODUCTION

Released on October 17, 1980, Columbia Records

Produced by Bruce Springsteen, Jon Landau, and Steven Van Zandt
Engineered by Neil Dorfman, Bob Clearmountain, and Jimmy Iovine
Recording Assistants: Garry Rindfuss, James Farber, Jeff Hendrickson, and Raymond Willhard Mixed by Clearmountain, Chuck Plotkin, and Toby Scott at the Power Station
Mixing Assistants: Dana Bisbee at Clover Recorders
Mastered by Ken Perry at the Capitol Mastering
Recorded at the Power Station, New York City, April 1979 to May 1980

PERSONNEL

Bruce Springsteen: vocals, electric and acoustic guitars, piano, harmonica
Roy Bittan: piano, organ, backing vocals
Clarence Clemons: tenor saxophone, percussion, backing vocals
Danny Federici: organ, glockenspiel
Garry Tallent: electric bass
Steven Van Zandt: electric guitar, backing vocals
Max Weinberg: drums, percussion
Flo and Eddie (Mark Volman and Howard Kaylan): backing vocals

COVER ART AND PACKAGING

Cover design: Jimmy Wachtel
Photography: Frank Stefanko (cover photo), Amanda Flick, Barry Goldenberg, David Gahr, Jimmy Wachtel, and Joel Bernstein.

TRACK LISTING

All songs composed by Bruce Springsteen.
Side one
1. "The Ties That Bind"
2. "Sherry Darling"

No Nukes

Bruce Springsteen described the "No Nukes" shows as "one of the favorite shows that we ever did . . . because you could go like a runaway train for an hour." The concerts were held at New York City's Madison Square Garden between September 19 and 23, 1979. The sponsoring group was an organization recently founded by Jackson Browne, Graham Nash, Bonnie Raitt, and John Hall called Musicians United for Safe Energy (MUSE). Along with Springsteen and the aforementioned founders, the concerts featured such superstar artists of the 1970s as Crosby, Stills and Nash, the Doobie Brothers, James Taylor, Carly Simon, and Tom Petty. The concerts yielded a 1980 album on the Asylum label and a 1980 film released by Warner Brothers. The album featured the first live performance by Springsteen and the E Street Band released on vinyl, a concert favorite of theirs consisting of an assortment of songs by Mitch Ryder and the Detroit Wheels, listed on the album as "The Devil with a Blue Dress Medley." The film features Springsteen performing "Thunder Road," "The River," and a cover of Gary U.S. Bond's 1961 hit "Quarter to Three."

His involvement in the five-concert series of fundraisers for the anti-nuclear energy cause held in the aftermath of the near meltdown at the Three Mile Island nuclear reactor in Pennsylvania marked Springsteen's first tentative step toward using his music in the service of political activism. Springsteen does not say much about the concerts in his 2016 autobiography, *Born to Run*, but he does describe them as "our entrance into the public political arena." At first, Springsteen evinced a hesitancy about making an overt political statement, declining the opportunity to provide one for the concert program as other artists on the bill had done. He felt his presence at the concerts was statement enough and the concerts inspired him to write "Roulette," one of his most political songs to date.

3. "Jackson Cage"

4. "Two Hearts"

5. "Independence Day"

Side two

1. "Hungry Heart"

2. "Out in the Street"

3. "Crush on You"

4. "You Can Look (But You Better Not Touch)"

5. "I Wanna Marry You"

6. "The River"

Side three

1. "Point Blank"

2. "Cadillac Ranch"

3. "I'm a Rocker"

4. "Fade Away"

5. "Stolen Car"

Side four

1. "Ramrod"

2. "The Price You Pay"

3. "Drive All Night"

4. "Wreck on the Highway"

UNRELEASED OUTTAKES

"Be True": released on *Tracks* (1998); B-side of "Fade Away"

"Chain Lightning": released on *The Ties That Bind: The River Collection* (2015)

"Cindy": released on *The Ties That Bind: The River Collection* (2015)

"Dollhouse"

"From Small Things (Big Things One Day Come)": released on *Essential Bruce Springsteen* (2003)

"Held Up without a Gun": B-side of "Hungry Heart"

"I Wanna Be with You": released on *Tracks* (1998)

"Little White Lies": released on *The Ties That Bind: The River Collection* (2015)

"Living on the Edge of the World": released on *Tracks* (1998)

"The Man Who Got Away": released on *The Ties That Bind: The River Collection* (2015)

"Mary Lou": released on *Tracks* (1998)

"Meet Me in the City": released on *The Ties That Bind: The River Collection* (2015)

"Mr. Outside": released on *The Ties That Bind: The River Collection* (2015)

"Night Fire": released on *The Ties That Bind: The River Collection* (2015)

"Paradise by the 'C'": released on *The Ties That Bind: The River Collection* (2015)

"Party Lights": released on *The Ties That Bind: The River Collection* (2015)

"Restless Nights": released on *Tracks* (1998)

"Ricky Wants a Man of Her Own": released on *Tracks* (1998)

"Roulette": B-side of "One Step Up"

"Stray Bullet": released on *The Ties That Bind: The River Collection* (2015)

"Take 'Em as They Come": released on *Tracks* (1998)

"The Time that Never was": released on *The Ties That Bind: The River Collection* (2015)

"Where the Bands Are": released on *Tracks* (1998)

"Whitetown": released on *The Ties That Bind: The River Collection* (2015)

CONTEMPORARY REVIEWS

Sam Sutherland (*High Fidelity*, January 1981): "On *The River* he has done nothing less than summarize and extend the best features of his past work, fitting them into a brilliant conceptual framework. What makes that sense of formal purpose work is the seeming informality of the music itself. Alongside the deliberation of *Darkness on the Edge of Town* or the all-or-nothing fervor of *Born to Run*, these new songs often sound playful, off-the-cuff or even relaxed. Yet underneath the restored exuberance of its up-tempo rockers and the spare, low-keyed ache of its most introspective ballads lies a steady heartbeat. Throughout the four sides, Springsteen has attempted to expand the alternately wide-eyed and hard-boiled romanticism of his recent writing into a multileveled essay on love, identity, and commitment—the topics most common to rock both Before and After the Beatles, and the ones easiest to mouth without really saying much."

Ira Robbins (*Trouser Press*, January 1981): "Springsteen has two major stumbling blocks: stunningly bad vocals and perennially flawed lyrics. His wounded buffalo noises should be reserved for football grandstands. He also repeats lines mercilessly and meanders into a high register that is not his domain; the sound of his voice cracking and straining destroys any mood he might have built up (e.g., 'Drive All Night': on side four). Lyrically, Springsteen is capable of powerful tableaus and stories, but he insists on tossing in his crutchwords—'night,' 'street,' 'darkness,' 'drive'—as if he were totally unable to imagine the sunlit world not moving along a thoroughfare. That sort of monomania might be okay for an entire album, but not a career. *The River* paints a bleak picture of the American dream gone sour: kids forced into marriage and adulthood; people disgusted with their lives and jobs; lovers and families who know they're doomed to grow apart. Everything is wrapped in automotive settings and metaphors that are tenuous at best. All Springsteen's songs are about those same dismal lives in one way or another, just as the highway metaphor runs through his work. Almost all *The River*'s themes, in fact, could have been consolidated into one song."

Paolo Hewitt (*Melody Maker*, October 11, 1980): "So after two and a half years Springsteen delivers—and does it in a style that's breathtaking. *The River* fully encapsulates everything Springsteen has ever been about, which ultimately means the music, and he does it with a record that is the most vitally alive work I've heard this year. It's a full, panoramic screen of rock at its most glorious and passionate; its vanities, traditions, devices, pleas, humor and hopes are set triumphantly to a vibrant whirlwind of excitement, victory and defeat. . . . It pleads for a better world, sees there's no hope for one, cries for that fact and then gloriously recreates its own version. So nod your trilby to the musicians and producers who produced it, shake the hand of the small man with the guitar, and get to it."

Phil Sutcliffe (*Sounds*, October 11, 1980): "In his best songs, Springsteen's ordinary people fill the sky, the workaday thrown on to a giant movie screen and revealed as a true epic. Invariably at the heart of it is a relationship—or rather than that bland-out jargon word, I should say 'a passion'. Compare Springsteen's performance on *The River* with *Darkness* though and you find a huge shift. Where Springsteen used to run bare-naked through his emotions, now he wears a sober suit. He's been over the top, he knows he can do that. This time it seems he wanted to see whether he could tear it apart quietly. Brave again. Restraint might have called his bluff, exposed him as just plain noisy rather than soulful. It didn't. The feeling comes achieving through. The Federici/Bittan organ/piano axis responds in excelsis with an empathy which is potent even when they're not blowing down the walls—though they still get to swing the hammer often enough and with stupendous style.

Paul Nelson (*Rolling Sone*, December 11, 1980): "Bruce Springsteen's *The River* is a contemporary, New Jersey version of *The Grapes of Wrath*, with the Tom Joad/Henry Fonda figure—nowadays no longer able to draw upon the solidarity of family—driving a stolen car through a neon Dust Bowl 'in fear / That in this darkness I will disappear.' Quite often, he does. . . . What makes *The River* really special is Bruce Springsteen's epic exploration of the second acts of American lives. Because he realizes that most of our todays are the tragicomic sum of a scattered series of yesterdays that had once hoped to become better tomorrows, he can fuse past and present, desire and destiny, laughter and longing, and have death or glory emerge as more than just another story. By utilizing the vast cast of characters he's already established on the earlier LPs—and by putting a spin on the time span—Springsteen forces his heroes and heroines into seeing themselves at different and crucial periods in their lives. The connections are infinite (and, some would say, repetitious). . . . Though I consider *The River* a rock 'n' roll milestone, in a way I hope it's also Independence Day."

PROMOTION

In support of *The River*, Springsteen and the E Street Band toured from October 1980 through September 1981, performing 140 concerts.

Springsteen and the E Street Band marked *The River*'s thirty-fifth anniversary with an eighty-nine-show tour that ran from January 2016 through February 2017, in which they performed the album in its entirety. The tour earned some $307 million in receipts. During a September 2016 concert in Philadelphia, Vini "Mad Dog" Lopez briefly reunited with the E Street Band, playing drums during the encore for "It's Hard to Be a Saint in the City" and "Spirit in the Night."

CHART ACTION

Billboard Top LPs and Tape: number one.

Released on October 17, 1980, *The River* peaked at number one, achieving sales of more than five million copies, earning quintuple platinum status from RIAA. The album debuted on the album charts at number four on November 1, when the number-one album was Barbra Streisand's *Guilty*. During the following week, *The River* topped the *Billboard* charts.

The River spent 107 weeks on the *Billboard* charts.

COMMENTS FROM SPRINGSTEEN AND HIS CIRCLE

Springsteen: "I wanted to write for my age and that started very consciously with *Darkness* and continued through *The River*. I was moving forward, but in a funny way I was being inspired by things older than rock music at the time and that was where I was finding a lot of commonality, so I blended those two things and blended that sensibility with the excitement of what I did with the band. . . . The biggest change on *The River* I started the narrative writing where I would inhabit a character, was a very specific narrative story I would sing in that voice, you know, [of] the character that wasn't necessarily me, it was partly me and it was partly other people. Of course, *The River* was my touchstone for all of that writing that came later where you simply step into a character's shoes and try to get your listeners to walk in those shoes for a while" (*Creem*, January 1981).

Springsteen: "When I did *The River*, I tried to accept the fact that, you know, the world is a paradox, and that's the way it is. And the only thing you can do with a paradox is live with it. And I wanted to do that this time out. I wanted to live with particular conflicting emotions. Because I always, personally, in a funny kind of way, lean toward the *Darkness* kind of material—and when I didn't put the album out in 1979, it was because I didn't feel that was there. I felt that it was something where I just got a bigger picture of what things are, of the way things work, and I tried to learn to be able to live with it" (*Creem*, January 1981).

MISCELLANEOUS

After performing a concert at the Spectrum in Philadelphia on December 8, 1980, Springsteen learned that John Lennon had been murdered in New York City. The next night, as Springsteen and the band prepared to take the Spectrum stage yet again, a backstage argument broke out about whether they should be taking the stage at all in light of what had happened the night before.

Later, after the bandmates' tempers had cooled, a visibly shaken Springsteen walked onto the Forum stage, famously remarking that "it's a hard thing to come out and play tonight when so much has been lost. The first record that I ever learned was a record called 'Twist and Shout,'" said Springsteen, his voice audibly shaken. "And if it wasn't for John Lennon, we'd all be in some place very different tonight. It's an unreasonable world and you have to live with a lot of things

that are just unlivable, and it's a hard thing to come out and play. But there's just nothing else you can do." And with that, Springsteen and the band launched into an impassioned version of the anthemic "Born to Run."

The River's "Ramrod" served as a key influence for Stephen King's bestselling novel *Christine* (1983), which tells the story of a 1958 Plymouth Fury that has come under the possession of supernatural forces and begins terrorizing an unsuspecting world.

In 2015, Springsteen released *The Ties That Bind: The River Collection* to commemorate the 1979 album that he had originally envisioned.

SONG ANALYSES

SIDE ONE

"The Ties That Bind"
Bruce Springsteen: vocals, guitar
Roy Bittan: piano, backing vocals
Clarence Clemons: saxophone, percussion, backing vocals
Danny Federici: organ, glockenspiel
Garry Tallent: bass
Steven Van Zandt: guitar, backing vocals
Max Weinberg: drums, percussion

This up-tempo song introduces an album in which a thirty-one-year-old Springsteen seems to contemplate the possibility of commitment and settling down. In this particular number, he seems to suggest that a true and lasting love requires risk taking and courage in order to find something that "cheap romance" cannot offer. He references Johnny Cash's chart-topping song "Walk the Line," singing "You walk cool darlin' can you walk the line," which is exactly what Cash promised his love he would do in his country classic. There is at least a yearning for connection here and a recognition that the true "ties that bind" will be worth it and can never be broken once you find someone "who'll ease the sadness" and "quiet the pain." In its *Bruce Springsteen Collector's Edition* (2022), *Rolling Stone* listed "The Ties That Bind" as number seventy-nine among the artist's top 100 songs.

"Sherry Darling"

Bruce Springsteen: vocals, guitar
Roy Bittan: piano, backing vocals
Clarence Clemons: saxophone, percussion, backing vocals
Danny Federici: organ, glockenspiel
Garry Tallent: bass
Steven Van Zandt: guitar, backing vocals
Max Weinberg: drums, percussion

A fun, exuberant, rock and roll number, this song might be said to look at some of the downsides of a committed relationship, but in a lighthearted, humorous manner. In this song, the singer is stuck in traffic with his girl's (or wife's) mother as he drives her to pick up her welfare check at the unemployment agency. He threatens to make her get out and walk and take the subway "back to the ghetto tonight," all while reassuring Sherry that his love is real and encouraging her to "let the brokenhearted love again," a common theme in Springsteen's lyrics and in popular music more generally.

"Jackson Cage"

Bruce Springsteen: vocals, guitar, harmonica
Roy Bittan: piano, backing vocals
Clarence Clemons: percussion, backing vocals
Danny Federici: organ, glockenspiel
Garry Tallent: bass
Steven Van Zandt: guitar, backing vocals
Max Weinberg: drums, percussion

This song continues the rock and roll vibe of the beginning of the album, but the lyric is far more depressing than the two previous songs. In this song we detect a continuation of the themes that predominated on *Darkness on the Edge of Town*, particularly the difficulty of maintaining hope in the future when living every day proves such a struggle, as well as the theme of darkness itself. The song opens with a young woman driving home to "a house where the blinds are closed," closed to prevent her from "seeing things she don't want to know." The singer tries to offer some encouragement but, unlike those songs in which Springsteen offers some hope for a better life if the girl will come with him, here he confesses that "although there's nights when I dream of a better world," he is "so tired and confused" and "just waiting to see some sun never knowing if that day will ever come." Both the singer and the girl in the song are stuck in "the Jackson Cage," wasting away without any visible means of escape, with prison serving as a metaphor for life without the possibility of parole before death.

"Two Hearts"

Bruce Springsteen: vocals, guitar
Roy Bittan: piano, backing vocals
Clarence Clemons: percussion, backing vocals
Danny Federici: organ, glockenspiel
Garry Tallent: bass
Steven Van Zandt: guitar, backing vocals
Max Weinberg: drums, percussion

"Two Hearts" is an upbeat song that definitely falls on the rock and roll side of the divide in this album, as opposed to those with a more folk, singer-songwriter vibe. It carries the same message, though, that it can be tough to make it in a world that "turns you hard and cold," and it contains the same balance between despair and hope that characterizes so many of Springsteen's songs, especially those from this period. In the face of despair, hope keeps one moving forward and, in this song, since "two hearts are better than one," Springsteen concludes, "I'll keep searching till I find my special one."

"Independence Day"

Bruce Springsteen: vocals, guitar
Roy Bittan: piano, backing vocals
Clarence Clemons: saxophone, percussion,
  backing vocals
Danny Federici: organ, glockenspiel
Garry Tallent: bass
Steven Van Zandt: guitar, backing vocals
Max Weinberg: drums, percussion

"Independence Day" could easily have appeared on *Darkness on the Edge of Town* and is another song about Springsteen's strained and troubled relationship with his father while he was growing up. In fact, the song refers to the "darkness" that pervades the town and the house father and son share, both of which the singer seeks to escape by leaving and declaring his own "independence day." It is unclear in the song what the future holds, as it would be to any young adolescent leaving home, but in the song "the rooms are all empty down at Frankie's joint" and there is no one on the highway because so many other people are leaving town, abandoning their homes and their friends.

But in an important sense, it is the past, not the future, that is significant in this song, an acknowledgment of all that has passed between father and son, all the things they could never say to each other as much as they might have wanted to, and that they could not have acted any differently than they did because of who they were—too different but also "too much of the same kind." Finally, although the song signals a decisive break, its plaintive words and somber music contain both a sadness and a longing that at least imply that independence from one another could also contain hope for reconciliation. In its *Bruce Springsteen Collector's Edition* (2022), *Rolling Stone* listed "Independence Day" as number fifty-five among the artist's top 100 songs.

SIDE TWO

"Hungry Heart"

Bruce Springsteen: vocals, guitar
Roy Bittan: piano, backing vocals
Clarence Clemons: saxophone, percussion,
  backing vocals
Danny Federici: organ, glockenspiel
Garry Tallent: bass
Steven Van Zandt: guitar, backing vocals
Max Weinberg: drums, percussion
Flo and Eddie [Howard Kaylan and Mark Volman]:
  backing vocals

"Hungry Heart" offers a happy-go-lucky rocker whose joyful sound and playful lyric belies yet more darkness and longing. Springsteen sings that "everybody's got a hungry heart" with exuberance, as if it were a positive thing, but in the song it has led the singer to abandon his wife and children and sabotage another relationship with a woman with whom he had fallen in love, leaving him once again alone. Springsteen's own ambivalence toward commitment in a relationship at this stage of his life manifests itself in the last verse where he acknowledges that "everyone wants to have a home" and, no matter what anyone says, presumably including himself, "Ain't nobody like to be alone." For all that, the infectious and energetic beat of the song, with words that can be belted out at concerts or along with the car radio, make it easy to see why this pop rock anthem became Springsteen's first top-ten single.

Springsteen originally composed "Hungry Heart" after a chance meeting in Asbury Park with Joey Ramone, a member of the eponymous American band. Springsteen originally intended to share the song with the Ramones, but opted to retain it for himself on the advice of Jon Landau, who recognized the song's potential hit-making status. During the postproduction process, the song was treated with varispeed to raise the pitch of Springsteen's vocal and imbue it with a brighter quality. Also known as "frequency control," varispeed is the recording technique in which the tape speed is altered in order to produce a different frequency during playback. In its *Bruce Springsteen Collector's Edition* (2022), *Rolling Stone* listed "Hungry Heart" as number fifty-three among the artist's top 100 songs.

CHART ACTION

Billboard Hot 100: number one.

"Hungry Heart" b/w "Held Up without a Gun" was released on October 21, 1980. The number-one song that week was Queen's "Another One Bites the Dust."

"Out in the Street"
Bruce Springsteen: vocals, guitar
Roy Bittan: piano, backing vocals
Clarence Clemons: saxophone, percussion, backing vocals
Danny Federici: organ, glockenspiel
Garry Tallent: bass
Steven Van Zandt: guitar, backing vocals
Max Weinberg: drums, percussion

"Out in the Street" is a classic rock and roll song about a working-class guy who labors at his job "loading crates down on the dock" five days a week but who lives for the weekend, borrowing a lyric from a 1966 hit by the Easybeats called "Friday on My Mind." The weekend gives the singer a chance to get "out in the street" where he can dress, walk, talk the way he wants to instead of having to follow orders at his job the rest of the week. That he doesn't "feel sad or blue" when he is out on the street, unfortunately, implies that he does feel depressed the rest of the time. In its *Bruce Springsteen Collector's Edition* (2022), *Rolling Stone* listed "Out in the Street" as number eighty among the artist's top 100 songs.

"Crush on You"
Bruce Springsteen: vocals, guitar
Roy Bittan: piano, backing vocals
Clarence Clemons: saxophone, percussion, backing vocals
Danny Federici: organ, glockenspiel
Garry Tallent: bass
Steven Van Zandt: lead guitar, backing vocals
Max Weinberg: drums, percussion

"Crush on You" offers yet another breezy rock and roll song that fulfills Springsteen's aim of mixing that side of his music and himself with serious ballads such as "Independence Day" and "The River." The title and lyrics of the song are straightforward enough: the singer is a guy out looking to pick up a beautiful woman; sometimes he encounters one so irresistible he swears he would give everything for just one kiss. Furthermore, he declares that he does not care if a woman is an heiress or a bank teller, if she has "a lousy personality," if she is the queen of style or "makes Sheena of the Jungle look meek and mild," as long as she is beautiful, with the song ending in a kind of warning to "watch out" if the singer gets a "crush on you." In later years, Springsteen soured on "Crush on You," remarking that "we firmly believe this is the worst song we ever put on record" (Hiatt, *Bruce Springsteen*, 2019).

"You Can Look (But You Better Not Touch)"
Bruce Springsteen: vocals, guitar
Roy Bittan: piano, backing vocals
Clarence Clemons: percussion, backing vocals
Danny Federici: organ, glockenspiel
Garry Tallent: bass
Steven Van Zandt: guitar, backing vocals
Max Weinberg: drums, percussion

With "You Can Look (But You Better Not Touch)," Springsteen conjures up certain images of Americana like the shopping mall and the drive-in movie theater, which contribute to the theme of the song, the frustration of living in a society that seems to offer a paradise, which turns out to be an illusion. In other words, this song, despite being another upbeat rocker, provides yet another example of Springsteen's take on the American Dream. The protagonist accidentally knocks over a lamp in a store, but catches it before it hits the floor; the salesman admonishes him that if he had broken the lamp, he would have had to pay for it. At home watching television, he sees a pretty girl wiggling "back and forth across the screen," but instead of exciting him it makes him angry. He takes a girl nicknamed "Dirty Annie" to the drive-in, but his amorous intentions are interrupted by a knock on the window. The song, while admittedly not as serious as others in Springsteen's canon that contain social commentary, could still be interpreted as reflective and symbolic of a society that puts things within sight but not within reach of many who are left on the outside looking in, able to look but not touch.

"I Wanna Marry You"

Bruce Springsteen: vocals, guitar
Roy Bittan: piano, backing vocals
Clarence Clemons: saxophone, percussion, backing vocals
Danny Federici: organ, glockenspiel
Garry Tallent: bass
Steven Van Zandt: guitar, backing vocals
Max Weinberg: drums, percussion

When Springsteen released his monumental four-disc live album, *Bruce Springsteen and the E Street Band Live, 1975–1985*, the set included a cover of a 1980 song by Tom Waits called "Jersey Girl," which, in Springsteen's hands, became the definitive version. Waits offered a song about a single mother whom the singer falls in love with and wants to rescue from her mundane, exhausting life taking care of her children. With "I Wanna Marry You," Springsteen explores a similar subject. "I Wanna Marry You" takes the promise of a relationship one step further, though, by actually suggesting the idea of marriage, albeit a realistic and not overly romanticized version of the institution.

In the song, Springsteen talks about a couple raising a family and "facing up to its responsibilities," and acknowledges that it would be wrong "to say I'll make your dreams come true." This song demonstrates Springsteen at least considering the possibility of a committed relationship, at least at some point in his life, even if marriage, like life in general, holds only a promise of both happiness and sadness. The song ends with an affirmation that he would be proud to have his name attached to the girl to whom he proposes in the song.

"The River"

Bruce Springsteen: vocals, guitar, harmonica
Roy Bittan: piano, backing vocals
Clarence Clemons: percussion, backing vocals
Danny Federici: organ, glockenspiel
Garry Tallent: bass
Steven Van Zandt: guitar, backing vocals
Max Weinberg: drums, percussion

In his autobiography, *Born to Run* (2016), Springsteen described "The River" as a "breakthrough for my writing." Written from the perspective of a blue-collar worker, "The River" might have easily fit among the contents of *Darkness on the Edge of Town*. Springsteen said he wrote the song about his sister and brother-in-law, but the song also reflects the economic downturn that occurred in the United States more generally during the Carter administration.

Inspired by country legend Hank Williams's "Long Gone Lonesome Blues," "The River" is about a young man who marries his high school sweetheart right after graduation and immediately goes to work as a construction worker, only to find that the job does not provide the steady work and income he needs to support his family. This leads him to reminisce about a happier time, reflected in the shift in the tone of the music when he is reflecting on the past, which comes 3:05 minutes into the song, in contrast to the slow, plodding melody that accompanies the description of his present life. In its *Bruce Springsteen Collector's Edition* (2022), *Rolling Stone* listed "The River" as number five among the artist's top 100 songs.

SIDE THREE

"Point Blank"

Bruce Springsteen: vocals, guitar
Roy Bittan: piano, backing vocals
Clarence Clemons: percussion, backing vocals
Danny Federici: organ, glockenspiel
Garry Tallent: bass
Steven Van Zandt: guitar, backing vocals
Max Weinberg: drums, percussion

"Point Blank" offers a pointedly dark song about a relationship gone awry and the struggle of everyday life, when "you wake up and you're dying / You don't even know what from." It is about promises unfulfilled, about realizing you will never have the nicer things in life, while at the same time love fades and you begin telling "little white lies . . . to ease the pain." Like "The River," the song contrasts a time before, when "I was gonna be your Romeo, you were gonna be my Juliet," and the present, when all the promises have ended up "point blank."

Whereas in "The River," the singer reminisces about a romantic evening at the reservoir with his girl when he would "pull her close just to feel each breath she takes," in "Point Blank," the scene has shifted to "back home in those old clubs the way we used to be," when "I pulled you tighter I swore I'd never let you go." The song contains the same haunted memories evoked by "The River" in a composition that ends with either a metaphorical or an actual death, the last lines being "Bang bang, baby, you're dead." In its *Bruce Springsteen Collector's Edition* (2022), *Rolling Stone* listed "Point Blank" as number sixty-one among the artist's top 100 songs.

"Cadillac Ranch"

Bruce Springsteen: vocals, guitar
Roy Bittan: piano, backing vocals
Clarence Clemons: saxophone, percussion, backing vocals
Danny Federici: organ, glockenspiel
Garry Tallent: bass
Steven Van Zandt: guitar, backing vocals
Max Weinberg: drums, percussion

Cars play a huge role in Springsteen's work, and in "Cadillac Ranch," he shifts away from introspection to write an ode not only to the Cadillac, "long and dark, shiny and black," but to other classic cars, such as the Mercury '49 of James Dean and the black Trans Am of Burt Reynolds. Springsteen reinforces these images by setting them in the American heartland, referencing a girl wearing blue jeans "drivin' alone through the Wisconsin night." Another spirited rocker, the song allows Springsteen to display his less serious side, describing the Cadillac as "a little bit of heaven here on earth." Yet, even here, the song ends with loss, when that same Cadillac described in loving detail early in the song pulls up to his house and takes his girl away.

The song pointedly references the eponymous public art installation due west of Amarillo, Texas. A roadside attraction on Route 66 (now the Interstate 40 frontage road), the "Cadillac Ranch" was erected in 1974 by a hippie art collective that called themselves the Ant Farm. The brainchild of the art collective known as Ant Farm and funded by eccentric billionaire Stanley Marsh III, the Texas panhandle installation consists of ten Cadillacs ranging from a 1949 Club Sedan to a 1963 Sedan de Ville implanted in the ground and facing westward, ostensibly in ironic homage to the Great Pyramids of Giza. Over the years, the installation has become weathered and rusted, with tourists emblazoning the vehicles in garish Day-Glo paint.

"I'm a Rocker"

Bruce Springsteen: vocals, guitar
Roy Bittan: piano, organ, backing vocals
Clarence Clemons: percussion, backing vocals
Garry Tallent: bass
Steven Van Zandt: guitar, backing vocals
Max Weinberg: drums, percussion

If "Cadillac Ranch" is an ode to classic American cars, "I'm a Rocker" is a tribute to American popular culture. Among the television shows name-checked in the song, we find *I Spy* (1965–1968), *Columbo* (premiered 1968), *Kojak* (1973–1978), and *Mission Impossible* (1966–1973). The song opens with a reference to British super-spy James Bond, along with Johnny Rivers's 1966 hit song "Secret Agent Man." "I'm a Rocker" suggests that Springsteen can do more than the fictional heroes and detectives of these series because of his hard-rocking pedigree. In short, the song offers a hard-driving tribute to the power of rock and roll, another of Springsteen's favorite subjects and one of his core beliefs.

"Fade Away"

Bruce Springsteen: vocals, guitar
Roy Bittan: piano, backing vocals
Clarence Clemons: percussion, backing vocals
Danny Federici: organ, glockenspiel
Garry Tallent: bass
Steven Van Zandt: guitar, backing vocals
Max Weinberg: drums, percussion

In his autobiography, Springsteen recalled looking back on his life in the late 1970s, reflecting on "my experience with relationships and love to that point," and realizing that, "all told, I wasn't built for it" (*Born to Run*, 2016). With songs like "Fade Away," Springsteen seems to confirm this overarching belief on his part. "Fade Away" offers yet another song about love gone wrong, in which Springsteen acknowledges that the fault is entirely his. His girl is lonely and misses the good times when they used to go out dancing, "When you and I walked as two."

With "Fade Away," the singer acknowledges that he has lost his girl's trust after the song opens with him lamenting that he has just been told that the relationship is over and that she has found someone else. The message of "Fade Away," of course, as indicated in the title, is that the singer does not want to "fade away," that he misses the old days, too (as with "The River" and "Point Blank"), and he does not want to be "just another useless memory holding you tight." He also continues to explore the contrast between light and dark in lines such as "new rooms that were once so bright are filled with the coming night." In its *Bruce Springsteen Collector's Edition* (2022), *Rolling Stone* listed "Fade Away" as number eighty-five among the artist's top 100 songs.

CHART ACTION
Billboard Hot 100: number twenty.

"Fade Away" b/w "Be True" was released on January 22, 1981. The number-one song that week was John Lennon's "(Just Like) Starting Over."

"Stolen Car"

Bruce Springsteen: vocals, guitar
Roy Bittan: piano, backing vocals
Clarence Clemons: percussion, backing vocals
Danny Federici: organ, glockenspiel

Garry Tallent: bass
Steven Van Zandt: guitar, backing vocals
Max Weinberg: drums, percussion

During *The River* era, Springsteen recalled that "with the end of each affair, I'd feel a sad relief from the suffocating claustrophobia love had brought me" (*Born to Run*, 2016). While its title might seem like a misnomer, "Stolen Car" explores the notion of a broken love affair caused by some deep, undefinable yearning for freedom that leads to the end of a relationship. "At first I thought it was just restlessness that would fade," Springsteen wrote, but "in the end it was something more I guess that tore us apart."

The song's pervasive sadness finds its origins in the couple's marriage, which offers no easy escape, leading the narrator to steal a car, waiting for the moment when he will get caught. The song seems to ask: Are there times when an actual prison feels preferable to the metaphorical one of being trapped in a relationship? In the meantime, the narrator drives his stolen car into the darkness, afraid that he will "disappear," just another way of saying he does not want to "fade away," as in the preceding song. In its *Bruce Springsteen Collector's Edition* (2022), *Rolling Stone* listed "Stolen Car" as number twenty-five among the artist's top 100 songs.

SIDE FOUR

"Ramrod"

Bruce Springsteen: vocals, guitar
Roy Bittan: piano, backing vocals
Clarence Clemons: saxophone, percussion, backing vocals
Danny Federici: organ, glockenspiel
Garry Tallent: bass
Steven Van Zandt: guitar, backing vocals
Max Weinberg: drums, percussion

With "Ramrod," *The River* perceptibly shifts gears once again, reminding the listener that on this double album Springsteen intends to explore both the hard-driving, enthusiastic rock and roll side of his music and the reflective, introspective and poetic side of himself. In an interview with his biographer Dave Marsh in February 1981, he described this song as a "partner" to "Cadillac Ranch," with its "old big engine sound."

The lyric expresses a sentiment similar to "Out in the Street," that of a working-class man waiting for the weekend when he can let his "ramrod rock." Interestingly, though, the issue of commitment still emerges in the song, only this time the narrator ventures closer to a willingness to at least consider a larger commitment, as expressed in "I Wanna Marry You," promising that if the "little dolly with the blue jeans on" pledges herself to him, they will "go ramroddin' forevermore." In its *Bruce Springsteen Collector's Edition* (2022), *Rolling Stone* listed "Ramrod" as number ninety-one among the artist's top 100 songs.

"The Price You Pay"

Bruce Springsteen: vocals, guitar, harmonica
Roy Bittan: piano, backing vocals
Clarence Clemons: percussion, backing vocals
Danny Federici: organ, glockenspiel
Garry Tallent: bass
Steven Van Zandt: guitar, backing vocals
Max Weinberg: drums, percussion

"The Price You Pay" provides a profound illustration of the many ways in which Springsteen has begun viewing his music as a larger body of work, cross-referencing the lyrics that pervade his songs. This technique allows him to develop certain themes throughout his music, some consistently throughout his career and others more adapted to a particular time in his life and the broader cultural and historical contexts of the times. "The Price You Pay" considers the general themes expressed in *Darkness on the Edge of Town*, of learning to live with the sins one has committed, of learning "to sleep at night with the price you pay."

In "The Price You Pay," Springsteen asks the listener to "remember the story of the promised land," in reference, of course, to the song by that name on *Darkness*. He refers to the inability of the song's male subject to enter the chosen land because he has to stay by the banks of "the river," "to face the price you pay." The title of the song can mean many things, and perhaps has multiple meanings within the song itself, but the closing verse suggests once again that the singer might be ready for commitment—as long as he realizes the price he has to pay for it. Perhaps that price was what he was referring to in his autography when he wrote, "You simply can't stop imagining other worlds, other loves, other places than the one you are comfortably settled in at any given moment, the one holding all your treasures" (Springsteen, *Born to Run*, 2016).

"Drive All Night"
Bruce Springsteen: vocals, guitar, piano
Roy Bittan: organ
Clarence Clemons: saxophone, percussion,
  backing vocals
Garry Tallent: bass
Steven Van Zandt: guitar, backing vocals
Max Weinberg: drums, percussion

Springsteen is not known for writing traditional love songs, although "Drive All Night" comes as close to being a romantically inclined composition as anything else in his corpus. In "Drive All Night," he promises his love to his girl "through the wind, through the rain, the snow, the wind, the rain." In the chorus,

he sings that he would "drive all night" just to "sleep tonight again in your arms." Pop songwriters have found myriad ways to express the same thing (take, for example, the 1969 hit "I'd Wait a Million Years," written by Gary Zekley and Mitchell Bottler for the Grass Roots), and Springsteen finds a way to verbalize this sentiment in his own style, drawing on his own uniquely coded language.

When Springsteen sings "Dry your eyes and c'mon, c'mon, c'mon, let's go to bed, baby," he means something different than any other singer singing those lines. In the context of the minor keys and the vocal expressionism of the song, it is less a sexual invitation and more of a simple desire of a lonely man who has lost his love, who simply wants to be with her again and would do anything to get her back. In its *Bruce Springsteen Collector's Edition* (2022), *Rolling Stone* listed "Drive All Night" as number eighty-two among the artist's top 100 songs.

"Wreck on the Highway"
Bruce Springsteen: vocals, guitar
Roy Bittan: piano, backing vocals
Clarence Clemons: percussion, backing vocals
Danny Federici: organ, glockenspiel
Garry Tallent: bass
Steven Van Zandt: guitar, backing vocals
Max Weinberg: drums, percussion

"Wreck on the Highway" concludes the album with a simple song with sparse but rich lyrics about a man driving home from work who comes across a car crash on the highway and, seeing the "blood and glass all over," stops and discovers in the middle of a driving rainstorm an injured man lying by the road who pleads for help. After an ambulance arrives, the man drives home thinking about the state trooper who will inform the victim's wife or girlfriend about the accident. At home, he sits in the darkness watching his own beloved as she sleeps and goes to bed holding her and thinking about "the wreck on the highway." The song offers a meditation on the precariousness and preciousness of life and potentially on the randomness and apparent lack of meaning in the universe.

In retrospect, "Wreck on the Highway" seems to serve less as a conclusion to *The River* and more as a transition or an introduction to his next album, *Nebraska*. In its *Bruce Springsteen Collector's Edition* (2022), *Rolling Stone* listed "Wreck on the Highway" as number thirty among the artist's top 100 songs.

Nebraska (Alamy) [LP cover]

NEBRASKA

Released in September 1982, *Nebraska* marks an unusual artistic turn in Springsteen's evolving catalog, astutely described by critic William Ruhlmann as "one of the most challenging albums ever released by a major star on a major record label." With its stark, simple arrangements, the LP exists in dramatic contrast with the vast majority of his recorded output.

Having read Howard Zinn's *A People's History of the United States* (1980), Springsteen was inspired to think deeply about the desultory nature of contemporary American life, especially in terms of its inherent socioeconomic disparities. He later recalled that "*Nebraska* began as an unknowing meditation on my childhood and its mysteries. I had no conscious political agenda or social theme. I was after a feeling, a tone that felt like the world I'd known and still carried inside me. The remnants of that world were still only ten minutes and ten miles from where I was living. The ghosts of *Nebraska* were drawn from my many sojourns into the small-town streets I'd grown up on. My family, [Bob] Dylan, Woody [Guthrie], Hank [Williams], the American gothic short stories of Flannery O'Connor, the noir novels of James M. Cain, the quiet violence of the films of Terrence Malick and the decayed fable of director Charles Laughton's *The Night of the Hunter* all guided my imagination" (Springsteen, *Born to Run*, 2016).

Armed for the most part with his acoustic guitar, Springsteen captured a series of home demos in Colts Neck, New Jersey, on a portable Teac four-track recorder, planning to rerecord them later with the E Street Band. With their somber thematics and solemn storylines, Springsteen's latest batch of contents reflected the dark, hard-boiled textual landscapes of O'Connor and Cain. The songwriter's bevy of down-and-out characters pursue hopeless lives of crime and iniquity in search of an elusive American Dream. Having completed his solo demos, Springsteen convened the E Street band at New York City's Power Station and the Hit Factory to create full-band renditions of his new material, the unreleased recordings of which have come to be known among fans as *Electric Nebraska*.

After listening to the playbacks from the *Electric Nebraska* sessions, Springsteen found himself drawn to his original, sparsely recorded arrangements of the songs. "All popular artists get caught between making records and making music," he later recalled. "If you're lucky, sometimes it's the same thing. When you learn to craft your music into recordings, there's always something gained and something lost. The ease of an unself-conscious voice gives way to the formality of presentation. On certain records, that trade-off may destroy the essential nature of what you've done. At the end of the day, satisfied

I'd explored the music's possibilities and every blind alley, I pulled out the original cassette I'd been carrying around in my jeans pocket and said, 'This is it'" (Springsteen, *Born to Run*, 2016).

With its ten songs exploring a unique story about working-class life in the American heartland, *Nebraska* enjoyed some of the most effusive critical praise that Springsteen would earn across his storied career. With his next album, he would surpass all expectations, generating the greatest commercial success among the works in his enviable discography.

HISTORICAL CONTEXT

Springsteen's *Nebraska* is yet another example of how an album can reflect the unfolding zeitgeist of a society even if the artist did not set out specifically with a goal of capturing it or with a particular political message in mind. The early years of Ronald Reagan's presidency betokened an even harsher economic climate than that which permeated the late 1970s, with its emphasis on a free-market economy and a reduction of welfare benefits. This period also saw a widening gulf between the rich and the poor that particularly affected the working class. Factories began closing throughout a region that had become known as the Rust Belt, which stretched from New York State to Indiana. Unemployment and crime rates rose simultaneously; at the time of *Nebraska*'s 1982 release, the prison population in the United States was the largest in its history. The prison population of the country had increased by more than 12 percent in 1981 alone. A disproportionate percentage of that population consisted of African Americans, who suffered from the backlash against the civil rights movement that had started to set in during this reactionary period of US history.

Springsteen had already begun to explore some of the themes that appear on *Nebraska* on *The River*, particularly in songs such as "Point Blank, "Stolen Car," and "Wreck on the Highway." Since the release of *The River* in 1980, he had begun to explore aspects of America's past, familiarizing himself with legendary American musicians such as Jimmie Rodgers, Woody Guthrie, and Hank Williams, who had roots deep in folk and country music. Those genres seemed better suited for what Springsteen wanted to convey on *Nebraska*, a musically sparse album that contains none of the feel-good rockers that had appeared on each of his previous albums, even *Darkness on the Edge of Town*. He considered punching the songs up by half, by bringing the E Street Band in to record them, but decided the gray material called for the toned-down solo acoustic recordings he had made on a cassette recorder in his home in Colts Neck, New Jersey. Once again, Springsteen ignored the expectations of fans and critics to make an album that reflected what he wanted to do and say at the time.

Springsteen drew inspiration from his reading of American literature, particularly the morally ambiguous stories of Flannery O'Connor, and from films, such as John Ford's adaptation of John Steinbeck's novel *The Grapes of Wrath* and the 1973 true crime drama *Badlands*, directed by Terence Malick. The latter film's treatment of the 1957–1958 killing spree of mass murderer Charles Starkweather as he fled the law provided the inspiration for the title track of *Nebraska*. Springsteen's awakening historical consciousness led him to see the struggle of the working classes in Reagan's America as part of a larger and longer story that he was just beginning to address on *Nebraska*. He began to

feel as though he could hardly understand himself and his own place in American society and history without understanding the past.

PRODUCTION

Released on September 30, 1982, Columbia Records
Produced by Bruce Springsteen
Engineered by Mike Batlan
Mixed by Springsteen and Batlan

Springsteen recorded the album on a four-track Teac Portastudio 144, which he had purchased for $1,050, at his home studio in Colts Neck, New Jersey, between December 1981 and May 1982.

Springsteen recorded expanded arrangements of several *Nebraska* tracks with the E Street Band at New York City's Power Station and the Hit Factory. Known among fans as *Electric Nebraska*, the sessions also produced several songs that would be included on *Born in the U.S.A.* in 1984.

PERSONNEL

Bruce Springsteen: vocals, acoustic and electric guitars, harmonica, mandolin, glockenspiel, tambourine, organ, synthesizer

COVER ART AND PACKAGING

Design: Andrea Klein
Photography: David Michael Kennedy

TRACK LISTING

All songs composed by Bruce Springsteen.
Side one
1. "Nebraska"
2. "Atlantic City"

Heartland Rock

In the late 1970s and 1980s, a group of primarily male artists became associated with a subgenre of rock that became known as Heartland Rock, implying that it had its roots in American rock and roll, as opposed to that associated with the Beatles and the British Invasion, although the Rolling Stones are considered one of the key influences on its practitioners. The term suggests a strong connection with Middle America, and indeed some leading representatives of the genre, such as John Mellencamp, John Hiatt (both from Indiana), and Bob Seger (Detroit), came from the Midwest; however, others associated with the term included Tom Petty (Florida), John Fogerty (California), and Bruce Springsteen, who was, of course, from New Jersey. Although the term is associated with predominantly male rockers, Lucinda Williams (from Louisiana) could certainly be placed in this category. Although the style is generally regarded as having died out by the 1990s, in that decade the rock band Hootie and the Blowfish, from Columbia, South Carolina, could be considered as carrying on in the same vein. What distinguished Heartland Rock as a musical style was its combination of a generally buoyant and upbeat rock vibe and some kind of social message, which often involved criticisms of the direction in which America was headed. Songs by John Mellencamp, who initially gained fame under the pseudonym John Cougar, such as "Jack and Diane," "Pink Houses," "Rain on the Scarecrow," and "Small Town," not only celebrated small-town and rural America but also conveyed a sense of resistance against the exploitation of rural, blue-collar, and minority Americans amid the unbridled capitalism of the Reagan administration. It was his own identification with blue-collar workers and the critique of the political and economic landscape in many of his songs that earned Springsteen his association with Heartland Rock.

3. "Mansion on the Hill"
4. "Johnny 99"
5. "Highway Patrolman"
6. "State Trooper"

Side two

1. "Used Cars"
2. "Open All Night"
3. "My Father's House"
4. "Reason to Believe"

UNRELEASED OUTTAKE

"The Big Payback": B-side of the UK single "Open All Night"

CONTEMPORARY REVIEWS

Chris Bohn (*New Musical Express*, September 25, 1982): "Of course, the bigger he gets the farther away he shifts from the roots he undoubtedly cherishes. There is no way back and thankfully *Nebraska* doesn't pretend there is; but by bravely ditching the excesses of the E Street Band for solo guitars, harmonica and voice, he's made a valuable sideways leap, allowing him space to breathe free again. Not that an acoustic guitar automatically implies soul searching integrity. On the contrary, the staples he works in here provide a sensible distancing device. He focuses his continuing obsessions through the third person dustbowl updates, prison ballads and personal country blues."

Joel Selvin (*San Francisco Chronicle*, October 17, 1982): "*Nebraska* is an artist's sketchbook. On this record, Springsteen fouls up time and meter on frequent occasion, mumbles inarticulate lyrics at points, and generally includes stray marks and moments of human fallibility anybody else would have taken the time to record over. Not that Springsteen is lazy, but rather, the obvious intention of this work is to let the listener in on the creative process at a tender, fragile moment that can never be recaptured. There were hints of his growing interest in simple, unadorned folk music at his most recent West Coast appearances last year at the Los Angeles Sports Arena, where Springsteen strapped on a harmonica cage, strummed his guitar and—without an additional note from his formidable band—sang Woody Guthrie's 'This Land Is Your Land.' But *Nebraska* only recalls the early works of Bob Dylan and his folk movement colleagues as far as the instrumental approach. The ten songs are rich Springsteen, full of automobiles, working class heroes, and the dreams and nightmares of everyday people."

Steve Pond (*Rolling Stone*, October 28, 1982): "After ten years of forging his own brand of fiery, expansive rock 'n' roll, Bruce Springsteen has decided that some stories are best told by one man, one guitar. Flying in the face of a sagging record industry with an intensely personal project that could easily alienate radio, rock's gutsiest mainstream performer has dramatically reclaimed his right to make the records he wants to make, and damn the consequences. This is the bravest of Springsteen's six records; it's also his most startling, direct, and chilling. And if it's a risky move commercially, *Nebraska*

is also a tactical masterstroke, an inspired way out of the high-stakes rock 'n' roll game that requires each new record to be bigger and grander than the last. Until now, it looked as if 1973's dizzying *The Wild, the Innocent, and the E Street Shuffle* would be the last Springsteen album to surprise people. Ensuing records simply refined, expanded, and deepened his artistry. But *Nebraska* comes as a shock, a violent, acid-etched portrait of a wounded America that fuels its machinery by consuming its people's dreams. It is a portrait painted with old tools: a few acoustic guitars, a four-track cassette deck, a vocabulary derived from the plain-spoken folk music of Woody Guthrie and the dark hillbilly laments of Hank Williams. The style is steadfastly, defiantly out-of-date, the singing flat and honest, the music stark, deliberate and unadorned. *Nebraska* is an acoustic triumph, a basic folk album on which Springsteen has stripped his art down to the core. It's as harrowing as *Darkness on the Edge of Town*, but more measured. Every small touch speaks volumes: the delicacy of the acoustic guitars, the blurred sting of the electric guitars, the spare, grim images. He's now telling simple stories in the language of a deferential common man, peppering his sentences with 'sir's.' 'My name is Joe Roberts,' he sings. 'I work for the state.'"

Jon Young (*Trouser Press*, January 1983): "One thing has not changed. Springsteen still treats life as a big deal, full of high drama with inner meaning for those intent on finding it. The consequent generalizing and mythologizing undermines his ability to evoke a specific situation. 'Highway Patrolman,' a flat account of two brothers, takes on almost Biblical dimensions but is no more interesting for it. 'My Father's House' strives so hard to chisel a lesson in forgiveness that its slight story crumbles.

When Springsteen searches for the point of essentially meaningless crimes in the title track and 'Johnny 99,' he comes up empty-handed. Elsewhere, however, he shows signs of growth. Like the Clash and so many others, Springsteen has been influenced by film—in this case, director Terrence Malick. The silence and space in *Badlands* and *Days of Heaven* may well have inspired the spareness of *Nebraska*. The title cut and *Badlands* have the same subject matter; 'Mansion on the Hill' parallels *Days of Heaven*'s study of the inarticulate poor fascinated by the rich."

Richard C. Walls (*Creem*, January 1983): "I like this album. Its singular gloom seems appropriate to the times and its underlying compassion is restrained and moving, though I suspect that most people will find it more admirable than likeable. Those, that is, who don't dismiss it as an example of one of Springsteen's most problematic traits—his implacable sincerity—gotten out of hand. It seems to me to be honest and rather brave—not just because it goes against the commercial tide but because with its willfully un-grand nuances of light and dark it risks beings seen by most people only as gray."

PROMOTION

As with *Darkness on the Edge of Town*, Springsteen opted to engage in limited publicity, choosing not to tour in support of *Nebraska*.

CHART ACTION

Billboard Top LPs and Tape: number three.

Released on September 30, 1982, *Nebraska* debuted at number twenty-nine on October 9, with John Cougar's *American Fool* holding down the top spot. On October 30, the album peaked at number three, with *American Fool* still lording over the charts. *Nebraska* achieved sales of more than one million copies, earning platinum status from RIAA.

Nebraska spent twenty-nine weeks on the *Billboard* charts.

COMMENTS FROM SPRINGSTEEN AND HIS CIRCLE

Springsteen: "I was just doing songs for the next rock album, and I decided that what always took me so long in the studio was the writing. I would get in there, and I just wouldn't have the material *written*, or it wasn't written well enough, and so I'd record for a month, get a couple of things, go home write some more, record for another month—it wasn't very efficient. So this time, I got a little Teac four-track cassette machine, and I said, I'm gonna record these songs, and if they sound good with just me doin' 'em, then I'll teach 'em to the band. I could sing and play the guitar, and then I had two tracks to do somethin' else, like overdub a guitar or add a harmony. It was just gonna be a demo. Then I had a little Echoplex that I mixed through, and that was it. And that was the tape that became the record. It's amazing that it got there, 'cause I was carryin' that cassette around with me in my pocket without a case for a couple of weeks, just draggin' it around. Finally, we realized, 'Uh-oh, that's the album.' Technically, it was difficult to get it on a disc. The stuff was recorded so strangely, the needle would read a lot of distortion and wouldn't track in the wax. We almost had to release it as a cassette" (*Rolling Stone*, December 6, 1984).

Max Weinberg: "The E Street Band actually did record all of *Nebraska* and it was killing. It was all very hard-edged. As great as it was, it wasn't what Bruce wanted to release. There is a full band *Nebraska* album; all of those songs are in the can somewhere" (*Rolling Stone*, June 10, 2010).

Jon Landau: "Before Bruce made the decision to put out the *Nebraska* sessions as is, we sort of looked at the possibility of it as a blueprint for a studio album. We spent a certain amount of time in the studio recording band versions of a few of the songs. They weren't, in my judgment, [appropriate for release]. We made the right decision. The right version of *Nebraska* came out" (*Time Off*, July 29, 2006). After Springsteen spent considerable effort attempting to record an E Street Band version of "Atlantic City," Landau reportedly said, "No way was it as good as what he had going on that demo tape."

Springsteen: "That whole *Nebraska* album was just that isolation thing, and what it does to you. The record was just basically about people being isolated from their jobs, from their friends, from their families, their fathers, their mothers, just not feeling connected to anything that's going on. Your government. And when that happens, there's just a whole breakdown. When you lose that sense of community, there's some spiritual breakdown that occurs. And when that occurs, you just get shot off somewhere where nothing seems to matter" (*International Musician and Recording World*, October 1984).

MISCELLANEOUS

Directed by Barry Ralbag, the music video "Atlantic City" marked one of Springsteen's earliest entries in the video age, which can be traced to the August 1981 launch of MTV (Music Television Network). In contrast with future MTV-era videos, Springsteen did not feature in the promo, which established a stark palette in keeping with *Nebraska* via black-and-white images of Atlantic City, punctuated by footage of the October 1978 demolition of the immaculate dome of the city's Marlborough Blenheim Hotel and Casino.

In 1983, country star Johnny Cash released cover versions of "Johnny 99" and "Highway Patrolman," which were included on his sixty-ninth LP titled *Johnny 99*.

In 1989, *Rolling Stone* ranked *Nebraska* at number forty-three among the 100 Great Albums of the 1980s.

Academy Award–winning actor Sean Penn modeled his 1991 film *The Indian Runner* on Springsteen's story about the Roberts brothers in "Highway Patrolman." Written and directed by Penn, the crime drama *The Indian Runner* starred David Morse and Viggo Mortensen as two brothers—one a lawman and the other a hardened criminal.

In 1993, the Band recorded a cover version of "Atlantic City" for their album *Jericho*. Hank Williams III followed suit in 2002, featuring the song on his album *Lovesick, Broke, and Driftin'*.

"State Trooper" is played over the closing credits in the January 1999 pilot episode of acclaimed television drama *The Sopranos*, which featured E Street Band guitarist Steven Van Zandt in the role of Silvio Dante.

In 2000, a host of artists contributed to the critically acclaimed LP titled *Badlands: A Tribute to Bruce Springsteen's Nebraska*. Produced by Jim Sampas, the album included selections from Los Lobos, Ani DiFranco, Ben Harper, Aimee Mann, and Michael Penn, among others.

In 2003, *Rolling Stone* ranked *Nebraska* at number 224 among its 500 Greatest Albums of All

Time. In 2020, *Rolling Stone* listed the album at number 150 in an updated version of the rankings.

Written by Tennessee Jones, the 2005 collection of short stories titled *Deliver Me from Nowhere* drew its inspiration from *Nebraska*. The book's title was derived from a lyric that appeared both in "Open All Night" and "State Trooper."

In 2021, the Killers drew on *Nebraska* as a central influence during the composition and production of *Pressure Machine*. In October 2022, Springsteen joined the Killers for a three-song set during their concert at New York City's Madison Square Garden. Springsteen performed duets with lead singer Brandon Flowers on the Killers' "Dustland Fairytale," as well as his own "Badlands" and "Born to Run," for which they were joined onstage by saxophonist Jake Clemons, Clarence Clemons's nephew.

In 2022, singer-songwriter Ryan Adams released a track-by-track cover version of *Nebraska*, which he distributed as a free download on his website.

SONG ANALYSES

SIDE ONE

"Nebraska"
Bruce Springsteen: vocals, acoustic guitar, harmonica, mandolin, glockenspiel

"Nebraska" traces the story of Charles Starkweather, a convicted murderer who killed ten people with his girlfriend during an eight-day spree in 1958. In the song, Springsteen takes on Starkweather's voice, narrating the story of meeting Caril Ann Fugate, a baton-twirling teenager who would join him on his murderous rampage. Springsteen was inspired to tell their story after seeing Terence Malick's *Badlands* (1973) on television. Springsteen was also inspired to tell Starkweather's story after reading Flannery O'Connor's classic short story "A Good Man Is Hard to Find," which concerns an enigmatic spree-killer known as the Misfit. At the story's conclusion, the Misfit blithely remarks that "it's nothing for you to do but enjoy the few minutes you got left the best way you can—by killing somebody or burning down his house or doing some other meanness to him. No pleasure but meanness." Springsteen echoes this perspective via Starkweather's parting words in "Nebraska," when he soberly concludes that "I guess there's just a meanness in this world."

"Atlantic City"
Bruce Springsteen: vocals, acoustic guitar, harmonica, mandolin

Originally titled "Fistful of Dollars," in homage to the 1964 Clint Eastwood Spaghetti Western of the same name, "Atlantic City" traces the story of young couple's desperate sojourn to New Jersey's seaside gambling town. As the song proceeds, the narrator sizes up his impending danger, singing, "Well, they blew up the chicken man in Philly last night," referring to the 1981 mob killing of Phil "The Chicken Man" Testa.

In "Atlantic City," Springsteen's narrator, struggling with "debts that no honest man can pay," makes his escape to the Jersey Shore, where he hopes to pull off one last score that will square things up with the Philly underworld before it's too late. The song's chorus—"Everything dies, baby, that's a fact, / But maybe everything that dies someday comes back"—acts as the narrator's ongoing mantra about his desperate circumstances, as well as his capacity for surviving against increasingly perilous odds. In its

Bruce Springsteen Collector's Edition (2022), *Rolling Stone* listed "Atlantic City" as number seven among the artist's top 100 songs.

"Mansion on the Hill"
Bruce Springsteen: vocals, acoustic guitar, harmonica

For "Mansion on the Hill," the first song that he completed for the album, Springsteen addresses a childhood memory about his father driving with him to the outskirts of Freehold, where he would gaze at a rich man's imposing hillside house: "My father was always transfixed by money. He used to drive out of town and look at this big white house. It became a kind of touchstone for me. Now, when I dream, sometimes I'm on the outside looking in—and sometimes I'm the man on the inside." Springsteen drew the song's name from Hank Williams's 1948 jukebox hit "Mansion on the Hill."

"Johnny 99"
Bruce Springsteen: vocals, acoustic guitar, harmonica

"Johnny 99" explores the story of a laid-off autoworker from Mahwah, New Jersey, who drunkenly murders a convenience store clerk. Subsequently sentenced to ninety-nine years in prison, the narrator begs the judge to execute him instead. In addition to drawing on Jimmie Rodgers's "Ninety-Nine Year Blues," Springsteen was inspired to compose "Johnny 99" after learning about the 1980 closure of a Ford auto plant after more than twenty-five years in operation. He drew the judge's name, "Mean John Brown," from Bob Marley's "I Shot the Sheriff," in which "John Brown" is the titular character in the reggae master's classic song. In its *Bruce Springsteen Collector's Edition* (2022), *Rolling Stone* listed "Johnny 99" as number forty-nine among the artist's top 100 songs.

"Highway Patrolman"
Bruce Springsteen: vocals, acoustic guitar, harmonica, mandolin

Set in the late 1960s, "Highway Patrolman" tells the story of Joe Roberts, a highway patrolman, and his wayward brother, Frankie, a Vietnam veteran who struggles with civilian life, turning to a life of crime. Much of the song concerns Joe's dilemma over upholding the law and coming to his brother's aid, soberly concluding that when a "man turns his back on his family, well, he just ain't no good."

A subplot in the song explores the brothers' attraction to Maria, a hometown girl who marries Joe—presumably, while Frankie is away in Southeast Asia. Joe fondly recalls a happier time with his brother, when he and Frankie took turns dancing with Maria to "Night of the Johnstown Flood," a mournful folk tune about the May 1889 failure of the South Fork Dam that led to the loss of more than 2,000 lives in Johnstown, Pennsylvania. In "Highway Patrolman," things come to a head after Frankie commits an act of violence in a roadhouse, forcing Joe to give chase as his brother speeds away toward the Canadian border. As he gazes at the taillights of Frankie's getaway car, Joe ponders the moral question regarding whether or not to bring his brother to justice. In its *Bruce Springsteen Collector's Edition* (2022), *Rolling Stone* listed "Highway Patrolman" as number twenty-seven among the artist's top 100 songs.

"State Trooper"
Bruce Springsteen: vocals, acoustic guitar

On an album chockful of foreboding songs about murder and mayhem, "State Trooper" may be the most menacing of them all. It traces the experience of a desperate man driving along the New Jersey Turnpike. When a state trooper begins tailing him, the narrator begins praying that the officer won't pull him over—"Maybe you got a kid, maybe you got a pretty wife?"—with the implication that the driver will most likely kill the trooper if there is any sort of confrontation. Name-checked by Springsteen in "State Trooper," the New Jersey Turnpike passes by the songwriter's hometown of Freehold, which is located at Exit 8. In its *Bruce Springsteen Collector's Edition* (2022), *Rolling Stone* listed "State Trooper" as number eighteen among the artist's top 100 songs.

SIDE TWO

"Used Cars"

Bruce Springsteen: vocals, acoustic guitar, harmonica, glockenspiel

"Used Cars" depicts the image of Springsteen's father, who devoted much of his time to keeping the Springsteen family's used cars in working condition. During a 2005 concert, Springsteen recalled that "when I was growing up, he had every kind of used car possible. He had the used car without the heat, he had the used car without the muffler, he had the used car with the bad brakes, he had the used car that doesn't go in reverse. Then of course, let's not forget the used car that just won't start. And the worst part, my room was out over the backyard, and I'd hear him in the morning out on that ice-cold ground in the middle of winter trying to get the thing started. Then he would take us on a forced march on Sunday—our family day—and we would go for a ride. It was brutal. The used car without the muffler, when we passed a police car, he used to have to turn the thing off and coast by."

Springsteen's father, Doug, was a regular fixture in his compositions, a touchstone from his past

and his family life back in Freehold. "I slammed the old bastard so much in so many songs," Springsteen later observed. "I made such a fortune on him, I gotta say some good things about him once in a while. What would I have written about if all things had gone well?"

"Open All Night"

Bruce Springsteen: vocals, electric guitar

Originally titled "Wanda," "Open All Night" is the only song to feature an electric guitar on *Nebraska*. Played with an up-tempo guitar riff in the style of Chuck Berry, "Open All Night" is rife with New Jersey imagery, including a reference to the Route 60 location of a Bob's Big Boy, the hamburger restaurant chain with the distinctive statue of its titular mascot. Brimming with longing and nostalgia, the song traces the narrator's all-night drive, with a Texaco road map open on his lap, to meet his New Jersey girlfriend.

"My Father's House"

Bruce Springsteen: vocals, acoustic guitar, synthesizer, harmonica

In his autobiography, Springsteen recalled writing songs "from a child's point of view. 'Mansion on the Hill,' 'Used Cars,' and 'My Father's House' were all stories that came out of my experience with my family" (Springsteen, *Born to Run*, 2016). In "My Father's House," the composer draws upon a key biblical phrase from John 14:2: "My Father's house has many rooms; if that were not so, would I have told you that I am going there to prepare a place for you?"

In a 1990 concert, Springsteen introduced "My Father's House," recalling that "I had this habit for a long time: I used to get in my car and drive back through my old neighborhood in the town I grew up in. I'd always drive past the old houses that I used to live in, sometimes late at night. I got so I would do it really regularly—two, three, four times a week for years. I eventually got to wondering, 'What the hell am I doing?' So, I went to see the psychiatrist. I said, 'Doc, for years I've been getting in my car and driving past my old houses late at night. What am I doing?'" In the story, Springsteen's psychiatrist told him that "something bad happened and you're going back thinking you can make it right again. Something went wrong and you keep going back to see if you can fix it or somehow make it right. . . . Well, you can't."

"Reason to Believe"
Bruce Springsteen: vocals, acoustic guitar, harmonica

Working in a bluesy mode, Springsteen considers the nature of earthly existence in "Reason to Believe" after seeing the image of a dead dog lying in the sun along the highway. Eventually, the song explores the nature of religion, from baptism to internment, with Springsteen singing "Lord, won't you tell us, tell us what does it mean." In another sense, "Reason to Believe" examines the notion of the American Dream and individual success as cultural touchstones—as different sorts of pillars of faith for humanity. In its *Bruce Springsteen Collector's Edition* (2022), *Rolling Stone* listed "Reason to Believe" as number fifty-nine among the artist's top 100 songs.

BORN IN THE U.S.A./BRUCE SPRINGSTEEN

INCLUDES THE SINGLE
DANCING IN THE DARK

Born in the U.S.A. (Alamy) [LP cover]

BORN IN THE U.S.A.

Released in June 1984, *Born in the U.S.A.* sold seventeen million copies in the United States, easily notching it as Springsteen's most successful album, as well as one of the most successful albums in the history of recorded music. In addition, *Born in the U.S.A.* generated seven top ten singles: "Dancing in the Dark," "Cover Me," "Born in the U.S.A.," "I'm on Fire," "Glory Days," "I'm Goin' Down," and "My Hometown."

Eight of *Born in the U.S.A.*'s songs have their roots in the *Electric Nebraska* sessions at New York City's Power Station and the Hit Factory. Chuck Plotkin, who had participated in the mixing sessions for *Darkness on the Edge of Town*, joined Jon Landau as coproducer of Springsteen's latest LP. The album's iconic cover shot, with a red cap tucked into the rear pocket of the musician's blue jeans, was taken by Annie Leibovitz.

Springsteen found inspiration for the album from reading Ron Kovic's Vietnam-era memoir, *Born on the Fourth of July* (1976), as well as a script by Paul Schrader with the working title of *Born in the U.S.A.* With these works in mind, Springsteen later recalled, "I wrote and recorded my soldier's story. It was a protest song, and when I heard it thundering back at me through the Hit Factory's gargantuan studio speakers, I knew it was one of the best things I'd ever done. It was a GI blues, the verses an accounting, the choruses a declaration of the one sure thing that could not be denied . . . birthplace. Birthplace, and the right to all of the blood, confusion, blessings and grace that come with it. Having paid body and soul, you have earned, many times over, the right to claim and shape your piece of home ground."

Many of *Born in the U.S.A.*'s songs were recorded in the space of three weeks, with Springsteen putting the finishing touches to the LP after overcoming a bout of writer's block, which he later described as a protracted "brain freeze." For Springsteen, the resulting album and the release of his biggest hit single, "Dancing in the Dark," proved to be a revelation. "This was the record and song that'd take me my farthest into the pop mainstream," he later wrote. "I was always of two minds about big records and the chance involved in engaging a mass audience. You should be. There's risk. Was the effort of seeking that audience worth the exposure, the discomfort of the spotlight and the amount of life that'd be handed over? What was the danger of dilution of your core message, your purpose, the reduction of your best intentions to empty symbolism or worse?"

An overwhelming commercial and critical success, *Born in the U.S.A.* found Springsteen and the E Street Band connecting with the malingering despair associated with the post-Vietnam zeitgeist and a growing socioeconomic unrest in the American Heartland.

HISTORICAL CONTEXT

The nation and the rock universe were both undergoing an important transformation in the early 1980s. The conservative movement within the Republican Party led by President Ronald Reagan sought to revive traditional American or family values and renew a sense of patriotism, combined with a laissez-faire economic agenda that favored business and free-market capitalism. Reagan sought to take government out of people's lives and stop the expansion of regulations, famously saying in his 1981 inaugural address, "Government is not the solution to our problem; government is the problem." Reagan and his conservative allies sought to move beyond the humiliation of the Vietnam War and the disgrace of Watergate and restore the American people's pride in their country. The Democrats in 1984 would try to exploit the so-called gender gap, referring to the lack of support for Reagan among women, by nominating Geraldine Ferraro as the first female vice-presidential candidate in history, but Reagan won a second term in the White House by defeating Walter Mondale by a landslide in the 1984 presidential election.

Meanwhile, to many people at that time, rock had lost its edge as it had gotten older, while a new generation of rockers created a smoother, more technologically advanced and pop-oriented form of rock known as "New Wave." Billy Joel may have sung "It's still rock and roll to me" in reference to the new-wave aesthetic, but many rock fans did not agree. Furthermore, after the debut of MTV in August 1981, rock and pop came prepackaged in music videos as well, becoming even more associated with the crass commercialism that the British rock band Dire Straits would lampoon in their 1985 hit "Money for Nothing."

Bruce Springsteen had demonstrated a great deal of bravado in bucking this trend in putting out his folk-inspired *Nebraska* in 1982, though he did approve a music video to promote the song "Atlantic City" from the album. By 1984, though, Springsteen was ready to not only join but to conquer the pop universe with his spectacularly successful album *Born in the U.S.A.* He even infused the title track, lyrically a searing indictment of American society and in particular its continued shabby and shameful treatment of Vietnam War veterans, with an energetic rock beat that belied the somber message of the lyric.

Misunderstanding "Born in the U.S.A." as a patriotic anthem, Reagan attempted to appropriate the song on a campaign stop in New Jersey and Chrysler Corporation CEO Lee Iacocca sought permission to use it to sell cars. Springsteen made clear that he did not support Reagan's use of the song and refused, as usual, to allow his songs to be used for commercial purposes, but in other ways Springsteen seemed to have sold out for financial success, even getting famed Hollywood director Brian De Palma to direct the music video for "Dancing in the Dark," the most popular of the seven singles released from the album.

PRODUCTION

Released on June 4, 1984, Columbia Records
Produced by Bruce Springsteen, Jon Landau, Chuck Plotkin, and Steven Van Zandt
Engineered by Toby Scott, Mike Batlan, Neil Dorfsman, and Bill Scheniman
Recording Assistants: John Davenport, Jeff Hendrickson, Bruce Lampcov, Billy Straus, Zoe Yankas
Mixed by Bob Clearmountain at the Power Station, New York City
Mastered by Bob Ludwig at Masterdisk

Recorded at the Power Station and the Hit Factory in New York City, January 1982 to March 1984

PERSONNEL

Bruce Springsteen: lead vocals, electric and acoustic guitars
Roy Bittan: piano, synthesizer, background vocals
Clarence Clemons: tenor saxophone, percussion, background vocals
Danny Federici: organ, piano, glockenspiel
Garry Tallent: electric bass, background vocals
Steven Van Zandt: electric and acoustic guitars, mandolin, background vocals
Max Weinberg: drums, background vocals
Richie "La Bamba" Rosenberg: background vocals
Ruth Davis: background vocals

COVER ART AND PACKAGING

Cover design: Andrea Klein
Photography: Annie Leibovitz (cover) and David Gahr
Born in the U.S.A. marked Springsteen's first LP to be released as both a long-playing record and a compact disc.

Leibovitz: Springsteen chose the "picture for the album, which is to me like a 'grab' shot. And he really liked that. I took a lot of pictures that I liked better. He doesn't really like to look at himself" (*Backstreets*, 1985).

Springsteen: "The flag is a powerful image, and when you set that stuff loose, you don't know what's gonna be done with it." Some detractors suggested that the cover photo depicted Springsteen urinating on the flag, which he denied, insisting that "the picture of my ass looked

Springsteen and Reagan

Bruce Springsteen's initial foray into the political arena in his participation in the No Nukes concerts continued when he proclaimed his resistance to the political views of Ronald Reagan during a concert at Arizona State University on November 5, 1980, the night following Reagan's victory over incumbent Jimmy Carter for the presidency. An extremely extroverted performer on stage, Springsteen overcame his introversion when it came to politics by telling the crowd, "I don't know what you thought about what happened last night, but I thought it was pretty terrifying." He then launched into a performance of "Badlands," allowing his music to not only speak for itself as usual but this time to amplify his previous comment.

Springsteen's initial negative appraisal of Reagan did not deter the president from lauding Springsteen as just the kind of example of a hard-working, self-made, self-reliant individual that fueled his particular version of laissez-faire economics. Reagan was a strong advocate for small government, a core Conservative belief at the time. The fact that this view directly clashed with Springsteen's indictment of the failure of government to do more for Vietnam War veterans in his 1984 smash hit "Born in the U.S.A." did not prevent Reagan from appropriating it as an anthem for his campaign for reelection that same year. On stage in Pittsburgh on the night he heard about Reagan's compliment, Springsteen disavowed it, although he largely eschewed the controversy about the misappropriation of his song. But something had changed, nonetheless, in Springsteen's mind from which there would be no turning back.

In his 2016 memoir, *Born to Run*, he cited that night in Pittsburgh as one of a kind of political awakening, fueled more, he says, by an illuminating meeting with a remarkable union organizer named Ron Weisen than by his anger over Reagan's acclaim for Springsteen in support of his Republican cause and reelection. Either way, Springsteen and Reagan would be forever linked by their indirect association in 1984 and the very year in which Springsteen enjoyed his greatest commercial success at a climactic moment of his career also saw him take a further step toward an openness to political activism that would prove important to his life and music for years to come.

better than the picture of my face, [so] that's what went on the cover" (*Rolling Stone*, 1984).

TRACK LISTING

All songs composed by Bruce Springsteen.
Side one
1. "Born in the U.S.A."
2. "Cover Me"
3. "Darlington County"
4. "Working on the Highway"
5. "Downbound Train"
6. "I'm on Fire"
Side Two
1. "No Surrender"
2. "Bobby Jean"
3. "I'm Goin' Down"
4. "Glory Days"

5. "Dancing in the Dark"
6. "My Hometown"

UNRELEASED OUTTAKES

"Brothers under the Bridges": released on
   Tracks (1998)
"Car Wash": released on *Tracks* (1998)
"County Fair": released on *Essential Bruce
   Springsteen* (2003)
"Cynthia": released on *Tracks* (1998)
"Frankie": released on *Tracks* (1998)
"Janey, Don't You Lose Heart": released as the
   B-side for "I'm Goin' Down"; released on
   Tracks (1998)
"Johnny Bye Bye": released as the B-side for
   "I'm on Fire"; released on *Tracks* (1998)
"Lion's Den": released on *Tracks* (1998)
"Man at the Top": released on *Tracks* (1998)
"Murder Incorporated": released on *Greatest
   Hits* (1995)
"My Love Will Not Let You Down": released on
   Tracks (1998)
"None but the Brave": released on *Essential
   Bruce Springsteen* (2003)
"Pink Cadillac": released as the B-side for
   "Dancing in the Dark"; released on *Tracks*
   (1998)
"Rockaway the Days": released on *Tracks* (1998)
"Shut out the Light": released as a B-side for
   "Born in the U.S.A."; released on *Tracks* (1998)
"Stand on It": released as the B-side for "Glory
   Days"; released on *Tracks* (1998)
"This Hard Land": released on *Tracks* (1998);
   rerecorded for *Greatest Hits* (1995)
"TV Movie": released on *Tracks* (1998)
"Wages of Sin": released on *Tracks* (1998)

CONTEMPORARY REVIEWS

Sandy Robertson (*Sounds*, June 9, 1984):
"The title tune is a wildly declaimed,

drum-punctuated rock anthem, and if it lacks
the irony of a Chuck Berry geography lesson
it's hardly a major fault in a blast this full of
life. 'Cover Me,' a raucous shuffle melodrama
full of self-consciously 'hot' blues licks, can't
follow with much hope, but then nothing could—
Springers has learned the art of pacing his
albums. Lyrical analysis is out for me, mostly. In
spite of a heavy rep in that department, I think
most people hear this stuff as radio rock, car-
motorvating music . . . and this is a pinnacle of
that genre. Most of the tunes here could be covered by other artists, the way Beatles LPs used
to be stripped within days of release by young
hopefuls."

Debby Miller (*Rolling Stone*, July 19, 1984):
"Though it looks at hard times, at little people
in little towns choosing between going away and
getting left behind, *Born in the U.S.A.*, Bruce
Springsteen's seventh album, has a rowdy,
indomitable spirit. Two guys pull into a hick town
begging for work in 'Darlington County,' but
Springsteen is whooping with sha-la-las in the
chorus. He may shove his broody characters out
the door and send them cruising down the turnpike, but he gives them music they can pound on
the dashboard to. He's set songs as well-drawn as
those on his bleak acoustic album, *Nebraska*, to
music that incorporates new electronic textures
while keeping as its heart all of the American
rock 'n' roll from the early Sixties. Like the guys
in the songs, the music was born in the U.S.A.:
Springsteen ignored the British Invasion and
embraced instead the legacy of Phil Spector's
releases, the sort of soul that was coming from
Atlantic Records and especially the garage bands
that had anomalous radio hits. He's always
chased the utopian feeling of that music, and
here he catches it with a sophisticated production and a subtle change in surroundings—the

E Street Band cools it with the saxophone solos and piano arpeggios—from song to song. The people who hang out in the new songs dread getting stuck in the small towns they grew up in almost as much as they worry that the big world outside holds no possibilities—a familiar theme in Springsteen's work. But they wind up back at home, where you can practically see the roaches scurrying around the empty Twinkie packages in the linoleum kitchen. In the first line of the first song, Springsteen croaks, 'Born down in a dead man's town, the first kick I took was when I hit the ground.' His characters are born with their broken hearts, and the only thing that keeps them going is imagining that, as another line in another song goes, 'There's something happening somewhere.'"

Charles Shaar Murray (*New Musical Express*, August 4, 1984): "No one's going to get high on fantasy or rebellion from listening to *Born in the U.S.A.* There are no moments of delirious abandon here; the music is as dry and contracted as the state of mind it describes. It is very rare to see an artist take a clearcut choice between selling his audience the same old bullshit that he knows they love and telling them the truth even if it means letting go of stuff that sells. By abandoning all that 'rebel triumphant' blabber 'n' smoke, Bruce Springsteen displays the kind of moral and artistic integrity that rock music rarely shows any more. The power of *Born in the U.S.A.* is less flashy and less intoxicating, but it is far more real than the power of Springsteen's early work; this is the power of an artist telling the truth."

Jeff Nesin (*Creem*, September 1984): "The most meaningful question for an LP like *Born in the U.S.A.* is, 'is it worth its weight, is it worth its popularity?' My answer is 'absolutely yes.' If I don't in my secret heart, agree with Bruce Springsteen that extraordinary individual will

and passion can somehow overcome bleak-to-no prospects, these songs will still be good to hear in the months to come. And if Springsteen, in his secret heart, knows he has to find a better metaphor for aging than 'hearts of fire grow cold,' . . . I'm sure that his upcoming live-till '85 touring will help both him and the multitudes flocking to see him feel younger and better able to cope. So, however dark its core, I'm glad to have *Born in the U.S.A.* You don't have to be Bruceish to love it."

PROMOTION

The *Born in the U.S.A.* tour commenced in June 1984 and concluded in October 1985, and including 157 shows, the performance of eighty-four different songs, and grossing $90 million in receipts before an audience of some 3.9 million.

CHART ACTION

Billboard Top 200 Albums: number one.

Released on June 4, 1984, *Born in the U.S.A.* debuted at number nine on June 23; the number-one album that week was the *Footloose* soundtrack. The album peaked at number one on July 7, holding down the top spot on the charts for seven weeks. Overall, *Born in the U.S.A.* spent 143 weeks on the *Billboard* charts. The album sold more than thirty million copies worldwide, including seventeen million in the United States alone, where it earned multiplatinum status from RIAA.

COMMENTS FROM SPRINGSTEEN AND HIS CIRCLE

Springsteen: "What I've tried to do in this new music is that I've previously written a lot about certain things that were caught up in my past. I came out of a working-class environment, played in working-class bars, and my history just drew me towards those topics naturally. I didn't have any particular worldview or any rhetoric that I was trying to get across in any way. It was just those things that felt urgent. I wrote a lot about that and I'm proud of that music. But I felt at the end of *Born in the U.S.A.* that I'd said all I wanted to say about those things. My battles were elsewhere" (*Q*, 1992).

Max Weinberg: "We recorded about 80 songs for *Born in the U.S.A.* Some of them are great. 'This Hard Land,' which didn't make it on the record, is just fantastic. That's probably my favorite song we've done. . . . Bob Clearmountain mixed it. On the record you hear everything—it's a very clean sounding record. It's more contemporary sounding than what we've been doing in the past. We got some good drum sounds. I got in the studio, and I hit the drum about as hard as I can hit it. The rest is just momentum" (*Backstreets*, 1984).

Roy Bittan: "We started recording in the beginning of '83. Digital technology was just coming in then, but I had a feeling that we were going to hold onto the CS-80 (synthesizer) because of its warmth. Anyway, for 'Born in the U.S.A.' Bruce came into the studio and said, 'I got this song,' and he played the thing on the guitar. . . . The first thing I noticed was there was no third in it, and that invoked this sort of Oriental sound. I don't know; maybe there was some subliminal thing about Vietnam behind it when Bruce wrote that riff" (*Keyboard* magazine, 1986).

Jon Landau: "He [Springsteen] has strong feelings for his country, which he has tried to reconcile in that song with certain hard facts from reality. Someone wrote, '"Born in the

U.S.A." is a patriotic song, not a nationalistic one.' Bruce is not a nationalist. He loves America, but he is fully aware of the limitations and problems of the system and wants people to think about it" (*OOR* [Netherlands], 1987).

MISCELLANEOUS

Midway through the production of *Born in the U.S.A.*, Van Zandt left the E Street Band to strike out on his own. For the impending world tour, Springsteen added guitarists Nils Lofgren and Patti Scialfa to the lineup.

In 1985, Springsteen earned his first Grammy Award for "Dancing in the Dark," which was honored for Best Male Vocal.

In 2020, *Rolling Stone* ranked *Born in the U.S.A.* at number 142 among its 500 Greatest Albums of All Time.

SONG ANALYSES

SIDE ONE

"Born in the U.S.A."
Bruce Springsteen: vocals, guitar
Roy Bittan: synthesizer, backing vocals
Clarence Clemons: percussion, backing vocals
Danny Federici: piano, glockenspiel
Garry Tallent: bass, backing vocals
Steven Van Zandt: guitar, mandolin, backing vocals
Max Weinberg: drums, backing vocals

Springsteen composed the album's title track after meeting disabled Vietnam veteran Ron Kovic in 1980. Springsteen had recently read Kovic's *Born on the Fourth of July* (1976) and was moved by the plight of veterans. Kovic invited him to visit a California veterans' center, and Springsteen couldn't believe his eyes. As he later remarked during his *Springsteen on*

Broadway residency, "I'm usually pretty easy with people, but once we were at the center, I didn't know how to respond to what I was seeing. Talking about my own life to these guys seemed frivolous. There was homelessness and drug problems and post-traumatic stress—guys my age dealing with life-changing physical injuries."

Originally titled "Vietnam," "Born in the U.S.A." was based on Springsteen's experiences at the center, as well as the overall impact of Kovic's book. The songwriter recalled, "The verses are just an accounting of events. The chorus is a declaration of your birthplace, and the right to all the pride and confusion and shame and grace that comes with it." When Springsteen first unveiled the song in the studio, Bittan fashioned an accompaniment on his new Yamaha CS-80 synthesizer, the instrument that he deployed on several of the songs on *Born in the U.S.A.* The result was "a riff—a very succinct, simplistic riff. I was always intensely listening to the lyrics to see what the hell the song was about. So I heard what he was talking about, and what I tried to conjure up is a Southeast Asian sort of synthesized, strange sound. And I played the riff on that" (*Rolling Stone*, 1984). In its *Bruce Springsteen Collector's Edition* (2022), *Rolling Stone* listed "Born in the USA" as number nine among the artist's top 100 songs.

CHART ACTION
Billboard Hot 100: number nine. The song also notched a number-eight showing on the magazine's Mainstream Rock chart.

"Born in the U.S.A." b/w "Shut out the Light" was released on October 30, 1984. The number-one song that week was Stevie Wonder's "I Just Called to Say I Loved You."

"Cover Me"
Bruce Springsteen: vocals, guitar
Roy Bittan: piano, synthesizer, backing vocals
Clarence Clemons: saxophone, percussion, backing vocals
Danny Federici: organ, glockenspiel
Garry Tallent: bass, backing vocals
Steven Van Zandt: guitar, mandolin, backing vocals
Max Weinberg: drums, backing vocals
Richie "La Bamba" Rosenberg: backing vocals

Originally composed for disco superstar Donna Summer, "Cover Me" explores the unforgiving nature of a contemporary world consumed with greed and self-satisfaction. After he recorded a demo for the song, he opted to keep it for himself, sharing with Summer another tune called "Protection" instead; Springsteen played the guitar solo on Summer's recording. In *Songs* (1998), Springsteen observed that Summer "could really sing, and I disliked the veiled racism of the anti-disco movement."

Springsteen composed "Cover Me" at the tail end of a writing spurt that came to an end when he began questioning himself about the overtly commercial nature of his latest batch of songs. After "Cover Me," a "brain freeze settled in," he recalled. "I was uncomfortable with the pop aspect of my finished material and wanted something deeper, heavier and more serious. I waited, I wrote, I recorded, then I waited some more. Months passed in writer's block, with me holed up in a little cottage I'd bought by the Navesink River, the songs coming like the last drops of water being pumped out of a temporarily dry well" (Springsteen, *Born to Run*, 2016).

CHART ACTION
Billboard Hot 100: number seven. The song also registered a number-two showing on the magazine's Mainstream Rock chart and number eleven on the Hot Dance/Disco chart.

"Cover Me" b/w "Jersey Girl (live)" was released on July 31, 1984. The number-one song that week was Prince's "When Doves Cry."

B-side: "Jersey Girl"

Bruce Springsteen: vocals, electric guitar
Roy Bittan: piano, backing vocals
Clarence Clemons: saxophone, maracas, backing vocals
Danny Federici: organ, glockenspiel
Garry Tallent: electric bass, backing vocals
Steven Van Zandt: electric guitar, backing vocals
Max Weinberg: drums, backing vocals

Often associated with Springsteen, "Jersey Girl" was originally composed and recorded by American singer-songwriter Tom Waits for his 1980 album *Heartattack and Vine*. Springsteen's version of the song was recorded on July 9, 1981, at Brendan Byrne Arena in East Rutherford, New Jersey. "Jersey Girl" has become a beloved staple of Springsteen's live performances.

"Darlington County"

Bruce Springsteen: vocals, guitar
Roy Bittan: piano, synthesizer, backing vocals
Clarence Clemons: saxophone, percussion, backing vocals
Danny Federici: organ, glockenspiel
Garry Tallent: bass, backing vocals
Steven Van Zandt: guitar, mandolin, backing vocals
Max Weinberg: drums, backing vocals

"Darlington County" was originally composed for *Darkness on the Edge of Town*. The song shares many of the fatalistic storytelling devices from that era, as well as *The River* and *Nebraska*, in which Springsteen's characters come face to face with the unknown. In "Darlington County," two working-class men from New York City take a road trip to Darlington County, South Carolina. With their big city panache, they brag to the local girls that their fathers each own one of the World Trade Center towers. The narrator's carefree nonchalance is broken when they begin searching for love and work, only to see his buddy arrested at the hands of a state trooper, suggesting that their city-wise sophistication hasn't prepared them for the world outside of the metropolis.

"Working on the Highway"

Bruce Springsteen: vocals, guitar
Roy Bittan: piano, synthesizer, backing vocals
Clarence Clemons: saxophone, percussion, backing vocals
Danny Federici: organ, glockenspiel
Garry Tallent: bass, backing vocals
Steven Van Zandt: guitar, mandolin, backing vocals
Max Weinberg: drums, backing vocals

Originally titled "Child Bride," "Working on the Highway" was originally written for *Nebraska* and finds Springsteen exploring the "meanness in the world" that pervades that album. Over the years, "Working on the Highway" has emerged as a popular concert staple. During a July 26, 1992, performance of the song at the Brendan Byrne Arena, Springsteen danced with his mother, Adele. When the song ended, Springsteen quipped that "a boy's best friend is his mother," referencing Alfred Hitchcock's *Psycho* (1960).

"Downbound Train"

Bruce Springsteen: vocals, guitar
Roy Bittan: piano, synthesizer, backing vocals
Clarence Clemons: percussion, backing vocals
Danny Federici: organ, glockenspiel
Garry Tallent: bass, backing vocals
Steven Van Zandt: guitar, mandolin, backing vocals
Max Weinberg: drums, backing vocals

As with several *Born in the U.S.A.* songs, "Downbound Train" was first attempted during the 1982 *Electric Nebraska* sessions. The song offers a melancholic study of the American Dream and its elusive, even toxic nature. Having lost his job at the lumberyard, as well as his girl in the bargain,

Springsteen's narrative contemplates our desperate attempts at love and an overarching loss that pervades our lives. In its *Bruce Springsteen Collector's Edition* (2022), *Rolling Stone* listed "Downbound Train" as number forty-four among the artist's top 100 songs.

"I'm on Fire"
Bruce Springsteen: vocals, guitar
Roy Bittan: piano, synthesizer, backing vocals
Clarence Clemons: percussion, backing vocals
Danny Federici: organ, glockenspiel
Garry Tallent: bass, backing vocals
Steven Van Zandt: guitar, mandolin, backing vocals
Max Weinberg: drums, backing vocals

Springsteen drew the lyrics for "I'm on Fire" from another tune, "Spanish Eyes." As for the music, he composed "I'm on Fire" live in the studio with keyboard player Roy Bittan and drummer Max Weinberg. As Springsteen concocted the song, Bittan and Weinberg began fashioning a moody, tension-filled accompaniment with a rockabilly air. "I'm on Fire" was supported by a popular video that enjoyed heavy rotation on MTV. Directed by John Sayles, the video depicted Springsteen as a working-class mechanic who is mixed up in a dangerous flirtation with a beautiful married woman. In 1985, "I'm on Fire" was honored with the MTV Video Music Award for Best Male Video. In its *Bruce Springsteen Collector's Edition* (2022), *Rolling Stone* listed "I'm on Fire" as number twenty-one among the artist's top 100 songs.

CHART ACTION
Billboard Hot 100: number six. The song also registered a number-six showing on the magazine's Adult Contemporary chart.

"I'm on Fire" b/w "Johnny Bye Bye" was released on February 6, 1985. The number-one song that week was Philip Bailey and Phil Collins's "Easy Lover."

"No Surrender"
Bruce Springsteen: vocals, guitar
Roy Bittan: piano, synthesizer, backing vocals
Clarence Clemons: saxophone, percussion, backing vocals
Danny Federici: organ, glockenspiel
Garry Tallent: bass, backing vocals
Max Weinberg: drums, backing vocals
Richie "La Bamba" Rosenberg: backing vocals

Originally titled "Brothers under the Bridges," "No Surrender" celebrates the power of friendship and rock and roll music. Springsteen reportedly included the song on *Born in the U.S.A.* at Van Zandt's insistence. "No Surrender" features one of the composer's most oft-quoted lines, "We learned more from a three-minute record, baby, than we ever learned in school." With Springsteen's permission, John Kerry employed the song as the anthem for his failed 2004 presidential bid. In its *Bruce Springsteen Collector's Edition* (2022), *Rolling Stone* listed "No Surrender" as number thirty-seven among the artist's top 100 songs.

"Bobby Jean"
Bruce Springsteen: vocals, guitar
Roy Bittan: piano, synthesizer, backing vocals
Clarence Clemons: saxophone, percussion, backing vocals
Danny Federici: organ, glockenspiel
Garry Tallent: bass, backing vocals
Max Weinberg: drums, backing vocals

As with "No Surrender," Springsteen considered "Bobby Jean" to be a paean to his longstanding friendship with Van Zandt and "the bonding power of rock" (*Born to Run*, 2016). With a poignant piano figure from Bittan and Clemons's mournful saxophone solo, "Bobby Jean" stands as one of the LP's most emotional tunes. In its *Bruce Springsteen Collector's Edition* (2022), *Rolling Stone* listed

"Bobby Jean" as number eighty-seven among the artist's top 100 songs.

"I'm Goin' Down"

Bruce Springsteen: vocals, guitar
Roy Bittan: piano, synthesizer, backing vocals
Clarence Clemons: saxophone, percussion, backing vocals
Danny Federici: organ, glockenspiel
Garry Tallent: bass, backing vocals
Steven Van Zandt: guitar, mandolin, backing vocals
Max Weinberg: drums, backing vocals

With a sizzling country and western crossover feel, the up-tempo "I'm Goin' Down" finds Springsteen bemoaning his sexual frustration amid the last act of a fading romantic relationship. As if to underscore the narrator's disgust and irritation, the word "down" appears more than eighty times in the song. In its *Bruce Springsteen Collector's Edition* (2022), *Rolling Stone* listed "I'm Goin' Down" as number fifty-two among the artist's top 100 songs.

CHART ACTION

Billboard Hot 100: number nine.

"I'm Goin' Down" b/w "Janey, Don't Lose Your Heart" was released on August 27, 1985. The number-one song that week was Huey Lewis and the News's "The Power of Love."

"Glory Days"

Bruce Springsteen: vocals, guitar
Roy Bittan: piano, synthesizer, backing vocals
Clarence Clemons: saxophone, percussion, backing vocals
Danny Federici: organ, glockenspiel
Garry Tallent: bass, backing vocals
Steven Van Zandt: guitar, mandolin, backing vocals
Max Weinberg: drums, backing vocals

Springsteen was inspired to compose "Glory Days" after a chance meeting with Joe DePugh, a star baseball player that he knew in high school. At the Headliner, a bar in Neptune, New Jersey, they reminisced about the summer of 1973. Over the years, the two men had drifted apart, but Springsteen held fond memories for their time together at Freehold's St. Rose of Lima School, where they played baseball together in the Babe Ruth league.

The song originally included a fourth verse about his father Doug Springsteen's lack of any discernible "glory days," but Springsteen deleted it, believing that it didn't cohere with the rest of the song's lighthearted feel. As with "I'm on Fire," the "Glory Days" video was directed by filmmaker John Sayles. Springsteen's girlfriend, actress and model Julianne Philips, made a cameo appearance in the video, along with E Street Band newcomers Nils Lofgren and Patti Scialfa. In its *Bruce Springsteen Collector's Edition* (2022), *Rolling Stone* listed "Glory Days" as number sixty-six among the artist's top 100 songs.

CHART ACTION

Billboard Hot 100: number five. The song also registered a number-three showing on the magazine's Mainstream Rock chart.

"Glory Days" b/w "Stand on It" was released on May 31, 1985. The number-one song that week was Simple Minds' "Don't You (Forget about Me)."

"Dancing in the Dark"

Bruce Springsteen: vocals, guitar
Roy Bittan: piano, synthesizer, backing vocals
Clarence Clemons: saxophone, percussion, backing vocals
Danny Federici: organ, glockenspiel
Garry Tallent: bass, backing vocals
Max Weinberg: drums, backing vocals

"Dancing in the Dark" was the last song recorded for the *Born in the U.S.A.* LP. The song was written at the urging of Landau, who felt that the album needed a lead-off single.

"Look," Bruce reportedly barked at Landau, "I've written 70 songs. You want another one, you write it" (Marsh, *Two Hearts*, 2004). That night, Springsteen retired to his hotel room and wrote "Dancing in the Dark" in one sitting. The song was recorded in six takes on February 14, 1984, at the Hit Factory.

Directed by celebrated filmmaker Brian De Palma, the video for "Dancing in the Dark" was shot on June 28–29, 1984, at the Civic Arena in St. Paul, Minnesota. For the purposes of the video, actress and future *Friends* star Courteney Cox was stationed in the audience so that Springsteen could invite her onstage to dance with him. Although the concept was later scrapped, the video originally included a storyline in which Cox and her friends get ready to go to the concert. In 1985, the video won the MTV Video Music Award for Best Stage Performance. In 2010, the Rock and Roll Hall of Fame ranked "Dancing in the Dark" among the 500 Songs that Shaped Rock.

CHART ACTION
Billboard Hot 100: number two. The song also registered a number-one showing on the magazine's Mainstream Rock chart and a number-seven showing on the Hot Dance/Disco chart.

"Dancing in the Dark" b/w "Pink Cadillac" was released on May 9, 1984. The number-one song that week was Phil Collins's "Against All Odds (Take a Look at Me Now)."

"My Hometown"
Bruce Springsteen: vocals, guitar
Roy Bittan: piano, synthesizer, backing vocals
Clarence Clemons: saxophone, percussion, backing vocals
Danny Federici: organ, glockenspiel
Garry Tallent: bass, backing vocals
Max Weinberg: drums, backing vocals
Ruth Jackson: backing vocals

Originally titled "Your Hometown," "My Hometown" found Springsteen reflecting on his uneasy relationship with Freehold, New Jersey, as well issues involving economic despair and racial strife. Reflecting on "My Hometown" during his *Springsteen on Broadway* show, the composer remarked that "everybody has a love/hate relationship with their hometown. It's just built into the equation of growing up." Springsteen addresses several historical occurrences, including a 1965 incident of race-baiting that he witnessed—"Two cars at a light on a Saturday night"—as well as the 1964 closure of Freehold's A&M Karagheusian Rug Mill after six decades in operation.

In 1985, the year after the release of the *Born in the U.S.A.* LP, 3M shuttered their Freehold factory. Springsteen subsequently held a benefit for the displaced workers. As he introduced "My Hometown," he remarked that "the marriage between a community and a company is a special thing that involves a special trust. What do you do after ten years or 20 years, you wake up in the morning and see your livelihood sailing away from you, leaving you standing on the dock? What happens when the jobs go away, and the people remain? What goes unmeasured is the price that unemployment inflicts on people's families, on their marriages, on the single mothers out there trying to raise their kids on their own. The 3M company: it's their money, it's their plant. But it's the 3M workers' jobs. I'm here to say that I think that after 25 years of service from a community, there is a debt owed to the 3M workers and to my hometown." In its *Bruce Springsteen Collector's Edition* (2022), *Rolling Stone* listed "My Hometown" as number seventy-eight among the artist's top 100 songs.

Billboard Hot 100: number six. The song also registered a number-one showing on the magazine's Adult Contemporary chart, as well as number six on the Album Rock Tracks chart.

"My Hometown" b/w "Santa Claus Is Comin' to Town (live)" was released on November 21, 1985. The number-one song that week was Stevie Wonder's "I Just Called to Say I Loved You."

B-side: "Santa Claus Is Comin' to Town"
Bruce Springsteen: vocals, electric guitar, harmonica
Roy Bittan: piano, backing vocals
Clarence Clemons: saxophone, backing vocals
Danny Federici: organ, glockenspiel
Garry Tallent: electric bass, backing vocals
Max Weinberg: drums, backing vocals
Steven Van Zandt: electric guitar, backing vocals

Springsteen's rendition of the holiday classic was originally recorded on December 12, 1975, at C. W. Post College in Brookville, New York. Springsteen fashioned the chorus after the Crystals' 1963 recording of "Santa Claus Is Comin' to Town." Springsteen's version was originally released in 1982 as a selection on *In Harmony 2*, a Sesame Street record compilation. Over the years, Springsteen's cover version of "Santa Claus Is Comin' to Town" has emerged as a perennial seasonal favorite.

CONTEMPORANEOUS RELEASES

"War"
Bruce Springsteen: vocals, electric guitar
Roy Bittan: piano, backing vocals
Clarence Clemons: saxophone, backing vocals
Danny Federici: organ
Nils Lofgren: electric guitar, backing vocals
Patti Scialfa: guitar, backing vocals
Garry Tallent: electric bass, backing vocals
Max Weinberg: drums, backing vocals

Released in support of *Live 1975–1985* album, Springsteen and the E Street Band's cover version of "War" was recorded live on September 30, 1985, at the Los Angeles Memorial Coliseum. The song was written by Norman Whitfield and Barrett Strong as an antiwar anthem during the Vietnam era. Originally earmarked as a vehicle for the Temptations, "War" topped the charts in 1970 with Edwin Starr handling lead vocals.

Billboard Hot 100: number eight.

"War" b/w "Merry Christmas Baby" was released on November 10, 1986. The number-one song that week was Boston's "Amanda."

"Fire"
Bruce Springsteen: vocals, electric guitar
Roy Bittan: piano, backing vocals
Clarence Clemons: saxophone, backing vocals
Danny Federici: organ
Garry Tallent: electric bass, backing vocals
Max Weinberg: drums, backing vocals
Steven Van Zandt: electric guitar, backing vocals

Released in support of *Live 1975–1985* album, Springsteen and the E Street Band recorded "Fire" live at the Winterland Ballroom in San Francisco on December 16, 1978. Springsteen had originally composed "Fire" after attending Elvis Presley's concert in Philadelphia on May 28, 1977, hoping that the King would record a cover version (Presley died on August 16). Later that summer, he recorded a studio version of his own during the *Darkness on the Edge of Town* sessions. That take was later included on *The Promise* (2010). "Fire" came to prominence in 1979 after the Pointer Sisters notched a number-two showing with the song, which had been produced by Richard Perry for the singers' *Energy* album (1978).

"Fire," *Billboard* Hot 100: number forty-six. The song also notched a number-eight showing on the magazine's Mainstream Rock chart.

"Fire" b/w "Incident on 57th Street (live)" was released on January 1, 1987. The number-one song that week was the Bangles' "Walk Like an Egyptian."

"We Are the World"

An international chart-topping 1985 charity record featuring a cavalcade of pop-music luminaries, "We Are the World" included a standout vocal performance from Springsteen. Composed by Lionel Richie and Michael Jackson, "We Are the World" was produced by Quincy Jones and Michael Omartian. Credited to USA for Africa, the multiplatinum single was spearheaded by musician and activist Harry Belafonte in support of African famine relief.

In addition to Springsteen, "We Are the World" included contributions from Ray Charles, Billy Joel, Diana Ross, Cyndi Lauper, and Tina Turner.

Billboard Hot 100: number one.

"We Are the World" b/w "Grace" was released on March 7, 1985. The number-one song that week was "Careless Whisper" by Wham! featuring George Michael.

Tunnel of Love (Alamy) [LP cover]

TUNNEL OF LOVE

Released in October 1987, *Tunnel of Love* continued *Born in the U.S.A.*'s commercial juggernaut, notching a chart-topping LP and a trio of hit singles in "Brilliant Disguise," "Tunnel of Love," and "One Step Up." For his eighth studio album, Springsteen recorded most of the instrumentation himself, which he supplemented with drum machines and synthesizers. For his efforts, he earned a Grammy Award in 1988 for Best Rock Vocal Performance.

Tunnel of Love found Springsteen at an interpersonal crossroads. His 1985 marriage to Julianne Phillips was in jeopardy and the singer-songwriter was posing larger questions about the nature of romance and erotic relationships in the face of an encroaching middle age. Springsteen later observed that "the twin issues of love and identity form the core of *Tunnel of Love*, but *time* is *Tunnel*'s unofficial subtext. In this life (and there is only one), you make your choices, you take your stand and you awaken from the youthful spell of 'immortality' and its eternal present. You walk away from the nether land of adolescence. You name the things beyond your work that will give your life its context, meaning . . . and the clock starts. You walk, now, not just at your partner's side, but alongside your own mortal self. You fight to hold on to your newfound blessings while confronting your nihilism, your destructive desire to leave it all in ruins. This struggle to uncover who I was and to reach an uneasy peace with time and death itself is at the heart of *Tunnel of Love*" (Springsteen, *Born to Run*, 2016).

With Chuck Plotkin and Jon Landau joining him as coproducers, Springsteen recorded the album between January and July 1987. As with *Born in the U.S.A.*, *Tunnel of Love* benefited from the video zeitgeist. The album's promotional videos were shot in Asbury Park, New Jersey, including "Brilliant Disguise," which was nominated for five MTV Video Music Awards, including Video of the Year. Directed by Irish filmmaker Meiert Avis, "Brilliant Disguise" came up short, losing out to Peter Gabriel's groundbreaking "Sledgehammer" video. *Tunnel of Love* was certified triple platinum, a far cry from the epoch-making sales enjoyed by *Born in the U.S.A.*, but impressive nonetheless in a crowded and highly competitive pop-music landscape.

HISTORICAL CONTEXT

In the music video for "Tougher than the Rest," which charted as a single in Australia and a number of European countries (it was not released as a single in the United States), Bruce Springsteen and his backing singer Patti Scialfa sing emotionally and passionately to one another in a too-convincing performance in which it was unclear if art was imitating life or vice versa. The significance of this performance lies in the portrayal of a reciprocal and equal relationship that came toward the end of a

decade that saw heterosexual couples striving to adjust and renegotiate their relationships in the wake of the feminist movement of the late 1960s and 1970s. Significantly, the video also included same-sex couples in a series of candid scenes of lovers displaying their affection for one another, a major comment coming from the overtly heterosexual Springsteen.

In this social and historical context, it seems appropriate, in keeping with the times, that Springsteen would follow up the mischievously masculine, rock-oriented, semiaggressive tone of *Born in the U.S.A.* with an inward-looking album that would focus on the fraught nature of interpersonal relationships at a time of social and cultural change. This was one way for him to answer his critics who had conjectured that he had abandoned his authentic singer-songwriter credentials to appeal to a broader pop audience. But it was also a way of staying relevant at a time when younger bands and artists were starting to encroach on the culture's attention, including groups like R.E.M., which continued to expand its popular appeal with the release of its fifth album, *Document*, just weeks before Springsteen released *Tunnel of Love* on October 6, 1987.

Also released about the same time as Springsteen's new album was a new volume by the soothsayer of sexuality, Shere Hite, who had previously garnered both great publicity and multimillion-dollar sales with *The Hite Report: A Nationwide Study on Female Sexuality* (1976) and *The Hite Report on Male Sexuality* (1981). In 1987, she released *Women and Love: A Cultural Revolution in Progress*, in which her data (challenged by some as being skewed by self-selective questionnaire responders) seemed to suggest that gender relations in the 1980s had started to unravel as women were becoming increasingly dissatisfied with the men in their relationships.

If Hite was to be believed, women were becoming stronger, more self-sufficient, and making gains in the workplace, while men were becoming more emotional, vulnerable, and dependent, expecting women now to fulfill a dual role as a wage earner and a nurturer of the male ego.

Listening to *Tunnel of Love* in this light makes for an interesting experience that suggests the album transcends whatever personal crisis Springsteen himself was experiencing around this time. Regarded as one of his most autobiographical albums, *Tunnel of Love* came out while Springsteen was apparently reassessing his recent marriage to the model and actor Julianne Phillips. *Tunnel of Love* explores the many ways in which he channeled his own experiences, questions, and insights into human nature and himself in lyrics and music that spoke to others living through a comparable shift in gender roles and societal expectations for relationships.

PRODUCTION

Released on June 4, 1984, Columbia Records
Produced by Bruce Springsteen, Jon Landau, and Chuck Plotkin
Engineered by Toby Scott, assisted by Tim Leithner, Roger Talkov, Squeek Stone, and Rob Jacobs
Mixed by Bob Clearmountain at A&M Studios
Mastered by Bob Ludwig at Masterdisk, assisted by Heidi Cron
Recorded at Thrill Hill Recording and A&M Studios, January-July 1987

PERSONNEL

Bruce Springsteen: vocals, electric and acoustic guitars, mandolin, electric bass, keyboards, harmonica, percussion, drum machines

Clarence Clemons: backing vocals
Danny Federici: organ
Nils Lofgren: guitar, backing vocals
Garry Tallent: electric bass
Max Weinberg: drums, percussion
Patti Scialfa: backing vocals
Roy Bittan: keyboards
The Schiffer family of Point Pleasant, New Jersey: roller coaster vocals

COVER ART AND PACKAGING

Cover design: Sandra Choron
Photography: Annie Leibovitz (cover), Bob Adelman, Kryn Taconis, and Elliott Erwitt

TRACK LISTING

All songs composed by Bruce Springsteen.

1. "Ain't Got You"
2. "Tougher than the Rest"
3. "All that Heaven Will Allow"
4. "Spare Parts"
5. "Cautious Man"
6. "Walk Like a Man"
7. "Tunnel of Love"
8. "Two Faces"
9. "Brilliant Disguise"
10. "One Step Up"
11. "When You're Alone"
12. "Valentine's Day"

UNRELEASED OUTTAKES

"The Honeymooners": released on *Tracks* (1998)
"Lucky Man": released on *Tracks* (1998)
"When You Need Me": released on *Tracks* (1998)
"The Wish": released on *Tracks* (1998)

CONTEMPORARY REVIEWS

Steve Pond (*Rolling Stone*, October 3, 1987): "So Bruce Springsteen met a girl, fell in love, got married and made an album of songs about meeting a girl, falling in love and getting married. And if you think it's that cut and dried, you don't know Springsteen. Far from being a series of hymns to cozy domesticity, *Tunnel of Love* is an unsettled and unsettling collection of hard looks at the perils of commitment. A decade or so ago, Springsteen acquired a reputation for romanticizing his subject matter; on this album he doesn't even romanticize romance. *Tunnel of Love* is precisely the right move for an artist whose enormous success gloriously affirmed the potential of arena rock 'n' roll but exacted a toll on the singer. *Born in the U.S.A.* sold 12 million copies mostly because it was the best kind of thoughtful, tough, mainstream rock and roll record—but also because it was misinterpreted and oversimplified by listeners looking for slogans rather than ideas. When Springsteen hit the road to support that album, his sound got bigger, his gestures larger, his audience huger. The five-record live set that followed that tour was a suitably oversize way to sum up Bruce Springsteen, the Boss, American Rock Icon. But where do you go from there? Trying to top *Born in the U.S.A.* with another collection of rock anthems would have been foolhardy artistically; on the other hand, to react the way Springsteen did after the breakthrough 1980 success of *The River*—with a homemade record as stark and forbidding as *Nebraska*— would have turned an inspired gesture into a formula. So *Tunnel of Love* walks a middle ground. The most intelligently arranged album Springsteen has made, it consists mostly of his own tracks, sparingly overdubbed; he uses the members of the E Street Band when they fit. It's not, as was rumored, a country album, though Springsteen sings it in the colloquial, folkish voice he used on *Nebraska*, and it's not a rock 'n' roll album, though 'Spare Parts' and 'Brilliant Disguise' come close to the full-bodied E Street Band sound. Instead, this is a varied, modestly scaled, modern-sounding pop album; it is a less ambitious work than *Born in the U.S.A.*, but its simpler sound is perfectly suited to the more intimate stories Springsteen is telling. Although you could often hear the sweat on his previous records, this LP came surprisingly quickly and feels effortless and elegant rather than belabored. Crucially, it demystifies Springsteen's often arduous album-making process."

Richard Williams (*The Times*, October 5, 1987): "Of the individual songs, 'Walk Like a Man' returns with great success to a favorite theme, Springsteen's difficult relationship with his father. 'Ain't Got You,' just voice and guitar, rewrites Billy Boy Arnold's old rhythm and blues hit of the same name, over a chopping Bo Diddley beat. 'All That Heaven Allows' has a sort of pre-Beatles charm, while 'One Step Up' is a moving snapshot of a washed-up marriage, pitched against a slowly resolving chord cycle. On the other hand, the title song finds nothing new in its chosen metaphor, and the closing 'Valentine's Day' muffs the big romantic gesture. Is it legitimate to hope that he will one day again give us songs as rich in conception and detail as 'Thunder Road'? While providing some reassurance, *Tunnel of Love* falls short of satisfying the highest expectations, which in this case are the only sort worth having."

Neil Taylor (*New Musical Express*, October 10, 1987): "But what does the man who has everything do now? The answer is of course to do exactly what he's always done. Take the same seemingly hackneyed subject matter, refresh them and re-present them. It's elevated Bruce Springsteen into rock's Hall of Fame and rightly so. Why, even on the cover here—posing on a beach in a pencil tie and cowboy outfit while leaning on a fast car—Springsteen has got It. He's discovered the formula for selling you the basic elements of a life itself, and sometimes he almost achieves that with titles alone. 'Walk Like A Man' and 'When You're Alone' are both polished ballads (falling into the 'Downbound Train' tradition) whose monikers sum up their whole purpose. Bruce Springsteen is Elvis, Marlon, and Johnny 99 all rolled into one—the kid with the sneer who's his own man, the street hassled Wayne who won his ribbons in the wars of the heart by riding a fender and strumming a loaded guitar—in smalltown, anytown, your town. Pop music is all about simple tunes and Springsteen's are worth every last cent of his billions. Fifty million Bruce Springsteen fans can't be wrong, yet even they can't begin to see just how right they are."

PROMOTION

In February 1988, Springsteen was joined by the E Street Band for sixty-seven concerts on the subsequent Tunnel of Love Express tour, which concluded that August. Pointedly, the E Street Band shared the stage with the Horns of Love. The Tunnel of Love Express tour would mark their last performances together for more than eleven years.

Garry Tallent: "The Tunnel of Love Express tour was unlike anything we'd ever done in that so much of it was staged. The band had fixed positions onstage; unlike every other time we performed live, there was really no spontaneity. We had our parts and needed to stick to them if the show was going to make any sense" (Santelli, *Greetings from E Street*, 2006).

CHART ACTION

Billboard Top Pop Albums: number one. Released on October 9, 1987, *Tunnel of Love* peaked at number one, achieving sales of more than three million copies, earning platinum status from RIAA. The album debuted on the album charts at number sixteen on October 24, when the number-one album was Michael Jackson's *Bad*. On November 7, *Tunnel of Love* reached its peak position at number one.

Tunnel of Love spent forty-five weeks on the *Billboard* charts.

COMMENTS FROM SPRINGSTEEN AND HIS CIRCLE

Springsteen: "After '85, I'd had enough and turned inward to write about men, women and love, things that have previously been on the periphery of my work" (Humphries, *Bruce Springsteen*, 1996).

Springsteen: "I reached a point where I thought I knew myself very well and I had a variety of things happen where I realized I actually didn't. It was a very good eye-opener because it throws everything wide open; it's not that you don't know parts of yourself, but very few people can confront themselves very accurately. We all live life with our illusions and our self-image, and there's a good percentage of that that's a pipe dream. If you can cut that stuff away, which I've tried to do in my music, and realize that I do this well but I'm taking baby steps in this other part of my life, it gets you closer to feeling a certain fullness in your life that I always felt that I was missing. . . . So basically, the music has been based around somebody in pursuit of whatever that thing is" (*Q*, 1992).

Chuck Plotkin: "Every song is about figuring out how to keep things beautiful, so not to betray the truth at the heart of something that, in your sloppiness, you can crash out of existence. This is something that Bruce has always been dealing with" (*Mojo*, September 2022).

Roy Bittan: "On *Tunnel of Love*, I play on two songs, the title song and "Brilliant Disguise." I'm quite a bit proud of what these two singles have become. . . . It took me some effort to convince Bruce that the synth can also be used for his music in a good way. When we started it there were two camps, the bands that used them and the bands that didn't. There was no in-between. Finally, Bruce went through a change because he realized that synths could also give the music extra color in a very tasteful and modest way, without affecting the sound beyond recognition" (*Music Maker*, 1988).

Gary Tallent: "I only played on one song on the album *Tunnel of Love*. It really was a solo album; it wasn't an E Street band album. And at the time of the tour, it was approached that way. The staging, initially, they were trying to stage it in a more theatrical way and have the band just kind of be a backdrop, it wasn't the same" (*Backstreets*, 2006).

Max Weinberg: "Things had been changing for a while in terms of the band. We had done the *Tunnel of Love* project, which was Bruce's solo album, and then we went on tour to accompany him. Although it was great fun . . . it felt at the time like something was winding down, so I made plans to go back to Seton Hall University" (*Modern Drummer*, 1999).

MISCELLANEOUS

In October 1984, Springsteen met actress Julianne Philips, and married her in her Oregon hometown in 1985. "She was twenty-four, tall,

blond, educated, talented, a beautiful and charming young woman," he later recalled. "We hit it off and began seeing each other regularly. Six months into our dating, I proposed on my cottage balcony in Laurel Canyon. We were married in Lake Oswego, Oregon, where a scene straight out of a Preston Sturges film unfolded. Our pending betrothal had leaked, and the little town exploded" (Springsteen, *Born to Run*, 2016).

Howard Kramer on Springsteen's debt to Elvis Presley: "When you're dealing with the subject of Bruce Springsteen, Elvis Presley is a good place to start. Springsteen might not exist as we know him if not for Presley. Springsteen was just shy of his seventh birthday when he saw Presley's first appearance on the Ed Sullivan Show, an admitted watershed moment for the young kid from New Jersey. Springsteen's embrace of rock and roll as defining purpose in life was all-encompassing. The pure energy of the music held hands with the myths that rock and roll conjured about itself and the people who made the music. Springsteen keenly used mythology and imagery for his own ongoing metamorphoses. Hell, you could sing half of Springsteen's catalog in an Elvis-styled voice and you'd swear that he wrote the songs with Elvis in mind. Try it. It's a fun game to play at parties. (Skip 'Fire' and try 'Atlantic City' or 'Tougher than the Rest')" (Womack, Zolten, and Bernard, *Bruce Springsteen, Cultural Studies, and the Runaway American Dream*, 2012).

SONG ANALYSES

"Ain't Got You"
Bruce Springsteen: vocals, guitar, mandolin, bass, keyboards, harmonica, percussion, drum machines

With Springsteen handling all of the instrumentation, "Ain't Got You" signals a key shift in his sound from working with the E Street Band to crafting his ideas in a pure studio setting. The composer drew his inspiration from bluesman Billy Boy Arnold's 1956 release "I Ain't Got You," a song that was covered by the Animals in 1965. When he introduced the song at a Philadelphia concert in November 2005, he remarked, "When I'm approached out on the streets, I'm often asked the same question: 'What is it like to be the Boss?' I have a standard bullshit humble answer that I always give, it goes something like, 'It's no big deal, somebody's gotta do it, it's just like anything else.' Lies, lies, all lies. I don't want to lord it over anybody—I like to do that in private. But I did write about it once."

"Tougher than the Rest"

Bruce Springsteen: vocals, guitar, mandolin, bass, keyboards, synthesizer, harmonica, drum machines
Danny Federici: organ
Max Weinberg: percussion

With its moody synthesizer belying the song's rockabilly feel, "Tougher than the Rest" has emerged as a concert staple in the ensuing years. During the Tunnel of Love Express tour, "Tougher than the Rest" was performed as a duet between Springsteen and Scialfa. In 2017, they reprised the duet as a centerpiece of *Springsteen on Broadway*. During the 1988 tour, director Meiert Avis filmed a video accompaniment for the song. To tell the story of love's trials and tribulations, the video featured a range of couples, including heterosexuals and gay and lesbian couples, a bold statement during an era in which conservative elements often challenged the liberalism of the arts in the media. Released as a single exclusively in the UK marketplace, "Tougher than the Rest" b/w "Roulette" landed

a top twenty hit. In its *Bruce Springsteen Collector's Edition* (2022), *Rolling Stone* listed "Tougher than the Rest" as number thirty-five among the artist's top 100 songs.

"All that Heaven Will Allow"

Bruce Springsteen: vocals, guitar, mandolin, bass, keyboards, harmonica, percussion
Max Weinberg: drums

Drawing his song's title from the 1955 romantic drama *All that Heaven Allows*, starring Jane Wyman and Rock Hudson, "All that Heaven Will Allow" acts as a tenderhearted third entry in the *Tunnel of Love* song cycle. In the album's progress to this point, the narrator has realized that he has all the riches that the world portends, "But I ain't got you." With "Tougher than the Rest" and "All that Heaven Will Allow," Springsteen highlights love's rewards in a world of heartbreak and missed opportunities. In its *Bruce Springsteen Collector's Edition* (2022), *Rolling Stone* listed "All that Heaven Will Allow" as number ninety-five among the artist's top 100 songs.

"Spare Parts"

Bruce Springsteen: vocals, guitar, mandolin, keyboards, drum machines
Danny Federici: organ
Garry Tallent: bass
Max Weinberg: percussion
Jimmie Wood: harmonica

The *Tunnel of Love* song cycle takes a bitter turn with "Spare Parts," a song about a young unwed mother who suffers abandonment at the hands of her boyfriend. In her despair, she begins to contemplate drowning her baby, only to think better of it and accept the responsibilities that life has dealt to her. "Spare Parts" may have roots in Raymond Carver's short story "Popular Mechanics," which explores similar terrain with even more ominous results. Released as a single exclusively in the UK marketplace, "Spare Parts" b/w "Pink Cadillac" landed a top forty hit.

"Cautious Man"
Bruce Springsteen: vocals, guitar, mandolin, bass, keyboards, harmonica, percussion, drum machines

"Cautious Man" traces the story of a married man who cherishes his beloved, on the one hand, only to be overcome with concern about her fidelity, on the other. The cautious man pointedly sports a pair of conspicuous tattoos, with the word "love" inked on one of his hands, while the other reads "fear." Introducing the song in 2005 at a Hollywood concert, Springsteen described "Cautious Man" as being about the concept of "brinksmanship," remarking that "those were the kinds of characters that interested me—on the brink of learning something."

"Walk Like a Man"
Bruce Springsteen: vocals, guitar, mandolin, bass, keyboards, harmonica, drum machines
Max Weinberg: percussion

Drawing his title from the Four Seasons' 1963 hit "Walk Like a Man," Springsteen tackles the difficulties inherent in social constructions of manhood—in this instance, in a largely positive sense centering on the narrator's wedding day. But for Springsteen, the conception of manhood was fraught, as he explained in his autobiography: "I learned many a rough lesson from my father. The rigidity and the blue-collar narcissism of 'manhood' 1950s-style. An inner yearning for isolation, for the world on your terms or not at all. A deep attraction to silence, secrets and secretiveness. You always withhold something, you do not lower your mask. The distorted idea that the beautiful things in your life, the love itself you struggled to win, to create, will turn and possess you, robbing you

of your imagined long-fought-for freedoms" (Springsteen, *Born to Run*, 2016). In its *Bruce Springsteen Collector's Edition* (2022), *Rolling Stone* listed "Walk Like a Man" as number sixty-five among the artist's top 100 songs.

"Tunnel of Love"
Bruce Springsteen: vocals, guitar, mandolin, bass, keyboards, harmonica, percussion, drum machines
Roy Bittan: synthesizer
Nils Lofgren: lead guitar
Patti Scialfa: backing vocals
Max Weinberg: percussion
The Schiffer family of Point Pleasant, New Jersey: roller coaster vocals

The latter half of the LP takes an ominous turn, as demonstrated by the title track's description of the rocky roads of romance, especially as lovers grow older and confront their own mortality. Inspired by the melodic bridge from the Moody Blues' "New Horizons" from *Seventh Sojourn* (1972), "Tunnel of Love" transforms the carnival funhouse into an eerie, brutalizing metaphor for the politics of love and marriage. Backup singer Patti Scialfa made her recording debut on *Tunnel of Love*. As with "Brilliant Disguise," "One Step Up," and "Tougher than the Rest," "Tunnel of Love" was heavily promoted with a music video. Under the direction of Meiert Avis, the video was staged at Asbury Park's Palace Amusements in November 1987. "Tunnel of Love" received five nominations at the annual MTV Video Music Awards, including Video of the Year and Best Male Video. In its *Bruce Springsteen Collector's Edition* (2022), *Rolling Stone* listed "Tunnel of Love" as number twenty-six among the artist's top 100 songs.

CHART ACTION
Billboard Hot 100: number nine. The song also notched a number-one showing on the Mainstream Rock chart.

"Tunnel of Love" b/w "Two for the Road" was released in November 1987. The number-one song that week was Tiffany's "I Think We're Alone Now."

"Two Faces"
Bruce Springsteen: vocals, guitar, mandolin, bass, keyboards, harmonica, percussion
Danny Federici: organ (uncredited)
Max Weinberg: drums

"Two Faces" offers one of Springsteen's most candid and revealing descriptions of his periodic struggles with depression and mental health issues. For the song's musical structure, Springsteen drew upon Lou Christie's 1963 hit "Two Faces Have I" as a central influence. Back in the 1960s, Springsteen attended the falsetto legend's Greenwich Village concerts. In "Two Faces," Springsteen explores the incendiary way in which depression impinges on his life, forcing him to approach the world with two radically different "faces"—dueling personalities that leave him feeling, conversely, "sunny and wild" and beset by "dark clouds." The song's powerful conclusion finds Springsteen declaring his defiance and determination to overcome his mental woes. In its *Bruce Springsteen Collector's Edition* (2022), *Rolling Stone* listed "Two Faces" as number seventy-seven among the artist's top 100 songs.

"Brilliant Disguise"
Bruce Springsteen: vocals, guitar, mandolin, bass, harmonica, drum machines
Roy Bittan: keyboards
Danny Federici: organ
Max Weinberg: percussion

Originally entitled "Is That You," "Brilliant Disguise" was originally recorded on February 5, 1987, with Springsteen handling all of the instrumentation. The following month, additional players were added to the mix in the form of veteran E Streeters Bittan, Federici, and Weinberg. "Brilliant Disguise" explores the jealousy and confusion that emerge among human interpersonal relationships, especially in terms of the masks that we often wear as we confront the world. In particular, "Brilliant Disguise" examines the challenges associated with marital discord. Even as they dutifully play their roles as "faithful man" and "loving woman," the married couple in the song struggle with enduring issues involving intimacy and trust, as well as the larger threat of sexual betrayal. In its *Bruce Springsteen Collector's Edition* (2022), *Rolling Stone* listed "Brilliant Disguise" as number twenty-nine among the artist's top 100 songs.

CHART ACTION
Billboard Hot 100: number five.

"Brilliant Disguise" b/w "Lucky Man" was released in September 17, 1987. The number-one song that week was Michael Jackson's "I Just Can't Stop Loving You."

"One Step Up"
Bruce Springsteen: vocals, guitar, mandolin, bass, keyboards, harmonica, percussion, drum machines
Patti Scialfa: backing vocals

With "One Step Up," Springsteen continues his study of the trials and tribulations of marriage and human relationships. Recorded at A&M Studios with Scialfa providing backup against Springsteen's instrumentation, "One Step Up" reverses the phrase used by Russian revolutionary Vladimir Lenin, who introduced his conservative New Economic Policy, by saying it was necessary to take one step backwards in order to take two steps forward. In "One Step Up," Springsteen traces the corrosive nature of a couple's "dirty little war" and compares the dying embers of their romantic relationship to a house beset by a failing furnace, as well as a broken-down automobile. In February 1988, Springsteen appeared in a video for the song, which was filmed at the Wonder Bar in Asbury Park, New Jersey. In its *Bruce Springsteen Collector's Edition* (2022), *Rolling Stone* listed "One Step Up" as number fifty-one among the artist's top 100 songs.

CHART ACTION
Billboard Hot 100: number thirteen. The song also registered a number-two showing on the Album Rock Tracks chart, as well as a number-three showing on the Adult Contemporary chart.

"One Step Up" b/w "Roulette" was released on February 27, 1988. The number-one song that week was George Michael's "Father Figure."

"When You're Alone"
Bruce Springsteen: vocals, guitar, mandolin, bass, keyboards, harmonica, percussion
Clarence Clemons: backing vocals
Nils Lofgren: backing vocals
Patti Scialfa: backing vocals
Max Weinberg: drums

As *Tunnel of Love*'s song cycle enters its final stretch, "When You're Alone" extends the stories of the title track and "One Step Up" by addressing a relationship's demise in all its pain and anxiety. In the aftermath, "When You're Alone" demonstrates the demoralizing nature of romantic breakups. In the final verse, Springsteen ponders some distant future, when the narrator will find himself able to come to terms with romantic loss after the passage of time, even cherishing the good times that he once shared with his beloved.

"Valentine's Day"
Bruce Springsteen: vocals, guitar, mandolin, bass, keyboards, harmonica, percussion, drum machines

Springsteen composed "Valentine's Day" after receiving manager Jon Landau's jubilant telephone call announcing his son's birth. As the closing song on *Tunnel of Love*, "Valentine's Day" pointedly explores notions of mortality and our human potential for seeking out hope and the possibility of salvation. Rather than referencing annual Valentine's Day celebrations, Springsteen's song draws its influence from Saint Valentine's martyrdom, which led to the establishment of the feast of Roman priest Saint Valentine on February 14 in 496 CE. As a fervent symbol of the contemporary persecution of Christians, Saint Valentine's imprisonment, torture, and beheading in February 269 CE led to his eventual hagiography and sanctification.

In "Valentine's Day," Springsteen pointedly explores issues related to life and death. At the beginning of the song, the narrator thinks wistfully about his beloved, who awaits his return. In a key instant in the song, he ponders his mortality—and the possibility of losing not only his own life but the opportunity to be with his girlfriend: "They say if you die in your dreams you really die in your bed / But honey last night I dreamed my eyes rolled straight back in my head." But as he makes his way through his dreamscape, with "God's light . . . shining on through," he realizes that the only thing that he truly misses is his beloved. Her absence from his world looms even larger than his regrets—even the corrosive "bitterness of a dream that didn't come true." His one saving grace, his true solace, is the woman whom he wants to be "forever mine," his "lonely valentine."

HUMAN TOUCH

Released in March 1992 on the same day as Springsteen's *Lucky Town* LP, *Human Touch* is a rare instance of an artist delivering not one, but two new album's worth of material. Springsteen had originally intended to release *Human Touch* back in 1991, but delayed the album's appearance after he had begun working on *Lucky Town*.

The albums have their origins in October 1989, when Springsteen disbanded the E Street Band following the Tunnel of Love Express tour and after some sixteen years as a working rock and roll unit. "It was painful, but in truth, we all needed a break," he later recalled. "A reconsidering was in order. I left in search of my own life and some new creative directions. Many of the guys did that as well, finding second lives and second careers as musicians, record producers, TV stars and actors. We retained our friendships and stayed in touch. When we would come back together I would find a more adult, settled, powerful group of people. Our time away from one another gave us all a new respect for the man or woman standing next to us. It opened our eyes to what we had, what we'd accomplished and might still accomplish together."

As his ninth studio album, *Human Touch* proved to be slightly more successful than its counterpart. Indeed, it would be nominated for Best Rock Vocal Performance at the 1993 Grammy Awards. Spearheaded by the LP's hit title track, *Human Touch* features a pop-rock sound in comparison to *Lucky Town*'s folk tendencies. Both albums were produced during a two-year period in which Springsteen worked with a bevy of studio musicians, as well as with Roy Bittan, the sole E Street contributor.

Having shared a trio of instrumentals with Springsteen in "Roll of the Dice," "Real World," and "Trouble in Paradise," Bittan acted as Springsteen's chief collaborator and coproducer for several tracks. In all, Springsteen recorded twenty-five new songs for the projects. A number of top-flight LA studio players served as Springsteen's backing band, including Randy Jackson on bass and Toto's Jeff Porcaro on drums. Sam Moore, Bobby Hatfield, and Bobby King provided backing vocals.

In addition to the title track, *Human Touch* included "57 Channels (and Nothin' On)," Springsteen's commentary about the rise of consumer culture during the 1990s. The song would be released as a single and emerge as a hit in several countries. Years later, Springsteen considered "57 Channels" to be a failed experiment of sorts. "Shot back in the quaint days of only 57 channels and no flat screen TVs," he remarked, "I have no idea what we were aiming for in this one outside of some vague sense of 'hipness' and an attempt at irony. Never my strong suit, it reads now to me as a break from our usual approach and kind of a playful misfire."

HISTORICAL CONTEXT

By the early 1990s, Bruce Springsteen had seemingly reached the pinnacle of success. His concert tours routinely sold out and he had enough of a track record as a recording artist that his albums would always attract interest from his fans and the record-buying public. Having moved to California, to any outsider Bruce Springsteen was living the American Dream. But when he released two separate albums, *Human Touch* and *Lucky Town*, each with its own sticker price, on March 31, 1992, they debuted to a resounding lack of enthusiasm from both fans and critics. This could be attributed to a variety of factors. Certainly, some fans resented Springsteen's jettisoning of the E Street Band for a new band he put together in Los Angeles, where he was living at the time. Biographer Dave Marsh thought the US economy had something to do with it. Speaking of the opening track on *Lucky Town*, he wrote, "I probably wouldn't have sent off an album that opened with a song called 'Better Days' into the teeth of a Presidential election being contested amidst a national economic crisis, and might even have been daunted by putting out two discs simultaneously in the midst of a recession, but maybe that's where my mentality becomes analytic rather than artistic." Yet even the usually deferential Marsh thought *Human Touch* one of Springsteen's weakest albums. Others might have thought that Springsteen had lost his edge, continuing to write more about relationships and gender roles as he had on *Tunnel of Love* but this time from a happier, well-adjusted perspective. Finally, Springsteen, and other rock acts, faced intense competition from country music stars such as Garth Brooks and Randy Travis, who made the genre more popular than rock, even among baby boomers, in the 1990s.

Undeterred, Springsteen remained consistent in his concern for his own satisfaction rather than that of either the fans or the critics. And he was satisfied with *Human Touch*, even though it is still considered the weaker of the two albums released in 1992. He worked hard to craft the album and gave serious thought to what he wanted to say. In *Songs*, he explained, "Both *Human Touch* and *Lucky Town* came out of a moment in which to find what I needed, I was going to have to let things go, change, try new things, make mistakes—just live." He identified "Human Touch," "Real World," and "Soul Driver" as tracks that explored the tension between the need to have an emotional connection with another human being and giving up one's freedom in order to receive love. This was not exactly a new theme in Springsteen's work, but now he found himself in a position where he seemed ready to let go of his past in order to finally have the kind of connection that had been missing in his life before his marriage to Patti Scialfa. Yet he was still capable of expressing both confidence and self-doubt, sometimes within the same song, such as "Man's Job," and expressing scathing social commentary, such as on the searing "57 Channels (and Nothin' On)." On the whole, *Human Touch* was an album by an experienced artist who knew what he wanted to do and how to achieve it, even if others did not find it up to the very high standard set by Springsteen's previous albums.

PRODUCTION

Released on March 31, 1992, Columbia Records
Produced by Bruce Springsteen, Jon Landau, Chuck Plotkin, and Roy Bittan
Engineered by Toby Scott
Recording assistants: Robert "RJ" Jaczko, Greg Goldman, and Randy Wine
Mixed by Bob Clearmountain
Mastered by Bob Ludwig at Masterdisk
Digital editing by Dave Collins
Mastering digital editing by Scott Hull
Recorded at A&M Studios, Soundworks West, Oceanway Studios, One on One Studio, the Record Plant, Westlake Studios and Thrill Hill Recording, September 1989 to March 1991

PERSONNEL

Bruce Springsteen: vocals, electric and acoustic guitars, electric bass
Roy Bittan: keyboards
Randy Jackson: electric bass
Doug Lunn: fretless electric bass
Ian McLagan: piano
Jeff Porcaro: drums
David Sancious: keyboards
Patti Scialfa: backing vocals
Kurt Wortman: drums
Michael Fisher: percussion
Bobby Hatfield: backing vocals
Mark Isham: trumpet
Bobby King: backing vocals
Sam Moore: backing vocals
Tim Pierce: electric guitar

COVER ART AND PACKAGING

Art direction: Sandra Choron
Typography design: Victor Weaver
Cover photography: David Rose
Interior photography: David Rose, Annie Leibovitz, and Harvey Gruyaert

TRACK LISTING

All songs composed by Bruce Springsteen.

1. "Human Touch"
2. "Soul Driver"

3. "57 Channels (and Nothin' On)"
4. "Cross My Heart"
5. "Gloria's Eyes"
6. "With Every Wish"
7. "Roll of the Dice"
8. "Real World"
9. "All or Nothin' at All"
10. "Man's Job"
11. "I Wish I Were Blind"
12. "The Long Goodbye"
13. "Real Man"
14. "Pony Boy"

UNRELEASED OUTTAKES

"30 Days Out": released on *Leap of Faith* EP
    (Europe, 1992)
"Give it a Name": released on *Tracks* (1998)
"Goin' Cali": released on *Tracks* (1998)
"Leavin' Train": released on *Tracks* (1998)
"Loose Change": released on *Tracks* (1998)
"My Lover Man": released on *Tracks* (1998)
"Over the Rise": released on *Tracks* (1998)
"Part Man, Part Monkey": released on *Tracks*
    (1998)
"Sad Eyes": released on *Tracks* (1998)
"Seven Angels": released on *Tracks* (1998)
"Trouble in Paradise" released on *Tracks* (1998)
"Trouble River": released on *18 Tracks* (1999)
"When the Lights Go Out": released on *Tracks*
    (1998)

CONTEMPORARY REVIEWS

Stuart Bailie (*New Musical Express*, April 4,
1992): "There's no writing agenda on *Human
Touch*. . . . Instead of fresh, soulful wanderings,
you get masses of extra redundant metaphors;
tumbling dice ('Real World,' 'Roll of the Dice'),
meaningful car rides '('Soul Driver'), darkness and light ('I Wish I Were Blind), and all

that. It's like he's desperately, painfully trying
to remember what he used to be good at. I was
playing Bruce's *Greetings from Asbury Park*
recently, and it shocked me to remember just
how adventurous he was then—20 years ago. He
was bursting with sensations and stories and
weird visions. He had poetry. Then he got onto
his Normal Joe trip, and here we are at the awful
terminus of that excursion. How labored is the
crap grammar in 'I Wish I Were Blind'? Listening to *Human Touch* is like being harangued
across the garden fence by your boring bastard
neighbor who wants to tell you about his gera-
niums and seed packets and the rubbish road
movie he got out on video last weekend."

Anthony DeCurtis (*Rolling Stone*, April 30,
1992): "Beginning with the pulsing title track,
which stands among Springsteen's best work,
the 14 songs on *Human Touch* explore the
movement from disenchanted isolation to a willingness to risk love and its attendant traumas
again. At first the moves are tentative, motivated
more by loneliness—a need for 'a little of that
human touch'—than by love's golden promise
or, even more remote, the prospect of actual
lasting happiness with another human being.
Also, as the bluesy 'Cross My Heart' makes
clear, the certainties of the past ('Once you
cross your heart / You ain't ever supposed to lie')
are starting to be replaced by a more shaded
outlook: 'Well you may think the world's black
and white / And you're dirty or you're clean /
You better watch out you don't slip / Through
them spaces in between.' Aptly, the introspective, self-questioning mood of *Human Touch*
shifts near its midpoint with 'Roll of the Dice,'
the most generic-sounding Springsteen rocker—
glockenspiel and all—on either of these albums.
With renewed energy, even optimism, the singer
accepts the emotional dangers of love and his

own failings ('I'm a thief in the house of love / And I can't be trusted'), stops fretting and determines to get on with living. The superb 'Real World' then offers an inspiringly lucid vision of a love that can sidestep fantasy to take a dignified place in 'the real world,' and the slamming 'All or Nothin' at All,' graced by a soaring, catchy chorus, insists on commitment rather than flees it.... 'Pony Boy,' a traditional tune performed acoustically by Springsteen on guitar and harmonica, with his wife Patti Scialfa providing harmony, closes *Human Touch* on a tender, disarming note."

PROMOTION

In May 1992, the *New York Times* reported that the twin releases of *Human Touch* and *Lucky Town* had initially sold well, only to swiftly exit the charts in comparison to previous Springsteen releases. Music critics had debated that excitement over new Springsteen material may have given way to a dissatisfaction with the direction of his new material. Other critics contended that the lackluster sales—at least by Springsteen's standards—may have been because he had essentially flooded the market with the new LPs.

The *New York Times* took special notice of Springsteen's recent appearance on *Saturday Night Live*. "People assumed that the moderate response to his two new albums, *Human Touch* and *Lucky Town* (both Columbia) had forced him into it. Mr. Springsteen, known for being aloof when it comes to the media, had never done television. To some people his acceptance of the decades-old open offer from *Saturday Night Live* reduced him to the status of mere mortal. Whatever the reasons for his appearance, the performance of three songs on the show—estimated by NBC to have been watched by more than twenty-five million viewers—appears to have paid off. Music stores across the country have already noticed an increase in sales" (*New York Times*, May 13, 1992).

Springsteen supported the twin releases of *Human Touch* and *Lucky Town* with his 1992–1993 world tour, which ran from June 1992 through June 1993 and featured 107 performances.

CHART ACTION

Billboard Top Pop Albums: number two.

Released on March 31, 1992, *Human Touch* peaked at number two, achieving sales of more than one million copies, earning platinum status from RIAA. The album debuted on the album charts on April 18 at number two, its peak position. The number-one album was Def Leppard's *Adrenalize*.

Human Touch spent twenty-seven weeks on the *Billboard* charts.

COMMENTS FROM SPRINGSTEEN AND HIS CIRCLE

Springsteen: "I try to present what I stumbled around and groped my way into, and I try to get some of that into my music in some fashion and that's when I feel good about releasing the stuff and committed to going on the road and getting involved in that life. I feel this is something that's not going to waste people's time. They may like it or not like it; it may be what you think rock and roll is or not. But it's very centered and real. So if you want to slice them up like that, there's a lot of groping around on *Human Touch* . . . about finding your place and re-finding yourself, getting back in touch with your humanity and the good things that you feel about yourself" (*Q*, August 1992).

MISCELLANEOUS

Having divorced Julianne Phillips in 1989, Springsteen married Patti Scialfa on June 8, 1991. He had known Scialfa since he was twenty-one and she was nineteen, looking for opportunities to sing background vocals. "Patti was a musician, was close to my age, had seen me on the road in all of my many guises and viewed me with a knowing eye," he wrote years later. "She knew I was no white knight (perhaps a dark gray knight at best), and I never felt the need to pretend around her." For Springsteen, Scialfa represented new possibilities in life, including a potential family life that had long since eluded him. "I looked at Patti and saw something different, something new, something I'd missed and hadn't experienced before," he recalled. "Patti is a wise, tough, powerful woman, but she is also the soul of fragility, and there was something in that combination that opened up new possibilities in my heart. In my life, Patti is a singularity" (Springsteen, *Born to Run*, 2016).

On May 9, 1992, Springsteen performed three songs on *Saturday Night Live*, including *Human Touch*'s "57 Channels (and Nothin' On)."

In 1993, *Human Touch* was nominated in the category of Best Rock Vocal Performance at the Grammy Awards.

SONG ANALYSES

"Human Touch"
Bruce Springsteen: vocals, guitar
Roy Bittan: keyboards

Randy Jackson: bass
Jeff Porcaro: drums
Patti Scialfa: backing vocals

The album opens with the title track, which contains a number of themes characteristic of Springsteen's songwriting. A catchy rock number that would have drawn raves had any other artist released it, the song focuses on that longing for connection that had haunted Springsteen since childhood, as it does most of us, and which is probably what drove him to write songs in the first place. He would later speak of his long-lasting and continual need to share parts of himself with the world, to communicate with whatever audience was out there willing to listen.

Also present in the song is the self-deprecation heard in lines such as "Thunder Road's" "I ain't no hero, that's understood," replaced here with "I ain't nobody's bargain." But just as in "Thunder Road," and many of his other songs, the lyrics hold out the promise that the singer has something to offer, despite his flaws. What the singer offers here is "somebody that you can just talk to and a little of that human touch," but at the end he reveals that he needs it as much as the girl addressed in the song, admitting, "I just want to feel you in my arms."

CHART ACTION
Billboard Hot 100: number sixteen. The song also registered a number-one showing on the Mainstream Rock chart and number eight on the Adult Contemporary chart.

"Human Touch" b/w "Souls of the Departed" was released on March 9, 1992. The number-one song that week was Mr. Big's "To Be with You."

"Soul Driver"
Bruce Springsteen: vocals, guitar
Michael Fisher: percussion

Randy Jackson: bass
Sam Moore: backing vocals
Tim Pierce: rhythm guitar
Jeff Porcaro: drums
David Sancious: keyboards

"Soul Driver" sees Springsteen again looking for connection, recognizing the risk in exposing his vulnerability but here saying it is a risk he is willing to take. Unlike "Human Touch," this song is laden with religious imagery, implied in its title and overt in the opening line, in which Springsteen sings that he "rode forty nights through the gospel's rain." From the biblical flood, the song jumps to the plagues God sent to Egypt before the Exodus, "Black sky pourin' snakes, frogs and love in vain."

Having survived these metaphorical catastrophes unscathed, the singer now informs the woman that he is qualified to be her "soul driver." The rest of the song addresses the theme of the uncertainty of how a love affair will end when it starts and even seems to acknowledge that it likely will end badly, whether because "the angels are unkind or the season is dark" or simply because "love just falls apart." Yet by acknowledging this in the beginning, he is making his case that it will be worth it anyway, even singing in the penultimate line, "Here's to our destruction," before his final plea to "just let me be your soul driver."

"57 Channels (and Nothin' On)"
Bruce Springsteen: vocals, guitar, bass
Roy Bittan: keyboards
Jeff Porcaro: drums

Perhaps more than any Springsteen song, this one expresses the dissatisfaction with living the materialistic version of the American Dream. Based on both personal experience and general observations about his times and human nature, a combination found in so many of his songs,

this song takes the listener through a series of verses that build on the theme that material goods, wealth, and worldly success do not bring happiness, but loneliness, emptiness, and frustration. Having attained fame and riches beyond his own wildest dreams as a young rocker on the Jersey Shore and having moved to what the Eagles famously dubbed "Hotel California," Springsteen opens the song referring to his having "bought a bourgeois house" (use of the term "bourgeois" perhaps symbolizing his betrayal of his working-class roots), "with a trunkload of hundred thousand dollar bills."

In the second verse, dissatisfied with the offerings on standard cable television, he goes out and buys a satellite dish, but when he gets it home there are still "57 channels and nothing on." This theme continues to the end of the song, with a direct reference to Elvis Presley and his penchant for shooting at his televisions to symbolize the anger at the emptiness of American mass culture, which Springsteen imitates, landing him before a judge who says, "I can see by your eyes, friend, you're just about gone." One might expect a song like this from a young rocker expressing their teenage angst, but not perhaps from a rock superstar at the pinnacle of his profession.

CHART ACTION
Billboard Hot 100: number sixty-eight. The song also registered a number-six showing on the magazine's Mainstream Rock chart.

"57 Channels (and Nothin' On)," b/w "Part Man, Part Monkey" was released in June 1992. The number-one song that week was the Red Hot Chili Peppers' "Under the Bridge."

"Cross My Heart"
Bruce Springsteen: vocals, guitar
Roy Bittan: keyboards

Randy Jackson: bass
Jeff Porcaro: drums

The lyrics of this song are about as sparse as one will find from a Springsteen number, with a message both simple and profound. One thing Springsteen had always explored is the ambiguity in the line between good and bad, and the areas of gray that represent the complexity of his moral universe. "Little boys" and "little girls" might know right from wrong, he says in the song, but there are "spaces in between" the "world's black and white," that are easy to fall into. For children, the act of crossing one's heart is a promise that one is not telling a lie. Here the singer promises the girl/woman that he will cross his heart even though 'life ain't nothin' but a cold hard ride." The only ambiguity is at the end of the song, when he crosses his heart that he "ain't leavin' till I'm satisfied," meaning that his promise is only conditional? And, what exactly, would that satisfaction entail?

"Gloria's Eyes"
Bruce Springsteen: vocals, guitar
Roy Bittan: keyboards
Randy Jackson: bass
Jeff Porcaro: drums

Without doing an exact count, it seems like half of Springsteen's relationship-centered songs deal with the promise of starting a new relationship and half deal with the end of an old one, probably pretty close to the statistical division of popular love songs in general. "Gloria's Eyes" falls into the second category, and like in many other Springsteen songs, the fault lies mainly with the protagonist for not living up to what he originally promised. Starting out as "Prince Charming, King on a white horse," he is now "just a fool in Gloria's Eyes." He admits to trying to trick her into a relationship in the first place and then using sweet talk to cover up his lies to try to get her back, but now, he avers, he realizes he has to prove his love really is true and prays that someday he will once again see love in Gloria's eyes. The sentiment is the same as that of such classic love songs as Paul McCartney's "Yesterday," a man realizing too late what he had and lamenting the loss in a profoundly sad way, his own role in his fall from grace only compounding the sorrow.

"With Every Wish"
Bruce Springsteen: vocals, guitar
Roy Bittan: keyboards
Mark Isham: muted trumpet
Doug Lunn: fretless bass
Kurt Wortman: drums

This song consists of three verses, with an instrumental bridge separating the second from the third verses. Each of the verses deals with a stage of life, starting with childhood, continuing with romance, and concluding with maturity. The basic message of the song could be summed up as "be careful what you wish for." The first wish to come true is when the singer skips church to go fishing and catches a long-coveted catfish the singer refers to as "Big Jim." But at the end of the verse an angel whispers in his ear to remember "with every wish there comes a curse." The wish that comes true in the second verse is the hope that he would get together with a pretty girl named Doreen, but when he does, the singer becomes jealous, making him "treat her cruel and mean." The third verse finds the singer reflecting on all the mistakes he has made, but in the end, he is still willing to take a chance and "leave the angels to worry with every wish."

"Roll of the Dice"
Bruce Springsteen: vocals, guitar
Roy Bittan: keyboards
Randy Jackson: bass
Bobby King: backing vocals

Tim Pierce: rhythm guitar
Jeff Porcaro: drums

As the title of this song indicates, "Roll of the Dice" offers another song about the importance of taking chances in life, even though there is always some risk involved in whatever we choose. But this song also incorporates other themes that reach back into Springsteen's songwriting past, especially issues of self-doubt, identity, and the flaws we all carry with us as human beings. Here he sings that he knows that the odds are not in his favor, but he is still willing to take one more "roll of the dice," perhaps inspired by his relationship with his wife Patti Scialfa in the wake of his failed marriage to Julianne Phillips. If so, the song would seem to indicate the persistence of doubt and uncertainty. In 1987's "Brilliant Disguise," he had sung "I damn sure don't trust myself." Here he confesses to being "a thief in the house of love" who "can't be trusted."

"Real World"

Bruce Springsteen: vocals, guitar
Roy Bittan: keyboards
Randy Jackson: bass
Sam Moore: backing vocals
Jeff Porcaro: drums

This song consists of four verses, each followed by the chorus, with a refrain tacked on to the end of the song. The message of the chorus is that marriage is not about "church bells ringing" or having "flags unfurled," but about living in the "real world." The verses trace the singer's past history that have led him to the point where he is ready to face the reality he sings about in the chorus. The first verse finds the singer fleeing "heartbreak city" only to build "a roadside carnival out of hurt and self-pity."

In the second verse, he still has a trace of faith remaining, despite the memory of past hurts and broken hearts, enough to try to find it in his lover's eyes. Doubt returns in the third verse but, unlike in the past, he is able to move past it "to stand at your side with my arms open wide." In the fourth and final verse, the singer is still unsure that love isn't hopeless, but he is willing to go "to hell and heaven and back" to find out and invites his love to go out with him "with the tumblin' dice," repeating the metaphor from the previous song for continuing to take a chance on love.

"All or Nothin' at All"

Bruce Springsteen: vocals, guitar
Roy Bittan: keyboards
Randy Jackson: bass
Jeff Porcaro: drums

The simple message of this song, its title self-explanatory, is identical to that of Carly Simon's 1987 hit, "Give Me All Night." Simon had sung, "If I can't take the whole of you, give it to me anyway." Here Springsteen sings, "You ain't gonna get what you want with one foot in bed and one foot out." It is a relatively short song for Springsteen (3:23), over a third of the lyric consisting of the simple phrase in the song's title. It could be interpreted as a plea for sex, a familiar enough theme in pop and rock music (the Beatles' "Day Tripper" comes to mind), but in the context of the rest of the album and Springsteen's concerns at this time in his life, it could just as easily represent a desire for true commitment, as he started to become aware of having reached middle age. "I only got a little time," he sings in the last verse, hence his plea is "for all or nothing at all."

"Man's Job"

Bruce Springsteen: vocals, guitar
Roy Bittan: keyboards
Randy Jackson: bass
Bobby King: backing vocals

Sam Moore: backing vocals
Jeff Porcaro: drums

In a chapter of *Born in the U.S.A.: Bruce Springsteen and the American Tradition*, Jim Cullen argues that Springsteen redefined masculinity and offers "Man's Job" as a prime exhibit, where Springsteen offers a reconsideration of what a "man's job" really is. Cullen also notes the progression for the terms he uses to describe the female he addresses in the song, beginning with "baby" to "darlin'" to "woman," encapsulating in one song a change from so much of his earlier songs that generally referred to females as "girl" (or even "little girl" or other such diminutives). As with "Point Blank," among other previous Springsteen songs, the girl the singer is addressing is actually with someone else and he is trying to convince her that she would be better off with him.

Like "Thunder Road," among other Springsteen songs, he acknowledges that he is not a hero, that he has feet of clay, and the only reason to consider him is that he has something in his soul, in this case that "something" being his willingness to accept his limitations but still to get up the nerve to ask her to give him a chance. Thus, the song continues the importance of risk taking as a major theme of the album, since it turns out that a "man's job" is to be vulnerable, even in the face of the possibility or even likelihood it will lead to hurt and rejection.

"I Wish I Were Blind"
Bruce Springsteen: vocals, guitar
Roy Bittan: keyboards
Bobby Hatfield: backing vocals
Randy Jackson: bass
Jeff Porcaro: drums

Here we have yet another song that could easily be interpreted as a continuation of the song preceding it on the album. In "Man's Job," he watches the woman he desires dancing with her man and all his "illusions slip away." Here he takes that image one step further by singing, "I wish I were blind when I see you with your man." The song has an unusual structure, in that it repeats the refrain at the end of each verse but has no chorus. It has eight lines in each of the first three verses and only two in the last verse, and a bridge that comes two lines into the third verse, instead of between any of the verses, and is then repeated at the end of the song before the final refrain. Lyrically, the song contains a contradiction between the singer's affirmation that he wishes he were blind and yet he cannot seem to stop watching the very thing he does not want to see, as in the line, "I watch how you touch him as you start to dance." It also implies that in a way the pain of seeing the woman he loves with another man has already made him blind, figuratively if not literally, because the pain of it has plunged his heart into darkness "and the light that once entered here is banished from me." If this is meant or interpreted as a sequel to "Man's Job," the singer is no longer capable of "getting up the nerve," but has succumbed to a hopeless depression that has him wishing for blindness "though this world is filled with a grace and beauty of God's hand."

"The Long Goodbye"
Bruce Springsteen: vocals, guitar
Roy Bittan: keyboards
Randy Jackson: bass
Jeff Porcaro: drums

Lyrically, "The Long Goodbye" represents perhaps the most profound song on the album. It deals with the recurring theme of love, loss, growth, maturity, and commitment. The song is about regret and the "long goodbye" referred to in the song is an attempt at the singer's farewell to his younger self in order to forge a better version of himself. Its subject is the end of a long-term relationship that the protagonist has been reluctant to end, although he believes it should have ended a long time ago. "Well I went to leave twenty years ago," Springsteen sings, continuing, "Since then I guess I been packin' kinda slow." The song contains the usual dose of self-reproach encountered in many of Springsteen's songs. He refers to himself "chippin' away at this chain of my own lies" as he waits for "words of forgiveness from some God above." Those words don't come, a least in this song, which ends with the singer having a drink and just sitting around and waiting for "the long goodbye."

"Real Man"
Bruce Springsteen: vocals, guitar
Randy Jackson: bass
Ian McLagan: piano
Jeff Porcaro: drums
David Sancious: organ

At the beginning of "Real Man," Springsteen introduces a stereotype of a real man in the figure of Sylvester Stallone's character Rambo gunning down all of his opponents in a bloody killing spree. By contrast, Springsteen avers that he does not need a gun to be a real man, just the "sweet kiss" from the woman to whom he addresses the song. In the second verse, another take on the many times he professes in his music not to be a hero, Springsteen sings that he is not "some smooth-talkin' cool walkin' private eye"; in contrast to the fictional heroes one watches on television or a movie screen, the one thing he can promise his woman is that he is at least real and qualifies as a real man because of the love she gives him. In the song he even dehumanizes the stereotype of what a real man might be in the popular imagination, referring in a chorus repeated three times in the song that any monkey can beat his chest, but it is as a lover, not a fighter, that he wishes to be remembered and that is actually what makes him a "real man."

"Pony Boy"
Bruce Springsteen: vocals, guitar
Patti Scialfa: backing vocals

A simple Western-style lullaby, with a harmonica bridge between the second and third final verse, sung with a country twang, Springsteen concludes an album filled with considerations related to his growing maturity and marriage to Patti Scialfa with a nod to fatherhood that reflects his almost lifelong fascination with cowboys, horses, and the American West.

Lucky Town (Alamy) [billboard advertisement]

LUCKY TOWN

Released in March 1992 on the same day as Springsteen's *Human Touch* LP, *Lucky Town* is a rare instance of an artist delivering not one, but two new album's worth of material. Springsteen had originally intended to release *Human Touch* back in 1991, but delayed the album's appearance after he had begun working on *Lucky Town*.

The albums have their origins in October 1989, when Springsteen disbanded the E Street Band following the Tunnel of Love Express tour and after some sixteen years as a working rock and roll unit. "It was painful, but in truth, we all needed a break," he later recalled. "A reconsidering was in order. I left in search of my own life and some new creative directions. Many of the guys did that as well, finding second lives and second careers as musicians, record

producers, TV stars and actors. We retained our friendships and stayed in touch. When we would come back together I would find a more adult, settled, powerful group of people. Our time away from one another gave us all a new respect for the man or woman standing next to us. It opened our eyes to what we had, what we'd accomplished and might still accomplish together."

As his tenth studio album, *Lucky Town* proved to be slightly less successful than its counterpart, though it still earned platinum sales status in the American marketplace. Spearheaded by the LP's hit single "Better Days," *Lucky Town* features a more soulful, folk-oriented sound in comparison to *Human Touch*'s pop-rock tendencies. Both albums were produced during a two-year period in which

Springsteen worked with a bevy of studio musicians, as well as with Roy Bittan, the sole E Street contributor to both projects.

Having originally shared a trio of instrumentals with Springsteen in "Roll of the Dice," "Real World," and "Trouble in Paradise," Bittan acted as Springsteen's chief collaborator and coproducer for several tracks. In all, Springsteen recorded twenty-five new songs for the projects. A number of top-flight LA studio players served as Springsteen's backing band, including Randy Jackson on bass and Gary Mallaber on drums. E Street bandmate Patti Scialfa provided backing vocals, along with Soozie Tyrell and Lisa Lowell.

"Better Days" would land a top twenty hit for Springsteen, serving as the anthem, in many ways, for his overarching desire to start over and derive new creative directions after nearly two decades with the E Street Band, as well as following his divorce from Julianne Phillips. Other standout tracks include "Souls of the Departed," Springsteen's commentary on the traumas associated with the Gulf War, and "Living Proof," a meditation on the birth of his first son.

HISTORICAL CONTEXT

Lucky Town contains two songs in particular that directly relate to the historical context for its release, along with *Human Touch*, on the last day of March 1992. "The Big Muddy" echoes Pete Seeger's gritty 1967 anti-Vietnam War song "Waist Deep in the Big Muddy," foreshadowing Springsteen's 2006 album *We Shall Overcome: The Pete Seeger Sessions*. Although it does not specifically mention the invasion of Kuwait by the United States under President George H. W. Bush, it provided a reminder of the costs of foreign wars; the *Seeger Sessions* album came out in the midst of another war with Iraq initiated by the elder Bush's son, George W. Bush. "The

Souls of the Departed" more directly referenced the Persian Gulf War, the first verse telling of a soldier ordered to go through the clothes of those killed in action who is haunted in his dreams by their souls rising "like dark geese in the Oklahoma skies." In addition, the second chilling verse tells of a seven-year-old shot dead in an East Compton schoolyard, leaving his mother to cry, "My beautiful boy is dead." Later in the song, the singer proclaims his desire "to build a wall so high nothing can burn it down" to protect his son, fear providing the flip side of the joy expressed over the birth of a child in another song on the album, "Living Proof."

In his memoir, *Born to Run*, Springsteen devotes a chapter to the Rodney King riots that began just days after the release of *Human Touch* and *Lucky Town*, sparked by the acquittal of the four police officers involved in the helpless King's brutal beating after a traffic stop. An amateur film of the incident permeated the culture and exacerbated race relations in the early 1990s. Springsteen wrote of word of the riots reaching him in the studio, causing him and his bandmates to leave in an effort to make their way home in a tense atmosphere rife with the possibility of violence spilling throughout the city and its environs.

In the last verse of "Souls of the Departed," the narrator sings, "Now I ply my trade in the land of king dollar / Where you get paid and your silence passes as honor." Rob Kirkpatrick speculates that this may or may not refer to Oliver North, Ronald Reagan's deputy-director of the National Security Council, who, was heavily implicated in the 1986 Iran-Contra scandal and charged with sixteen felony accounts, including attempting to defraud the US government (Kirkpatrick, *Magic in the Night*, 2009). North later had his convictions reversed on appeal. However, Kirkpatrick asserts, "The general implications against George Bush Senior's America, though, are all too clear." Indeed, early signs of trouble for Bush had appeared at the New Hampshire primary when he won a meager 53 percent of the vote, an astonishingly low number for an incumbent president in his party's first primary. Bush would go on to secure the Republican nomination but would be defeated by the upstart governor of Arkansas, Bill Clinton, in the 1992 general election.

Although *Lucky Town*, like *Human Touch*, deals largely with relationships and personal issues, the Gulf War, the Rodney King incident and its aftermath, the country's economic recession, and a general moral crisis stemming from the loss of a clear national purpose when the Cold War ended in 1989, all provide important historical context for Springsteen's 1992 releases and would play a much greater role in his next album, *The Ghost of Tom Joad*, released three years later.

PRODUCTION

Released on March 31, 1992, Columbia Records
Produced by Bruce Springsteen, Jon Landau, Chuck Plotkin, and Roy Bittan
Engineered by Toby Scott
Recording assistants: Greg Goldman, Robert "RJ" Jacko, and Randy Wine
Mixed by Bob Clearmountain
Mastered by Bob Ludwig at Masterdisk
Digital editing by Scott Hull
Recorded at Thrill Hill Recording and A&M Studios, September 1991 to January 1992

PERSONNEL

Bruce Springsteen: vocals, electric and acoustic guitars, electric bass, keyboards, harmonica, percussion

Roy Bittan: keyboards
Randy Jackson: electric bass
Gary Mallaber: drums
Ian McLagan: organ
Patti Scialfa: backing vocals
Lisa Lowell: backing vocals
Soozie Tyrell: backing vocals

COVER ART AND PACKAGING

Art direction: Sandra Choron
Typography design: Victor Weaver
Cover photography: David Rose and Alexander Vitlin
Interior photography: Pam Springsteen and David Rose

TRACK LISTING

All songs composed by Bruce Springsteen.
1. "Better Days"
2. "Lucky Town"
3. "Local Hero"
4. "If I Should Fall Behind"
5. "Leap of Faith"
6. "The Big Muddy"
7. "Living Proof"
8. "Book of Dreams"
9. "Souls of the Departed"
10. "My Beautiful Reward"

UNRELEASED OUTTAKE

"Happy": released on *Tracks* (1998)

CONTEMPORARY REVIEWS

Stuart Bailie (*New Musical Express*, April 4, 1992): "Then comes along the *Lucky Town* LP, and Bruce put his shoulder to the maggoty old edifice—a bit. Good points: he looks like Shane

MacGowan on the cover, and there are at least three great songs, notably the opener, 'Better Days,' which is like a reprise of 'Tougher Than the rest'—all guts and resolve in the face of compromising circumstances. . . . We are told that *Lucky Town* was a kind of afterthought, an extended B-sides session that got sparky and creative, and made a better album than the parent project. There's certainly a bit more welly to the music, and the words aren't always so boringly contrived. . . . So don't expect anything new, just play and admire 'Souls of the Departed' (gunfire and conscience) and skip around the rest according to your preferences."

Anthony DeCurtis (*Rolling Stone*, April 30, 1992): "The childlike charm of 'Pony Boy' provides an effective, understated transition to *Lucky Town*, on which Springsteen examines his life as a family man, negotiates a truce with his demons, and achieves a hard-won sense of fulfillment. Dedicated to Scialfa and the couple's two children, the album's ten songs paint a convincing—and only rarely cloying—portrait of domestic life and its contents. The rousing opener, 'Better Days,' ably sets the tone; it's a bracing anti-nostalgia blast that asserts, "these are better days baby / Better days with a girl like you.' The song also takes on, with impressive candor, the Springsteen myth ('It's a sad funny ending to find yourself pretending / A rich man in a poor man's shirt') and the immeasurable degree of his material comfort ('A life of leisure and a pirate's treasure / Don't make much for tragedy'). With characteristic sure-footedness, however, Springsteen does not permit heartfelt satisfaction to slip into self-satisfaction. If 'Leap of Faith,' 'If I Should Fall Behind,' 'Living Proof,' and 'Book of Dreams' all convey a nearly swooning appreciation of the pleasures that a settled home life affords, 'The Big Muddy,' 'Souls of the

Departed,' and 'My Beautiful Reward' intimate that, for Springsteen at least, the attainment of love is inextricable from the fear of its loss. A brooding blues evocatively colored by Springsteen's acoustic slide guitar, 'The Big Muddy' takes a knowing look at infidelity, greed, and moral compromise, concluding, 'There ain't no one leavin' this world, buddy / Without their shirttail dirty or their hands bloody.' The churning, guitar-driven 'Souls of the Departed' depicts the singer, one of 'the self-made men' in the Hollywood Hills, under siege as violence rages in the Middle East and, closer by, in East Compton. The death of a child in a barrio shooting causes him to wonder, in an aching drawl, 'Tonight as I tuck my own son in bed / All I can think of is what if it would've been him instead.' 'My Beautiful Reward,' an elegant, folkish ballad, ends *Lucky Town* on an almost surreally unsettled note. The calm, gentle music belies dreamlike imagery of falling, wandering and abandonment . . . and hints of a darkness on the edge of *Lucky Town*."

Greg Kot (*Chicago Tribune*, February 26, 1995): "*Human Touch* tried to re-create the stadium-rocking aura of an E Street album, with session musicians unsuccessfully replacing the road-tested band. But the sparer, more introspective *Lucky Town* is highly underrated; though it didn't penetrate the national consciousness the way *Born to Run* and *Born in the U.S.A.* did, it contains some of the strongest songwriting of Springsteen's career and ranks as one of his most completely realized albums."

PROMOTION

In May 1992, the *New York Times* reported that the twin releases of *Human Touch* and *Lucky Town* initially sold well, only to swiftly exit the charts in comparison to previous Springsteen releases. Music critics had debated that excitement over new Springsteen material may have given way to a dissatisfaction with the direction of his new material. Other critics contended that the lackluster sales—at least by Springsteen's standards—may have been because he had essentially flooded the market with the new LPs.

The *New York Times* took special notice of Springsteen's recent appearance on *Saturday Night Live*. "People assumed that the moderate response to his two new albums, *Human Touch* and *Lucky Town* (both Columbia) had forced him into it. Mr. Springsteen, known for being aloof when it comes to the media, had never done television. To some people his acceptance of the decades-old open offer from *Saturday Night Live* reduced him to the status of mere mortal. Whatever the reasons for his appearance, the performance of three songs on the show—estimated by NBC to have been watched by more than twenty-five million viewers—appears to have paid off. Music stores across the country have already noticed an increase in sales" (*New York Times*, May 13, 1992).

Springsteen supported the twin releases of *Human Touch* and *Lucky Town* with his 1992–1993 world tour, which ran from June 1992 through June 1993 and featured 107 performances.

CHART ACTION

Billboard Top Pop Albums: number three.

Released on March 31, 1992, *Lucky Town* peaked at number three, achieving sales of more than one million copies, earning platinum status from RIAA. The album debuted on the album charts on April 18 at number three. The number-one album was Def Leppard's *Adrenalize*.

Lucky Town spent twenty-three weeks on the *Billboard* charts.

COMMENTS FROM SPRINGSTEEN AND HIS CIRCLE

Springsteen: "I wrote and recorded the whole thing in about three weeks. It's just one of those records that comes pouring out of you and they always tend to be more direct [when that happens]. Maybe the songwriting was a little better on it [*Lucky Town*], maybe I was fishing around less to see what I wanted to see, and I think I had focused in real well on it by that time and knew what I wanted to communicate, and then it finally just kind of came out, and it happened real fast" (RTÉ 2FM Radio [Ireland], May 14, 1993).

MISCELLANEOUS

Having divorced Julianne Phillips in 1989, Springsteen married Patti Scialfa on June 8, 1991. He had known Scialfa since he was twenty-one, and she was nineteen, looking for opportunities to sing background vocals. "Patti was a musician, was close to my age, had seen me on the road in all of my many guises and viewed me with a knowing eye," Springsteen later wrote. "She knew I was no white knight (perhaps a dark gray knight at best), and I never felt the need to pretend around her." For Springsteen, Scialfa represented new possibilities in life, including a potential family life that had long since eluded him. "I looked at Patti and saw something different, something new, something I'd missed and hadn't experienced before," he recalled. "Patti is a wise, tough, powerful woman, but she is also the soul of fragility, and there was something in that combination that opened up new possibilities in my heart. In my life, Patti is a singularity" (Springsteen, *Born to Run*, 2016).

On May 9, 1992, Springsteen performed three songs on *Saturday Night Live*, including *Lucky Town*'s title track and "Living Proof."

SONG ANALYSES

"Better Days"
Bruce Springsteen: vocals, guitar, keyboards, harmonica, percussion
Randy Jackson: bass
Gary Mallaber: drums
Patti Scialfa: backing vocals
Lisa Lowell: backing vocals
Soozie Tyrell: backing vocals

This is one of the most upbeat, happy, optimistic songs Springsteen has written, a song that could have come only from someone who felt content with his life and who had come to terms with many of the fears and anxieties that accompany the transition from young adulthood to middle age. Here, Springsteen is no longer searching for the Promised Land or seeking to hit the road and escape his life, town, relationship, or really anything. In this song he rejects the working-class persona he adopts in many of his songs, referring himself to "a rich man in a poor man's shirt." He later liked to joke that he always wore work clothes even though he never had a real job. The song contains the revelation that we are responsible for our own happiness ("Every fool's got a reason to feel sorry for himself") and expresses a serene sense of growth and satisfaction, thanks partly to his relationship with his wife Patti, but also to his own acceptance that life is best lived in the present

instead of sitting around and waiting for a better tomorrow.

In its *Bruce Springsteen Collector's Edition* (2022), *Rolling Stone* listed "Better Days" as number seventy among the artist's top 100 songs.

CHART ACTION
Billboard Hot 100: number sixteen. The song registered a number-two showing on the Mainstream Rock chart.

"Better Days" b/w "Tougher Than the Rest (live)" was released on March 21, 1992. The number-one song that week was Mr. Big's "To Be with You."

"Lucky Town"
Bruce Springsteen: vocals, guitar, keyboards, bass guitar, harmonica, percussion
Gary Mallaber: drums

"Lucky Town" evokes similar sentiments to those expressed in "Better Days," a determination to leave the blues behind, to make the most of today, and to build a new life out of the ashes of the old. Here Springsteen has reshaped his metaphor of stepping "out in the street" from one signaling a means of escape and forgetfulness to one that implies an actual life change: "I been a long time walking on fortune's cane" but "tonight I'm steppin' lightly and feeling no pain." In "Better Days," Springsteen sings that he is "tired of waiting for his ship to come in." Here he affirms that "when it comes to luck you make your own" and instead of waiting for some magic metaphorical gold strike, he's getting dirt on his hands building a new home for himself. It is another song about starting over and shaking off the past and the blues that came with it.

In its *Bruce Springsteen Collector's Edition* (2022), *Rolling Stone* listed "Lucky Town" as number fifty-six among the artist's top 100 songs.

"Local Hero"

Bruce Springsteen: vocals, guitar, keyboards, bass
  guitar, harmonica, percussion
Gary Mallaber: drums
Patti Scialfa: backing vocals
Lisa Lowell: backing vocals
Soozie Tyrell: backing vocals

This song finds Springsteen in a mode of storytelling that contains a message consistent with the first two songs on the album, based on the perspective he has gained from his own life experience. The song begins with the singer encountering a portrait of a man on a black velvet painting in the store (a reference to Elvis?), a face that he does not recognize "between the Doberman and Bruce Lee," although he recognizes the pose. When he inquires in the store about the identity of the man, the salesgirl tells him that it is just a portrait of a "local hero who used to live here for a while." As the song progresses, it becomes clear that Springsteen recognizes himself in the image of a "local hero" who is convinced to leave home by "a stranger dressed in black" (probably the devil, not Johnny Cash, despite the fact the country singer was famous for always dressing in black) because there is serious money to be made in "the big town 'cross the whiskey line." In the second verse, Springsteen even sings "They make us boss [his popular nickname], the devil pays off." He succeeds, in the song, just as he had in life, singing in the bridge, "They made me king, then they made me pope," continuing in the next line, "Then they brought the rope." In the final verse, though, he acknowledges that he has come through the experience bent but unbowed and that "these days I'm feeling all right." The song concludes with the singer ready to return to small-town life, to a place that just needs "a local hero," presumably as opposed to the rock megastar Springsteen had become in many people's eyes.

"If I Should Fall Behind"

Bruce Springsteen: vocals, guitar, keyboards, bass
  guitar, harmonica, percussion
Gary Mallaber: drums

"If I Should Fall Behind" can be understood as revisiting "The River," but here again Springsteen offers a different perspective than that expressed in so much of his earlier work. In "The River," he explored the theme of how love can turn sour over time when faced with the harsh realities of life, such as unemployment, the challenge of raising children, and general depression at getting older. "If I Should Fall Behind" does not ignore those realities; in fact, it explicitly acknowledges them. "Now everyone dreams of a love lasting and true / But you and I know what this world can do." But this song is the opposite of a song about escape or, in the case of "The River" about taking solace only in memories of how things used to be; it is a song about commitment and two people staying together even if they at times fall out of step with one another. In fact, here "the river" is not in the past: "There's a beautiful river in the valley ahead," where the singer suggests he and his partner wait for each other if "they lose each other in the shadow of the evening trees." The song could be a promise of a couple to reunite in the afterlife if one should die first, the "beautiful river" possibly referring to the River Jordan as a metaphor for the Promised Land. But it also works as a promise to persist in a marriage or relationship through tough times or individual changes.

In its *Bruce Springsteen Collector's Edition* (2022), *Rolling Stone* listed "If I Should Fall Behind" as number forty-one among the artist's top 100 songs.

"Leap of Faith"

Bruce Springsteen: vocals, guitar, bass guitar,
  harmonica, percussion

Roy Bittan: keyboards
Gary Mallaber: drums
Patti Scialfa: backing vocals
Lisa Lowell: backing vocals
Soozie Tyrell: backing vocals

Even in Springsteen's earliest work, two of the main preoccupations that dominate his songwriting are sex and religion. (On Springsteen and religion, see Azzan Yadin-Israel, *The Grace of God and the Grace of Man: The Theologies of Bruce Springsteen*.) Possibly in no other song, however, are these two themes more closely intermingled than in "Leap of Faith." While some might view the song and lyrics such as "your legs were heaven, your breasts were the altar, your body was the holy land" as sacrilegious, it is also possible to interpret these lyrics and the song as Springsteen's tendency to find the sacred in the profane, in the world and realities of daily life, a theme he goes on to pursue in some of his later work. The "leap of faith" in the song refers to the act of commitment and willingness to love again after hurting others and being hurt, with sex standing in for the beginning of a new life with someone. "Now you were the Red Sea, I was Moses . . . the waters parted and love rushed inside." Of course, Moses was in the process of leading the Hebrews to the Promised Land. The end of the song even refers to the singer being "born again," but here the secular is infused with religious imagery to emphasize just how important the choices of this life can be, with salvation coming not just in the next life, but in this one as well.

"The Big Muddy"
Bruce Springsteen: vocals, guitar, bass guitar,
  harmonica, percussion
Roy Bittan: keyboards
Gary Mallaber: drums

In 1967, the iconic American folk troubadour Pete Seeger released a song called "Waist Deep in the Big Muddy," the title of which constitutes the chorus of Springsteen's "The Big Muddy," repeated twice in the first and second choruses and three times in the third. Clearly inspired by Seeger's anti–Vietnam War song that Springsteen probably heard for the first time around the age of eighteen, this song foreshadows his actual recording of many songs written or recorded by Seeger, in his 2006 album *We Shall Overcome: The Seeger Sessions*. In Seeger's original, a captain tries to take his army through a ford in the river only to find it much deeper than he thought; the captain ends up drowning while his troops barely make it out alive. While the river keeps increasing in depth in Seeger's song, in Springsteen's song the river remains waist deep, but the other line in the chorus is "You start on higher ground but end up crawlin'." Each of the verses describes situations in which people start out with good intentions, but life always gets messier than we expect. In fact, in Springsteen's song, it is we, not the river, who are the "messier things," and nobody leaves this world "without their shirttail dirty or their hands bloody."

"Living Proof"
Bruce Springsteen: vocals, guitar, bass guitar,
  harmonica, percussion
Roy Bittan: keyboards
Gary Mallaber: drums

In *Songs*, Springsteen wrote, "Children are the 'living proof' of our belief in one another, that love is real" (rev. ed., 2003, 218). In this song, he writes of the birth of his son as "a little piece of the Lord's undying light" that helped to restore his faith and lift him out of "some kind of darkness." Springsteen addresses his past mistakes, "The sad and hurtful things he'd done," but speaks of his newborn child as shooting "through my anger and rage to show me my prison was just an open cage." Sin, faith, mercy, salvation had for a long time found their way into Springsteen's music as themes, but this is the first song in which he is able to write that he has found "living proof" of God's mercy. He also uses the song to shift from the image of a "lonely rider" out on the boulevard, "where life is just a house of cards," to the metaphor of a train that contains "treasures of the Lord," one he plans to board when it comes for him.

"Book of Dreams"
Bruce Springsteen: vocals, guitar, keyboards, bass
  guitar, harmonica, percussion
Gary Mallaber: drums

Written from the perspective of a man about to get married, the singer of "Book of Dreams," stands outside in the yard while a party goes on inside the house without him. If "Living Proof" views the birth of a child as a sign of God's mercy, this song sees the same promise in a wedding vow, quite a different take on marriage than we find in Springsteen's earlier work, where it was approached with sadness or at least a sense of resignation, without much hope that love would last or life would get better because of it. Instead, this song finds Springsteen, or the singer anyway, "drinkin' in the forgiveness this life provides." Reminders of the past survive, but while we may still show the scars, the pain is gone. The song is not naïve about marriage as a panacea; at the wedding, "The dance floor is alive with beauty," but also with "mystery and danger." The song seems to be saying we cannot know what the future holds, but we can dream about the one we want, as he invites his partner into his "book of dreams."

"Souls of the Departed"
Bruce Springsteen: vocals, guitar, keyboards, bass
  guitar, harmonica, percussion
Gary Mallaber: drums

This is by far the darkest song on the album, but that is appropriate for a song with references to the Persian Gulf War of 1991 and gang warfare in Los Angeles. If "Living Proof" is about birth and hope and love, "Souls of the Departed" provides the counterpoint, a song about death and fear and the hatred that leads to wars and violence on the streets. Springsteen offers the song as a "prayer for the souls of the departed," while he puts his son to bed at night, realizing that it could have been him instead of the child a mother grieves because he has been shot in a schoolyard in East Compton. Despite his career success, fame, money, and now some peace and contentment with a new wife and family, here Springsteen pays tribute to his social conscience, the lines "Now I ply my trade in the land of king dollar / Where you get paid and your silence passes as honor," revealing an uneasiness with selling out, something of which his critics would accuse him in the 1990s.

"My Beautiful Reward"
Bruce Springsteen: vocals, guitar, keyboards, bass
  guitar, harmonica, percussion
Gary Mallaber: drums
Ian McLagan: organ

There is a danger in treating the songs on this album as autobiographical, although it is hard not to do so, given how closely many of them correlate to Springsteen's own life around the time of its release. It is important to recognize that each of these songs deals with general human situations as well and that when Springsteen writes in the first person in a song, that person does not have to be him per se, and often is not (see most of the songs on *Nebraska*, for instance). "My Beautiful Reward" provides a good example of a song that could be listened to either way. It describes a man searching for something to "ease the pain that living brings," first in wealth and items of material value, but not finding it there, he searches elsewhere "from the mountain to the valley floor." He does not find it "walking down empty hallways," and even after finding love, and considering himself lucky to do so, he comes "crashing down like a drunk on a ballroom floor." The distance between author and character emerges clearly in the last verse though, as the narrator finds himself transformed into a bird with long black feathers flying over the world, still searching for his "beautiful reward," something perhaps unattainable in this life but symbolic of that yearning for something more or better that never completely goes away.

THE GHOST OF TOM JOAD

Released in November 1995, *The Ghost of Tom Joad* is a largely folk- and acoustic-oriented album in the style of 1982's *Nebraska*. *The Ghost of Tom Joad* followed the April 1995 release of Springsteen's *Greatest Hits*, for which the E Street band reunited in the studio to record "Blood Brothers" and "This Hard Land."

The Ghost of Tom Joad was written and recorded between March and September 1995 at Thrill Hill West, his home studio in California. The new LP found Springsteen exploring present-day socioeconomic struggles in the United States and Mexico. For the project, he drew on the character of Tom Joad from John Steinbeck's classic novel *The Grapes of Wrath* (1939), which traced the economic despair associated with the Great Depression. The

film adaptation of *The Grapes of Wrath* starred Henry Fonda and inspired Woody Guthrie to compose "The Ballad of Tom Joad," which proved to be a signal influence on the course of Springsteen's new album. Springsteen would also cite Dale Maharidge and Michael Williamson's *Journey to Nowhere: The Saga of the New Underclass* (1985) as a key influence.

For Springsteen, *The Ghost of Tom Joad* "was the result of a decade-long inner debate I'd been having with myself after the success of *Born in the U.S.A.* That debate centered on a single question: Where does a rich man belong? If it was true that it's 'easier for a camel to go through the eye of a needle than for a rich man to enter the kingdom of God,' I wouldn't be walking through those pearly gates any time soon,

The Reunion of the E Street Band and the Greatest Hits Album

Springsteen fans disappointed by Springsteen's move to California and the release of his two 1992 albums, *Human Touch* and *Lucky Town*, backed by musicians other than the E Street Band, had reason for excitement when he got the band back together to record some new tracks for his *Greatest Hits* album, released in February 1995.

The album included eighteen tracks and featured such standards as "Born to Run," "Badlands," and "Hungry Heart," as well as five tracks that had not appeared on any of Springsteen's earlier albums. In addition to the Oscar-winning "Streets of Philadelphia," the album featured an unreleased track from the *Born in the U.S.A.* sessions called "Murder Incorporated," a song Springsteen described as "darkly erotic" called "Secret Garden," and two songs that speak directly to his reconciliation with the E Street Band, "Blood Brothers"

and "This Hard Land." The album came at another crossroad in Springsteen's life and career, one that found him looking back at what he had achieved thus far while considering what new challenge he might decide to take on next. Those reflections included the realization that a decade had passed since he had last recorded with the E Street Band. He got the band together in January 1992, even renewing his relationship with Steve Van Zandt, who unexpectedly joined in to play mandolin on "This Hard Land." The album sold well and gained Springsteen extra midcareer attention. Springsteen was even accommodating in allowing "Secret Garden" not only to be used in the film *Jerry Maguire* but also to be played on the radio in a schmaltz-tinged version overlaid with dialogue from the film between the characters played by Tom Cruise and Renee Zellweger. As it turned out, Springsteen had other things on his mind. He and the E Street Band would have many years of concerts and recording still ahead of them, but this particular reunion did not provide the spark for his next project, which turned out to be the socially conscious solo acoustic album, *The Ghost of Tom Joad*.

The Reunion of the E Street Band and the *Greatest Hits* (Alamy) [LP sales rack]

but that was okay; there was still plenty of work to be done down here on Earth. That was the premise of *The Ghost of Tom Joad*. What is the work for us to do in our short time here?" (Springsteen, *Born to Run*, 2016).

Springsteen viewed *The Ghost of Tom Joad* as a clear successor to *Nebraska* in terms of both its thematics and its production. "I'd pick up where I'd left off with *Nebraska*," he later wrote, and "set the stories in the mid-90s and in the land of my current residence, California. The music was minimal, the melodies uncomplicated; the austere rhythms and arrangements defined who these people were and how they expressed themselves. They traveled light; they were lean, direct in their expression, yet with most of what they had to say left in the silence between words. They were transient and led hard, complicated lives, half of which had been left behind in another world, in another country" (Springsteen, *Born to Run*, 2016).

While several of the songs on *The Ghost of Tom Joad* would be solo acoustic efforts, other compositions featured full band recordings. Several E Street Band members and studio musicians contributed to the LP, including E Streeters Danny Federici and Garry Tallent, as well as Chuck Plotkin, Gary Mallber, Marty Rifkin, Jim Hanson, and Jennifer Condos. As with *Lucky Town*, Patti Scialfa, Soozie Tyrell, and Lisa Lowell provided backing vocals.

HISTORICAL CONTEXT

The Ghost of Tom Joad puts forth a series of stories about contemporary America with deep resonances from the American past. It also provides another Springsteen take on the American Dream. Springsteen wrote that the album "chronicled the increasing economic division of the '80s and '90s and the hard times

and consequences for many of the people whose work and sacrifice helped build the country we live in." The album explores many of the same themes as many of his earlier songs and albums, but with added resonances from American folk icons Woody Guthrie and Bob Dylan.

The title track refers to the main character in John Steinbeck's 1939 novel *The Grapes of Wrath* and the film on which it was based, directed by John Ford. Woody Guthrie had previously written a song called "Tom Joad," which provided further inspiration for Springsteen's "The Ghost of Tom Joad." The title of the song recalls the Depression and the period in which Steinbeck and Ford set the novel and film, but immediately Springsteen brings us into the present with references to "highway patrol choppers" and the "new world order," a phrase coined by President George H. W. Bush in the aftermath of the fall of the Soviet Union in 1991.

Even though the album deals with broader social themes of economic and social justice, Springsteen still finds room to explore relationships on this album, as he does in "Straight Time." Other songs on the album that explore relationships include "The Line" and "My Best Was Never Good Enough," while "Dry Lightning" deals with the theme of lost love. But one thing Springsteen does differently on this album is to consider the perspectives of immigrants and minorities. In the song "Across the Border," the use of "my corazón" ("my heart") establishes the Hispanic identity of the singer. At the end of this song, we really start to see the American Dream from the immigrant perspective, in which for many the United States really is "the land of hope and dreams."

One of the most interesting songs on the album is "Galveston Bay," which tells the story of a Vietnamese immigrant who had fought alongside American soldiers in the Vietnam

War but who confronts racism and the Klan as he tries to make a living with a shrimp boat off the coast of Texas. In this song, significantly, his friend Bobby has threatened to kill him, but makes the choice "to let him pass" when he has the chance. This choice partially reaffirms the ability of each of us to choose to do the right thing, even if it means going against the sentiments of the crowd, especially if, as in this case, the crowd is nothing more than a racist mob. The experiences of Vietnam War veterans chronicled in "Born in the U.S.A." reappear here as well, with similar effect. Unlike in the earlier song, the singer in "Youngstown" comes home from the war to a job, but one "that'd suit the devil as well." In short, the historical context for this album goes much deeper and further back than for any previous Springsteen album but still speaks to the specific historical context in which he wrote it in the mid-1990s.

PRODUCTION

Released on November 21, 1995, Columbia Records
Produced by Bruce Springsteen and Chuck Plotkin
Engineered by Toby Scott with assistance from Greg Goldman
Mixed by Scott at Thrill Hill West
Mastered by Dave Collins at A&M Mastering Studios
Recorded at Thrill Hill West, March to September 1985

PERSONNEL

Bruce Springsteen: vocals, electric and acoustic guitars, keyboards, harmonica
Jennifer Condos: electric bass
Danny Federici: keyboards, accordion

Jim Hanson: electric bass
Gary Mallaber: drums, percussion
Chuck Plotkin: keyboards
Marty Rifkin: pedal steel guitar
Patti Scialfa: backing vocals
Garry Tallent: electric bass
Lisa Lowell: backing vocals
Soozie Tyrell: violin, backing vocals

COVER ART AND PACKAGING

Design: Sandra Choron, Eric Dinyer, and Harry Choron
Photography: Pam Springsteen

TRACK LISTING

All songs composed by Bruce Springsteen.

1. "The Ghost of Tom Joad"
2. "Straight Time"
3. "Highway 29"
4. "Youngstown"
5. "Sinaloa Cowboys"
6. "The Line"
7. "Balboa Park"
8. "Dry Lightning"
9. "The New Timer"
10. "Across the Border"
11. "Galveston Bay"
12. "My Best Was Never Good Enough"

UNRELEASED OUTTAKES

"Brothers under the Bridges": released on *Tracks* (1998)

CONTEMPORARY REVIEWS

Phil Sutcliffe (*MOJO*, December 1995): "But entertainment value? Sorry, wrong queue. *The*

Ghost of Tom Joad's musical content is minimal and uniform. It is quiet. Turn it up to 11, it's still quiet. Small-room production sets Springsteen down beside you, muttering in your ear. Other sounds shade the background almost subliminally; the "Streets of Philadelphia" keyboard lowers along, sometimes violin or pedal steel sigh and moan. The aural effect of this album could be restful or downright monotonous, according to taste. So it all depends on the lyrics. Good thing, then, that they're magnificent."

Mikal Gilmore (*Rolling Stone*, December 28, 1995): "Plaintive, bitter epiphanies like these are far removed from the sort anthemic cries that once filled Springsteen's music, but then these are not times for anthems. These are times for lamentations, for measuring how much of the American promise has been broken or abandoned and how much of our future is transfigured into a vista of ruin. These are pitiless times. *The Ghost of Tom Joad* is Springsteen's response to this state of affairs. Maybe even his return to arms. In any event, this is his first overtly social statement since *Born in the U.S.A.* The atmosphere created is as merciless in its own way as the world the lyrics describe, and you will have to meet or reject that atmosphere on your own terms. I'm convinced it's Springsteen's best album in ten years, and I also think it's among the bravest work that anyone has given us this decade. *Tom Joad* bears an obvious kinship with Springsteen's 1982 masterwork, *Nebraska*. The musical backing is largely acoustic, and the sense of language and storytelling owes much to the Depression-era sensibility of Woody Guthrie. The stories are told bluntly and sparsely, and the poetry is broken and colloquial—like the speech of a man telling the stories he feels compelled to tell if only to try to be free of them. On *Tom Joad*, there are few

escapes and almost no musical relief from the numbing circumstances of the characters' lives. You could almost say that the music gets caught in meandering motions or drifts into circles that never break. The effect is brilliant and lovely; there's something almost lulling in the music's blend of acoustic arpeggios and moody keyboard textures, something that lures you into the melodies' dark dreaminess and loose mellifluence. But make no mistake—what you are being drawn into are scenarios of hell. American hell. . . . By climbing into their hearts and minds, Springsteen has given voice to people who rarely have one in this culture. And giving voice to people who are typically denied expression in our other arts and media has always been one of rock 'n' roll's most important virtues. As we move into the rough times and badlands that lie ahead, such acts will count for more than ever before."

Mark Cooper (*Q*, January 1996): "Inevitably, happy endings are in short supply as Springsteen's narrative leans more to Hubert Selby, Jr. and the hopelessness of *Last Exit to Brooklyn* than the jaunty "gather round" approach of Guthrie's calls to resistance. As a result, *The Ghost of Tom Joad* is ultimately rather hard going. The title track, 'Youngstown' and the almost-love song, 'Dry Lightning,' are by far the best tunes here but there are too many long narratives with thrown-together melodies, mumbled lyrics and grim resolutions. There's a drab uniformity about Springsteen's approach throughout the album, perhaps because the narratives tend to end the same way and be delivered in the same deadpan mumble. . . . Curiously, however, Springsteen seems so determined to step out of Beverly Hills and into the world of Guthrie and the West of the contemporary dispossessed that he's been unable to freight these songs with anything but the bleakest of emotional undercurrents. Perhaps the true ghost here is neither the Boss nor Tom Joad but Bruce Springsteen himself, the man who found happiness in his family but then could only see misery in the world around him."

PROMOTION

Springsteen supported *The Ghost of Tom Joad* with a 128-date solo tour that spanned November 1995 through May 1997.

CHART ACTION

Billboard Top Pop Albums: number eleven.

Released on November 21, 1995, *The Ghost of Tom Joad* debuted at number eleven, its peak position, on December 9; the number-one album that week was the Beatles' *Anthology I*. The album sold more than 500,000 copies, earning gold status from RIAA.

The Ghost of Tom Joad spent fourteen weeks on the *Billboard* charts.

COMMENTS FROM SPRINGSTEEN AND HIS CIRCLE

Bruce Springsteen: "I think you have to feel like there's a lot of different ways to reach people, help them think about what's really important in this one-and-only life we live. There's pop culture—that's the shotgun approach, where you throw it out and it gets interpreted in different ways and some people pick up on it. And then there's a more intimate, focused, approach like I tried on *Tom Joad*. I got a lot of correspondence about the last album from a lot of different people—writers, teachers, those who have an impact on shaping other people's lives" (*The Advocate*, April 2, 1996).

MISCELLANEOUS

In March 1994, "Streets of Philadelphia" won an Academy Award for Best Original Song, later going on to win Grammy Awards in four categories, including Song of the Year, Best Rock Song, Best Rock Vocal Performance (Solo), and Best Song Written Specifically for a Motion Picture or Television.

In 1997, *The Ghost of Tom Joad* earned the Grammy Award for Best Contemporary Folk Album.

In 1997, Rage Against the Machine released a hit cover version of "The Ghost of Tom Joad," which was later included on their 2000 LP *Renegades*.

SONG ANALYSES

"The Ghost of Tom Joad"
Bruce Springsteen: vocals, guitar, harmonica
Danny Federici: keyboards
Gary Mallaber: drums
Marty Rifkin: pedal steel guitar
Garry Tallent: bass

Springsteen drew his inspiration for "The Ghost of Tom Joad" from Henry Fonda's famous "I'll Be There" speech in *The Grapes of Wrath* (1940), directed by John Ford. As Tom Joad, Fonda turns in a bravura performance, especially when his character vows to fight for the rights of working people and the impoverished: "I'll be all around in the dark—I'll be everywhere. Wherever you can look—wherever there's a fight, so hungry people can eat, I'll be there. Wherever there's a cop beatin' up a guy, I'll be there. I'll be in the way guys yell when they're mad. I'll be in the way kids laugh when they're hungry and they know supper's ready, and when the people are eatin' the stuff they raise and livin' in the houses they build—I'll be there, too."

In "The Ghost of Tom Joad," Springsteen references Fonda's speech, while conjuring up 1930s-era images of the Dust Bowl in comparison to the socioeconomic travails of the 1990s. The song was originally intended to be an E Street Band vehicle and included on his *Greatest Hits* (1995) compilation. Instead, Springsteen reworked the composition as a folk-rock performance. He would later record yet another version of the song with the E Street Band (including guitarist Tom Morello) for *High Hopes* (2014).

"Straight Time"
Bruce Springsteen: vocals, guitar
Danny Federici: keyboards
Jim Hanson: bass
Gary Mallaber: drums, percussion
Soozie Tyrell: violin

For the LP's second song, Springsteen drew his title and his inspiration from *Straight Time* (1978), a neo-noir film directed by Ulu Grosbard. Based on Edward Bunker's novel *No Beast So Fierce*, *Straight Time* starred Dustin Hoffman as a lifelong criminal who struggles as a parolee to assimilate back into society. "Straight Time" traces the brutal story of a convict who finds himself unable to adapt to a quiet family life, a man who is in near-constant temptation of falling into his hard-wired criminal ways.

During his solo tour in support of *The Ghost of Tom Joad*, Springsteen introduced "Straight Time" as being "about a fellow who gets out of prison and comes home and is trying to find out how he can find a way to integrate himself back into the world, back into his family. You know, old habits, they die really hard, because those are the things that somehow give us a feeling of who we are no matter how destructive or harmful they may be. Everybody's laid awake at night and had the worst of them feel like their only

hope sometimes, like their only chance, only breath of fresh air."

"Highway 29"
Bruce Springsteen: vocals, guitar, keyboards

"Highway 29" traces the story, if only obliquely, of Bonnie and Clyde, the notorious 1930s-era bank robbers who were known to travel Highway 29 during their long-running crime spree. Springsteen's song explores their tragic romance and the death and destruction that it wrought, including the fatal ambush that brought their nefarious activities to an end.

"Youngstown"
Bruce Springsteen: vocals, guitar
Jim Hanson: bass
Gary Mallaber: drums, percussion
Chuck Plotkin: keyboards
Marty Rifkin: pedal steel guitar
Soozie Tyrell: violin

Springsteen had been inspired to compose "Youngstown" after reading Dale Maharidge and Michael Williamson's *Journey to Nowhere: The Saga of the New Underclass* (1985). The book includes discussion of Joe Marshall Jr., an unemployed Youngstown, Ohio, steelworker. The reference to "my sweet Jenny" concerns the nickname for Youngstown's Jeanette blast furnace rather than a romantic counterpart.

During a 1995 performance at New York City's Beacon Theatre, Springsteen introduced the song, remarking that "there were people coming in who'd made good livings previously and been able to support their wives and their kids and who'd played by all the rules and done all the right things and were coming up empty-handed. I read the book and I put it down and I laid awake and I thought, 'I only know how to do one thing. What if somebody came and told me that that one thing that I could do wasn't necessary anymore, after I was 30 years or 40 years down the road. That I wasn't needed, wasn't useful now. How would I come home at night and face my family and see my children if they needed something to eat or something to wear?' How directly it would affect the core sense of who I am and what my place is. These were people that built the bridges that we cross, the buildings we live in. Who gave up their sons to the wars that we fought."

"Sinaloa Cowboys"
Bruce Springsteen: vocals, guitar, keyboards

For "Sinaloa Cowboys," Springsteen drew his inspiration from a March 1995 *Los Angeles Times* story about Southern California's growing array of methamphetamine labs, which are operated by the cowboys of Mexico's Sinaloa state. According to the article, "These 'Sinaloa Cowboys,' with their beaver hats, boots, and ostrich-skin belts are armed and dangerous. 'Stay out if you value your ass!' read the spray-painted message in Spanish and English on the side of a large shed in rural Firebaugh, west of Fresno." In particular, Springsteen was intrigued by the methamphetamine epidemic's hold on Southern California, especially the inherent dangers of the deadly hydriodic acid fumes that it produced as a byproduct and that often resulted in the deaths of its manufacturers. In "Sinaloa Cowboys," Springsteen traces the story of Miguel and Louis Rosales, Mexican brothers who cross the border to work the fields as migrant workers only to come into the orbit of California's flourishing meth trade, which leads to tragic ends.

"The Line"
Bruce Springsteen: vocals, guitar, keyboards

As with "Sinaloa Cowboys," "The Line" addresses contemporary issues related to immigration, especially the ongoing challenges associated with his country's international border with Mexico. For Springsteen, border issues come down to heartfelt human quandaries as opposed to political brinksmanship. "I don't like the soapbox stuff," he explained to *Mother Jones*. "I don't believe you can tell people anything. You can show them things. I don't set out to make a point, I set out to create compassion and understanding and present something that feels like the world. I set out to make sure something is revealed at the end of the song, some knowledge gained. That's when I figure I'm doing my job."

For "The Line," Springsteen adapted the melody from Bob Dylan's "Love Minus Zero/No Limit," from the folk musician's *Bringing It All Back Home* (1965). In his song, Springsteen traces the story of a California Border Patrol officer who finds himself in an ethical conundrum after he meets Luisa, an illegal immigrant, in a bar and decides to assist her and her family in crossing the border line. A widower and military veteran, Carl is forced to weigh his well-honed ethics in comparison with his genuine desire to help out Luisa and her family.

"Balboa Park"
Bruce Springsteen: vocals, guitar, keyboards

Drawing on an April 1993 *Los Angeles Times* article as his inspiration, Springsteen composed "Balboa Park" as a means for examining San Diego's freeway subculture. The article, as with "Balboa Park," offers an exposé on the homeless youth who often live beneath the city's freeway interchanges, where their only solace arrives in the form of drugs and prostitution. In "Balboa Park," which highlights the city's 1,200-acre urban parklands, Springsteen explores a youth culture beset by crime and despair.

"Dry Lightning"

Bruce Springsteen: vocals, guitar
Danny Federici: keyboards
Gary Mallaber: drums
Garry Tallent: bass
Soozie Tyrell: violin

In this song, Springsteen explores the concept of "dry lightning" or a "dry thunderstorm," a phenomenon that often occurs in desert-like conditions and is the frequent source of wildfires because much of the storm's precipitation has dissipated before it reaches the ground. In "Dry Lightning," Springsteen employs the phenomenon as a metaphor for his character's intense, apparently unquenchable inner sadness. The song concerns a seemingly happy romantic relationship between the narrator and his beloved, a quest for love and redemption that, in spite of everything, seems hopeless and has inevitably gone awry.

"The New Timer"

Bruce Springsteen: vocals, guitar

Having found his inspiration in *Journey to Nowhere*, Springsteen explores the notion of a "new timer," which, according to the book, is a "new breed of street person, forced to the bottom by economic hardship." In "New Timer," Springsteen traces the story of a hobo who has left his family back in Pennsylvania to live an itinerant life on freight trains. In the song, Springsteen examines that painful nature of a transient existence and a fruitless longing for human connection among the hobo class. The song also finds its roots in the words and music of Woody Guthrie, as well as the true story of Thomas Jefferson "Alabama" Glenn, a hobo like Springsteen's character Frank, who is the victim of a senseless murder in an insensate, uncaring world.

"Across the Border"

Bruce Springsteen: vocals, guitar, harmonica
Jennifer Condos: bass
Danny Federici: keyboards, accordion
Lisa Lowell: backing vocals
Gary Mallaber: drums
Marty Rifkin: pedal steel guitar
Patti Scialfa: backing vocals
Soozie Tyrell: violin, backing vocals

As with "The Line," "Across the Border" considers the artificial nature of border lines and what they represent across different cultures. In "Across the Border," Springsteen's narrator leaves his beloved and his homeland to begin a new life in America, a heavenly place, to his mind, filled with endless fortune and possibility, whether they await him in his current world or some kind of afterlife.

"Galveston Bay"

Bruce Springsteen: vocals, guitar, keyboards

A song about the plight of Vietnamese immigrants who settle on the Texas Gulf Coast in the postwar years, "Galveston Bay" traces a brutalizing story of vengeance and murder with a glint of hopefulness. In many ways, "Galveston Bay" concerns the nature of violence and trauma and their unsettling, insidious penchant for eclipsing generations and geography. Yet in others, it examines what it means to be a veteran and to assimilate into civilian culture.

"My Best Was Never Good Enough"

Bruce Springsteen: vocals, guitar, keyboards

Inspired by Jim Thompson's hardboiled crime novel *The Killer Inside Me* (1958), "My Best Was Never Good Enough" finds Springsteen pondering the slippery nature of human identity and the complicated selves that we hide behind carefully constructed veneers. In addition to Thompson's novel, Springsteen was motivated by the rise of cable news and its incessant need to establish news stories no matter what the interpersonal cost. "It was my parting joke," Springsteen commented in *Songs* (1998), "and [a] shot at the way pop culture trivializes complicated moral issues, how the nightly news 'sound bytes' [*sic*] and packages life to strip away the dignity of human events."

CONTEMPORANEOUS RELEASES

"Streets of Philadelphia"
Bruce Springsteen: vocals, guitar, bass, synthesizer, drum machine
Ornette Coleman: tenor saxophone
"Little" Jimmy Scott: backing vocals
Tommy Sims: backing vocals

Director Jonathan Demme originally solicited Neil Young to compose the theme of his 1993 film *Philadelphia*. When Young was forced to bow out, Springsteen accepted the challenge, composing one of his most powerful and affecting songs in the process. "Streets of Philadelphia" finds Springsteen adopting the voice and experience of an AIDS victim as he ponders a bleak future. Demme later recalled receiving Springsteen's demo in the mail. "My wife and I sat down and listened to it, and we were literally weeping by the end" (Sandford, *Springsteen*, 1999). "Streets of Philadelphia" marked Springsteen's first top-ten hit since "Tunnel of Love."

CHART ACTION
Billboard Hot 100: number nine. The song registered a number-three showing on the magazine's Adult Contemporary and Mainstream Rock charts, respectively, as well as a number-thirteen showing on the Mainstream Top 40 chart.

"Streets of Philadelphia" b/w "If I Should Fall Behind" was released on February 2, 1994. The number-one song that week was Bryan Adams, Rod Stewart, and Sting's "All for Love."

"Murder Incorporated"
Bruce Springsteen: vocals, electric guitar
Roy Bittan: piano, synthesizer, backing vocals
Clarence Clemons: saxophone, percussion, backing vocals
Danny Federici: organ, synthesizer, backing vocals
Garry Tallent: electric bass, backing vocals
Steven Van Zandt: electric guitar, backing vocals
Max Weinberg: drums, backing vocals

With "Murder Incorporated," Springsteen assails the place of violence in American life as an accepted reality at the hands of corporations and broken mores. As he explained at the Beacon Theatre in 1995, "There's a body count incorporated into our way of life. We've come to accept the expendability of some of our citizens' lives and dreams as just a part of the price of doing business." Drawing its title from *Murder, Inc.* (1960), a gangster film directed by Burt Balaban and Stuart Rosenberg, the song was originally recorded in 1982 for the *Born in the U.S.A.* project, for which it was considered as a potential title track.

CHART ACTION
Billboard Hot 100: did not chart.

"Murder Incorporated" was released as a promotional single on February 24, 1995. The number-one song that week was Madonna's "Take a Bow."

"Secret Garden"
Bruce Springsteen: vocals, guitar
Roy Bittan: piano, synthesizer
Clarence Clemons: saxophone, percussion, backing vocals
Danny Federici: organ, glockenspiel, synthesizer

"Streets of Philadelphia"

Bruce Springsteen's fame brought him myriad opportunities to expand beyond his normal professional routine of writing songs, recording albums, and touring with the E Street Band. Other artists recorded many of his songs, some of which he occasionally wrote specifically for them, such as "This Little Girl," which he offered to Gary U.S. Bonds to help revive the classic rocker's career in the 1970s. His habitual refusal to allow his songs to be used in insipid commercials, though, sent a message that his talents were not for sale and indicated a reluctance to have his songs used outside of the context for which he originally intended them. In 1994, however, he received an offer from film director Jonathan Demme to compose a song for his new movie, a serious venture that dramatically portrayed the plight of a gay and relatively young attorney in Philadelphia suffering from the (at the time) incurable disease of AIDS. It took little deliberation for Springsteen to agree, but he had trouble accommodating Demme's desire for a rock song for the beginning of the film. He responded instead with a somber and melancholy song with a subtle rock undertone that seemed more in keeping with the serious nature of the subject addressed in the film than a rollicking rock song like "Badlands" or "Born to Run" would have been. "Streets

"Streets of Philadelphia" (Alamy) [Academy Award photo]

of Philadelphia" captured the inner dialogue and hopelessness of a man experiencing the dissolution of all of the physical attributes he used to associate with his personal identity. Written in the first person, the singer finds he is "unrecognizable to myself," his clothes "don't fit me no more," and he feels himself "fading away" in a slow and agonizing death. Springsteen had always had the ability to write through the eyes of his characters, and in this case he took the, at the time, bold step of identifying with a gay man dying from AIDS, helping, along with the film, to raise AIDS awareness and to humanize those who suffered from this affliction. The song won Springsteen an Academy Award, and garnered four Grammy awards, including Song of the Year and Best Rock Song.

Nils Lofgren: guitar
Patti Scialfa: backing vocals
Garry Tallent: electric bass
Steven Van Zandt: guitar
Max Weinberg: drums, backing vocals

Featured in Cameron Crowe's romantic comedy *Jerry Maguire* (1996), "Secret Garden" offers a poignant interpretation of womankind from a male narrator's perspective. In particular, the song addresses the challenges of loving a person who has built unassailable boundaries to conceal past hurts. Springsteen originally composed the song in the early 1990s for inclusion on *Human Touch*, later featuring it along with "Streets of Philadelphia" and "Murder Incorporated" on his *Greatest Hits* (1995) release.

CHART ACTION

Billboard Hot 100: number nineteen. The song notched a number-five showing on the Adult Contemporary chart, number forty on the Adult Top 40 chart, and number twelve on the Mainstream Top 40 chart.

"Secret Garden" b/w "Thunder Road (live)" was released on April 11, 1995. The number-one song that week was Dionne Farris's "I Know."

"Blood Brothers"
Bruce Springsteen: vocals, electric guitar
Roy Bittan: piano, synthesizer, backing vocals

Clarence Clemons: saxophone, percussion, backing vocals
Danny Federici: organ, synthesizer, backing vocals
Garry Tallent: electric bass, backing vocals
Steven Van Zandt: electric guitar, backing vocals
Max Weinberg: drums, backing vocals
Frank Pagano: percussion

Another one of the five unreleased songs on *Greatest Hits*, "Blood Brothers" was composed by Springsteen prior to reuniting the E Street Band. In the song, Springsteen sings poignantly about working with the group again and the time-eclipsing power of friendship: "We stood side by side each one fighting for the other / And we said until we died we'd always be blood brothers."

"This Hard Land"
Bruce Springsteen: vocals, electric guitar
Roy Bittan: piano, synthesizer, backing vocals
Clarence Clemons: saxophone, percussion, backing vocals
Danny Federici: organ, synthesizer, backing vocals
Garry Tallent: electric bass, backing vocals
Steven Van Zandt: mandolin, backing vocals
Max Weinberg: drums, backing vocals

As with "Murder Incorporated," "This Hard Land" dates back to the early 1980s, when Springsteen originally considered it for *Born in the U.S.A.* "This Hard Land" has much in common with "The Line" and "Across the Border," songs that ponder border relations between the United States and Mexico. During a 1996 introduction in Berlin, Springsteen described "This Hard Land" as being "about, faith, hope, love, brotherhood, sisterhood, community, every Western I ever saw, a little tequila mixed in there somewhere, and old friends."

"Sad Eyes"
Bruce Springsteen: vocals, guitar
Michael Fisher: percussion
Randy Jackson: electric bass
Jeff Porcaro: drums
David Sancious: keyboards

Released as a single in support of the *Tracks* compilation, "Sad Eyes" was recorded in 1990 during the *Human Touch* sessions. Enrique Iglesias enjoyed moderate chart success after recording a cover version for his 1999 debut LP.

CHART ACTION
Billboard Hot 100: did not chart.

"Sad Eyes" b/w "I Wanna Be with You" was released on June 8, 1999. The number-one song that week was Ricky Martin's "Livin' la Vida Loca."

The Rising (Shutterstock) [performance photo]

THE RISING

Released in July 2002, *The Rising* marked Springsteen's first studio album in nearly seven years, the longest expanse between releases since the onset of his recording career in 1973. Produced by Brendan O'Brien between January and March 2002 at Atlanta's Southern Tracks Recording Studio, *The Rising* was the first of several highly regarded collaborations between Springsteen and O'Brien. The album earned two Grammy Awards in 2003.

The album served as Springsteen's musical response to the atrocities of the 9/11 terrorist attacks. As Springsteen later recalled, "*The Rising* had its origins in the national telethon [*America: A Tribute to Heroes*] we were invited to be a part of the week after September 11. I wrote 'Into the Fire' for that show. Of the many tragic images of that day, the picture I couldn't let go of was of the emergency workers going up the stairs as others rushed down to safety. The sense of duty, the courage, ascending into . . . what? The religious image of ascension, the crossing of the line between this world, the world of blood, work, family, your children, the breath in your lungs, the ground beneath your feet, all that is life, and . . . the next, flooded my

Induction into the Rock and Roll Hall of Fame (Getty) [with Joel and McCartney]

Induction into the Rock and Roll Hall of Fame

In January 1999, Bruce Springsteen was inducted into the Rock and Roll Hall of Fame in Cleveland, Ohio, along with Bob Wills and His Texas Playboys, Charles Brown, Billy Joel, George Martin, Curtis Mayfield, Paul McCartney, Del Shannon, Dusty Springfield, and the Staple Singers. One would be hard pressed to find a more striking or impressive group of rock aristocracy inducted in any other year since the hall's foundation in 1983. Paul McCartney, George Martin, and Billy Joel alone would have made this a formidable group, but adding Springsteen and the other names on this list to the roster elevated it to near perfection.

To this point, Springsteen had certainly enjoyed an illustrious career that had spanned a quarter of a century since the release of his first two albums, but the question as the 1990s drew to a close and that hung over Springsteen's induction concerned where that career was headed. He had last released an album in 1995, an eternity ago in the music industry.

Furthermore, that album, *The Ghost of Tom Joad*, had marked another radical departure from his rock and roll roots, raising the question of whether his days as a rocker were perhaps behind him even as the rock industry commemorated his considerable output and legendary reputation as a performer in Cleveland. Of course, we now know that nothing could have been further from the truth. After receiving the validation conferred by his induction, Springsteen, never one to rest on his laurels, embarked a month later for a European tour with the E Street Band, having assuaged some bitterness and hurt feelings that Springsteen had been inducted as a solo artist without formal recognition of his collaboration with the band. Three years later, in the aftermath of 9/11, Springsteen got the E Street Band back together to record *The Rising*, which many critics consider one of his best albums. Springsteen was not done, and he has continued to record and perform with the E Street Band into the present. In 2014, the E Street Band finally earned their induction into the Rock and Roll Hall of Fame. The person who inducted them was Bruce Springsteen.

imagination. If you love life or any part of it, the depth of their sacrifice is unthinkable and incomprehensible. Yet what they left behind was tangible. Death, along with all its anger, pain, and loss, opens a window of possibility for the living. It removes the veil that the 'ordinary' gently drapes over our eyes. Renewed sight is the hero's last loving gift to those left behind."

The album concludes with a powerful trilogy that includes "The Rising," "Paradise," and "My City of Ruins"—a meditation on finding redemption in the wake of tragedy. *The Rising* features several compositions that verge on the experimental, including "The Fuse," with its hip-hop beat, and "Worlds Apart," with a Middle Eastern flavor courtesy of a troupe of Qawwali singers. Meanwhile, "Mary's Place" draws its origins from Sam Cooke's "Meet Me at Mary's Place," and "My City of Ruins" borrows its melody from Curtis Mayfield's gospel anthem "People Get Ready."

Springsteen credited O'Brien with fashioning the album's distinctive sound. "Brendan brought a fresh power and focus to the band's sound and playing," Springsteen later wrote. "He didn't comment on the subject matter; he just said, 'These are good. Now go home and write some more.' I knew from the beginning if I was going to continue to write thematically, my songs could not depend on simply being tied to the event. They needed an independent life, a life where their internal coherency would be completely understood even if there'd been no 9/11. So I wrote rock music, love songs, breakup songs, spirituals, blues, hit songs, and I allowed my theme and the events of the day to breathe and find their place within the framework I created. I went home, searched my book for unfinished songs and continued to write" (Springsteen, *Born to Run*, 2016).

HISTORICAL CONTEXT

On August 5, 2002, Springsteen appeared on the cover of *Time* magazine again, almost three decades since his visage had first graced the magazine following the 1975 release of *Born to Run*. This time the focus was no longer on the hype surrounding Springsteen, but because he had just released an album, *The Rising*, that, according to Nancy Gibbs, who wrote the cover story, was "the first significant piece of pop art to respond to the events of [September 11, 2001]. The United States was approaching the first anniversary of the terrible and shocking events of that day, when two hijacked airliners flew into the World Trade Center's Twin Towers in New York City, while a third crashed into the Pentagon in Virginia and a fourth headed for Washington crashed in Pennsylvania thanks to the determined efforts of passengers to prevent terrorists aboard the plane from achieving their mission of destruction.

Within a week of the attacks, Springsteen appeared on a telethon from New York City, where he performed a song he had written within the past year called "My City of Ruins." Springsteen had written the song about his beloved Asbury Park, but the lyric now seemed perfectly suited for a grieving audience appalled by the tragic and sudden manner in which their world, and that of the entire country, had been turned upside down. He had already started writing a song called "Into the Fire" about the heroics of the first responders who had courageously ascended the Twin Towers as others trapped in the buildings scurried downward in a too-often futile attempt to reach safe ground before the towers crumbled to the ground.

Springsteen later wrote other songs directly related to the terrorist attacks that appeared on the album, including "You're Missing," "Empty Sky," "Worlds Apart," and "Paradise." The album was well received not only by Springsteen fans but by the public as a whole, some of whom had become diffident if not outwardly hostile to Springsteen because of a song he had begun performing in concert in 1999 called "American Skin (41 Shots)." The song became divisive because it examined the death of an immigrant from Guinea named Amadou Diallo at the hands of four New York City police officers who fired forty-one shots at Diallo because they mistakenly thought he was reaching for a weapon instead of his wallet.

The controversy surrounding the song did not seriously affect Springsteen's popularity among his fan base, many of whom got the nuances in the song that his critics missed, but it did not help him either, given the seemingly downward arc of his career since 1984's *Born in the U.S.A.* To the extent that this was true,

Springsteen restored himself to the graces of his fans and the country at large with *The Rising*, partly because of the quality of the songs on the album and his reunion with the ever-popular E Street Band and partly also because it provided a compelling and emotional response to events Americans were still struggling with less than a year after 9/11.

PRODUCTION

Released on July 30, 2002, Columbia Records
Produced by Brendan O'Brien
Engineered by Nick Didia and Toby Scott
Recording Assistants: Billy Bowers and Karl Egsieker
Mixed by O'Brien at Southern Tracks Recording Studio and Silent Sound Studios
Mastered by Bob Ludwig at Masterdisk
Recorded at Southern Tracks Recording Studio, Atlanta, January to March 2002

PERSONNEL

Bruce Springsteen: vocals, guitar, harmonica
Roy Bittan: piano, mellotron, Kurzweil, pump organ, Korg M1 synthesizer, Crumar synthesizer
Clarence Clemons: tenor saxophone, backing vocals
Danny Federici: Hammond B3, Vox Continental, and Farfisa organs
Nils Lofgren: guitar, dobro, slide guitar, banjo, backing vocals
Patti Scialfa: backing vocals
Garry Tallent: electric bass
Soozie Tyrell: violin, backing vocals
Steven Van Zandt: guitar, mandolin, backing vocals
Max Weinberg: drums
Jere Flint: cello

Larry Lemaster: cello

Ed Manion: baritone saxophone

Brendan O'Brien: hurdy-gurdy, glockenspiel, orchestra bells

Mark Pender: trumpet

Richie "La Bamba" Rosenberg: trombone

Jane Scarpantoni: cello

Mike Spengler: trumpet

Jerry Vivino: tenor saxophone

The Alliance Singers: Corinda Carford (also contractor), Tiffeny Andrews, Michelle Moore (choir solo), Antoinette Moore, Antonio Lawrence, Jesse Moorer

Nashville String Machine: Ricky Keller (arranger/conductor); Carol Gorodetzky (contractor concert manager); Pam Sixfin, Leo Larrison, Conni Ellisor, Alan Umstead, Dave Davison, Mary Kathryn Vanosdale, and David Angell (violins); Kris Wilkinson, Gary Vanosdale, Jim Grosjean, and Monica Angell (violas); Bob Mason, Carol Rabinowitz, Julie Tanner, and Lynn Peithman (cellos)

Asif Ali Khan and Group: Asif Ali Khan (lead singer), Manzoor Hussain Shibli, Sarfraz Hussain, Raza Hussain, Imtiaz Shibli, Chahnawaz Hussain Khan, Bakat Fayyaz Hussain, Omerdroz Hussain Aftab (singers), Karamat Ali Asad (harmonium player), Haji Nazir Afridi (tabla player), Waheed Hussain Mumtaz

COVER ART AND PACKAGING

Design: Dave Bett and Michelle Holme
Photography: Danny Clinch

TRACK LISTING

All songs composed by Bruce Springsteen.

1. "Lonesome Day"
2. "Into the Fire"
3. "Waitin' on a Sunny Day"
4. "Nothing Man"
5. "Countin' on a Miracle"
6. "Empty Sky"
7. "Worlds Apart"
8. "Let's Be Friends (Skin to Skin)"
9. "Further on (Up the Road)"
10. "The Fuse"
11. "Mary's Place"
12. "You're Missing"
13. "The Rising"
14. "Paradise"
15. "My City of Ruins"

CONTEMPORARY REVIEWS

Kurt Loder (*Rolling Stone*, July 30, 2002): "The heart sags at the prospect of pop stars weighing in on the subject of September 11th. Which of them could possibly transmute the fiery horror of that day with the force of their art, or offer up anything beyond a dismal trivialization? The answer, it turns out, is Bruce Springsteen. With his new album, *The Rising*, Springsteen wades into the wreckage and pain of that horrendous event and emerges bearing fifteen songs that genuflect with enormous grace before the sorrows that drift in its wake. The small miracle of his accomplishment is that at no point does he give vent to the anger felt by so many Americans: the hunger for revenge. The music is often fierce in its execution, but in essence it is a requiem for those who perished in that sudden inferno, and those who died trying to save them. Springsteen grandly salutes their innocence and their courage and holds out a hand to those who mourn them, who seek the comfort of an explanation for the inexplicable. It's wonderful to hear these finely calibrated lyrics borne aloft by the E Street Band, brought back at last for a record that rocks as broadly as *Born in the*

U.S.A., the last studio album for which they all gathered, 18 years ago. However heavy of heart the new songs may be, this three-guitar incarnation of the band (with Steve Van Zandt and Nils Lofgren standing shoulder-to-shoulder with Springsteen—never a slouch in the screaming-guitar department himself) propels them with resounding power. Like *Born in the USA* before it, *The Rising* sounds unlike any other record of its time; in an era of rock murk and heavy synthetics, it flaunts its hard, bright guitars and positively walloping beats."

Sylvie Simmons (*MOJO*, September 2002): "Yes, the band the Boss let go in 1990 are with him here; wife Patti Scialfa too. Maybe the musical equivalent of the post-disaster desire to be with friends and family; maybe the realization that a stark, solo *Nebraska*-style treatment might have been too desolate. The E Streeters sound much as ever—lots of rousing build-ups, soaring sax, big backbeats, bombast. There are more retro-sounding pop-R&B numbers with 'sha la la' backing vocals than the subject matter might indicate, a stadium-rocker, some soulful ballads recalling early Van Morrison, and stirring gospel. Closer 'My City of Ruins,' urging us to 'rise up,' is particularly rousing. In the end *The Rising*'s message—as the other frequently recurring words 'hope,' 'strength,' 'faith,' and 'love' indicate—is one of indomitability."

PROMOTION

In addition to appearances on CBS-TV's *Late Night with David Letterman*, ABC-TV's *Nightline*, and NBC-TV's *Saturday Night Live*, Springsteen conducted a world tour from August 2002 through October 2003 in support of *The Rising*. The tour included 120 concerts and grossed some $221 million. Springsteen later

reflected on the tour, writing that "for the next year, the E Street Band crisscrossed the nation trying to contextualize the uncontextualizable. Perhaps the physical and psychic horrors were beyond music and art's ability to communicate, explain, heal or even comment upon. I don't know. Coming from a place that had been hit so hard, speaking to firemen who served at Ground Zero, ships' captains whose ferries crossed Sandy Hook Bay bringing back survivors, their decks inch-deep in ash, and my own desire to use the language I learned as a musician to sort through what was in my own head turned me to writing those songs. First, you write for yourself . . . always, to make sense of experience and the world around you. It's one of the ways I stay sane. Our stories, our books, our films are how we cope with the random trauma-inducing chaos of life as it plays" (Springsteen, *Born to Run*, 2016).

CHART ACTION

Billboard Top Pop Albums: number one.

Released on July 30, 2002, *The Rising* debuted at number one on August 17, unseating Toby Keith's *Unleashed*. The album sold more than two million copies, earning double-platinum status from RIAA.

The Rising spent thirty-seven weeks on the *Billboard* charts.

COMMENTS FROM SPRINGSTEEN AND HIS CIRCLE

Springsteen: "In the late afternoon, I drove to the Rumson–Sea Bright Bridge. There, usually, on a clear day the Twin Towers struck two tiny vertical lines on the horizon at the bridge's apex. Today, torrents of smoke lifted from the end of Manhattan Island, a mere fifteen miles away by boat. I stopped in at my local beach and walked to the water's edge, looking north; a thin gray line of smoke, dust and ash spread out due east over the water line. It appeared like the smudged edge of a hard blue sheet folding and resting upon the autumn Atlantic. I sat for a while, alone, the September beach empty beneath the eerie quiet of silent skies. We live along a very busy air corridor. Planes are constantly flying just off the Eastern Seaboard on their way to Kennedy and Newark airports, and the low buzz of airplane engines is as much a part of the sound tapestry at the Shore as are the gently crashing waves. Not today. All air traffic grounded. A deadly *On the Beach*, science fiction–like quiet unfolded over the sand. After a short while, I headed home to join Patti and pick up our children from school. As I drove over the gravel of the beach club parking lot, I hesitated before pulling into traffic on Ocean Boulevard. Just then a car careening off Rumson–Sea Bright Bridge shot past, its window down, and its driver, recognizing me, shouted, 'Bruce, we need you.' I sort of knew what he meant" (Springsteen, *Born to Run*, 2016).

Springsteen: "When you're putting yourself in shoes you haven't worn, you have to be very thoughtful, you call on your craft, and you search for it, and hopefully what makes people listen is that over the years you've been serious and honest. This album is the opposite end of the lyrical spectrum. There's detail, but it was a different type of writing than I've done in a while.... The lyrics want to be at the center and there is a minimal amount of music. The music is very necessary, but it wants to be minimal, and so with *The Rising* I was trying to make an exciting record with the E Street Band, which I hadn't done in a long time, so that form was

kind of driving me" (*American Songwriter*, March/April 2003).

Soozie Tyrell: "[Bruce] was very definite on the parts he wanted; when we were demoing, he'd have me come in and have specific parts he would have laid down on the keyboard and have me do the same parts on the violin—and double it or octave it, make it more into a string sections kind of thing. He was very specific about the parts and had great liners for me to play. It was great to hear him say that violin would be integral in [*The Rising*]" (*Backstreets*, Spring 2004).

MISCELLANEOUS

The Rising was feted at the annual Grammy Awards, earning the statuette for Best Rock Album, while placing second in the Album of the Year sweepstakes to Norah Jones's blockbuster debut *Come Away with Me*.

SONG ANALYSES

"Lonesome Day"

Bruce Springsteen: vocals, guitar, harmonica
Roy Bittan: piano, mellotron, Kurzweil, pump organ, Korg M1 synthesizer, Crumar
Clarence Clemons: saxophone, backing vocals
Danny Federici: Hammond B3, Vox Continental, and Farfisa organs
Nils Lofgren: guitar, dobro, slide guitar, banjo, backing vocals
Patti Scialfa: backing vocals
Garry Tallent: bass
Steven Van Zandt: guitar, mandolin, backing vocals
Max Weinberg: drums
Jere Flint: cello
Larry Lemaster: cello
Brendan O'Brien: hurdy-gurdy
Soozie Tyrell: violin, backing vocals

"Lonesome Day" was inspired by the distinctive riff in John Cougar Mellencamp's "Paper in Fire," the lead single from his 1987 LP *The Lonesome Jubilee*. With O'Brien playing the hurdy-gurdy—the medieval, hand-cranked string instrument—"Lonesome Day" kicks the LP into motion with a forlorn, albeit potentially triumphant sound. While it may not have been written expressly to connote the sad realities of post-9/11 life for the victims' families, "Lonesome Day" strikes notes of concern about waging war—"House is on fire, vipers in the grass" and "a little revenge, and this too shall pass"—while challenging the listener to seek solace in community and strive to persevere after experiencing the unthinkable. In its *Bruce Springsteen Collector's Edition* (2022), *Rolling Stone* listed "Lonesome Day" as number eighty-three among the artist's top 100 songs.

CHART ACTION

Billboard Hot 100: did not chart. The song registered a number-three showing on *Billboard*'s Adult Alternative Songs chart and number twenty-six on the Adult Top 40.

"Lonesome Day" was released on December 2, 2002. The number-one song that week was Eminem's "Lose Yourself."

"Into the Fire"

Bruce Springsteen: vocals, guitar, harmonica
Roy Bittan: piano, mellotron, Kurzweil, pump organ, Korg M1 synthesizer, Crumar synthesizer
Clarence Clemons: saxophone, backing vocals
Danny Federici: Hammond B3, Vox Continental, and Farfisa organs
Nils Lofgren: guitar, dobro, slide guitar, banjo, backing vocals
Patti Scialfa: backing vocals
Garry Tallent: bass
Steven Van Zandt: guitar, mandolin, backing vocals
Max Weinberg: drums
Brendan O'Brien: hurdy-gurdy, glockenspiel
Jane Scarpantoni: cello
Soozie Tyrell: violin, backing vocals

Dedicated to the New York City firefighters who bravely climbed the World Trade Center's stairwells, "Into the Fire" marked Springsteen's first post-9/11 composition. Springsteen was likely inspired by the widely publicized photograph of FDNY's Mike Kehoe, a thirty-three-year-old firefighter climbing the stairs of the North Tower. "Our job was to get up to the floor where the plane hit to reach people there," Kehoe recalled. "That's what we were determined to do. As we were going up people kept saying, 'good luck,' 'lots of luck.' But I must admit that even at that stage, I was frightened. Then over the radio [my boss] Roy said, 'everybody evacuate the building now.' We all turned around immediately. It was frightening. We managed to get into the lobby, it was like Beirut, there was rubble everywhere."

While Kehoe survived the rescue operation, some 343 firemen were not so fortunate, including Chief Orio Palmer, a forty-five-year-old fireman who was seen making his way into the upper reaches of the South Tower only to die in the building's collapse a short time later.

"Waitin' on a Sunny Day"

Bruce Springsteen: vocals, guitar, harmonica
Roy Bittan: piano, mellotron, Kurzweil, pump organ, Korg M1 synthesizer, Crumar synthesizer
Clarence Clemons: saxophone, backing vocals
Danny Federici: Hammond B3, Vox Continental, and Farfisa organs
Nils Lofgren: guitar, dobro, slide guitar, banjo, backing vocals
Patti Scialfa: backing vocals
Garry Tallent: bass
Steven Van Zandt: guitar, mandolin, backing vocals
Max Weinberg: drums
Brendan O'Brien: glockenspiel, orchestra bells
Soozie Tyrell: violin, backing vocals

Written in the style of Smokey Robinson, "Waitin' on a Sunny Day" predated *The Rising* by three years, having been performed by the

E Street Band during various soundchecks for 1999's Reunion Tour. Unabashedly upbeat and ebullient, "Waitin' on a Sunny Day" explores the simple joys of being alive with those you love: "Without you, I'm working with the rain falling down / I'm half a party in a one dog town." In the ensuing years, "Waitin' on a Sunny Day" has emerged as a concert staple, often prompting Springsteen to invite children onstage to sing the chorus along with him.

CHART ACTION
Billboard Hot 100: did not chart. The song registered a number-twenty showing on *Billboard*'s Adult Alternative Airplay chart.

"Waitin' on a Sunny Day" was released on April 22, 2003. The number-one song that week was 50 Cent's "In da Club."

"Nothing Man"
Bruce Springsteen: vocals, guitar, harmonica
Roy Bittan: piano, mellotron, Kurzweil, pump organ, Korg M1 synthesizer, Crumar synthesizer
Clarence Clemons: saxophone, backing vocals
Danny Federici: Hammond B3, Vox Continental, and Farfisa organs
Nils Lofgren: guitar, dobro, slide guitar, banjo, backing vocals
Patti Scialfa: backing vocals
Garry Tallent: bass
Steven Van Zandt: guitar, mandolin, backing vocals
Max Weinberg: drums

Based on Jim Thompson's hardboiled novel *The Nothing Man* (1953), the song's composition predates the atrocities of 9/11 by nearly a decade, although its story about survivor's guilt and posttraumatic stress certainly comports with *The Rising*'s overall theme. Thompson's novel traced the story of a disfigured military veteran who struggles to make it through each and every day, buoyed only by his chronic alcoholism. In Springsteen's song, the nothing man admits to a daily contemplation about suicide and his unquenchable sadness about living when so many other comrades have fallen. In short, "The Nothing Man," Springsteen later wrote, "captured the awkwardness and isolation of survival."

"Countin' on a Miracle"
Bruce Springsteen: vocals, guitar, harmonica
Roy Bittan: piano, mellotron, Kurzweil, pump organ, Korg M1 synthesizer, Crumar synthesizer
Clarence Clemons: saxophone, backing vocals
Danny Federici: Hammond B3, Vox Continental, and Farfisa organs
Nils Lofgren: guitar, dobro, slide guitar, banjo, backing vocals
Patti Scialfa: backing vocals
Garry Tallent: bass
Steven Van Zandt: guitar, mandolin, backing vocals
Max Weinberg: drums
Nashville String Machine: Ricky Keller (arranger/ conductor); Carol Gorodetzky (contractor concert manager); Pam Sixfin, Leo Larrison, Conni Ellisor, Alan Umstead, Dave Davison, Mary Kathryn Vanosdale, and David Angell (violins); Kris Wilkinson, Gary Vanosdale, Jim Grosjean, and Monica Angell (violas); Bob Mason, Carol Rabinowitz, Julie Tanner, and Lynn Peithman (cellos)

With a soaring score performed by the Nashville String Machine, "Countin' on a Miracle" offers one of Springsteen's most heartrending vocal performances. In many ways, the song finds the narrator at his wit's end, desperately hoping for a sense of solace that will never arrive for the bereaved. In the days after 9/11, Springsteen recalled that "Monmouth County had lost one hundred fifty husbands, brothers, sons, wives, daughters. For weeks, the long black limousines pulled up to churches, and candlelit vigils were held in the neighborhood park. In Rumson, a town full of Wall Street commuters, almost everyone knew someone who lost somebody. A benefit was held at the Count Basie Theatre, where local musicians met and played to raise funds for many of the surviving families. Here I was introduced to the Jersey Girls, who would soon do so much to push the government to be openly accountable for the events of that day; their efforts would lead to the formation of the 9/11 Commission. The nation owes them a debt of gratitude" (Springsteen, *Born to Run*, 2016).

"Empty Sky"
Bruce Springsteen: vocals, guitar, harmonica
Roy Bittan: piano, mellotron, Kurzweil, pump organ, Korg M1 synthesizer, Crumar synthesizer
Clarence Clemons: saxophone, backing vocals
Danny Federici: Hammond B3, Vox Continental, and Farfisa organs
Nils Lofgren: guitar, dobro, slide guitar, banjo, backing vocals
Patti Scialfa: backing vocals
Garry Tallent: bass
Steven Van Zandt: guitar, mandolin, backing vocals
Max Weinberg: drums
Brendan O'Brien: hurdy-gurdy

With a pounding drumbeat that Weinberg describes as being like "Ringo all the way," "Empty Sky" was the final song that Springsteen composed for *The Rising* as he and the E Street Band completed the album at Southern Tracks Recording Studio. "My art director had sent me a photo of clouds in an empty sky," he later recalled, "and in a few days, sitting on the edge of my hotel bed in Atlanta, I had the song." "Empty Sky" painstakingly captures the ineffability of loss, the heartbreaking finality of personal loneliness and isolation writ large across the face of international tragedy.

"Worlds Apart"
Bruce Springsteen: vocals, guitar, harmonica
Roy Bittan: keyboards, piano, mellotron, Kurzweil, pump organ, Korg M1 synthesizer, Crumar
Clarence Clemons: saxophone, backing vocals
Danny Federici: Hammond B3, Vox Continental, and Farfisa organs
Nils Lofgren: guitar, dobro, slide guitar, banjo, backing vocals
Patti Scialfa: backing vocals
Garry Tallent: bass
Soozie Tyrell: violin
Steven Van Zandt: guitar, mandolin, backing vocals
Max Weinberg: drums
Asif Ali Khan and Group: Asif Ali Khan (lead singer), Manzoor Hussain Shibli, Sarfraz Hussain, Raza Hussain, Imtiaz Shibli, Chahnawaz Hussain Khan, Bakat Fayyaz Hussain, Omerdroz Hussain Aftab, Karamat Ali Asad (harmonium player), Haji Nazir Afridi (tabla player), Waheed Hussain Mumtaz

Part of the refreshing complexity inherent in *The Rising* involves Springsteen's efforts to understand 9/11's geopolitical and religious underpinnings, particularly in the hands of the radicals who carried out the terror attacks. And he understood implicitly that imagining world unity in the wake of 9/11's overwhelming tragedy meant drawing upon a diversity of voices. "For 'Worlds Apart,' I wanted other voices, other situations than just American ones. The Eleventh was an international tragedy. I wanted Eastern voices, the presence of Allah. I wanted to find a place where worlds collide and meet. My old friend Chuck Plotkin assisted me in getting the voices of Pakistani Qawwali singers, Asif Ali Khan and his group, onto 'Worlds Apart'" (Springsteen, *Born to Run*, 2016).

"Let's Be Friends (Skin to Skin)"
Bruce Springsteen: vocals, guitar, harmonica
Roy Bittan: piano, mellotron, Kurzweil, pump organ, Korg M1 synthesizer, Crumar synthesizer
Clarence Clemons: saxophone, backing vocals
Danny Federici: Hammond B3, Vox Continental, and Farfisa organs
Nils Lofgren: guitar, dobro, slide guitar, banjo, backing vocals
Patti Scialfa: backing vocals
Garry Tallent: bass
Steven Van Zandt: guitar, mandolin, backing vocals

Max Weinberg: drums
Soozie Tyrell: violin, backing vocals
The Alliance Singers: Corinda Carford (also contractor), Tiffeny Andrews, Michelle Moore (choir solo), Antoinette Moore, Antonio Lawrence, Jesse Moorer

With "Let's Be Friends (Skin to Skin)," Springsteen offers an up-tempo shift in *The Rising*'s generally bracing proceedings. A song about sexual desire and tearing down the boundaries that separate us, "Let's Be Friends" sports a beach-music vibe that undergirds the song's sensual and serious intentions.

"Further on (Up the Road)"
Bruce Springsteen: vocals, guitar, harmonica
Roy Bittan: piano, mellotron, Kurzweil, pump organ, Korg M1, Crumar synthesizer
Clarence Clemons: saxophone, backing vocals
Danny Federici: Hammond B3, Vox Continental, and Farfisa organs
Nils Lofgren: guitar, dobro, slide guitar, banjo, backing vocals
Patti Scialfa: backing vocals
Garry Tallent: bass
Steven Van Zandt: guitar, mandolin, backing vocals
Max Weinberg: drums

In his memoirs, Springsteen describes "Further on (Up the Road)" as the E Street Band "tearing down the house." With the song's raw musical power, "Further On" explores the dark roads at society's periphery, where the "seed is sowed / Where the gun is cocked, and the bullets load / Where the miles are marked in the blood and the gold." Springsteen's lyrics bemoan a world where everyone seeks dominion over each other, where wealth and power reign supreme. In contrast with "Born to the Run" in the mid-1970s, "Further On" depicts a runaway American dreamscape for the new century, a place where obsession and unchecked ambition exist within increasingly vague ethical straits.

"The Fuse"
Bruce Springsteen: vocals, guitar, harmonica
Roy Bittan: piano, mellotron, Kurzweil, pump organ, Korg M1 synthesizer, Crumar synthesizer
Clarence Clemons: saxophone, backing vocals
Danny Federici: Hammond B3, Vox Continental, and Farfisa organs
Nils Lofgren: guitar, dobro, slide guitar, banjo, backing vocals
Patti Scialfa: backing vocals
Garry Tallent: bass
Steven Van Zandt: guitar, mandolin, backing vocals
Max Weinberg: drums
Soozie Tyrell: violin, backing vocals

With Bittan and Federici working a fusillade of different keyboards, "The Fuse" prepares the listener for the trilogy that closes *The Rising*. The song quite literally accounts for the before-and-after effect that took place in September 2001. With the ignition of an unimaginable tragedy, the world changes in the blink of any eye; ways of living that were in vogue only days earlier recede into distant memories in an instant. For Springsteen, "The Fuse" incorporated "images of life at home during wartime immediately following the Eleventh," a time and place that would simply never be the same again.

"Mary's Place"
Bruce Springsteen: vocals, guitar, harmonica
Roy Bittan: piano, mellotron, Kurzweil, pump organ, Korg M1 synthesizer, Crumar synthesizer
Clarence Clemons: saxophone, backing vocals
Danny Federici: Hammond B3, Vox Continental, and Farfisa organs
Nils Lofgren: guitar, dobro, slide guitar, banjo, backing vocals
Patti Scialfa: backing vocals
Garry Tallent: bass
Steven Van Zandt: guitar, mandolin, backing vocals
Max Weinberg: drums
Ed Manion: baritone saxophone
Mark Pender: trumpet
Richie "La Bamba" Rosenberg: trombone
Jane Scarpantoni: cello

Mike Spengler: trumpet
Soozie Tyrell: violin
Jerry Vivino: tenor saxophone
The Alliance Singers: Corinda Carford (also contractor), Tiffeny Andrews, Michelle Moore (choir solo), Antoinette Moore, Antonio Lawrence, Jesse Moorer

As *The Rising* enters its final spate of songs, "Mary's Place" depicts the nature of human behavior during times of crisis. Drawing its origins from Sam Cooke's "Meet Me at Mary's Place," the song is set inside a rollicking "house party," in Springsteen's words, merging straight-on "party music with the blues hidden inside. I wanted some of the warmth and familiarity of *The Wild, the Innocent and the E Street Shuffle*, a home place, the comfort music and friendship may bring in a crisis."

"You're Missing"
Bruce Springsteen: vocals, guitar, harmonica
Roy Bittan: piano, mellotron, Kurzweil, pump organ, Korg M1 synthesizer, Crumar synthesizer
Clarence Clemons: saxophone, backing vocals
Danny Federici: Hammond B3, Vox Continental, and Farfisa organs
Nils Lofgren: guitar, dobro, slide guitar, banjo, backing vocals
Patti Scialfa: backing vocals
Garry Tallent: bass
Steven Van Zandt: guitar, mandolin, backing vocals
Max Weinberg: drums
Jere Flint: cello
Larry Lemaster: cello
Soozie Tyrell: violin, backing vocals
Nashville String Machine: Ricky Keller (arranger/conductor); Carol Gorodetzky (contractor concert manager); Pam Sixfin, Leo Larrison, Conni Ellisor, Alan Umstead, Dave Davison, Mary Kathryn Vanosdale, and David Angell (violins); Kris Wilkinson, Gary Vanosdale, Jim Grosjean, and Monica Angell (violas); Bob Mason, Carol Rabinowitz, Julie Tanner, and Lynn Peithman (cellos)

As the last track before the onset of the brilliant trilogy that concludes "The Rising," "You're Missing" offers one final glimpse of the gaping absences wrought by 9/11. Images of loss and despair pock the song's lyrics about families and friends torn asunder, a world interrupted by sudden tragedy and inexplicable change. In its *Bruce Springsteen Collector's Edition* (2022), *Rolling Stone* listed "You're Missing" as number sixty among the artist's top 100 songs.

"The Rising"
Bruce Springsteen: vocals, guitar, harmonica
Roy Bittan: piano, mellotron, Kurzweil, pump organ, Korg M1, Crumar synthesizer
Clarence Clemons: saxophone, backing vocals
Danny Federici: Hammond B3, Vox Continental, and Farfisa organs
Nils Lofgren: guitar, dobro, slide guitar, banjo, backing vocals
Patti Scialfa: backing vocals
Garry Tallent: bass
Steven Van Zandt: guitar, mandolin, backing vocals
Max Weinberg: drums
Jane Scarpantoni: cello
Soozie Tyrell: violin, backing vocals

With the title track and the succeeding "Paradise" and "My City of Ruins," Springsteen concludes *The Rising* with a trio of songs that has been aptly described as his "spiritual litany" in 9/11's awful wake. As Springsteen later recalled, "'The Rising' was written late in the record as a bookend to 'Into the Fire.' Secular stations of the cross, steps of duty irretraceable, the hard realization of all the life and love left behind . . . the opening sky." In the song, the narrator assumes the voice of a New York City firefighter ascending into the malaise, where he "can't see nothing in front of me."

By the end of the composition, as the music reaches its fever-pitch, the narrator's fear of the unknown and of his own mortality is transformed into a rallying call for unity and resolve in the face of fearsome odds. "The Rising" received Grammy Awards for Best Rock Song and Best Male Rock Vocal Performance. In its *Bruce Springsteen Collector's Edition* (2022), *Rolling Stone* listed "The Rising" as number twenty-eight among the artist's top 100 songs.

CHART ACTION

Billboard Hot 100: number fifty-two. The song notched a number-one showing on *Billboard*'s Adult Alternative Songs chart, number twenty-four on Mainstream Rock, and number twenty-six on Adult Contemporary.

"The Rising" b/w "Land of Hope and Dreams" was released on July 16, 2002. The number-one song that week was Nelly's "Hot in Herre."

"Paradise"

Bruce Springsteen: vocals, guitar, harmonica
Roy Bittan: piano, mellotron, Kurzweil, pump organ, Korg M1 synthesizer, Crumar synthesizer
Clarence Clemons: saxophone, backing vocals
Danny Federici: Hammond B3, Vox Continental, and Farfisa organs
Nils Lofgren: guitar, dobro, slide guitar, banjo, backing vocals
Patti Scialfa: backing vocals
Garry Tallent: bass
Steven Van Zandt: guitar, mandolin, backing vocals
Max Weinberg: drums

Springsteen's "spiritual litany" establishes a form of oasis in "Paradise," a song about the swirl of cultures and religions that exist within 9/11's sociopolitical narrative. The song owes a clear debt to the melody from Simon and Garfunkel's "The Sound of Silence." As Springsteen later wrote, "'Paradise,' written late, was a study of different impressions of an afterlife. In the first verse, a young Palestinian

suicide bomber contemplates his last moments on Earth. In the second, a navy wife longs for her husband lost at the Pentagon, the absence of the physical, the smells, the human longing for a return to wholeness. In the last verse, my character swims deep into the water between worlds, where he confronts his lost love, whose eyes are 'as empty as paradise'" (Springsteen, *Born to Run*, 2016). In this way, Springsteen concludes, we are reminded that "the dead have their own business to do, as do the living."

"My City of Ruins"

Bruce Springsteen: vocals, guitar, harmonica
Roy Bittan: piano, mellotron, Kurzweil, pump organ, Korg M1 synthesizer, Crumar synthesizer
Clarence Clemons: saxophone, backing vocals
Danny Federici: Hammond B3, Vox Continental, and Farfisa organs
Nils Lofgren: guitar, dobro, slide guitar, banjo, backing vocals
Patti Scialfa: backing vocals
Garry Tallent: bass
Steven Van Zandt: guitar, mandolin, backing vocals
Max Weinberg: drums
Jane Scarpantoni: cello
Soozie Tyrell: violin, backing vocals

Borrowing its melody from Curtis Mayfield's gospel anthem "People Get Ready," "My City of Runs" brings the trilogy to a powerful and resounding close. Springsteen attributes the origins of "My City of Ruins" to "the soul gospel of my favorite sixties records, speaking not just of Asbury but hopefully of other places and other lands." Springsteen proudly observes that the E Street Band was a road-ready vehicle for addressing the nation's crisis in the wake of 9/11. "Our band was built well, over many years, for difficult times," he wrote. "When people wanted a dialogue, a conversation about events, internal and external, we developed a language that suited those moments. We were there. It was a language that I hoped would entertain, inspire, comfort, and reveal. The professionalism, the showmanship, the hours of hard work are all very important, but I always believed that it was this dialogue, this language, that was at the heart of our resiliency with our audience. *The Rising* was a renewal of that conversation and the ideas that forged our band" (Springsteen, *Born to Run*, 2016). In its *Bruce Springsteen Collector's Edition* (2022), *Rolling Stone* listed "My City of Ruins" as number thirty-nine among the artist's top 100 songs.

Devils & Dust (Alamy) [performance photo]

DEVILS & DUST

Released in April 2005, *Devils & Dust* marks Springsteen's second collaboration with coproducer Brendan O'Brien. One of his most critically acclaimed LPs, *Devils & Dust* features stark musical landscapes and penetrating, introspective lyrics.

For Springsteen, *Devils & Dust* was a continuation of his efforts on *The Ghost of Tom Joad*. "After two consecutive tours with the reconstituted E Street Band," he recalled, "I wanted to return to the music I had written during the *Tom Joad* tour. I went back; chose the best of it; wrote a new song, 'Devils & Dust'; and Brendan O'Brien helped me finish the record I'd started in my farmhouse at *Joad*'s end. Brendan wanted to cut the songs from scratch, but I'd grown very

fond of my home-recorded versions and decided to stick with those. We added some small embellishments, some subtle strings and horns; Brendan mixed; and there we were. I followed it with a solo tour of acoustic shows and came back home" (Springsteen, *Born to Run*, 2016).

As with *The Ghost of Tom Joad*, *Devils & Dust* featured sparse, largely acoustic arrangements. Springsteen supplemented his instrumentation with O'Brien's bass, tambura, and sitar. Steve Jordan provided drum accompaniment, along with a host of studio musicians performing string and horn parts. E Street Band members Danny Federici and Patti Scialfa performed on the album, as well as Lisa Lowell, who provided backing vocals.

The title track received considerable accolades for its explorations of faith, redemption, and the lifelong struggle to find one's place in the world. In particular, "Devils & Dust" offers a moving meditation on the experiences of soldiers during wartime. The song acts as a brutal reminder about the human cost of war, as well as the sacrifices that soldiers make in service to their country. *Devils & Dust* also afforded listeners extended studies of the abiding human struggle with matters of faith, including "Long Time Comin'," a soulful and reflective song about life's journey, and "All I'm Thinkin' About," a heartbreaking ballad about a man struggling to find his way back to the one he loves.

As with *Nebraska* and *The Ghost of Tom Joad*, *Devils & Dust* finds Springsteen continuing to adopt his storyteller persona in delivering his song-stories about the ongoing challenge of finding meaning in our deeply flawed world.

HISTORICAL CONTEXT

Springsteen first performed the somber title song of his 2005 album *Devils & Dust* at a concert in Vancouver in April 2003. A month earlier, the United States had launched an invasion of Iraq in a coordinated air and ground assault that resulted in the fall of Baghdad on April 9. At the end of February, Springsteen gave an interview to Ken Phillips of *Entertainment Weekly* in which he accurately predicted the coming invasion and speculated on the motivations that he suspected would lead the administration of George W. Bush to launch it. He told Phillips, "You try not to be cynical, but without the distraction of Iraq, [people] would notice that the economy is doing poorly, and the old-fashioned Republican tax cuts for the folks that are doin' well will seriously curtail services for people who are struggling out there."

To Springsteen, the war was connected to other issues that he cared about, just as had been the case with the war in Vietnam for many Americans in the 1960s and early 1970s. He continued to speak out on those issues during the presidential campaign of 2004, actively supporting the Democratic candidate John Kerry and calling that year's election the most important of his lifetime. Much of his political stance that year hinged on his opposition to the war in Iraq, a war that provoked energetic opposition and vociferous demonstrations and protests throughout the country, even if the crowds typically did not approach the size of the demonstrations that took place during the Vietnam War.

Hundreds of such demonstrations occurred on March 20, 2005, the second anniversary of the war, preceding the release of *Devils & Dust* by about a month. The title track of the album offers the perspective of an American soldier who is afraid that the war has corrupted him to the point where it has left his soul filled only with "devils and dust." The song does not specifically mention Iraq, but the imagery of the song, as well as the soldier's uncertainty, despite stating that he's got God on his side, would seem to allude to a war in which Americans were largely seen by others as in the wrong.

This view derived from the presentation of false evidence to the United Nations in 2003 to justify the war, the use of torture by American soldiers, and the large civilian death toll in Iraq. In addition to the thousands of Iraqi deaths, some 1,500 Americans had died in the war by the time the album was released. Springsteen's own outspoken opposition to the war had already made clear where he stood; he had no need to elaborate his viewpoint further on the album, leaving him free to view the war and early twentieth-century America from a more creative literary and musical perspective. The tone of this acoustic album sees Springsteen grappling with the tragedies and injustices of Bush's America just as *The Ghost of Tom Joad* had reflected an implicit critique of the 1990s and *Nebraska* those of Reagan's early years.

PRODUCTION

Released on April 26, 2005, Columbia Records
Produced by Brendan O'Brien, Bruce Springsteen, and Chuck Plotkin
Engineered by Nick Didia and Toby Scott
Recording Assistants: Tom Tapley, Billy Bowers, and Karl Egsieker
Mixed by O'Brien and Scott at Southern Tracks Recording Studio and Silent Sound Studios
Mastered by Bob Ludwig at Masterdisk
Recorded at Thrill Hill East, Southern Tracks Recording Studios, and Masterphonics Studios, 1996–1998, March to August 2004, and January 2005

PERSONNEL

Bruce Springsteen: vocals, guitar, keyboards, bass, drums, percussion
Brice Andrus: horn
Danny Federici: keyboards
Steve Jordan: drums, percussion
Lisa Lowell: backing vocals
Brendan O'Brien: bass, hurdy-gurdy, tambura, sitar, electric sarangi
Mark Pender: trumpet
Chuck Plotkin: piano
Marty Rifkin: steel guitar
Patti Scialfa: backing vocals
Donald Strand: horn
Soozie Tyrell: violin, backing vocals
Susan Welty: horn
Thomas Witte: horn
Nashville String Machine: strings

COVER ART AND PACKAGING

Design: Dave Bett, Michelle Holme, and Chris Austopchuk
Photography: Anton Corbijn

TRACK LISTING

All songs composed by Bruce Springsteen.
String and horn arrangements by Eddie Horst.

1. "Devils & Dust"
2. "All the Way Home"
3. "Reno"
4. "Long Time Comin'"
5. "Black Cowboys"
6. "Maria's Bed"
7. "Silver Palomino"
8. "Jesus Was an Only Son"
9. "Leah"
10. "The Hitter"
11. "All I'm Thinkin' About"
12. "Matamoros Banks"

CONTEMPORARY REVIEWS

Brian Hiatt (*Rolling Stone*, April 21, 2005): "Recorded without the E Streeters, *Devils* combines whispery acoustic story songs with stripped-bare, folk-and-country-inflected rock tunes. In many ways, Springsteen says, the album is a sequel to 1995's hushed *The Ghost of Tom Joad*, which inspired his first solo tour. . . . Springsteen had tried recording the title track as both an angry rock song and an acoustic ballad, but it took producer O'Brien—who also worked on *The Rising*—to bridge the gap. 'Brendan found something that put it in the middle, where it picks up a little instrumental beef as it goes,' says Springsteen. O'Brien took a similar approach to the rest of the album, helping Springsteen ditch *Joad's* low-fi sound and minimal arrangements for a more fleshed-out approach."

Alexis Petridis (*The Guardian*, April 22, 2005): "One school of thought suggests music fans in 2005 have become irreversibly jaded and that rock music is therefore incapable of delivering an eye-popping shock. Alumni of said school are advised to head directly to 'Reno,' the third track on Bruce Springsteen's 13th studio album, *Devils & Dust*. There, you can find the most astonishing sound you're likely to hear all year: Bruce Springsteen singing about anal sex. He's in character, of course, as a man visiting a prostitute, but somehow neither that, nor the song's delicate tune and wisps of slide guitar, softens the impact of hearing Springsteen's voice delivering the line: 'Two hundred dollars straight in, two-fifty up the ass.' Springsteen has professed bewilderment at any fuss caused by his sudden interest in sodomy: 'It's just what felt right,' he says, a line that wins top marks for nonchalance, but seems unlikely to wash if used in the marital boudoir. But you can't get around the fact that this particular conjunction of singer and subject matter is genuinely startling. For all the talk of gritty realism that rises up whenever Springsteen's songwriting is mentioned, his work largely inhabits a cozy and predictable world of blue-collar workers, small towns and dusty highways, in which off-color sexual practices never usually intrude. That was never more evident than on 2002's *The Rising*, which saw Springsteen coming to terms with 9/11 by reconvening the E Street Band after 15 years and seeking comfort in familiarity. It sounded like *Born in the U.S.A.*, but didn't sell like *Born in the U.S.A.*, which may have influenced the decision to dismiss the E Street Band once more and pilot its successor into the off-piste territories announced by 'Reno's lyric."

David Fricke (*Rolling Stone*, May 5, 2005): "Bruce Springsteen's thirteenth studio album is, in many ways, his most conventional singer-songwriter record since his 1973 debut, *Greetings from Asbury Park, N.J.*, *Devils & Dust* is twelve songs of assorted vintage and narrative setting, rendered with subdued, mostly acoustic flair that smells of wood smoke and sparkles in the right places like the stars in a clear Plains sky. There is no connected, redemptive urgency to these stories; this is not *The Rising*. And there is no E Street Band to turn Springsteen's trademark compulsion to save and be saved into fireball baptism. . . . Yet *Devils & Dust* is, in striking and affecting ways, also Springsteen's most audacious record since the home-demo American Gothic of 1982's *Nebraska*."

Phil Sutcliffe (*MOJO*, June 2005): "This alarming intimacy is the bedrock of *Devils & Dust*. 'Leah' and 'Maria's Bed' are simple, tremulous, mainly acoustic affirmations. 'Long Time Comin',' a band sing-along of nicely subdued rowdiness with Springsteen's hard innocence casting that 'heavenly light' he often refers to on earthy moments of tenderness: 'Two kids in a sleeping bag beside / Reach 'neath your shirt, lay my hands across your belly / And feel another one kickin' inside / I ain't gonna f-ck it up this time.' So Springsteen has stepped aside from party politics *pro tem*—and into the fiery heart of storytelling music where love is the hardest thing to hold on to, where that silver-lining God is everywhere and nowhere, baby: music that observes and feels life in the way that any worthwhile political vision must. In the great tradition of Woody Guthrie and Bob Dylan, Muddy Waters and John Lee Hooker, Johnny Cash and Willie Nelson, he was born to live into middle age, old age, and burn on down that road."

PROMOTION

Springsteen's team had originally considered Starbucks as a potential sales outlet for *Devils & Dust*. In 2004, the coffee conglomerate's in-store promotion of Ray Charles's *Genius Loves Company* drew strong sales returns, as did Starbucks' tenth-anniversary promotion of Alanis Morissette's *Jagged Little Pill*. But when it came to *Devils & Dust*, the coffee chain declined to offer the LP in its locations—in particular, citing the song "Reno" for its reference to anal sex, as well as Springsteen's refusal to co-brand the album with Starbucks. "There were a number of factors involved," Starbucks CEO Ken Lombard reported. "Lyrics was one of the factors, but not the only reason." Later, during a May 2005 concert at Philadelphia's Tower Theater, Springsteen slyly introduced the song by noting that the album could be purchased at "Dunkin Donuts and Krispy Kreme stores everywhere."

Springsteen conducted a solo tour in support of *Devils & Dust*, consisting of seventy-six shows, from April through November 2005. Springsteen played a variety of instruments, including acoustic and electric guitars, harmonica, piano, electric piano, pump organ, autoharp, ukulele, banjo, and stomping board. Springsteen concluded his concerts with a cover version of "Dream Baby Dream," a song that had been originally recorded in 1979 by electro-punk band Suicide.

CHART ACTION

Billboard Top Pop Albums: number one.

Released on April 26, 2005, *Devils & Dust* debuted at number one on May 14, unseating Rob Thomas's . . . *Something to Be*. The album sold more than 500,000 copies, earning gold status from RIAA.

Devils & Dust spent thirteen weeks on the *Billboard* charts.

COMMENTS FROM SPRINGSTEEN AND HIS CIRCLE

Springsteen: "I like to write about people whose souls are in danger, who are at risk. In every song on this record, somebody's in some spiritual struggle between the worst of themselves and the best of themselves, and everybody comes out in a slightly different place. That thread runs through the record, and it's what gives the record its grounding in the spirit" (*New York Times*, April 24, 2005).

Garry Tallent: "I think Brendan [O'Brien] does a great job, and Bruce has always got great songs. . . . It sounds good. Some good rockers up there—and it's not *Nebraska* revisited; it really is a different thing" (*Backstreets*, Winter 2005/2006).

MISCELLANEOUS

Devils & Dust earned five Grammy Award nominations, including three for the title track—Song of the Year, Best Rock Song, and Best Solo Rock Vocal Performance. The album was nominated for Best Contemporary Folk Album and Best Long Form Music Video, winning the former.

SONG ANALYSES

"Devils & Dust"
Bruce Springsteen: vocals, guitar, keyboards
Steve Jordan: drums
Brendan O'Brien: bass
Susan Welty: horn
Thomas Witte: horn
Nashville String Machine: strings

In keeping with the conflicted wars that the United States was engaging in at the time,

Springsteen's "Devils & Dust" considers the fate of a soldier who must reconcile his disillusionment about military life and the ethics of war with the harrowing circumstances of combat. With Springsteen's searing harmonica accompaniment, "Devils & Dust" conjures up images of the Old West in its contemporary representations of Iraq. Ultimately, the title track presents listeners with the soldier's crisis of faith, as Springsteen sings "I got my finger on the trigger, but I don't know who to trust / When I look into your eyes, there's just devils and dust." In its *Bruce Springsteen Collector's Edition* (2022), *Rolling Stone* listed "Devils & Dust" as number eighty-eight among the artist's top 100 songs.

CHART ACTION

Billboard Hot 100: number seventy-two.

"Devils & Dust" was released on March 28, 2005. The number-one song that week was Green Day's "Boulevard of Broken Dreams."

"All the Way Home"
Bruce Springsteen: vocals, guitar, keyboards, percussion
Steve Jordan: drums
Brendan O'Brien: bass, tambura, sitar, electric sarangi
Chuck Plotkin: piano
Marty Rifkin: steel guitar

Originally penned as a vehicle for Southside Johnny and the Asbury Jukes' 1991 LP *Better Days*, "All the Way Home" traces the story of a man offering to walk a woman home from a Jersey Shore bar—all the way home, he implies, to her bedroom. Springsteen's narrator recognizes the woman's plight as the refugee from an unhappy marriage, offering her the simple promise of good company, as opposed to a full-fledged romantic relationship, to pass the time.

CHART ACTION

Billboard Hot 100: did not chart.

"All the Way Home" was released on October 31, 2005. The number-one song that week was Kelly Clarkson's "Because of You."

"Reno"
Bruce Springsteen: vocals, guitar, keyboards, tambourine
Brice Andrus: horn
Donald Strand: horn
Susan Welty: horn
Thomas Witte: horn
Nashville String Machine: strings

Easily Springsteen's most graphic composition, "Reno" traces the story of its narrator's liaison with a prostitute. Set in the notorious Nevada gambling town, "Reno" finds the narrator seeking sexual solace for his loneliness, only to come away from the morally vacuous experience feeling even emptier and sadder than when he began.

"Long Time Comin'"
Bruce Springsteen: vocals, guitar, keyboards
Danny Federici: keyboards
Steve Jordan: drums
Brendan O'Brien: bass
Marty Rifkin: steel guitar
Patti Scialfa: backing vocals
Soozie Tyrell: violin, backing vocals

Whereas "Reno" speaks painfully about loss, "Long Time Comin'" brims with optimism. The narrator admits to his failures as a husband and father, but as the song reaches its full anthemic power, he rubs his wife's belly, where a new baby awaits, and vows that "I ain't gonna f-ck it up this time." The narrator sees his unborn child as an avenue for his own redemption, as well as a means for him to turn the page on his disappointment over his own father's lackluster performance when he needed him most.

"Black Cowboys"

Bruce Springsteen: vocals, guitar, keyboards, percussion
Brice Andrus: horn
Steve Jordan: percussion
Brendan O'Brien: bass
Donald Strand: horn
Susan Welty: horn
Thomas Witte: horn
Nashville String Machine: strings

"Black Cowboys" traces the story of young Rainey Williams, a kid growing up in the mean streets and drug dens of the South Bronx, where nothing—not even the life of a little boy—seems to carry any weight. Every day, he walks by the "melted candles and flower wreaths, names and photos of young black faces / Whose death and blood consecrated these places," as his mother waits for him at home, pining for her son to return home safely after yet another day in the battle zone of their neighborhood. With "Black Cowboys," Springsteen thwarts our expectations with tragedy compounded by yet more tragedy as Rainey's mother succumbs to heroin, forcing her son to begin a new and even riskier journey to save himself before it's too late.

"Maria's Bed"

Bruce Springsteen: vocals, guitar, keyboards
Steve Jordan: drums
Brendan O'Brien: bass, hurdy-gurdy, tambura
Patti Scialfa: backing vocals
Soozie Tyrell: violin, backing vocals

As with "Long Time Comin'," "Maria's Bed" finds Springsteen's narrator on an existential search for meaning and redemption in a broken world. With fire and conviction—as well as O'Brien's hurdy-gurdy holding up the rear—the narrator recognizes the salvation, sexual and otherwise, that he has experienced in Maria's company. In contrast with "Reno," where the sexual encounter produces lackluster results, leaving the narrator feeling empty, "Maria's Bed" bristles with carefree abandon and elevates the power of human connection as a tonic for living well and flourishing.

"Silver Palomino"

Bruce Springsteen: vocals, guitar, keyboards, percussion
Nashville String Machine: strings

"Silver Palomino" finds its roots in the untimely death of Fiona Williams-Chappel at age thirty-seven in 1996. Springsteen had been plagued by her death, especially by the even more tragic fact that she left behind two young sons. Williams-Chappel had left a considerable impression on Springsteen, who recalled her fondly during a 2005 episode of VH1's *Storytellers*. "My wife and I had a friend, a young lady who lived next door to us and passed away at a very young age. And she used to come over to our house regularly, every night, and there was a moment when she would be framed in the front window just before she was gonna knock on the door. And I would look up, and she was this very tall and elegant lady—and I still wait to see her in that window."

"Silver Palomino" traces the story of a thirteen-year-old boy whose mother dies at a tragically young age, leaving him alone to face the world. To assuage his pain, the boy begins to juxtapose his mother's loss with the taming of a wild horse, suggesting that he might yet reconnect with her absent spirit by taking the seemingly untamable palomino for a ride.

During this same period, Springsteen and Scialfa had begun stabling horses on their property, and one horse in particular proved to be his Achilles' heel. "We were told by the kindly gentleman doing the selling they were all of fine stock and could be ridden by an inebriated chimpanzee. Okay. With no riding experience, I climbed on. I'd seen a million Westerns; how hard could it be?" he recalled. Unable to make any progress with the wayward horse, "We hired an instructor who put me through my paces on one of our nags, but no good came of it. My back was killing me, and I had no idea of where the half ton under me might go next. Then a miracle occurred. Patti found a dusty old palomino. As I sat astride him, I felt at home. He had a beautiful light gait, smooth as a Cadillac, and was extremely quiet, old and confident. He was unruffled by the clumsy reining of the neophyte on his back" (Springsteen, *Born to Run*, 2016).

"Jesus Was an Only Son"

Bruce Springsteen: vocals, guitar, keyboards, bass, drums
Lisa Lowell: backing vocals
Patti Scialfa: backing vocals
Soozie Tyrell: backing vocals

On a 2005 episode of VH1's *Storytellers*, Springsteen observed that "on *Devils & Dust* I wrote several songs about mothers and sons," including most notably "Jesus Was an Only Son." In particular, "I was kind of interested in the relationship between parent and child. That is why Mary figures so prominently in the song. I felt if I approached the song from the secular side that the rest of it would come through."

As with "Silver Palomino," "Jesus Was an Only Son" examines the relationship between parents and their children—in this case, the story of a child who is outlived by his mother and the terrible nature of that kind of loss. "Our children have their own destiny apart from us," Springsteen explained, "and I think my idea was to try and reach into the idea of Jesus as son, as somebody's boy because I think that whatever divinity we can lay claim to is hidden in the core of our humanity. And when we let go, when we let our compassion go, we let go of what little claim we have to the divine. So, it's spooky out there sometimes. End of sermon."

"Leah"

Bruce Springsteen: vocals, guitar, keyboards, percussion
Mark Pender: trumpet

In contrast with earlier songs in which Springsteen found his characters to be inadequate in accepting both love's bounty, as well as its inherent responsibilities, "Leah" demonstrates the hopeful possibilities of inner growth and maturity. With Mark Pender's plaintive trumpet solo as its backdrop, "Leah" depicts the narrator not only appreciating the solace of a mature relationship with Leah, but also the inner peace that he enjoys when he comes to terms with himself.

"The Hitter"

Bruce Springsteen: vocals, guitar, keyboards, percussion
Brice Andrus: horn
Donald Strand: horn
Susan Welty: horn
Thomas Witte: horn
Nashville String Machine: strings

"The Hitter" traces the brutal life and times of a professional boxer whose only language, it seems, is audible in his fisticuffs and in the execution of violence. Written as a conversation with his mother, "The Hitter" finds the narrator confessing to throwing a fight and ceding his morality for money. As the song progresses, it becomes increasingly clear that the boxer might not be standing in his mother's doorway at all—that he might be hallucinating—suggesting that the pursuit of his brutal business may have been the fighter's undoing in more ways than one.

"All I'm Thinkin' About"

Bruce Springsteen: vocals, guitar, keyboards, drums
Lisa Lowell: backing vocals
Brendan O'Brien: bass
Patti Scialfa: backing vocals
Soozie Tyrell: backing vocals

With "All I'm Thinkin' About," Springsteen contributes his own composition to rock and roll's long tradition of songs covertly written about masturbation, a roster that includes Fleetwood Mac's "Rattlesnake Shake," Cyndi Lauper's "She Bop," and the Vapors' "Turning Japanese." "All I'm Thinkin' About" painstakingly traces the story of a young man discovering his sexuality in the bed of a truck, where his imagination runs wild as he pleasures himself. Springsteen alludes to the narrator's private moment through a series of euphemisms about "a little boy carrying a fishing pole" and other, not-so-veiled imagery.

"Matamoros Banks"

Bruce Springsteen: vocals, guitar, keyboards
Nashville String Machine: strings

In many ways, "Matamoros Banks" serves as the sequel to "Across the Border," the composition from *The Ghost of Tom Joad* in which a Mexican migrant worker thinks wistfully about his beloved as he prepares to cross the border line. In "Matamoros Banks," we learn the migrant worker's fate through the words of his beloved, who mourns his death at the hands of the unruly river currents. She imagines his corpse as "the turtles eat the skin from your eyes," until "every trace of who you ever were is gone." "Matamoros Banks" is a tragic song, to be sure, serving as a powerful vehicle for Springsteen's ongoing critique of US border practices, which he perceives to be inhumane.

In December 2019, Springsteen evoked the song on his website when he observed that in the intervening years since the release of *Devils & Dust*, the border crisis has only worsened. "More than 2,500 asylum-seekers are living in a state of intense danger on the streets of Matamoros, Mexico," he wrote. "Many of the most vulnerable people fleeing danger and persecution in Central America and the Caribbean end up in Matamoros because of the widespread belief that the crossing at that point is relatively easier than desert ports of entry. The majority of people waiting at the makeshift refugee camp on the river's edge are single mothers with multiple young children seeking to reunite with their extended family in the United States. This problem is worsening, as more than 100 new migrants arrive each day and are forced to remain (potentially for up to two years) pursuant to new US government policies."

We Shall Overcome: The Seeger Sessions (Alamy) [performance photo]

WE SHALL OVERCOME: THE SEEGER SESSIONS

Released in April 2006, *We Shall Overcome: The Seeger Sessions* is Springsteen's first album entirely comprising cover versions. In 2007, the album earned a Grammy Award for Best Traditional Folk Album. For Springsteen, Seeger's music had taken on a special meaning after the two musicians performed "This Land Is Your Land" on the occasion of President Barack Obama's 2009 inauguration. Springsteen took notice when Pete Seeger insisted that "we sing all of Woody's controversial verses. He wanted to reclaim the song's radical text."

The LP finds its origins back in 1997, when Springsteen recorded "We Shall Overcome" for the compilation entitled *Where Have All the Flowers Gone: The Songs of Pete Seeger*. For Springsteen, learning about Seeger (1919–2014), the American activist and folk musician, had been a revelation. "Growing up a rock 'n' roll kid," Springsteen later wrote, "I didn't know a lot about Pete's music or the depth of his influence. But once I started listening, I was overwhelmed by the wealth of songs, their richness and their power. It changed what I thought I knew about 'folk music.'"

Through his frequent collaborator Soozie Tyrell, Springsteen came into the orbit of some top-flight folk players. "I met a group of musicians out of New York City who occasionally came down and played at our farm," he recalled. "Accordion, fiddle, banjo, upright bass, washboard—this is the sound I was envisioning for the Pete Seeger project. We set up next to one another in the living room of our farmhouse (horns in the hall), counted off the opening chords to 'Jesse James' and away we went."

The album was produced by Springsteen at Thrill Hill, his home studio in Colts Neck,

New Jersey. With Tyrell, Scialfa, and the Miami Horns in tow, the group came to be known as the Seeger Sessions Band.

The album's title track, "We Shall Overcome," provides Springsteen's moving take on the classic civil rights anthem that has been sung by activists and protestors around the world. Intentionally stripped down and heartfelt, Springsteen's version features his voice and a plaintive piano accompaniment. In addition to paying tribute to Seeger's remarkable achievements in American folk music, *We Shall Overcome: The Seeger Sessions* addresses the sociopolitical conflicts that continue to plague American life.

HISTORICAL CONTEXT

Bruce Springsteen was inspired to do this album by getting acquainted in the 1990s with the songs of the folk icon Pete Seeger, having admittedly had little interest in folk music when younger. Of course, in the late 1970s and early 1980s, Springsteen had become acquainted with the music of Seeger's precursor, Woody Guthrie, whose music and populist politics had a great influence on the trajectory of Springsteen's career, especially heard in his live performances of Guthrie's "This Land is Your Land" and on 1995's *The Ghost of Tom Joad*. The historical context for *The Seeger Sessions*, therefore, like *Tom Joad*, extends well before the time Springsteen released the album. In fact, he first began recording songs that went on the album at a session that took place in 1997; the rest were laid down at individual sessions in 2005 and 2006.

That is not to say that the date of release on April 25, 2006, had no connection with the material on the album, given that Seeger was a strong social activist with a long track record of supporting labor unions, civil rights, and the antiwar movement during Vietnam. The Iraq War was still ongoing three years after it had begun. Despite the prospect of the United States becoming involved in a prolonged civil war in Iraq between Sunni and Shiite Muslims that seemed all too similar to the situation in Vietnam, President Bush was insisting that the country stay the course, still convinced that he could fulfill the neoconservative agenda favored by his vice president, Dick Cheney, and remake the Middle East to resemble American democracy. This situation made this a propitious time for the release of an album of songs by one of the leading voices of the antiwar movement from the 1960s.

On the other hand, there is no question that Springsteen was also simply having fun doing songs with musicians with whom he enjoyed making music. He expressed at the time a certain sense of freedom that came with doing an album for which he did not need to write the songs. While he included songs that formed an important part of the civil rights movement such as "Eyes on the Prize" and "We Shall Overcome," he also included a wide range of nonpolitical songs that ranged from a sea shanty like "Pay Me My Money Down" to folk standards like "Froggie Went-a Courting," which dates to the sixteenth century. "Mrs. McGrath," an Irish folk standard from the perspective of a mother whose son loses both his legs in the Napoleonic Wars, fits the antiwar theme, but does not dominate the album in the same way that the title song had on his previous effort, *Devils & Dust*.

On *The Seeger Sessions*, Springsteen wanted to stay true to the roots and spirit of the material, making the album drastically different from either the rock and roll albums he did with the E Street Band and his own solo acoustic projects. "Accordion, fiddle, banjo, upright bass, washboard—this is the sound I was envisioning for the Pete Seeger project," he wrote in his autobiography, *Born to Run*. A more sustained critique of the Iraq War and the Bush administration would wait until his next album, *Magic*, released the following year.

PRODUCTION

Released on April 25, 2006, Columbia Records
Produced by Bruce Springsteen
Engineered by Toby Scott
Mixed by Bob Clearmountain
Mastered by Bob Ludwig at Masterdisk
Recorded at Thrill Hill East, 1997, 2005–2006

PERSONNEL

Bruce Springsteen: vocals, acoustic guitar, harmonica, Hammond B3 organ, percussion
Sam Bardfeld: violin
Art Baron: tuba
Frank Bruno: acoustic guitar, backing vocals
Jeremy Chatzky: electric upright bass, backing vocals
Mark Clifford: banjo, backing vocals
Larry Eagle: drums, percussion, backing vocals
Charles Giordano: accordion, piano, Hammond B3 organ, pump organ
Lisa Lowell: backing vocals
Ed Manion: saxophone, backing vocals
Mark Pender: trumpet, backing vocals
Richie "La Bamba" Rosenberg: trombone, backing vocals
Patti Scialfa: backing vocals
Soozie Tyrell: violin, backing vocals

COVER ART AND PACKAGING

Design: Meghan Foley
Art direction: Chris Austopchuck
Photography: Danny Clinch

TRACK LISTING

All songs are traditional, except where indicated.

1. "Old Dan Tucker" (attributed to Dan Emmett)
2. "Jesse James"
3. "Mrs. McGrath"
4. "O, Mary Don't You Weep"
5. "John Henry"
6. "Erie Canal" (Thomas S. Allen)
7. "Jacob's Ladder"
8. "My Oklahoma Home" (Bill and Agnes Cunningham)
9. "Eyes on the Prize" (Alice Wine)
10. "Shenandoah"
11. "Pay Me My Money Down"
12. "We Shall Overcome" (attributed to Charles Tindley)
13. "Froggie Went a Courtin'"
14. "Buffalo Gals" (bonus track)
15. "How Can I Keep from Singing?" (bonus track)

CONTEMPORARY REVIEWS

Phil Sutcliffe (*MOJO*, June 2006): "It takes easily five seconds to discover this is Springsteen as you've never heard him before. A quick count-in, a chortle, a campfire plink of banjo, and nonsense knees-up 'Old Dan Tucker"s hurtling down the chute—"Combed his hair with a wagon wheel / Died with a toothache in his heel." Springsteen bellows it like the best fun he ever had. A big band of little-knowns tumbles and jumbles diverse folk idioms all around him: Cajun accordion, country bull fiddle, hot New Orleans horns (though supplied by familiar Jerseyites including trombonist Richie Rosenberg), even a touch of New York Jewish klezmer from fiddler Sam Bardfeld and drummer Larry Eagle."

Jonathan Ringen (*Rolling Stone*, May 19, 2006): "*We Shall Overcome*—which was recorded live in Springsteen's New Jersey home with a fourteen-piece band, including horns, banjo, fiddles, washboard, organ and accordion—is his most jubilant disc since *Born in the U.S.A.* and more fun than a tribute to Pete Seeger has any right to be. But as on *Born in the U.S.A.*, seemingly triumphant anthems are paired with lyrics of pain and protest that champion the oppressed and the exploited (not to mention the calamity-prone protagonist of 'My Oklahoma Home,' whose wife, house and crops get blown away by a tornado, leaving him with nothing but a mortgage). Springsteen has always mined a deep vein of Americana, from the hot-rod-and-B-movie-obsessed early albums to the Steinbeckian social realism of *The Ghost of Tom Joad* and last year's *Devils & Dust*. But with his first-ever album of songs written by other people, it feels like he's turned to the music of our shared past to find a moral compass for a nation that's gone off the rails. The protest anthems 'Eyes on the Prize' and 'We Shall Overcome' are performed with an understated urgency; the gospel standard 'O, Mary, Don't You Weep'—which Springsteen sings in a gruff Tom Waits-ish baritone and to which the Seeger Sessions Band gives a Dixieland treatment with Stephane Grappelli-style violin—promises, 'Brothers and sisters, don't you cry / There'll be good times by and by.'"

PROMOTION

Springsteen embarked upon an extensive tour in support of the album with the "Seeger Sessions Band" from April through November 2006. The tour featured sixty-two concerts and was billed as "an all-new evening of gospel, folk, and blues."

CHART ACTION

Billboard Top Pop Albums: number one.

Released on April 25, 2006, *We Shall Overcome: The Seeger Sessions* debuted at number three, its peak position, on May 13; the number-one album that week was the Godsmack's *IV*. The album sold more than 500,000 copies, earning gold status from RIAA.

We Shall Overcome: The Seeger Sessions spent twenty-two weeks on the *Billboard* charts.

COMMENTS FROM SPRINGSTEEN AND HIS CIRCLE

Springsteen: "A lot of this music was written a long time ago, but I felt I could make it feel essential right now. I've always got an eye toward the future and an eye to the past. That's how you know where you've come from and where you want to go. If you look at our recent history, it seems there's been so much disregard of past experience in the way the country has conducted itself" (*USA Today*, June 6, 2006).

MISCELLANEOUS

On October 3, 2006, an extended version of the album was released as *We Shall Overcome: The Seeger Sessions—American Land Edition*. The extended version included videos, a documentary, and three additional tracks: "How Can a Poor Man Stand Such Times and Live?" "Bring 'Em Home," and "American Land."

In 2007, *We Shall Overcome: The Seeger Sessions* earned a Grammy Award for Best Traditional Folk Album.

SONG ANALYSES

"Old Dan Tucker"

Bruce Springsteen: vocals, guitar, harmonica, Hammond B3 organ, percussion
Sam Bardfeld: violin
Frank Bruno: guitar, backing vocals
Jeremy Chatzky: electric upright bass, backing vocals
Mark Clifford: banjo, backing vocals
Larry Eagle: drums, percussion, backing vocals
Charles Giordano: accordion, piano, Hammond B3 organ, pump organ
Ed Manion: saxophone, backing vocals
Mark Pender: trumpet, backing vocals
Richie "La Bamba" Rosenberg: trombone, backing vocals
Patti Scialfa: backing vocals
Soozie Tyrell: violin, backing vocals

Springsteen kicks off the album with a song that dates from the 1840s, but which he described in a 2006 interview with Dave Marsh as characterized by "surrealism," with lyrics that "are so modern." Springsteen sings a rousing version infused with energy that provides an energetic and energizing start to the album. The lyrics, however modern Bruce found them, are secondary to the fact that this fiddle tune was clearly meant for dancing at a country hoedown. The verses take you through a series of minor, everyday misadventures of the title character, with some nonsense thrown in ("washed his face in a frying pan" or "died with a toothache in his heel," for example). The chorus tells Old Dan Tucker to "get out of the way" because he is too late for supper, presumably because it was now time for music and dancing.

"Jesse James"

Bruce Springsteen: vocals, guitar, harmonica, Hammond B3 organ, percussion
Sam Bardfeld: violin
Frank Bruno: guitar, backing vocals
Jeremy Chatzky: electric upright bass, backing vocals
Mark Clifford: banjo, backing vocals
Larry Eagle: drums, percussion, backing vocals
Charles Giordano: accordion, piano, Hammond B3 organ, pump organ
Ed Manion: saxophone, backing vocals
Richie "La Bamba" Rosenberg: trombone, backing vocals
Patti Scialfa: backing vocals
Soozie Tyrell: violin, backing vocals

"Jesse James" was one of several songs that Springsteen recorded in 1997 while involved with the tribute album, *Where Have All the Flowers Gone: The Songs of Pete Seeger*. According to Springsteen, it was the first song recorded for this album. It was another nineteenth-century piece of Americana about the reviled outlaw and antihero who terrorized Missouri and other Midwestern states, robbing stagecoaches, banks, and trains until he met a violent end in 1882. The song had been adapted by both Huddie Ledbetter, better known as Lead Belly, and Woody Guthrie, whose version most influenced Springsteen's rendition. The song has been covered by numerous artists, including Pete Seeger, the American folk group the Kingston Trio, and the Irish band the Pogues.

The song portrays Jesse James as a Robin Hood figure, who stole from the rich and gave to the poor, though history does not support this interpretation. It also villainizes Robert Ford as a "dirty little coward" trusted by James who killed him in collaboration with the authorities in hopes of receiving the reward placed on James's head. It is a rousing number that humanizes an outlaw, thief, murderer, and defender of the Confederacy, but the song speaks to an antiestablishment tradition in American popular culture that finds sympathy with those who operate outside the law, from Western outlaws to Bonnie and Clyde to Mafia gangsters. Springsteen's own song "Nebraska" could be interpreted as part of that tradition.

"Mrs. McGrath"

Bruce Springsteen: vocals, guitar, harmonica, Hammond B3 organ, percussion
Sam Bardfeld: violin
Frank Bruno: guitar, backing vocals
Jeremy Chatzky: electric upright bass, backing vocals
Mark Clifford: banjo, backing vocals
Larry Eagle: drums, percussion, backing vocals
Charles Giordano: accordion, piano, Hammond B3 organ, pump organ
Ed Manion: saxophone, backing vocals
Patti Scialfa: backing vocals
Soozie Tyrell: violin, backing vocals

With "Mrs. McGrath," Springsteen shifts from the American tradition to a more somber Irish folk song set during the Napoleonic Wars of the early nineteenth century. Mrs. McGrath is asked at the beginning of the song if she would like for her son to enlist in the English army, where he would get to wear "a scarlet coat" and "a big cocked hat." Despite its local setting, and traditional Irish chorus adding a "too-ri-a, fol-diddle-di-a, too-ri ooh-ri, ooh-ri-a," this is a classic antiwar song with which anyone could identify, including the mothers of those American sons and daughters fighting in the Iraq War taking place when this album was released. In the song, Ted McGrath does indeed go to war and returns home having lost both his legs to a cannonball. To drive home the universality of the message the last verse includes the lines, "All foreign wars, I do proclaim, live on the blood of a mother's pain." Springsteen's vocal performance on the song

is impeccable, reminiscent of the pathos with which he sung "The Ghost of Tom Joad," for example.

"O, Mary Don't You Weep"

Bruce Springsteen: vocals, guitar, harmonica, Hammond B3 organ, percussion
Sam Bardfeld: violin
Frank Bruno: guitar, backing vocals
Jeremy Chatzky: electric upright bass, backing vocals
Mark Clifford: banjo, backing vocals
Larry Eagle: drums, percussion, backing vocals
Charles Giordano: accordion, piano, Hammond B3 organ, pump organ
Ed Manion: saxophone, backing vocals
Mark Pender: trumpet, backing vocals
Richie "La Bamba" Rosenberg: trombone, backing vocals
Patti Scialfa: backing vocals
Soozie Tyrell: violin, backing vocals

Given how many times Springsteen uses the name Mary in his own music, it is perhaps no surprise that he would select "O, Mary Don't You Weep" from among the traditional folk songs he chose to include on this album. This particular song was an African American spiritual that Aretha Franklin included on her 1972 Gospel album *Amazing Grace*.

The song dates originally from the first half of the nineteenth century and refers to the biblical story of Mary of Bethany's pleas to Jesus to raise her brother Lazarus from the dead. The lyric, though, mainly focuses on the Old Testament examples of the drowning of Pharaoh's army in the Red Sea during the Exodus and the rainbow that appeared to Noah after the Flood. Springsteen gives it his usual passionate interpretation, backed by an enthusiastic chorus and inspired playing by the musicians accompanying him, making this one of the standout performances on the album, along with "Old Dan Tucker,"

"Mrs. McGrath," "Erie Canal," and "Pay Me My Money Down."

"John Henry"

Bruce Springsteen: vocals, guitar, harmonica, Hammond B3 organ, percussion
Sam Bardfeld: violin
Frank Bruno: guitar, backing vocals
Jeremy Chatzky: electric upright bass, backing vocals
Mark Clifford: banjo, backing vocals
Larry Eagle: drums, percussion, backing vocals
Charles Giordano: accordion, piano, Hammond B3 organ, pump organ
Ed Manion: saxophone, backing vocals
Mark Pender: trumpet, backing vocals
Richie "La Bamba" Rosenberg: trombone, backing vocals
Patti Scialfa: backing vocals
Soozie Tyrell: violin, backing vocals

"John Henry" is perhaps one of the best-known songs on the album, having been recorded previously by Woody Guthrie, Lonnie Donegan, Johnny Cash, and, of course, Pete Seeger. This is another traditional song set to a sixteenth-century spiritual, though the lyric is based on a large Black man who worked hammering away at rock so dynamite could be inserted to help create the mile-and-a-quarter Big Bend Tunnel near Talcott, West Virginia, which was begun in 1870 and completed a mere three years later.

The narrative arc of the song begins with John Henry's birth, shortly after which he picks up a hammer and cries that it will be the cause of his death. While working, he refuses to give way to the steam drill his captain tries to introduce and continues to swing his hammer until at the end of his song, he dies, with the sound of his hammering ringing throughout eternity. In essence, it is about the working life Springsteen himself so often wrote about, which frequently ends only when someone has worked themselves to death.

The lyrics might be depressing, but the music and the performance are not, perhaps echoing the kind of defiance and determination evinced by the character of John Henry in the song.

"Erie Canal"

Bruce Springsteen: vocals, guitar, harmonica, Hammond B3 organ, percussion
Sam Bardfeld: violin
Art Baron: tuba
Frank Bruno: guitar, backing vocals
Jeremy Chatzky: electric upright bass, backing vocals
Mark Clifford: banjo, backing vocals
Larry Eagle: drums, percussion, backing vocals
Charles Giordano: accordion, piano, Hammond B3 organ, pump organ
Ed Manion: saxophone, backing vocals
Mark Pender: trumpet, backing vocals
Richie "La Bamba" Rosenberg: trombone, backing vocals
Patti Scialfa: backing vocals
Soozie Tyrell: violin, backing vocals

This popular folk song was written by Thomas Allen in 1905 and provides an almost romanticized view of working-class life in the nineteenth century: "You'll always know your neighbor and you'll always know your pal if you've ever navigated on the Erie Canal." Completed in 1825, the Erie Canal connected the Hudson River to Lake Erie at a time when the region was in the heart of an America that was industrializing, especially after the Civil War ended in 1865. Often sung almost as a kind of dirge, Springsteen infuses it with a soulful and optimistic tone that probably comes much closer to capturing the original spirit of the song, perhaps as a result of his ability to connect with working-class people through his music, but also no doubt as a result of the excitement he felt about recording these songs that sounded new to him because they were not what he tended to listen to when he was growing up.

"Jacob's Ladder"

Bruce Springsteen: vocals, guitar, harmonica, Hammond B3 organ, percussion
Sam Bardfeld: violin
Art Baron: tuba
Frank Bruno: guitar, backing vocals
Jeremy Chatzky: electric upright bass, backing vocals
Mark Clifford: banjo, backing vocals
Larry Eagle: drums, percussion, backing vocals
Charles Giordano: accordion, piano, Hammond B3 organ, pump organ
Lisa Lowell: backing vocals
Ed Manion: saxophone, backing vocals
Mark Pender: trumpet, backing vocals
Richie "La Bamba" Rosenberg: trombone, backing vocals
Patti Scialfa: backing vocals
Soozie Tyrell: violin, backing vocals

"Jacob's Ladder" offers another African American spiritual that Springsteen and his band infuse with their own jazz, rock, and folk elements. The song may date as far back as the late eighteenth century. It is based on the biblical story in the book of Genesis in which Jacob has a vision of a ladder extending to heaven itself. The lyric is extremely repetitive, with the refrain that "We are climbing Jacob's ladder," an obvious metaphor for being on the right path toward salvation in the afterlife. In his rendition of the song, Springsteen manages to infuse his vocals with the pure joy and happiness that would actually be associated with a strong belief in the promise of deliverance to the Promised Land free of earthly trials and vicissitudes.

"My Oklahoma Home"

Bruce Springsteen: vocals, guitar, harmonica, Hammond B3 organ, percussion
Sam Bardfeld: violin
Frank Bruno: guitar, backing vocals
Jeremy Chatzky: electric upright bass, backing vocals
Mark Clifford: banjo, backing vocals
Larry Eagle: drums, percussion, backing vocals
Charles Giordano: accordion, piano, Hammond B3 organ, pump organ
Ed Manion: saxophone, backing vocals
Richie "La Bamba" Rosenberg: trombone, backing vocals
Patti Scialfa: backing vocals
Soozie Tyrell: violin, backing vocals

Springsteen probably came to "My Oklahoma Home," as he did with so many others on the album, through the music of Pete Seeger. Seeger recorded this song in 1996, shortly before Springsteen recorded a version of "We Shall Overcome" for the Pete Seeger tribute album. In *Born to Run*, Springsteen says that when he started listening to Seeger's music around this time "it changed the way I thought about 'folk music.'"

Originally written by Sis and Bill Cunningham during the period of the Great Depression, "My Oklahoma Home" must have certainly appealed to Springsteen's connection with Woody Guthrie and his songs about the Dust Bowl, which Bruce featured in "The Ghost of Tom Joad." This song, despite its upbeat melody, is from the perspective of a farmer whose Oklahoma home was blown away during the Dust Bowl. The singer tells of how he, in fact, lost everything—crops, chickens, his wife—everything, in fact, except his mortgage. In a sentiment similar to Tom Joad's famous speech at the end of *The Grapes of Wrath*, where he says he will be everywhere, the song ends with the profession that his Oklahoma home will now be "in the sky" and "in that dust cloud rolling by."

"Eyes on the Prize"

Bruce Springsteen: vocals, guitar, harmonica, Hammond B3 organ, percussion
Sam Bardfeld: violin
Art Baron: tuba
Frank Bruno: guitar, backing vocals

Jeremy Chatzky: electric upright bass, backing
vocals
Mark Clifford: banjo, backing vocals
Larry Eagle: drums, percussion, backing vocals
Charles Giordano: accordion, piano, Hammond
B3 organ, pump organ
Lisa Lowell: backing vocals
Ed Manion: saxophone, backing vocals
Mark Pender: trumpet, backing vocals
Richie "La Bamba" Rosenberg: trombone, backing
vocals
Patti Scialfa: backing vocals
Soozie Tyrell: violin, backing vocals

Although the album clearly pays homage to America's historical and cultural heritage, Springsteen would tell biographer Dave Marsh that he "didn't choose anything as a historical piece." Instead, he replied to a question about "Eyes on the Prize" in particular: "I think you're choosing things you can make 'of the moment' and so connected to the present world." He was referring to the fact that a song that did not start out as a "freedom song" became, as with "We Shall Overcome," one of the anthems of the Civil Rights movement. A woman named Alice Wine had updated this song, originally a spiritual called "Gospel Plow" dating from the early twentieth century, to make it more applicable to the African American struggle for equality and freedom.

Springsteen's version still contains the line, "I got my hand on the gospel plow," and includes several biblical references, beginning with the imprisonment of the early Christian missionaries Paul and Silas. But in the updated lyrics the singer vows "to board that big Greyhound" to "carry the love from town to town" and says "the only thing we did right was the day we started to fight." The song returns to its Gospel origins in the final verse with a reference to the streets of heaven being "paved with gold." Springsteen

and the band's performance on this song is slightly more understated than in most songs on the album, perhaps to reflect the fact that full racial equality had still yet to be achieved.

"Shenandoah"
Bruce Springsteen: vocals, guitar, harmonica,
Hammond B3 organ, percussion
Sam Bardfeld: violin
Art Baron: tuba
Frank Bruno: guitar, backing vocals
Jeremy Chatzky: electric upright bass, backing
vocals
Mark Clifford: banjo, backing vocals
Larry Eagle: drums, percussion, backing vocals
Charles Giordano: accordion, piano, Hammond
B3 organ, pump organ
Ed Manion: saxophone, backing vocals
Mark Pender: trumpet, backing vocals
Richie "La Bamba" Rosenberg: trombone, backing
vocals
Patti Scialfa: backing vocals
Soozie Tyrell: violin, backing vocals

With "Shenandoah," Springsteen returns to the traditional American folk songbook with another song with nineteenth-century origins that had become well known by the end of that century. The song finds the singer crying about his absence from his homeland in the Shenandoah Valley of Virginia as he has crossed "the wide Missouri" and been roaming the West for seven years, with his lone wish to see his "Shenandoah" again. Again, the tone of Springsteen's performance perfectly matches the lyrics of the song and its sad lament.

"Pay Me My Money Down"
Bruce Springsteen: vocals, guitar, harmonica,
Hammond B3 organ, percussion
Sam Bardfeld: violin
Frank Bruno: guitar, backing vocals
Jeremy Chatzky: electric upright bass, backing
vocals

Mark Clifford: banjo, backing vocals
Larry Eagle: drums, percussion, backing vocals
Charles Giordano: accordion, piano, Hammond
  B3 organ, pump organ
Ed Manion: saxophone, backing vocals
Mark Pender: trumpet, backing vocals
Richie "La Bamba" Rosenberg: trombone, backing
  vocals
Patti Scialfa: backing vocals
Soozie Tyrell: violin, backing vocals

According to Rob Kirkpatrick, "Pay Me My Money Down" is "a shanty that originated among black dock workers in Georgia and South Carolina, with a message to ship captains who might try to stiff them of their hard earned-pay" (*Magic in the Night*, 2009). A sprightly tune whose lightness and infectious melody lends itself to live performance, "Pay Me My Money Down" finds Springsteen and his band clearly having a lot of fun while recording this song, as they did in subsequent live renditions. Lyrically, Springsteen added the line, "I wish I was Mr. Gates," substituting for the names of previous individuals who must have been wealthy and known to the audience, which is followed by the line, "They'd haul my money in in crates." The song is another with deep working-class roots, with another verse containing the lines, "Well 40 nights, nights at sea . . . Captain worked very last dollar out of me."

"We Shall Overcome"
Bruce Springsteen: vocals, guitar, harmonica,
  Hammond B3 organ, percussion
Sam Bardfeld: violin
Frank Bruno: guitar, backing vocals
Jeremy Chatzky: electric upright bass, backing
  vocals
Mark Clifford: banjo, backing vocals
Larry Eagle: drums, percussion, backing vocals
Charles Giordano: accordion, piano, Hammond B3
  organ, pump organ

Ed Manion: saxophone, backing vocals
Richie "La Bamba" Rosenberg: trombone, backing
  vocals
Patti Scialfa: backing vocals
Soozie Tyrell: violin, backing vocals

"We Shall Overcome" offers another civil rights anthem associated with the freedom movement of the 1960s, here performed with exquisite harmonies between Springsteen and his wife and longtime band member Patti Scialfa, and relatively muted background singers adding fullness and support without overpowering Springsteen's own voice. The song's origins are somewhat obscure, but it seems to have begun as a gospel song written sometime around the turn of the twentieth century. The song was later popularized by white folk singers such as Pete Seeger and Joan Baez, who gave a famous performance during a civil rights gathering at the Lincoln Memorial in August 1963, backed by about 300,000 singers in the audience. It is either the most or least surprising aspect of the album that Springsteen was able to take familiar songs and make them sound characteristically his own with his vocal stylings, phrasings, and inflections, which he does particularly well on this song.

"Froggie Went a Courtin'"
Bruce Springsteen: vocals, guitar, harmonica,
  Hammond B3 organ, percussion
Sam Bardfeld: violin
Art Baron: tuba
Frank Bruno: guitar, backing vocals
Jeremy Chatzky: electric upright bass, backing
  vocals
Mark Clifford: banjo, backing vocals
Larry Eagle: drums, percussion, backing vocals
Charles Giordano: accordion, piano, Hammond B3
  organ, pump organ
Ed Manion: saxophone, backing vocals
Mark Pender: trumpet, backing vocals

Richie "La Bamba" Rosenberg: trombone, backing vocals
Patti Scialfa: backing vocals
Soozie Tyrell: violin, backing vocals

This Scottish ballad dates to the mid-sixteenth century, but one wonders if Springsteen got the idea to include it on the album because, in addition to Pete Seeger, Bob Dylan had featured a version of "Froggie Went a Courtin'" on his 1992 album *Good as I Been to You*. It is to Springsteen's credit that he sings the song with as much earnestness as he does all the other songs on the album, making it sound fresh, with lush instrumental strings backing him before taking prominence in the bridges between the verses and the song picking up momentum and energy as it goes along, instead of plodding along in the same meter. The song itself anthropomorphizes a series of animals: the frog courts a mouse, but needs the consent of a rat; the consent having been obtained, a moth and a "junie bug" arrive with a tablecloth and whiskey, before a big black snake arrives to chase all the animals away, while a cat eats the mouse and a duck swallows the frog. If there is any message contained in the song, I suppose it must be something along the lines of "be careful what you wish for," although it is doubtful that the song was ever meant to inspire deep contemplation.

"Buffalo Gals"
Bruce Springsteen: vocals, guitar, harmonica, Hammond B3 organ, percussion
Sam Bardfeld: violin
Frank Bruno: guitar, backing vocals
Jeremy Chatzky: electric upright bass, backing vocals
Mark Clifford: banjo, backing vocals
Larry Eagle: drums, percussion, backing vocals
Charles Giordano: accordion, piano, Hammond B3 organ, pump organ
Lisa Lowell: backing vocals
Ed Manion: saxophone, backing vocals

Mark Pender: trumpet, backing vocals
Richie "La Bamba" Rosenberg: trombone, backing vocals
Patti Scialfa: backing vocals
Soozie Tyrell: violin, backing vocals

"Buffalo Gals" offers another traditional American song with lyrics dating to the mid-nineteenth century set to a sixteenth-century English melody. Many will associate it with Jimmy Stewart's performance in a famous scene in Frank Capra's 1946 classic film *It's a Wonderful Life*. The song refers to prostitutes on the streets of Buffalo, New York, but lent itself to substituting the name of any city where a singer might happen to be performing the song. Still, it has come down to us as "Buffalo Gals," and Springsteen performs it here with as much zest and enthusiasm as he does the other songs on this album.

"How Can I Keep from Singing"
Bruce Springsteen: vocals, guitar, harmonica, Hammond B3 organ, percussion
Sam Bardfeld: violin
Frank Bruno: guitar, backing vocals
Jeremy Chatzky: electric upright bass, backing vocals
Mark Clifford: banjo, backing vocals
Larry Eagle: drums, percussion, backing vocals
Charles Giordano: accordion, piano, Hammond B3 organ, pump organ
Lisa Lowell: backing vocals
Ed Manion: saxophone, backing vocals
Mark Pender: trumpet, backing vocals
Richie "La Bamba" Rosenberg: trombone, backing vocals
Patti Scialfa: vocals
Soozie Tyrell: violin, backing vocals

This spiritual was written by the nineteenth-century Baptist hymn writer Robert Lowry (1826–1899). Perhaps the title prompted Springsteen to include it on the album because the short and sparse lyric expresses the simple sentiment that seems to have animated his whole career, that he had a truth inside of him that he needed to get out, the only outlet being his words and music. The song begins, "My life goes on in endless song above earth's lamentation." This could easily serve as Springsteen's epitaph. The song also speaks of hearing the truth "what though the darkness round me close," which must have resonated with someone who did so much with the theme of darkness in his songs, while at the same time never being willing to entirely give in to it. Even the song's religious message seems more in tune than at odds with Springsteen's spiritual sensibility, concluding that "since love is Lord in Heaven and Earth, / How can I keep from singing?"

MAGIC

Released in September 2007, *Magic* was Springsteen's first studio album with the E Street Band
since *The Rising* (2002). In 2008, the LP's lead
single, "Radio Nowhere," earned Best Solo
Rock Vocal Performance and Best Rock Song at
the Grammy Awards.

For Springsteen, the album began to come
into focus "at the end of the *Rising* tour, [when]
I had a few songs from my road writing," he
recalled. "Brendan O'Brien once again paid me
a visit. I played him what I had and we took it
from there. I remember working on a decent
amount of *Magic* at my worktable in Rumson,
but by this time I tended to write anywhere and
everywhere. I no longer separated touring and
writing as I had in my early years. I wrote in my
dressing room often before the show or after
in my hotel room. It became a way I meditated
before or after a raucous night. Quiet, lost in my
own thoughts, traveling to places I'd never been,
looking through the eyes of those I'd never met,
I dreamt the dreams of refugees and strangers.
Those dreams were somehow also mine. I felt
their fears, their hopes, their desires, and when
it was good, I'd lift off from my hotel digs and
find myself back on some metaphysical highway
searching for life and rock 'n' roll" (Springsteen,
Born to Run, 2016).

Working with O'Brien, Springsteen com-
menced the album's recording sessions in
March 2007 at Atlanta's Southern Tracks
Recording Studio. Over the span of two months,

Springsteen and the E Street Band laid down the tracks, often working separately in order to accommodate their conflicting schedules. Drummer Max Weinberg, for example, was constrained by weekday obligations as bandleader for *Late Night with Conan O'Brien*. During the production of *Magic*, a routine would develop in which Springsteen and O'Brien would handle technical issues and record the artist's lead vocals on weekdays, while working with Weinberg, bassist Garry Tallent, and pianist Roy Bittan on weekends to concoct the basic tracks. Meanwhile, Clarence Clemons continued to work closely with Springsteen to craft his saxophone parts, while O'Brien would supervise overdubbing sessions among the other E Streeters, including guitarists Steven Van Zandt and Nils Lofgren, as well as Scialfa, who handled backing vocals.

In addition to "Radio Nowhere," songs like "Girls in their Summer Clothes"—which was based on Irwin Shaw's classic 1939 *New Yorker* story "The Girls in Their Summer Dresses"— hint at an overarching sense of foreboding. Compositions in the vein of "Last to Die," "Gypsy Biker," and "Long Walk Home" address the plight of soldiers as they attempt to regain their humanity during their return to civilian life, a situation often complicated by internal psychological wounds and physical maladies wrought by wartime violence.

HISTORICAL CONTEXT

Like *The Seeger Sessions* and many of Bruce Springsteen's albums, *Magic*, released on October 2, 2007, was years in the making. In this case, the album's origins date back to the aftermath of 9/11 and the subsequent US invasion of Iraq in 2003. If the historical context of the Iraq War overshadowed *Devils & Dust* and provided part of the background to *The Seeger Sessions*, Springsteen addressed the war and his general dissatisfaction with the Bush administration much more directly on *Magic*. Springsteen acknowledged as much in his 2016 memoir, admitting, "*Magic* was my state-of-the-nation dissent over the Iraq War and the Bush years."

At the time of the album's release, much of the initial support for the war among the American people had dissipated and calls for the government to bring the troops home were becoming both louder and more frequent. The United States was pouring $3 billion a week into Iraq, which became even more troublesome when stories started to appear about corruption within the military, thanks to several high-profile bribery cases, and revelations that seventy-three separate investigations had revealed the tainting of military contracts by bribes or kickbacks with individuals taking advantage of the labyrinthine nature of the bureaucracy through which these contracts had to progress. Even more disturbing, from Springsteen's perspective, were the ways in which the war and the general post-9/11 reaction had compromised long-standing American ideals. The use of torture, the denial of habeas corpus rights, and the lies used to justify the Iraq War in the first place all drew rebukes from Springsteen.

Instead of pounding the listener with a political message, though, Springsteen as usual tried to balance his concern with politics, which had increased significantly in the years leading up to the album, with a steady stream of rock and pop numbers that his fans could enjoy for their own sake without focusing on the political content of the album. Songs like "Livin' in the Future," "Last to Die," "Long Walk Home," and "Magic" all had edgy political overtones but also pulsed with an infectious energy provided by a revitalized E Street Band, which had rejoined

Springsteen for their first album together since *The Rising*.

This aspect makes perfect sense given that any artist hopes their work will long outlast the specific historical circumstances that might have initially informed it. Yet it is also important to comprehend the historical context if one wants to gain a true appreciation and understanding of the piece. At the time of *Magic*'s release, the United States still had 160,000 troops in Iraq and the country was deeply divided over whether to pull them out in a complete withdrawal or escalate the conflict in order to attain the elusive final victory over the insurgents who had arisen against the American presence. Springsteen's album had something important to say about this situation, without compromising the long-term integrity of the album.

PRODUCTION

Released on October 2, 2007, Columbia Records
Produced by Brendan O'Brien
Engineered by Nick Didia
Recording Assistants: Toby Scott, Billy Bowers, Glenn Pittman, Kevin Mills, and Matt Serrecchio
Mixed by Brendan O'Brien at Southern Tracks Studio
Mastered by Bob Ludwig at Masterdisk
Recorded at Southern Tracks Studio in Atlanta, March to May 2007

PERSONNEL

Bruce Springsteen: vocals, acoustic and electric guitars, pump organ, harmonica, synthesizer, piano, glockenspiel, percussion
Roy Bittan: piano, organ
Clarence Clemons: saxophone, backing vocals
Danny Federici: organ, keyboards
Nils Lofgren: guitar, backing vocals
Patti Scialfa: backing vocals
Garry Tallent: electric bass
Steven Van Zandt: guitar, mandolin, backing vocals
Max Weinberg: drums
Jeremy Chatzky: upright bass
Daniel Laufer: cello
Soozie Tyrell: violin
Patrick Warren: Chamberlin, tack piano
Magic String Section: Eddie Horst (string arrangement); Justin Bruns, Jay Christy, Sheela Iyengar, John Meisner, William Pu, Christopher Pulgram, Olga Shpitko, and Kenn Wagner (violins); Amy Chang, Tania Maxwell Clements, and Lachlan McBane (violas); Karen Freer, Charae Krueger, and Daniel Laufer (cellos)

COVER ART AND PACKAGING

Design: Bea Nettles
Photography: Danny Clinch and Mark Seliger

TRACK LISTING

All songs composed by Bruce Springsteen.

1. "Radio Nowhere"
2. "You'll Be Comin' Down"
3. "Livin' in the Future"
4. "Your Own Worst Enemy"
5. "Gypsy Biker"
6. "Girls in Their Summer Clothes"
7. "I'll Work for Your Love"
8. "Magic"
9. "Last to Die"
10. "Long Walk Home"

11. "Devil's Arcade"
12. "Terry's Song" (bonus track)

CONTEMPORARY REVIEWS

Amy Linden (*Village Voice*, October 3, 2007): "The answer, unfortunately, is *Magic*, a maddeningly uneven record that often sounds like legends coasting, most apparently on 'Living in the Future' and 'Last to Die.' The latter is Springsteen 101, echoing all those intros with understated strumming and/or tinkling sleigh-bell keyboards, all those quadruple-stacked choruses and slowly ascending, triumphantly screaming guitars. Oh, and there's something about a highway. Bruce, I love you—but unless you're giving directions, no more highways. 'Living in the Future,' meanwhile, is dragged down by Clarence Clemons's 'soulful' sax, which not only sounds dated but gives me a freaking headache. And speaking of headaches, *Magic*'s sound is so compressed and shitty that I seriously thought my speakers were busted—it's impossible sometimes to tell one instrument from another as producer Brendan O'Brien (who managed to not f-ck up *The Rising*) smashes Springsteen's Wall of Sound into rubble."

David Fricke (*Rolling Stone*, October 18, 2007): "Bruce Springsteen's first album of original songs with the E Street Band since he lost the vote for change in 2004 starts with guitars—a wall of anger, droning, treble that, for the three minutes of 'Radio Nowhere' is blessedly louder than the oceanic static of bent truths, partisan reporting and general bullshit that passes for life-and-death debate in the new wired order. Springsteen isn't just pissed about the state of rock and roll—that's like kicking a corpse—although he is blunt about

what's missing. . . . *Magic* is, in one way, the most openly nostalgic record Springsteen has ever made, the arrangements, the performances and Brendan O'Brien's wall-of-surf production are mined with echoes and near-direct quotes of classic records."

Andrew Mueller (*Uncut*, November 2007): "Probably as early as his fifth album, 1980's *The River*, Springsteen reached that sparsely populated stratosphere of artists recognized by surname alone, with a personal mythology so well entrenched that his newest records were best described in terms of their predecessors. *Magic*, then, Springsteen's 15th studio album, is *Born to Run* crossed with *Tunnel of Love*, an attempt to recover the indomitable youthful fury of the former, astutely tempered by the older, wiser, sadder resignation of the latter. The album's more exuberant intentions are telegraphed by opening track 'Radio Nowhere,' a glorious signature E Street Band tear-up in the manner of 'No Surrender,' clearly written in anticipation of shaking the seats at the back of the hangars they'll be touring in."

PROMOTION

The *Magic* tour commenced in October 2007 and concluded in August 2008, earning more than $235 million in receipts. The tour was feted at the 2008 *Billboard* Awards, where it won Top Tour, Top Draw, and Top Manager (for Jon Landau).

CHART ACTION

Billboard Top 200 Albums: number one.

Released on October 2, 2007, *Magic* debuted at number one on October 20, unseating Rascal

Flatts' *Still Feels Good*. The album earned platinum status from RIAA.

Magic spent twenty-six weeks on the *Billboard* charts.

COMMENTS FROM SPRINGSTEEN AND HIS CIRCLE

Springsteen: "*Magic* was my state-of-the-nation dissent over the Iraq War and the Bush years. Still, I aimed everywhere on *Magic* for the political and the personal to meld together. You can listen to the whole thing without ever thinking of the politics of the day, or you can hear them ticking deadly through the internal thread of the music" (Springsteen, *Born to Run*, 2016).

MISCELLANEOUS

Magic was nominated for Best Rock Album at the 2009 Grammy Awards, losing the statuette to the Foo Fighters' *Echoes, Silence, Patience, and Grace*. "Girls in Their Summer Clothes" was also nominated for Best Rock Song and Best Solo Rock Vocal Performance, winning the statuette for Best Rock Song.

SONG ANALYSES

"Radio Nowhere"
Bruce Springsteen: vocals, electric guitar
Roy Bittan: piano, organ
Clarence Clemons: saxophone, backing vocals
Danny Federici: organ, backing vocals
Nils Lofgren: guitar, backing vocals
Patti Scialfa: backing vocals
Garry Tallent: electric bass
Steven Van Zandt: guitar, mandolin, backing vocals
Max Weinberg: drums

For anyone who has ever wondered what would happen if the satellites all got shot out of the sky and we lost internet and all major communications networks went down, this song addresses that possibility and its potential ramifications. It is certainly a commentary on the possible over-reliance of modern civilization on technology. Springsteen grew up in an age in which you had to search the dial of your home or car radio for a station that was close enough or whose signal was strong enough for you to receive reception. When *Magic* came out, the world of satellite radio was still relatively new, but it opened up a much wider variety of musical and other programming options, coming through your car speakers with crystal clarity.

In "Radio Nowhere," deprived of something we all take for granted, Springsteen laments the appearance of radio nowhere, or the dead air that leads him to wonder if anybody is "alive out there." He longs for the reassurance of hearing music and expresses a desire to hear "a thousand guitars . . . poundin' drums, . . . [and] a million different voices speakin' in tongues." The song contrasts with his earlier "57 Channels (and Nothin' On)" on *Human Touch*, in its more positive attitude toward technology and the deep angst that would be caused if we suddenly lost it. In its *Bruce Springsteen Collector's Edition* (2022), *Rolling Stone* listed "Radio Nowhere" as number sixty-two among the artist's top 100 songs.

CHART ACTION
Billboard Hot 100: did not chart. The song notched a number-two showing on the magazine's Bubbling under the Hot 100 Singles chart.

"Radio Nowhere" was released on August 28, 2007. The number-one song that week was Sean Kingston's "Beautiful Girls."

"You'll Be Comin' Down"
Bruce Springsteen: vocals, guitar, pump organ, harmonica, synthesizer, glockenspiel, percussion

Roy Bittan: piano, organ
Clarence Clemons: saxophone, backing vocals
Danny Federici: organ, keyboards
Nils Lofgren: guitar, backing vocals
Patti Scialfa: backing vocals
Garry Tallent: bass
Steven Van Zandt: guitar, mandolin, backing vocals
Max Weinberg: drums

In "You'll Be Comin' Down," Springsteen sings of life's ups and downs and addresses his familiar theme of not putting too much stock in material possessions, youthful beauty, or the happenstance of good fortune, all of which can easily be lost or reversed. This is one of the songs on the album that could be heard without any political connotations or that could serve as a metaphor for the false prosperity of the Bush years that was about to come crashing down in the financial collapse that ruined so many lives and caused so much economic damage to the country and the world. "Easy street, a quick buck and true lies" would be a good description of the Wall Street brokers and investors who lent out so much money in high-risk mortgages and then divested themselves by selling them off so as not to incur the risk themselves. The song is a critique of the American Dream, the bill of sale that we can have it all; "A silver plate of pearls my golden child, it's all yours," Springsteen sings, before adding, "At least for a little while." The title of the song could as easily apply to the American economy as a whole as to the individual to whom he is ostensibly singing.

"Livin' in the Future"
Bruce Springsteen: vocals, guitar, pump organ,
  harmonica, synthesizer, glockenspiel, percussion
Roy Bittan: piano, organ
Clarence Clemons: saxophone, backing vocals
Danny Federici: organ, keyboards
Nils Lofgren: guitar, backing vocals
Patti Scialfa: backing vocals
Garry Tallent: bass

Steven Van Zandt: guitar, mandolin, backing vocals
Max Weinberg: drums
Soozie Tyrell: violin

"Livin' in the Future" mixes the personal and the political, sung in an upbeat, optimistic tone to the rock beat that characterizes this album as a whole. The song begins by referencing the possible end of a romantic relationship, the singer having just received a letter containing "somethin' 'bout me and you never seein' one another again." The structure of the song is verse/chorus/verse/chorus/verse/verse/chorus/refrain (repeated four times). The chorus refuses to accept the present and seeks to reassure the singer's partner not to worry about the future because "none of this has happened yet" (refrain). The second verse opens with the singer waking up on election day to "skies of gunpowder and shades of gray," a black cloud, and a "dirty sun" hanging over the country, signaling the same kind of ominous threat contained in the letter the singer receives in the first verse.

Ultimately, the third and fourth verses turn even more political, with the restrictions on freedom that accompanied the Patriot Act and the wars in Iraq and Afghanistan, not to mention the intrusions on personal privacy by the National Security Administration, all possibly implied when Springsteen sings, "My ship, Liberty, sailed away on a bloody red horizon." In the fourth verse, he confesses that his faith has been "torn asunder," but wonders if the sound he hears is "somethin' righteous goin' down under" (Barack Obama's presidential campaign, perhaps?) instead of "rollin' thunder" (a phrase with historical military resonances left over from the Vietnam War, to which the wars in Iraq and Afghanistan were drawing comparisons).

"Your Own Worst Enemy"

Bruce Springsteen: vocals, guitar, pump organ, harmonica, synthesizer, glockenspiel, percussion
Roy Bittan: piano, organ
Clarence Clemons: saxophone, backing vocals
Danny Federici: organ, keyboards
Nils Lofgren: guitar, backing vocals
Patti Scialfa: backing vocals
Garry Tallent: bass
Steven Van Zandt: guitar, mandolin, backing vocals
Max Weinberg: drums
Patrick Warren: Chamberlin, tack piano
Magic String Section: Eddie Horst (string arrangement); Justin Bruns, Jay Christy, Sheela Iyengar, John Meisner, William Pu, Christopher Pulgram, Olga Shpitko, and Kenn Wagner (violins); Amy Chang, Tania Maxwell Clements, and Lachlan McBane (violas); Karen Freer, Charae Krueger, and Daniel Laufer (cellos)

The lyrics for "Your Own Worst Enemy" are quite a bit vaguer than those of other songs on the album, with the recipient of the message and the identity of the enemy in the song's title remaining unclear. It could perhaps refer to those who lied and manipulated evidence to lead the country into the Iraq War in 2003, the use of torture by the Bush administration, or in general the belief on the part of political leaders that they can act with impunity, without regard for the consequences of their actions. In this reading of the song, it could contain a message similar to "You'll Be Comin' Down," that what goes around comes around and our actions, sins, and especially our hubris catch up to us.

This realization could be why Springsteen begins the song addressing someone who "can't sleep at night" because they left their "fingerprints clumsily at the scene." The song also provides a reminder that "you just can't get out of this skin," and we always see our own reflection when we look in the mirror. That is why, the song suggests, its subject has "removed all the mirrors," although to no avail because "everything is falling down" and "your own worst enemy has come to town." In its *Bruce Springsteen Collector's Edition* (2022), *Rolling Stone* listed "Your Own Worst Enemy" as number sixty-eight among the artist's top 100 songs.

"Gypsy Biker"

Bruce Springsteen: vocals, guitar, pump organ, harmonica, synthesizer, glockenspiel, percussion
Roy Bittan: piano, organ
Clarence Clemons: saxophone, backing vocals
Danny Federici: organ, keyboards
Nils Lofgren: guitar, backing vocals
Patti Scialfa: backing vocals
Garry Tallent: bass
Steven Van Zandt: guitar, mandolin, backing vocals
Max Weinberg: drums

There is always a danger in assigning specific meanings to a composition that the songwriter might not have originally intended, but it is hard to listen to the opening line of "Gypsy Biker" and not think of the billions of dollars made by US vice president Dick Cheney's former company, Halliburton, from the contracts it received from the US government as a result of the Iraq War. "The speculators made their money on the blood you shed," Springsteen sings to open the song. This song fits easily with "Born in the U.S.A." and Springsteen's earlier indictment of the treatment of war veterans after the Vietnam War. "To the dead, well, it don't matter much 'bout who's wrong and right," Springsteen sings later in the song, which is about a war veteran coming home to find a country divided ("The whole town's been rousted, which side you on?"). Some are "shoutin' victory for the righteous," while others just wait by the phone for news about the fate of those who remain overseas. In its *Bruce Springsteen Collector's Edition* (2022), *Rolling Stone* listed "Gypsy

Biker" as number seventy-two among the artist's top 100 songs.

"Girls in Their Summer Clothes"

Bruce Springsteen: vocals, guitar, pump organ, harmonica, synthesizer, glockenspiel, percussion
Roy Bittan: piano, organ
Clarence Clemons: saxophone, backing vocals
Danny Federici: organ, keyboards
Nils Lofgren: guitar, backing vocals
Patti Scialfa: backing vocals
Garry Tallent: bass
Steven Van Zandt: guitar, mandolin, backing vocals
Max Weinberg: drums
Patrick Warren: Chamberlin, tack piano
Magic String Section: Eddie Horst (string arrangement); Justin Bruns, Jay Christy, Sheela Iyengar, John Meisner, William Pu, Christopher Pulgram, Olga Shpitko, and Kenn Wagner (violins); Amy Chang, Tania Maxwell Clements, and Lachlan McBane (violas); Karen Freer, Charae Krueger, and Daniel Laufer (cellos)

This catchy pop tune could have easily been a hit if had been released at an earlier time, when such songs ruled the airwaves. Steven Van Zandt has commented that Springsteen could have been one of the great pop writers or artists of all time, but he chose a different path, carefully selecting songs to craft his albums to have meaning beyond a random collection of tunes supporting a couple of hit singles. "Girls in Their Summer Clothes" romanticizes young love from the perspective of an outside observer who seems to move unnoticed and unobserved among the "girls in their summer clothes." Perhaps the singer is reflecting on his own idealized youth, when the streets were alive, kids were playing ball in the street, and everything seemed perfect in the still and quiet air of a summer evening. In the song, he ends up in a diner, where the waitress sympathizes with him, calling him "poor, poor Bill." But the pity cuts him "like a knife," while at the same time he acknowledges that maybe, just maybe, she has saved his life. Why? There's a lot of mystery and potential hidden meaning in this song, but that perhaps is the largest one. Maybe a little kindness and sympathy was what an aging rocker needed to keep going, even if the "girls in their summer clothes" now just pass him by. In its *Bruce Springsteen Collector's Edition* (2022), *Rolling Stone* listed "Girls in Their Summer Clothes" as number ninety-six among the artist's top 100 songs.

CHART ACTION

Billboard Hot 100: number ninety-five. The song registered a number-sixty-seven showing on the magazine's Pop 100, number sixty-two on the Hot Digital Songs, and number twenty-seven on the Mainstream Rock charts.

"Girls in Their Summer Clothes" was released on January 15, 2008. The number-one song that week was Flo Rida's "Low" (featuring T-Pain).

"I'll Work for Your Love"

Bruce Springsteen: vocals, guitar, pump organ, harmonica, synthesizer, glockenspiel, percussion
Roy Bittan: piano, organ
Clarence Clemons: saxophone, backing vocals
Danny Federici: organ, keyboards
Nils Lofgren: guitar, backing vocals
Patti Scialfa: backing vocals
Garry Tallent: bass
Steven Van Zandt: guitar, mandolin, backing vocals
Max Weinberg: drums
Soozie Tyrell: violin

In "I'll Work for Your Love," the singer proclaims his intentions to reclaim his love not through roses and romance, but by putting in the work necessary to salvage a relationship, recalling the same kind of commitment Springsteen had previously sung about in songs like "Man's Job." What makes this song different from "Man's Job" and connects it more to a song like "Thunder Road" is the religious imagery that appears from the first verse, when he asks Teresa to fix him a drink while he watches "the bones in your back like the stations of the cross," while "the sun lifts a halo" from her head and a crown of thorns appears at her lips. As in a later song, "Jack of All Trades," Springsteen professes a willingness to work for "what others may want for free." In this song, however, the singer seems to be trying to reclaim his faith through the body of his lover; the religious imagery of the first verse continues in the second, where "the pages of Revelation lie open in your empty eyes of blue."

In *The Grace of God and the Grace of Man: The Theologies of Bruce Springsteen* (2016), Azzan Yadin-Israel sees the song as being about a married couple who "were joint authors of a book of faith, presumably a shared life based on trust, that has now been lost." The loss of faith has led their "city of peace" to crumble, while they exist in a state of perdition, the husband's "temple of bones" lying at his wife's feet. Suffused with religious imagery, including the metaphor of the fall from grace in the Garden of Eden, which condemned Adam to work for his living, the singer in the song now has to do the same to reclaim his place in his former marital paradise.

"Magic"

Bruce Springsteen: vocals, guitar, pump organ, harmonica, synthesizer, glockenspiel, percussion
Roy Bittan: piano, organ
Clarence Clemons: saxophone, backing vocals
Danny Federici: organ, keyboards
Nils Lofgren: guitar, backing vocals
Patti Scialfa: backing vocals
Garry Tallent: electric bass
Steven Van Zandt: guitar, mandolin, backing vocals
Max Weinberg: drums
Jeremy Chatzky: upright bass

Soozie Tyrell: violin
Patrick Warren: Chamberlin, tack piano

"Magic," as the song's title and lyrics suggest, is about the power of illusion, but whereas a song such as "Brilliant Disguise" stays solely with the themes of self-deceit and deception within the context of a relationship, "Magic" portrays a worldview where it is the powers that be who are not to be trusted. Again, with the wars in Iraq and Afghanistan ongoing—the former having begun on what turned out to be the falsely manipulated evidence of Iraqi dictator Saddam Hussein's manufacturing of weapons of mass destruction—Springsteen advises that it is best to "trust none of what you hear" and "less of what you see," perhaps a reference to the 1960s hit, "I Heard It through the Grapevine," written by Barrett Strong and Norman Whitfield, in which the singer cautions, "Believe half of what you see / And none of what you hear."

The idea behind magic is that one expects one thing and gets another; even if we know we are being tricked, we enjoy the power of illusion—"I'll cut you in half while you're smiling ear to ear." The problem comes in the song when reality intrudes upon the illusion and we realize that freedom is "drifting like a ghost amongst the trees," while actual bodies hang in the trees in the last verse, perhaps a reference to the loss of freedom at home and the carnage inflicted by war abroad.

"Last to Die"

Bruce Springsteen: vocals, guitar, pump organ, harmonica, synthesizer, glockenspiel, percussion
Roy Bittan: piano, organ
Clarence Clemons: saxophone, backing vocals
Danny Federici: organ, keyboards
Nils Lofgren: guitar, backing vocals
Patti Scialfa: backing vocals
Garry Tallent: bass
Steven Van Zandt: guitar, mandolin, backing vocals

Max Weinberg: drums
Soozie Tyrell: violin

If "Magic" implicitly challenges the extent to which we should trust authority, "Last to Die" explicitly affirms that the mistakes that send young men and women to war will lead to death. The only uncertainty is "whose blood will spill, whose heart will break, who'll be the last to die." The song has drawn comparisons with Springsteen's earlier antinuclear diatribe, "Roulette," written in the aftermath of the meltdown at the Three Mile Island nuclear facility in Pennsylvania in March 1979, which never appeared on any of Springsteen's studio albums. The inclusion of "Last to Die" here illustrates Springsteen's recent willingness to risk potential political controversy on his albums during a period in which he was becoming more vocal politically outside of his music. This song does not specifically mention the disaster that leads the bodies to pile up and the city to burn, though the reference to the New Mexico resort town of Truth or Consequences in the first verse conjures up the testing of nuclear weapons that took place in that state prior to the dropping of the first atomic bombs on Hiroshima and Nagasaki at the end of the Second World War, consequences with which the world was still dealing in the first decade of the twenty-first century.

"Long Walk Home"

Bruce Springsteen: vocals, guitar, pump organ,
  harmonica, synthesizer, glockenspiel, percussion
Roy Bittan: piano, organ
Clarence Clemons: saxophone, backing vocals
Danny Federici: organ, keyboards
Nils Lofgren: guitar, backing vocals
Patti Scialfa: backing vocals
Garry Tallent: electric bass
Steven Van Zandt: guitar, mandolin, backing vocals
Max Weinberg: drums
Patrick Warren: Chamberlin, tack piano

This song contrasts a kind of golden past that is receding further and further from view, making it symbolically a long walk to get home, or back to where we used to be. In the first verse, the singer can see his hometown in the distance, leading him to recall the smell of "the deep green of summer" and the glow in the familiar night sky. The references to Sal's Grocery and the barbershop on South Street tell us that Springsteen is indeed writing again about his hometown of Freehold, as he had in "My Hometown" in 1984. There are signs of change and loss: the Veteran's Hall "silent and alone," the diner closed. But in the last verse, Springsteen clings to a memory, real or imagined, of his father, who in "My Hometown" told his son to "take a good look around" at the town where he was born, telling him again that this was "a beautiful place to be born" because "nobody crowds you and nobody goes it alone." In the end, Springsteen uses the image of his hometown here to remind his listeners that there is an America worth preserving and perhaps even fighting for, but that in 2008, we were a long way from that America even if "the flag flyin' over the courthouse means certain things are set in stone." There are principles we will fight for, but not at any cost—there are things we will do and things we won't, he says in the last verse before two repetitions of the chorus affirming again that it is going to be "a long walk home."

"Devil's Arcade"

Bruce Springsteen: vocals, guitar, pump organ,
  harmonica, synthesizer, glockenspiel,
  percussion
Roy Bittan: piano, organ
Clarence Clemons: saxophone, backing vocals
Danny Federici: organ, keyboards
Nils Lofgren: guitar, backing vocals
Patti Scialfa: backing vocals

Garry Tallent: bass
Steven Van Zandt: guitar, mandolin, backing vocals
Max Weinberg: drums
Daniel Laufer: cello
Patrick Warren: Chamberlin, tack piano

"Devil's Arcade" is set in the desert and is full of rich imagery and a somber but driving beat that picks up energy and surges with power about halfway through in an instrumental bridge that links the first and second halves of the song. In the first half, we get glimpses into the lives and beliefs of the soldiers sent to the desert because "somebody made a bet" (that Saddam had nuclear weapons facilities) and "somebody paid" (the soldiers sent like chips pushed onto a table, an image reinforced by the poker game that constitutes part of the soldiers' daily activities). But the soldiers accept their fate—"heroes are needed so heroes get made." The song temporarily slows down to the rhythm of the opening stanzas coming out of the bridge, but again gathers momentum in the last verse to match the imagery of "a glorious kingdom of the sun" on the face of the soldier "rising from a long night as dark as the grave" until "something like faith" emerges out of the darkness that allows another day to begin, the soldier still alive with every beat of the heart ("the beat of your heart"

repeated a number of times) slowly triumphing over the hell fires of the devil's arcade.

"Terry's Song" (bonus track)
Bruce Springsteen: vocals, piano, acoustic guitar, harmonica

Springsteen wrote this song as a tribute to his longtime friend Terry McGovern, who had worked for him as part of his crew for a number of years and died in April 2007. Like many poems and songs about the passing of an individual, the song is also about death in general. It emphasizes the uniqueness of Terry, and Springsteen undoubtedly had him specifically in mind when he wrote the lyrics. As he got older, Springsteen would have plenty of other occasions to reflect on death, and would do so poignantly, particularly in some of the songs on 2020's *Letter to You*. Already, though, we see a familiar theme emerge in his treatment of that somber subject, the idea that love survives here ("Love is a power greater than death," he sings), and that one day we will be reunited with those we love. "They say you can't take it with you," Springsteen sings here, "But I think that they're wrong," as he imagines his friend Terry somewhere in "that dark ether" where Terry is "still young and hard and cold."

Working on a Dream (Alamy) [performance photo]

WORKING ON A DREAM

Released in January 2009, *Working on a Dream* completed a trilogy of LPs that included *The Rising* (2002) and *Magic* (2007). Steven Van Zandt yoked the albums together, describing *Working on a Dream*, *The Rising*, and *Magic* as a trilogy "in terms of sound, concept, and writing style, noting that they represented a movement "toward the pop-rock form—this one more than the other two." Thematically, the trio finds Springsteen shifting from the throes of international tragedy (9/11), ensuing war (the post-9/11 conflicts in Iraq and Afghanistan), and

an attempt to find solace in their wake—that is, "working on a dream." Sadly, *Working on a Dream* marked Danny Federici's last production with the E Street Band. He would succumb after a three-year bout with melanoma in April 2008. The album would be dedicated to Federici's memory, and his son Jason would contribute an accordion part on "The Last Carnival."

As Springsteen later noted, the events surrounding *Working on a Dream* were driven by change. "The rest of 2009 was taken up with the release of our *Working on a Dream* album and tour," he recalled. "Max's son, Jay, stepped in for his dad, who was taking care of business with Conan O'Brien, and at age eighteen Jay became only the second man to sit on that drum stool in thirty-five years. After a few ragged starts, it was obvious Jay had the power, the precision, the ears, the discipline, his father's work ethic and willingness to learn. Plus, he brought his own brand of young punk energy that kicked the shit out of our playbook. Still, something didn't feel quite right." Realizing that Jay was running roughshod over the band's arrangements, "I walked over to him and quietly explained that the drums are not part of the exoskeleton of these arrangements. The drums are the soul engine, buried down and breathing inside the band. You play not on top but immersed in the band. You power everything from within. I said, 'Take a breath, take it back down and dig deep. When you hit that right position, when the beat is placed correctly, you'll drop inside the band naturally.' That could be a pretty sophisticated idea for anyone to wrap their head around, much less an eighteen-year-old who up to this point had mostly played in front of approximately thirty people at a local club. But like father, like son."

For *Working on a Dream*, Springsteen, producer Brendan O'Brien, and the E Street Band continued the routine that they had established during the production of *Magic*. Recording with O'Brien during breaks from the *Magic* tour, Springsteen, Weinberg, bassist Garry Tallent, and pianist Roy Bittan worked in the studio as a primary unit, creating basic tracks, with additional adornments and overdubs laid down separately under O'Brien's supervision as time and the bandmates' competing schedules allowed.

Working on a Dream benefited from an unusually robust spate of promotional activities that included January 2009 appearances at the Golden Globe Awards, President Barack Obama's inauguration, and the Super Bowl XLIII halftime show, which included a performance of the title track. Afterward, Springsteen remarked that "this has probably been the busiest month of my life."

HISTORICAL CONTEXT

Springsteen released *Magic* toward the end of the Bush administration, which he openly deplored. He released his next album, *Working on a Dream*, at practically the same moment that the new administration led by Barack Obama, whom he supported, took office in January 2009. The unparalleled rise of Obama to become the first African American president of the United States provided inspiration and hope to Springsteen, as it did to millions of Americans. In many ways, the atmosphere surrounding Obama's inauguration, at which Springsteen performed "The Rising," was magical and seemed to herald the dawning of a new age that validated the civil rights movement of the previous half-century and offered a stinging rebuke of the politics and policies of the Bush administration, both foreign and domestic.

But not even Springsteen's rousing performance headlining the halftime show at the Super Bowl a few weeks later could mask the grim and sobering realities of a financial crisis the likes of which the country had not seen since the Great Depression. The alienation of the working classes and small-town and rural America would manifest itself fully only in the 2016 election of Donald J. Trump, but it was hard to ignore the foreclosures, layoffs, and credit shrinkage that brought real hardship to the lives of millions of Americans. Springsteen had spoken out for the disadvantaged in so many of his songs and albums, and if he failed to do so in *Working on a Dream* this was perhaps partly because he had been working on this set of songs since even before he had finished *Magic*, but partly because the election of Obama, for whom he had vigorously campaigned, gave him hope that conditions in the country would soon improve.

Yet if Springsteen did not directly address these issues on the album, which, like *Magic*, he recorded with the E Street Band, he did not shy away from doing so publicly. On the eve of Obama's inauguration, Springsteen gave an interview to Mark Hagen of *The Guardian*, in which he laid the blame for the financial crisis squarely at the feet of the Bush administration, attacking it for its love affair with "deregulation, the idea of the unfettered, free market" and for its "blind foreign policy." His outspokenness this time caused few political ripples; criticizing the Bush administration at this point was somewhat like disparaging the Nixon administration after he had resigned in the wake of the Watergate scandal.

Springsteen's participation in the Super Bowl, as much a unifying American ritual as Fourth of July celebrations, helped to situate him at the center of national attention, perhaps even more so than during the *Born in the U.S.A.* tour of 1984 or after the release of *The Rising* in the aftermath of 9/11. Despite all of this, *Working on a Dream* contributed little to the national conversation, nor did it serve to introduce Springsteen to a new generation of fans. He premiered the title track from the album earlier at an Obama campaign rally, but the rest of the album reflected more of Springsteen's personal concerns and hopes than it did those he had for the country. A more searing critique of the greed and corruption that led to the financial collapse

of 2008 would not emerge until his next album three years later.

PRODUCTION

Released on January 27, 2009, Columbia Records
Produced by Brendan O'Brien
Engineered by Nick Didia and Rick Kwan
Recording assistants: Darren Tablan, Tom Tapley, Toby Scott, Tom Syrowski, Billy Bowers, Derek Karlquist, Kevin Mills, Paul Lamalfa, and Tim Mitchell
Mixed by Brendan O'Brien at Southern Tracks Studio
Mixing assistant: Darren Tablan and Tom Tapley
Mastered by Bob Ludwig at Gateway Mastering and Bernie Grundman Mastering
Recorded at Southern Tracks Studio, Avatar Studios, Clinton Recording Studios, Henson Recording Studios, and Thrill Hill Recording, summer 2007 to fall 2008

PERSONNEL

Bruce Springsteen: vocals, acoustic and electric guitars, harmonica, keyboards, percussion, glockenspiel
Roy Bittan: piano, organ, accordion
Clarence Clemons: saxophone, backing vocals
Danny Federici: organ
Nils Lofgren: guitar, backing vocals
Patti Scialfa: backing vocals
Garry Tallent: electric bass
Steven Van Zandt: guitar, backing vocals
Max Weinberg: drums
Jason Federici: accordion
Soozie Tyrell: violin, backing vocals
Patrick Warren: organ, piano, keyboards
All string and horn arrangements by Eddie Horst

COVER ART AND PACKAGING

Design: Chris Austopchuck, Dave Bett, and
    Michelle Holme
Photography: Danny Clinch and Jennifer Tzar

TRACK LISTING

All songs composed by Bruce Springsteen.

1. "Outlaw Pete"
2. "My Lucky Day"
3. "Working on a Dream"
4. "Queen of the Supermarket"
5. "What Love Can Do"
6. "This Life"
7. "Good Eye"
8. "Tomorrow Never Knows"
9. "Life Itself"
10. " Kingdom of Days"
11. " Surprise, Surprise"
12. "The Last Carnival"
13. "The Wrestler" (bonus track)

CONTEMPORARY REVIEWS

Brian Hiatt (*Rolling Stone*, January 23, 2009):
"To understand the romantic sweep and swag-
gering musical ambition that define Bruce
Springsteen's first album of the Obama era,
you have to go all the way back to an artifact
of the Ford administration: 1975's *Born to Run*.
In those days, Springsteen was driving the
E Street Band without a seat belt, staying up
all night piling on overdubs: glockenspiel, surf
guitar, violins, motorcycle noises. With a few
exceptions, he's been paring down ever since.
But on much of *Working on a Dream*, Springsteen finally reignites his early infatuation with
the pop symphonies of Roy Orbison and Phil
Spector. It's all there from the first track, an
eight-minute-long, tragicomic Old West fable

called 'Outlaw Pete,' where he does everything
short of dragging an actual horse into the studio: There are tempo changes, chugging cellos,
Once Upon a Time in the West harmonica wails,
massed strings, crescendo after crescendo—and
a lyrical closing guitar solo worthy of 'Jungleland.' *Working on a Dream* is the richest of
the three great rock albums Springsteen has
made this decade with the E Street Band—and
moment for moment, song for song, there are
more musical surprises than on any Bruce
album you could name, from the Chess Records vocal distortion on the bluesy 'Good Eye'
to the joyous British Invasion pep of 'Surprise,
Surprise.' Producer Brendan O'Brien seems to
have shaken something loose in Springsteen,
who by the Nineties was so focused on his ever-
more-novelistic lyrics that melodies and chord
changes could feel like an afterthought."

Andrew Mueller (*Uncut*, March 2009): "It's
hard to imagine how Bruce Springsteen could
have conceived for this album a title much more
emblematic of himself and what he stands for
than *Working on a Dream*. In Springsteen's
moral universe, after all, the pursuit of happiness is always a job, not a hobby: he unveiled
the title track, appropriately, at a campaign
rally for Barack Obama, with whom he shares
a belief that working and dreaming are essentially the same thing. 'Working on a Dream'—the
Byrds-ish song in question—subscribes so
enthusiastically to this creed that it actually has
whistling on it, of the sort, presumably, that one
does while one is working. As it turns out, both
the song and the album title are *faux amis*, in no
way representative of what follows elsewhere.
Though a near-neighbor of *Magic*—as he was
finishing up on it, Springsteen was already writing tracks for *Dream*—it was recorded during
breaks on the 2007–2008 *Magic* tour . . . *Dream*

is something else entirely. His 16th full-length studio recording is, by some distance, Springsteen's weirdest, and most constantly startling to date."

PROMOTION

The *Working on a Dream* tour spanned seventy-two shows from April to November 2009, earning more than $167 million in receipts.

CHART ACTION

Billboard Top 200 Albums: number one.

Released on January 23, 2009, *Working on a Dream* debuted at number one on February 14, unseating Taylor Swift's *Fearless*. The album earned platinum status from RIAA.

The album spent eighteen weeks on the *Billboard* charts.

MISCELLANEOUS

"The Wrestler" won the statuette for Best Original Song at the 66th Golden Globe Awards. While there was intense speculation that Springsteen's recording would be nominated for an Oscar, "The Wrestler" was snubbed at the Academy Awards. His previous Oscar nomination for "Dead Man Walking" had seen Springsteen perform at the Academy Awards in 1996.

On February 1, 2009, Springsteen and the E Street Band performed before a TV audience of some ninety-nine million viewers during the halftime show at Super Bowl XLIII. Their four-song set including "Tenth Avenue Freeze-Out," "Born to Run," "Working on a Dream," and "Glory Days." Over the years, Springsteen

had declined numerous invitations to perform at the annual spectacle, finally reasoning that "I've said no for about 10 years or however long they've been asking, but, I tell you, we played on the last tour and there were some empty seats here and there and, well, there shouldn't be any empty seats at an E Street Band show. I hold pride that we remain one of the great wonders of the world . . . so sometimes you got to remind people a little bit" (*Los Angeles Times*, 2010).

In 2014, Springsteen published a graphic novel titled *Outlaw Pete*. Based on the leadoff track from *Working on a Dream*, the novel was illustrated by Frank Caruso.

COMMENTS FROM SPRINGSTEEN AND HIS CIRCLE

Springsteen (regarding the Super Bowl XLIII halftime performance, which marked the E Street Band's thirty-fifth anniversary)**:** "The theory of relativity holds. Onstage your exhilaration is in direct proportion to the void you're dancing over. A gig I always looked a little askance at and was a little wary of turned out to have surprising emotional power and resonance for me and my band. It was a high point, a marker of some sort, and went up with the biggest shows of our work life. The NFL threw us an anniversary party the likes of which we'd never have thrown for ourselves, with fireworks and everything! In the middle of their football game, they let us hammer out a little part of our story. I love playing long and hard, but it was the thirty-five years in twelve minutes . . . that was the trick. You start here, you end there, that's it. That's the time you've got to give it everything you have . . . twelve minutes . . . give or take a few seconds. The Super Bowl helped me sell a few new records and probably put a few extra fannies in the seats that tour. But what it was really about was this: I felt my band remained one of the mightiest in the land and I wanted you to know it. We wanted to show you . . . just because we could. By three A.M., I was back home, everyone in the house fast asleep. I was sitting in the yard in front of an open fire, watching the sparks light, fly and vanish into the black evening sky, my ears ringing good and hard . . . 'Oh yeah, it's all right'" (Springsteen, *Born to Run*, 2016).

SONG ANALYSIS

"Outlaw Pete"

Bruce Springsteen: vocals, guitar, harmonica, keyboards, percussion, glockenspiel
Roy Bittan: piano, organ, accordion
Clarence Clemons: saxophone, backing vocals
Danny Federici: organ
Nils Lofgren: guitar, backing vocals
Patti Scialfa: backing vocals
Garry Tallent: bass
Steven Van Zandt: guitar, backing vocals
Max Weinberg: drums
Soozie Tyrell: violin, backing vocals
Patrick Warren: organ, piano, keyboards

In a 2009 interview with Mark Hagen of *The Guardian*, Springsteen provided his own analysis of "Outlaw Pete," a song about a western antihero who tries to outrun his past but finds it difficult to do so with a bounty hunter on his trail. Paraphrasing William Faulkner, Springsteen said, "The past is never past. It is always present. And you better reckon with it in your life and in your daily experience, or it will get you." Springsteen had been exploring this concept at least since 1978's *Darkness on the Edge of Town*, but the difference between then and 2009 was that he now stressed the importance of the past to American history in general, making it a political as well as a personal statement.

In fact, he addressed the Iraq War and castigated the entire eight years of the Bush administration in terms of its failure to learn the lessons of the past. In the song, when the bounty hunter catches up with Pete, Pete draws a dagger and kills him, only to hear the man utter a dire warning before he dies: "We cannot undo these things we've done." The moral of the tale is to consider the long-range ramifications of our actions before we do anything we might end up later regretting.

"My Lucky Day"

Bruce Springsteen: vocals, guitar, harmonica, keyboards, percussion, glockenspiel
Roy Bittan: piano, organ, accordion
Clarence Clemons: saxophone, backing vocals
Danny Federici: organ
Nils Lofgren: guitar, backing vocals
Patti Scialfa: backing vocals
Garry Tallent: bass
Steven Van Zandt: guitar, backing vocals
Max Weinberg: drums
Soozie Tyrell: violin, backing vocals

At a time when Springsteen was becoming increasingly concerned about the direction of the country, he simultaneously embraced the degree of peace and contentment he had found in his personal life. This song offers the perspective of a man, who, whatever other concerns and troubles he has, feels fortunate to be with his wife or lover. "When I see strong hearts give way to the burdens of the day," he sings, "Honey, you're my lucky day." He compares his lot to that of a gambler who loses all his bets until one day he strikes it big, something he does not need to rely on because he has already found his "lucky day" with the woman by his side.

CHART ACTION
Billboard Hot 100: did not chart. The song notched a number-eighteen showing on the magazine's Adult Alternative Songs chart.

"My Lucky Day" was released on November 28, 2008. The number-one song that week was Beyoncé's "If I Were a Boy."

"Working on a Dream"

Bruce Springsteen: vocals, guitar, harmonica, keyboards, percussion, glockenspiel
Roy Bittan: piano, organ, accordion
Clarence Clemons: saxophone, backing vocals
Danny Federici: organ
Nils Lofgren: guitar, backing vocals
Patti Scialfa: backing vocals
Garry Tallent: bass
Steven Van Zandt: guitar, backing vocals
Max Weinberg: drums
Soozie Tyrell: violin, backing vocals

When you think about it, a dream is not really something you work on, it is something you have. Dreams certainly figure prominently in many Springsteen songs throughout the years, from the "runaway American dream" in "Born to Run" to his 2014 cover of Suicide's 1979 song "Dream Baby Dream." But this song does not treat a dream as something you have or wait for to come true but, along the lines of "I'll Work for Your Love," the singer here expresses the commitment to putting in the work to make his dream come true. "The sunrise come, I climb the ladder / The new day breaks, and I'm working on a dream," as if this is the first thing he will do each morning.

In the song Springsteen draws on other images of working-class life, referring to swinging his hammer and his hands being "rough from working on a dream." It is when he sings, "Our love will make it real someday" that it becomes clear that the song is about a personal relationship and not about some other dream about how life can be better in the future. It sends the message that if you take care of the ones who are close to you, the rest will fall into place.

CHART ACTION

Billboard Hot 100: number ninety-five. The song also registered a number-two showing on the Adult Contemporary chart.

"Working on a Dream" was released on November 21, 2008. The number-one song that week was Kanye West's "Heartless."

"Queen of the Supermarket"

Bruce Springsteen: vocals, guitar, harmonica, keyboards, percussion, glockenspiel
Roy Bittan: piano, organ, accordion
Clarence Clemons: saxophone, backing vocals
Danny Federici: organ
Nils Lofgren: guitar, backing vocals
Patti Scialfa: backing vocals
Garry Tallent: bass
Steven Van Zandt: guitar, backing vocals
Max Weinberg: drums
Soozie Tyrell: violin, backing vocals

This song shares a pop sensibility with a song like "Girls in their Summer Clothes" from *Magic*. It has a similar theme of desire for a girl who is out of reach, except in this song the love object is a single woman instead of a lament for lost youth. Springsteen said he was inspired to write the song by the fantasy land represented by modern supermarkets because they have so much abundance and variety; "Aisles and aisles of dreams await you / And the cool promise of ecstasy fills the air."

In this way, the queen represents the ultimate fantasy object, the ultimate object of desire in a place designed to fulfil the senses, giving the song a sexual subtext, which Springsteen himself has acknowledged. As with the "girls in their summer clothes," the cashier who qualifies as grocery store royalty is unaware of the admiration lavished on her by the singer, and in fact looks bored as she bags his groceries. To him, however, the "company cap [that] covers

her hair" cannot "hide the beauty waiting there."
It is a song about fantasy, but also about a real-
life person in a humble working-class job whose
beauty shines through and provides a little bit of
meaning and happiness so much that for him,
one smile from her "blows this whole f-cking
place apart."

"What Love Can Do"
Bruce Springsteen: vocals, guitar, harmonica,
    keyboards, percussion, glockenspiel
Roy Bittan: piano, organ, accordion
Clarence Clemons: saxophone, backing vocals
Danny Federici: organ
Nils Lofgren: guitar, backing vocals
Patti Scialfa: backing vocals
Garry Tallent: bass
Steven Van Zandt: guitar, backing vocals
Max Weinberg: drums
Soozie Tyrell: violin, backing vocals

In this song, Springsteen acknowledges the
realities of life and death that may be beyond
our control, but as the title indicates, he is more
concerned with "what love can do," though he
illustrates this notion by contrasting what love
can do with what it can't. The train is a frequent
metaphor for death in Springsteen's writing,
as it is here an example of something that love
cannot stop from "crashin' through." In addition, here is another song in which Springsteen
embraces religious imagery, from the "pillar in
the temple" into which he has carved the name
of his love that opens the song to the "mark of
Cain" he says we all bear at the end.

One might almost view "What Love Can Do,"
then, as a contrast between the Old Testament
and its "eye for an eye" (also quoted in the song)
mentality to the New Testament based on love
and forgiveness. Is Jesus, then, the light that the
song says shines through at the end of the song?
If not, Springsteen is at least using religious

imagery to offer reason for hope in "what love
can do," even in the face of the worst that the
world and humankind might throw at us, including death itself.

"This Life"
Bruce Springsteen: vocals, guitar, harmonica,
    keyboards, percussion, glockenspiel
Roy Bittan: piano, organ, accordion
Clarence Clemons: saxophone, backing vocals
Danny Federici: organ
Nils Lofgren: guitar, backing vocals
Patti Scialfa: backing vocals
Garry Tallent: bass
Soozie Tyrell: violin, backing vocals
Steven Van Zandt: guitar, backing vocals
Max Weinberg: drums
Patrick Warren: organ, piano, keyboards

On the one hand, as Springsteen became older
and more mature, he seemed to move beyond
the equation of an earthly paradise based on
love, sex, and romance, but, on the other hand,
some of the songs on this album seem to reflect
his desire to hold on to those as elements of a
good life. In *The Grace of God and the Grace
of Man*, Azzan Yadin-Israel, writes, "The idea
that salvific grace can be recovered from the
quotidian reality of our lives expresses itself
with particular clarity in a pair of songs from
Working on a Dream, that together constitute
Springsteen's meditations on the meaning of
love in the face of the vastness of time and
space." The two songs to which he refers are
"Kingdom of Days" and "This Life."

"This Life" literally opens with "a bang," referring to the Big Bang that still resonates in the
stardust of the eyes of his lover. For him a bil-
lion years has all led up to this one moment as
she eases into his car, a moment that leads the
singer to reflect on the miracle and blessings of
"this life." We might look to the stars for meaning or escape, but gravity keeps us "chained to

this earth," which is all right when he considers "the million suns cresting where you stood," singing "this lonely planet never looked so good." The message in the song is not to expect more than this world has to offer, but that what this world has to offer is enough when we take time to consider the everyday blessings in our lives.

"Good Eye"
Bruce Springsteen: vocals, guitar, harmonica, keyboards, percussion, glockenspiel
Roy Bittan: piano, organ, accordion
Clarence Clemons: saxophone, backing vocals
Danny Federici: organ
Nils Lofgren: guitar, backing vocals
Patti Scialfa: backing vocals
Garry Tallent: bass
Steven Van Zandt: guitar, backing vocals
Max Weinberg: drums
Soozie Tyrell: violin, backing vocals

This song has perhaps the simplest lyric and structure on the album: three verses, each followed by the refrain, "Had my good eye to the dark / And my blind eye to the sun." These lines imply that he was not looking where he should have been, staring into darkness and unable to see where the light was. In the first verse, the singer is standing by the river, by now a familiar motif in Springsteen's lyrics. In the second verse, he acknowledges that he has all the riches anyone could want, another echo from past Springsteen songs that emphasize that wealth, fame, and material possessions do not bring personal happiness. The concluding verse of the song has him swearing that his lover was the only one for him, apparently not the case because he "had my good eye to the dark / And my blind eye to the sun."

"Tomorrow Never Knows"
Bruce Springsteen: vocals, guitar, harmonica, keyboards, percussion, glockenspiel

Roy Bittan: piano, organ, accordion
Clarence Clemons: saxophone, backing vocals
Danny Federici: organ
Nils Lofgren: guitar, backing vocals
Patti Scialfa: backing vocals
Garry Tallent: bass
Steven Van Zandt: guitar, backing vocals
Max Weinberg: drums
Soozie Tyrell: violin, backing vocals
Patrick Warren: organ, piano, keyboards

As the song's title suggests, Springsteen addresses the uncertainty of the future in "Tomorrow Never Knows," a short and pleasant ditty that comes in at just over two minutes. The short lyric is full of rich imagery from nature (the cold wind, the green grass, the sound of thunder, the whispering tide), the works of humankind (a water tower, "the rusted spikes of that highway of steel"), and the "sweet smile" and "long hair" of the woman addressed in the song. The simple message of the song is as familiar as it is important, to be mindful of today and not to wait for anticipated riches but to find them where you can in the world and people around you.

"Life Itself"
Bruce Springsteen: vocals, guitar, harmonica, keyboards, percussion, glockenspiel
Roy Bittan: piano, organ, accordion
Clarence Clemons: saxophone, backing vocals
Danny Federici: organ
Nils Lofgren: guitar, backing vocals
Patti Scialfa: backing vocals
Garry Tallent: bass
Steven Van Zandt: guitar, backing vocals
Max Weinberg: drums
Soozie Tyrell: violin, backing vocals

"Life Itself" offers an appropriately titled love song that contains important aspects of Springsteen's philosophy about life in general. Similarly to "The River," the song begins with two lovers meeting "down in the valley," "where the wine of love and destruction flows." It also seems to follow the narrative of "The River," where temptation and sex lead to a monogamous relationship that at first feels "as good as life itself." However, the lyric shifts in the second verse to the singer reprising the role of the singer as flawed hero rescuing a woman in trouble, someone who, like Mary in "Thunder Road" is not "so young anymore." Here she is described as having "squandered all your riches, your beauty, and your wealth," making her want to give up on "life itself."

But in the chorus that follows the second and third verses and ends the song after a late bridge, the singer identifies his love with "life itself." The most meaningful verse in the song is the third verse, which asks, in typical Springsteen fashion, why we forsake the things we value the most, why we no longer hear the music we love, why we fail to appreciate God's beauty, and why we allow our relationships to fall apart "Till we fall away in our own darkness, a stranger to our own hearts." These are all good questions, if perhaps unanswerable, though still worth pondering from the perspective of an artist ever conscious of the need to take stock of life and all the blessings it has to offer. That is exactly what he does in the next song on the album.

"Kingdom of Days"

Bruce Springsteen: vocals, guitar, harmonica, keyboards, percussion, glockenspiel
Roy Bittan: piano, organ, accordion
Clarence Clemons: saxophone, backing vocals
Danny Federici: organ
Nils Lofgren: guitar, backing vocals
Patti Scialfa: backing vocals
Garry Tallent: bass
Steven Van Zandt: guitar, backing vocals
Max Weinberg: drums
Soozie Tyrell: violin, backing vocals

Like "This Life," with which Yadin-Israel paired this song in his analysis in *The Grace of God*

and the Grace of Man, "Kingdom of Days" celebrates the everyday joys of this life with a person you love, the singer oblivious to the rising and setting of the sun or the path of the moon through the sky, focusing instead on things like "the subtle change of light upon your face" and "my jacket 'round your shoulders . . . the wet grass on our backs." As Springsteen put it in his interview with Mark Hagen, "At certain moments time is obliterated in the presence of somebody you love." The phrase "Kingdom of Days" has biblical resonances, but Springsteen has once again transformed the secular into the sacred, everyday life and love into something eternal.

"Surprise, Surprise"

Bruce Springsteen: vocals, guitar, harmonica, keyboards, percussion, glockenspiel
Roy Bittan: piano, organ, accordion
Clarence Clemons: saxophone, backing vocals
Danny Federici: organ
Nils Lofgren: guitar, backing vocals
Patti Scialfa: backing vocals
Garry Tallent: bass
Steven Van Zandt: guitar, backing vocals
Max Weinberg: drums
Soozie Tyrell: violin, backing vocals

"Surprise, Surprise" acts as Springsteen's version of a "Happy Birthday" song, one that celebrates a special day at the same time that it recognizes the rhythm of every day and the potential it holds for the blessings life has to offer. What might seem at first hearing like a throwaway pop song included just for fun actually makes perfect sense following as it does "Kingdom of Days" on the album. The structure of the song is chorus/refrain/chorus/refrain; first verse/chorus/refrain; second verse/chorus refrain/chorus/refrain/refrain.

Most of the song, then, is a sequence of chorus and refrain, and the refrain mainly consists of the word "surprise" followed by an injunction to "open your eyes and let your love shine down." The first verse acknowledges the beginning of the day and the good wishes of a longtime friend. The second verse turns to the end of the day in poetic language, with a wish that "the evening stars scatter a shining light upon your breast" and that when the next day begins "the rising sun will caress and bless your soul for all your life." In graceful and expressive language, Springsteen has wished an old friend a happy birthday and many more as only he can do.

"The Last Carnival"

Bruce Springsteen: vocals, guitar, harmonica, keyboards, percussion, glockenspiel
Roy Bittan: piano, organ
Clarence Clemons: saxophone, backing vocals
Nils Lofgren: guitar, backing vocals
Patti Scialfa: backing vocals
Garry Tallent: bass
Steven Van Zandt: guitar, backing vocals
Max Weinberg: drums
Jason Federici: accordion
Soozie Tyrell: violin, backing vocals

It is not just the fact that "The Last Carnival" is addressed to someone named Billy that bookends it with "Wild Billy's Circus Story" from *The Wild, the Innocent and the E Street Shuffle*. It is full of the same kind of imagery as the 1973 song, from the tightrope walker to the daredevils on the flying trapeze to the knife thrower, but here all the tents are coming down and the carnival is leaving town. "Where are you now my handsome Billy?" the song asks. If "Surprise, Surprise," contains a birthday wish for a long and blessed life, this song serves as a eulogy with "every soul livin' and dead . . . gathered together by God to sing a hymn to your bones." Springsteen wrote the song in honor of long-time E Street Band keyboardist Danny

Federici, who died on April 17, 2008, to whom he dedicated the entire album.

"The Wrestler" (bonus track)

Bruce Springsteen: vocals, guitar, harmonica, keyboards, percussion, glockenspiel

All string and horn arrangements by Eddie Horst

Springsteen wrote "The Wrestler" for the 2008 movie of the same name directed by Darren Aronofsky and starring Mickey Rourke. The film traces the story of a down-and-out former professional wrestler who finds it difficult to accept the end of his glory days, while wrestling with his own self-destructive tendencies and seeking meaning through a late-life romance and an effort to reconnect with his estranged daughter. The lyric of the song, written in the first person, fits Rourke's character splendidly, the singer comparing himself to a one-trick pony, a one-legged dog, a scarecrow, and a one-armed man. He remembers when he could "make you smile when the blood hits the floor," but without his career he finds no place for himself in the world, his faith residing solely in "the broken bones and bruises," which are all he has left from his fading glory. It is a song that will resonate with anyone facing a major life change, in which they have lost their sense of purpose in life, or anyone feeling lonely, isolated, and alienated from a world that once celebrated them but no longer seems to have a need for what they have to offer.

CHART ACTION
Billboard Hot 100: did not chart. The song notched a number-twenty showing on the Bubbling Under the Hot 100 Singles chart.

"The Wrestler" was released on December 16, 2008. The number-one song that week was Beyoncé's "Single Ladies (Put a Ring on It)."

Wrecking Ball (Alamy) [performance photo]

WRECKING BALL

Released in March 2012, *Wrecking Ball* marked the beginning of a new collaboration between Springsteen and coproducer Ron Aniello, who recorded the LP at Thrill Hill, Springsteen's Colts Neck, New Jersey, home studio. Sadly, the album was the last Springsteen LP to feature saxophonist Clarence Clemons, who died in June 2011 after complications following a stroke. He final recordings included his sax solo on "Land of Hope and Dreams" and contributing to the rhythm section on the title track.

Wrecking Ball found Springsteen writing at a fever pitch in the wake of the 2008 financial crisis. The album's overarching mood is established by "We Take Care of Our Own," which contrasts the patriotic sentiment of its chorus— "Wherever this flag is flown / We take care of her own"—with the reality, as exemplified by the government's lackluster response to Hurricane Katrina, that perhaps we don't care for all of our citizens equally. Meanwhile, songs like "Death to My Hometown" underscore the slow demise of traditional American life because of the loss of manufacturing jobs across the country.

Overall, Springsteen "knew this was the music I should make now. It was my job. I felt the country was at a critical juncture. If this much damage can be done to average citizens with basically no accountability, then the game is off and the thin veil of democracy is revealed for what it is, a shallow disguise for a growing plutocracy that is here now and permanent. *Wrecking Ball* was received with a lot less fanfare than I thought it would be. I was sure I had it. I still think I do and did. Maybe my voice had been too compromised by my own success, but I don't think so. I've worked hard and long to write about these subjects and I know them well. I knew *Wrecking Ball* was one of my best, most contemporary and accessible albums since *Born in the U.S.A.* I'm no conspiracy theorist, so basically I realized that the presentation of these ideas in this form had a powerful but limited interest to a reasonably large but still select group of people, especially in the United States" (Springsteen, *Born to Run*, 2016).

HISTORICAL CONTEXT

If Springsteen sounded rejuvenated on *Working on a Dream*, especially on songs such as "This Life" and "Kingdom of Days," it was largely a result of a general contentment with his own life and perhaps partly because of a prevailing sense of optimism stemming from the rise of Barack Obama to the presidency of the United States. Those feelings did not hold, however, by the time he released his next album, appropriately titled *Wrecking Ball*, on March 6, 2012. On this album, he returned to the main themes that had preoccupied him for much of his career. "My work has always been about judging the distance between American reality and the American dream," he explained to a press conference held in Paris to promote the new album.

Springsteen was particularly upset that the recovery from the financial collapse of 2008 had proceeded so slowly and that what gains had returned accrued mainly to wealthy corporations and not to the working or even the middle classes. He was upset that so few of the culprits behind the crisis had answered for their crimes and shenanigans, although at the time of the album's release Preet Bharara, US Attorney for the Southern District of New York, had begun to investigate and charge some of the worst offenders of the manipulation of credit and mortgage financing that had led to the collapse. Springsteen was still upset about the policies of the Bush administration that had led to the crisis, as well as its prosecution of the unpopular war in Iraq and its slow and unsatisfactory response to the devastation of New Orleans by Hurricane Katrina in August 2005.

These concerns and critiques show up throughout the album, from the opening track, "We Take Care of Our Own," which, like his earlier "Born in the U.S.A.," is an infectious rocker that simultaneously evokes a sense of patriotism while offering a critique of the country's frequent failure to live up to the title of the song. The protagonist of "Easy Money" seeks to emulate "all of them fat cats," but without their resources to score a cool payday, he has to rely on a "Smith and Wesson .38." In going after the "fat cats" on Wall Street, Bharara attributed the economic collapse to "a creeping culture of corruption in our politics and also in Wall Street and in business generally," echoing the message Springsteen sought to promote in his Paris press conference and on the album, especially in a song like "Death to My Hometown."

When the album came out, unemployment still remained above 8 percent, even though other economic indicators had started to improve. The prolonged length of the supposed recovery, combined with its unequal benefits, meant that the backlash provoked by the crisis also continued, represented by both a movement like Occupy Wall Street, which began in September 2011, and Springsteen's *Wrecking Ball*. As Springsteen explained in Paris, "The genesis of the record was after 2008, when we had the huge financial crisis in the States, and there was really no accountability for years and years." This explains why the historical context for an album released in 2012 did not relate just to something that had happened four years earlier but to a problem of economic inequality that was both ongoing and deeply rooted in America's past, as this and other Springsteen albums sought to make clear.

PRODUCTION

Released on March 6, 2012, Columbia Records
Produced by Ron Aniello and Bruce Springsteen
Engineered by Aniello and Toby Scott
Recording assistants: Rob Lebret, Clif Norrell, and Ross Petersen
Mixed by Bob Clearmountain at Mix This!
Mixing assistant: Brandon Duncan
Mastered by Bob Ludwig at Gateway Mastering

Recorded at Stone Hill Studio, Very Loud House Studio, and MSR Studio B, January 2011 to January 2012

PERSONNEL

Bruce Springsteen: vocals, acoustic and electric guitars, banjo, piano, organ, drums, percussion, loops
Clarence Clemons: saxophone
Patti Scialfa: backing vocals
Steven Van Zandt: mandolin, backing vocals
Max Weinberg: drums
Tiffeny Andrews: backing vocals
Ron Aniello: guitar, bass, keyboards, loops, backing vocals, percussion, hurdy-gurdy
Art Baron: euphonium, tuba, sousaphone, penny whistle
Lilly "Crawford" Brown: backing vocals
Kevin Buell: drums, backing vocals
Corinda Carford: backing vocals
Matt Chamberlain: drums, percussion
Solomon Cobbs: backing vocals
Clark Gayton: trombone
Charles Giordano: piano, Hammond B3 organ, celeste, accordion
Stan Harrison: clarinet, alto saxophone, tenor saxophone
Steve Jordan: percussion
Rob Lebret: guitar, backing vocals
Greg Leisz: banjo, mandola, lap steel guitar
Darrell Leonard: trumpet, bass trumpet
Dan Levine: alto horn, euphonium
Lisa Lowell: backing vocals
Ed Manion: tenor saxophone, baritone saxophone
Jeremy McCoy: bass violin
Cindy Mizelle: backing vocals
Antoinette Moore: backing vocals
Michelle Moore: backing vocals
Tom Morello: guitar

Marc Muller: pedal steel guitar

Clif Norrell: tuba, backing vocals

Ross Petersen: backing vocals

Curt Ramm: trumpet, cornet

Mark Romatz: contra bassoon

Dan Shelly: bassoon

Soozie Tyrell: violin, backing vocals

Victorious Gospel Choir: choir vocals

New York String Section: Rob Mathes (orchestration); Sandy Park (string contractor); Lisa Kim (concertmaster); Hyunju Lee, Ann Lehmaan, Elizabeth Lim-Dutton, Joanna Maurer, Annaliesa Place, Fiona Simon, Sharon Yamada, and Jungsun Yoo (violins); Karen Dreyfus, Daniel Panner, and Robert Rinehart (violas); Mina Smith and Alan Stepansky (cellos)

COVER ART AND PACKAGING

Art direction and cover design: Dave Bett and Michelle Holme

Photography: Danny Clinch and Jo Lopez

TRACK LISTING

All songs composed by Bruce Springsteen

1. "We Take Care of Our Own"
2. "Easy Money"
3. "Shackled and Drawn"
4. "Jack of All Trades"
5. "Death to My Hometown"
6. "This Depression"
7. "Wrecking Ball"
8. "You've Got It"
9. "Rocky Ground"
10. "Land of Hope and Dreams"
11. "We Are Alive"
12. "Swallowed Up (in the Belly of a Whale)" (bonus track)
13. "American Land" (bonus track)

CONTEMPORARY REVIEWS

Phil Sutcliffe (*MOJO*, April 2012): "Greed rampant and American people burning up over the wealth-poverty divide; what can a songwriter do? Well, address it. Fiercely. Springsteen's not a manifesto man so *Wrecking Ball* starts from 'We Take Care of Our Own's goading ambiguity, the all-American blues disguised as an anthem; big, busy, anxious—every line giving the lie to the chorus, 'Wherever this flag's flown / We take care of our own.' An album of two halves, at first it tells the victims' stories. A broke suburban couple head for town with a gun looking for cash and 'fat cats' (sarcastic, angry 'Easy Money'). Blue-collar guys lose everything to invisible financier-thieves while 'on banker's hill the party's goin' strong' (chain-gang shouty 'Shackled and Drawn' and raging 'Death to My Hometown'). Then, in 'Jack of All Trades,' the archetypal Working Man, accompanied by a Grimethorpian brass band, humbly offers his services—'I'll mow your lawn. . . . I'll mend your roof'—but finally let's rip: 'If I had me a gun / I'd find the bastards and shoot 'em on sight.' You may know the feeling."

Peter Stone Brown (*Counter Punch*, February 24, 2012): "The landscape for *Wrecking Ball* is as bleak as *Nebraska* and ultimately angrier than anything he's yet produced. The characters are familiar and echo those on past albums and songs, though this time the struggle is harder, perhaps impossible, and the rewards, even the small ones, are not necessarily in sight or likely to appear. Despite this the overall effect of the album is curiously and strangely uplifting following the precept that songs are to elevate the spirit. In recording these songs, Springsteen channeled into the indefinable spirit of creation that goes way beyond the subject matter. Considering that Springsteen told *Rolling Stone* that the songs started as folk music, the production and instrumentation on the album . . . is massive. At times, it seems as if he's tapping into every sound he ever heard. The result is an ambience that is at times spooky and foggy, that casts an overall feeling of what the hell happened? . . . *Wrecking Ball* is easily the best album Springsteen has delivered in a very long time. Considering the daring creativity he took in recording the songs, and especially the context of the times in which it was created, it is also one of his most important."

David Fricke (*Rolling Stone*, March 6, 2012): "*Wrecking Ball* is the most despairing, confrontational, and musically turbulent album Bruce Springsteen has ever made. He is angry and accusing in these songs, to the point of exhaustion, with grave reason. The America here is a scorched earth: razed by profiteers and suffering a shameful erosion in truly democratic values and national charity. The surrender running through the chain-gang march and Springsteen's muddy-river growl in 'Shackled and Drawn'; the double meaning loaded into the ballad 'This Depression'; the reproach driving 'We Take Care of Our Own,' a song so obviously about abandoned ideals and mutual blame that no candidate would dare touch it: This is darkness gone way past the edge of town, to the heart of the republic. On *Wrecking Ball*, Springsteen throws nuance to the curb. 'Death to My Hometown' is an obvious allusion to the battered nostalgia of 'My Hometown,' on 1984's *Born in the U.S.A.* But even the vacant storefronts in the latter song are gone now; the place has been flattened. 'I never heard a sound / The marauders raided in the dark / And brought death to my hometown,' Springsteen sings, a blunt indictment of cold greed and congressional impotence. And he delivers it like delicious

revenge, with a robust Irish-wake rhythm and noble-warrior glaze: a sample from a 1959 Alan Lomax recording of the Alabama Sacred Harp Singers. The effect is a dance through ashes with a reminder: in a righteous fight, music is still good ammo. 'They'll be returning sure as the rising sun,' Springsteen warns. 'Get yourself a song to sing. . . . Sing it hard and sing it well / Send the robber barons straight to hell.'"

PROMOTION

The *Wrecking Ball* world tour ran from March 2012 through September 2013, earning $341 million in receipts across 133 dates. *Billboard* named the *Wrecking Ball* tour as the year's Top Draw.

CHART ACTION

Billboard Top 200 Albums: number one. March 6, 2012, *Wrecking Ball* debuted at number one on March 24, unseating Adele's *21* from the top spot. The album sold more than 500,000 copies, earning gold status from RIAA.

Wrecking Ball spent 143 weeks on the *Billboard* charts.

COMMENTS FROM SPRINGSTEEN AND HIS CIRCLE

Springsteen: "After the crash of 2008, I was furious at what had been done by a handful of trading companies on Wall Street. *Wrecking Ball* was a shot of anger at the injustice that continues on and has widened with deregulation, dysfunctional regulatory agencies and capitalism gone wild at the expense of hardworking Americans. The middle class? Stomped on. Income disparity climbed as we lived through a new Gilded Age. This was what I wanted to write about. I'd been following and writing about America's post-industrial trauma, the killing of our manufacturing presence and working class, for thirty-five years. So I went to work" (Springsteen, *Born to Run*, 2016).

MISCELLANEOUS

During his 2012 reelection effort, President Barack Obama deployed "We Take Care of Our Own" as one of his regular campaign songs on the stump. Springsteen performed an acoustic version of the song during several sets in support of President Obama's reelection campaign.

Wrecking Ball was nominated for Best Rock Album at the Grammy Awards, along with "We Take Care of Our Own," which was nominated for Best Rock Performance and Best Rock Song. *Rolling Stone* ranked *Wrecking Ball* as the number-one album on the magazine's Top 50 Albums of 2012.

SONG ANALYSES

"We Take Care of Our Own"

Bruce Springsteen: vocals, guitar, banjo, piano, organ, drums, percussion, loops
Ron Aniello: guitar, bass, keyboards, piano, drums, loops, backing vocals
Lisa Lowell: backing vocals
Patti Scialfa: backing vocals
Soozie Tyrell: backing vocals
New York String Section: Rob Mathes (orchestration); Sandy Park (string contractor); Lisa Kim (concertmaster); Hyunju Lee, Ann Lehmaan, Elizabeth Lim-Dutton, Joanna Maurer, Annaliesa Place, Fiona Simon, Sharon Yamada, and Jungsun Yoo (violins); Karen Dreyfus, Daniel Panner, and Robert Rinehart (violas); Mina Smith and Alan Stepansky (cellos)

No song from Springsteen since "Born in the U.S.A." has been more susceptible to misinterpretation than "We Take Care of Our Own." Springsteen explained at his 2012 press conference in Paris that the song, which he wrote in 2009–2010, was about "what's *supposed* to happen, but was not happening." In other words, we are supposed to take care of our own, but the country had failed those it had sent into war, the veterans who survived to return from overseas, and the many ordinary people whose lives were devastated by the 2008 financial collapse. The song reflects Springsteen's shift toward a larger concern with society as a whole rather than the more individualistic ethos he had celebrated earlier in his career. As in "Born in the U.S.A.," if the chorus sounds like a celebration of American patriotism, the rest of the lyric belies that notion, as Springsteen describes the "road to good intentions . . . gone dry as a bone" and sings that "from the shotgun shack to the Superdome" no help is coming because "the cavalry stayed home." Like Bob Dylan's classic protest song "Blowin' in the Wind," the song also contains a series of questions asking where are the eyes to see, the hearts flowing with mercy, "the love that has not forsaken me," and "the work that'll set my hands [and] my soul free."

CHART ACTION
Billboard Hot 100: did not chart. The song notched a number-six showing on the Bubbling Under the Hot 100 Singles chart, number eleven on the Adult Alternative Songs chart, and number forty-three on the Hot Rock and Alternative Songs chart.

"We Take Care of Our Own" was released on January 19, 2012. The number-one song that week was Rihanna's "We Found Love" (featuring Calvin Harris).

"Easy Money"
Bruce Springsteen: vocals, guitar, banjo, piano, organ, drums, loops
Tiffeny Andrews: backing vocals
Ron Aniello: guitar, bass, keyboards, piano, drums, loops, backing vocals
Lilly "Crawford" Brown: backing vocals
Corinda Carford: backing vocals
Solomon Cobbs: backing vocals
Steve Jordan: percussion
Lisa Lowell: backing vocals
Antoinette Moore: backing vocals
Michelle Moore: backing vocals
Patti Scialfa: backing vocals
Soozie Tyrell: violin, backing vocals

Springsteen described "Easy Money" as about a serial thief who is merely "imitating your guys on Wall Street the only way he knows how." The character in the song invites a girl out on a date, saying he has gotten himself a gun and is taking her out to look for "easy money." He expects the "fat cats" to "just think it's funny," obviously because they would presumably consider this small-town robber a kindred spirit.

"Shackled and Drawn"
Bruce Springsteen: vocals, guitar, banjo, loops
Ron Aniello: guitar, bass, keyboards, loops, backing vocals
Art Baron: euphonium, tuba, sousaphone, penny whistle
Matt Chamberlain: drums, percussion
Clark Gayton: trombone
Charles Giordano: piano, Hammond B3 organ
Stan Harrison: clarinet, alto saxophone, tenor saxophone
Dan Levine: alto horn, euphonium
Lisa Lowell: backing vocals
Ed Manion: tenor saxophone, baritone saxophone
Cindy Mizelle: backing vocals
Clif Norrell: backing vocals
Ross Petersen: backing vocals
Curt Ramm: trumpet, cornet

Patti Scialfa: backing vocals
Soozie Tyrell: violin, backing vocals

This song alternates verse and chorus four times until the chorus is repeated at the end. The chorus repeats the title phrase, "shackled and drawn," twice at the beginning and returns to it in the last line. There is some variation in the middle two lines but they all amount to the feeling that the singer is groping in the dark to find his way in a "world gone wrong." The song is narrated from a working man's perspective, making it clear that his troubles are not his own fault, with the echoes of slavery contained in the title probably meant to refer to its modern-day equivalent—a feeling of the odds being stacked against the individual in a way over which he or she has no control. The verses advocate working hard as the only way out of this trap, or at least the only alternative to succumbing to it and giving up on life. The line "Let a man work, is that so wrong," though, provides a reminder that not everyone even has that choice. Springsteen even refers to his own trade in the line, "What's a poor boy to do but keep singing his song?" which could be his way of offering up this album to his listeners as an acknowledgment of their own pain and suffering through the financial crisis that hovers over the entire album.

"Jack of All Trades"
Bruce Springsteen: vocals, guitar, banjo, piano, organ, drums, percussion, loops
Ron Aniello: guitar, bass, keyboards, piano, drums, loops, backing vocals
Art Baron: euphonium, tuba, sousaphone, penny whistle
Clark Gayton: trombone
Stan Harrison: clarinet, alto saxophone, tenor saxophone
Dan Levine: alto horn, euphonium

Ed Manion: tenor saxophone, baritone
  saxophone
Tom Morello: guitar
Curt Ramm: trumpet, cornet
Soozie Tyrell: violin
New York String Section: Rob Mathes
  (orchestration); Sandy Park (string contractor);
  Lisa Kim (concertmaster); Hyunju Lee, Ann
  Lehmaan, Elizabeth Lim-Dutton, Joanna Maurer,
  Annaliesa Place, Fiona Simon, Sharon Yamada,
  and Jungsun Yoo (violins); Karen Dreyfus, Daniel
  Panner, and Robert Rinehart (viola); Mina Smith
  and Alan Stepansky (cellos)

Here Springsteen offers up another take on the theme of songs like "I'll Work for Your Love" and "Man's Job." I heard a priest recite lyrics from this song at a funeral in 2022, paying tribute to a man who was described as going out of his way to help other people; thus he interpreted the song in the metaphorical way in which it was no doubt intended, instead of being literally about someone who can clean your gutters, fix your roof, harvest your crop, and repair your car, some other skills mentioned in the song. However, there is another way to interpret the song more in keeping with the financial difficulties besetting many average Americans at the time, "The banker man grows fat, working man goes thin," Springsteen sings, "It's happened before and it'll happen again."

This is why one needs to be a "jack of all trades," because we live in a society in which we cannot depend on others, especially those with the political and economic clout not to suffer when the cyclical nature of the capitalistic economy reaches bottom again. The song grows even darker at the end. "If I had a gun, I'd find the bastards and shoot 'em on sight," Springsteen sings in the last verse, no doubt expressing the frustration many people felt that led to the rise of populist politics later in the decade. In its

Bruce Springsteen Collector's Edition (2022), *Rolling Stone* listed "Jack of All Trades" as number seventy-one among the artist's top 100 songs.

"Death to My Hometown"
Bruce Springsteen: vocals, guitar, banjo, loops
Ron Aniello: guitar, bass, keyboards, loops, backing
  vocals
Art Baron: euphonium, tuba, sousaphone, penny
  whistle
Kevin Buell: drums, backing vocals
Matt Chamberlain: drums, percussion
Charles Giordano: piano, Hammond B3 organ
Rob Lebret: backing vocals
Clif Norrell: backing vocals
Ross Petersen: backing vocals
Soozie Tyrell: violin

This song deals with the impact on people's lives of events beyond their control. Whether it's Vietnam, the Depression, 9/11, or the economic collapse and recession of 2007–2008, it is frequently ordinary working-class people who suffer the most, not the wealthy bankers, CEOs, and lawyers who often find ways to benefit themselves in the midst of hardship and suffering of ordinary Americans. In this song, Springsteen talks about the factories and families destroyed, not by cannon balls, rifles, and bombs, nor the invasion of foreign dictators, but by "robber barons" and "greedy thieves," who just as surely and effectively brought death to his hometown. The song not only relates to important aspects of recent American history but shows that history is not over and we are all living it (as we have been reminded by the COVID pandemic and political upheaval of the Trump era), but living through troubled times is at least made easier by understanding it, which with his lyrics and music Springsteen helps us in his own way to do. In its *Bruce Springsteen Collector's Edition* (2022),

Rolling Stone listed "Death to My Hometown" as number fifty among the artist's top 100 songs.

CHART ACTION
Billboard Hot 100: did not chart.

"Death to My Hometown" was released in May 2012. The number-one song that week was Gotye's "Somebody that I Used to Know" (featuring Kimbra).

"This Depression"
Bruce Springsteen: vocals, guitar, banjo, piano, organ, drums, percussion, loops
Ron Aniello: guitar, bass, keyboards, piano, drums, loops, backing vocals
Lisa Lowell: backing vocals
Tom Morello: guitar
Patti Scialfa: backing vocals
Soozie Tyrell: violin, backing vocals

In recent years, we have witnessed a long overdue movement in our society toward awareness of the seriousness and importance of mental health issues, with a number of sports and entertainment celebrities acknowledging their own individual struggles with problems such as depression and anxiety. Springsteen came to recognize that his father had struggled with depression and has acknowledged his own intermittent bouts with this malady throughout his life. This song brings the subject further out into the open, Springsteen even singing in the song, "This is my confession." The song is a cry for help from the perspective of someone who has been down before "but never this down," lost before "but never this lost." In it, Springsteen also falls back on religious imagery, his prayers unanswered, a feeling of being utterly forsaken, the sentiment Jesus was reported to have uttered from the cross. The one positive note in the song is that the singer is able to ask for help, expressed in the last line of the chorus and the song, "I need your heart."

"Wrecking Ball"
Bruce Springsteen: vocals, guitar, banjo, percussion, loops
Ron Aniello: guitar, bass, keyboards, loops, backing vocals
Clarence Clemons: saxophone
Charles Giordano: piano, Hammond B3 organ
Rob Lebret: guitar, backing vocals
Lisa Lowell: backing vocals
Clif Norrell: backing vocals
Ross Petersen: backing vocals
Curt Ramm: trumpet, cornet
Patti Scialfa: backing vocals
Soozie Tyrell: violin, backing vocals
Steven Van Zandt: backing vocals
Max Weinberg: drums
New York String Section: Rob Mathes (orchestration); Sandy Park (string contractor); Lisa Kim (concertmaster); Hyunju Lee, Ann Lehmaan, Elizabeth Lim-Dutton, Joanna Maurer, Annaliesa Place, Fiona Simon, Sharon Yamada, and Jungsun Yoo (violins); Karen Dreyfus, Daniel Panner, and Robert Rinehart (violas); Mina Smith and Alan Stepansky (cellos)

In a 2012 Paris press conference, Springsteen had this to say about the title song. "'Wrecking Ball' seemed like a metaphor for what had occurred—it's an image where something is destroyed to build something new, and it was also an image [of] just the flat destruction of some fundamental American values and ideas that occurred over the past 30 years." As revealed in the 2010 documentary, *Inside Job*, directed by Charles Ferguson, the country had become one in which political connections and clout had rendered those most responsible for the financial collapse virtually untouched and frequently vastly enriched from a crisis that had cost millions of people their homes and livelihoods. The metaphor in the song is the demolition of Giants Stadium in the New Jersey Meadowlands in 2010, replaced by the new MetLife Stadium that opened the same year.

In "Wrecking Ball," Springsteen revisits the "swamps of Jersey" he immortalized in "Rosalita," where "Through the mud and the beer and the blood and the cheers I've seen champions come and go." He then challenges the powers that be to "bring on your wrecking ball," while exhorting his listeners to hold on to their anger, reminding them that "hard times come and hard times go." Just as sports fans in the New York metropolitan area can hope for the return of past glories (more of the Giants than the Jets, where football is concerned!), so we can all hope to recover from the destruction wrought by the wrecking ball that people in government and Wall Street had taken to the American economy. In its *Bruce Springsteen Collector's Edition* (2022), *Rolling Stone* listed "Wrecking Ball" as number forty-three among the artist's top 100 songs.

"You've Got It"

Bruce Springsteen: vocals, guitar, piano, organ, loops
Ron Aniello: guitar, bass, keyboards, piano, loops, backing vocals
Matt Chamberlain: drums, percussion
Clark Gayton: trombone
Stan Harrison: clarinet, alto saxophone, tenor saxophone
Rob Lebret: backing vocals
Greg Leisz: banjo, mandola, lap steel guitar
Ed Manion: tenor saxophone, baritone saxophone
Marc Muller: pedal steel guitar
Clif Norrell: backing vocals
Ross Petersen: backing vocals
Curt Ramm: trumpet, cornet

One of Springsteen's more cryptic songs, he never defines the "it" that is repeated throughout the lyric. Whatever "it" is, the woman he addresses in the song has "it," which is solely defined here by what "it" is not. "It" cannot be taught in school or read in a book, dreamed in a dream, or even given a name, but "it" should not be wasted or taken for granted. Is "it" a spiritual presence, an ineffable, mystical quality like love that can be felt but not truly defined, or simply that *je ne sais quoi* that leads us to fall in love or feel a powerful attraction or affinity with a certain person? Or is it a tribute to one of Springsteen's early rock and roll icons, Roy Orbison—to whom he paid homage in "Thunder Road"—and Orbison's posthumously released song "You Got It"?

"Rocky Ground"

Bruce Springsteen: vocals, guitar, banjo, drums, percussion, loops
Ron Aniello: guitar, bass, keyboards, drums, loops, backing vocals
Art Baron: euphonium, tuba, sousaphone, penny whistle
Lilly "Crawford" Brown: backing vocals
Clark Gayton: trombone
Charles Giordano: piano, Hammond B3 organ
Stan Harrison: clarinet, alto saxophone, tenor saxophone
Dan Levine: alto horn, euphonium
Ed Manion: tenor saxophone, baritone saxophone
Michelle Moore: vocals
Curt Ramm: trumpet, cornet
Victorious Gospel Choir: choir vocals

In this gospel-tinged tune, written in the voice of an Old Testament prophet, Springsteen sings of a people seeking refuge from the rocky ground over which they have traversed in search of a promised land. He calls for a shepherd to rise up, like Moses, to lead the people to higher ground in some foothills that will allow them to survive the flood that has washed over the land for a biblical forty days and forty nights. When Springsteen does bring the New Testament to bear on "Rocky Ground," it is not the merciful and loving Jesus that he recalls, but the angry Jesus who went ballistic over the presence of money changers in the temple. The song does not promise redemption for a people the "prophet" considers so tarnished with sin that, even if they cross the metaphorical river to safety, "the blood on our hands will come back on us twice."

The only consolation that "Rocky Ground" offers and that makes our current situation bearable is that we continue to do our best and "pray . . . that your best is good enough." Yet, just as the sun came out for Noah and the survivors of the flood, the song ends with the reassurance that "a new day's coming." In summary, the song follows a familiar narrative arc of sin, struggle, chastisement, the search for forgiveness, and ultimately the possibility of redemption and a fresh start. In its *Bruce Springsteen Collector's Edition* (2022), *Rolling Stone* listed "Rocky Ground" as number seventy-three among the artist's top 100 songs.

"Land of Hope and Dreams"

Bruce Springsteen: vocals, guitar, banjo, drums, percussion, loops
Ron Aniello: guitar, bass, keyboards, drums, loops, backing vocals
Art Baron: euphonium, tuba, sousaphone, penny whistle
Lilly "Crawford" Brown: backing vocals
Matt Chamberlain: drums (uncredited)
Clarence Clemons: saxophone solo
Clark Gayton: trombone
Charles Giordano: piano, Hammond B3 organ
Stan Harrison: clarinet, alto saxophone, tenor saxophone
Dan Levine: alto horn, euphonium
Lisa Lowell: backing vocals
Ed Manion: tenor saxophone, baritone saxophone
Michelle Moore: backing vocals
Curt Ramm: trumpet, cornet
Patti Scialfa: backing vocals
Soozie Tyrell: violin, backing vocals
Steven Van Zandt: backing vocals
Victorious Gospel Choir: choir vocals

After the bleak dirge-like cadences of "Rocky Ground," Springsteen lifts us up by inviting his listeners collectively to join Woody Guthrie's train "bound for glory," headed for a "land of hope and dreams." Here again we see Springsteen's shift from an individualistic ethos to a collective one. The song emphasizes the message of the New Testament stressed by the sixteenth-century German reformer Martin Luther that Jesus had come not to save the righteous but to bestow righteousness on sinners who merely had to accept God's grace to merit forgiveness. Those individuals smug enough to set themselves up in judgment of other people would be the ones most in danger of losing God's grace.

It is not that people who have lived up to high ethical standards would be excluded, for the train of which Springsteen sings "carries saints and sinners," "winners and losers," including "whores and gamblers." As in other songs, the train is a metaphor for death: "you don't know where you're going but you know you won't be back." But both musically and lyrically, it is also a life-sustaining song offering hope and comfort to all who know they may not have lived a perfect life but still might find some grace and mercy at the end of it; at least, that seems to be Springsteen's wish for all of us.

"We Are Alive"

Bruce Springsteen: vocals, guitar, percussion, loops
Ron Aniello: guitar, bass, keyboards, loops, backing vocals
Charles Giordano: piano, Hammond B3 organ
Greg Leisz: banjo, mandola, lap steel guitar
Darrell Leonard: trumpet, bass trumpet
Patti Scialfa: backing vocals
Soozie Tyrell: violin
Max Weinberg: drums

In "Land of Hope and Dreams" we find a train carrying people to their final destination; in this song we find people who have already arrived there and lie buried in their graves. And yet, invoking the death of Christ on "a cross up yonder on Calvary hill" in the very first line, the song affirms that the spirit of those who have died lives on and that they are, in fact, still alive. This is a message and a theme Springsteen will revisit in his album *Letter to You* a decade later and one that echoes the sentiments of Tom Joad at the end of *The Grapes of Wrath* that he sang about fifteen years prior. The more specific theme of the legacy of the poor and oppressed, of those fighting for their rights or social justice, comes through in the second verse, which refers to a railroad worker who died in a strike in 1877, to the young African Americans girls who died in a church bombing in Birmingham in 1963, and to a Mexican migrant who the previous year died crossing "the southern desert." It is another song that stresses the collective nature of humanity and the ways in which one death diminishes us all, although the memory of their spirit affirms something important in our own lives.

In its *Bruce Springsteen Collector's Edition* (2022), *Rolling Stone* listed "We Are Alive" as number seventy-five among the artist's top 100 songs.

"Swallowed Up (in the Belly of a Whale)" (bonus track)

Bruce Springsteen: vocals, guitar, banjo, piano, organ, drums, percussion, loops
Ron Aniello: guitar, bass, keyboards, piano, drums, loops, backing vocals
Charles Giordano: accordion
Rob Lebret: backing vocals
Lisa Lowell: backing vocals
Jeremy McCoy: bass violin
Clif Norrell: tuba, backing vocals
Ross Petersen: backing vocals
Mark Romatz: contra bassoon
Patti Scialfa: backing vocals
Dan Shelly: bassoon
Soozie Tyrell: violin, backing vocals

"Swallowed Up (in the Belly of a Whale)" is clearly based on the book of Jonah from the Old Testament, in which Jonah's ability to survive in the belly of a big fish (now commonly referred to as a whale) has been interpreted as a metaphor for the survival through captivity of the Israelites in the kingdom of Babylon or for the period of captivity of the Jews in Egypt prior to the Exodus. The biblical account interprets Jonah's individual plight as resulting from his disobedience to God in refusing to risk his life by preaching to the inhabitants of the Assyrian capital of Nineveh, as God had commanded him. Both Jewish and Christian interpretations of the book have emphasized the story as illustrative of the power and mercy of God in his ability to have the fish disgorge Jonah on the shores of Nineveh, where he is able to fulfill God's plan for him.

Azzan Yadin-Israel calls this song by Springsteen "a strong revisionist reading of the story of Jonah." Yadin-Israel explains that in contrast to the biblical account, in which Jonah initially flees from God but repents and returns to his faith as a result of his traumatic experience, the sailor in Springsteen's narrative starts out enjoying a peaceful sea voyage enveloped by God's mercy but loses his faith when he finds himself in a "dark cave" that turns out to the belly of a whale. Although a bonus track, the song fits with the theme of the album having to do with the rewards reaped by the wicked and the suffering of the innocent in an unjust world. (See Yadin-Israel, *The Grace of God and the Grace of Man*, for a much fuller exposition of the Book of Jonah and its relationship to this song.)

"American Land" (bonus track)

Bruce Springsteen: vocals, guitar, banjo, percussion, loops
Ron Aniello: guitar, bass, keyboards, loops, backing vocals, percussion, hurdy-gurdy

Art Baron: sousaphone, penny whistle
Charles Giordano: piano, Hammond B3 organ, celeste
Rob Lebret: backing vocals
Clif Norrell: backing vocals
Ross Petersen: backing vocals
Soozie Tyrell: violin, backing vocals
Steven Van Zandt: mandolin, backing vocals
Max Weinberg: drums

This song provides a reminder of all of the hard-working men and women who came from all over the world to build the cities and farms that made this country what it became. It is more of a celebration of the version of American history that influenced Springsteen's thinking, particularly Howard Zinn's *A People's History of the United States*. The song starts by asking, "What is this land America?" from the perspective of a presumably young man who has decided to start a new life there, as so many had done before him. But the song also contrasts this image of an America with the streets paved with gold or, in Springsteen's version, a land where "all the women wear silk and satin to their knees," while sweets grow on trees and rivers flow with gold. Instead of gold, "there's diamonds in the side-walk" and "beer flows through the faucets all night long."

Of course, the singer discovers a different reality after arriving at Ellis Island, finding "steel and fire" instead of diamonds and gold and instead of an easy life, the immigrants "worked to bones and skin" and "died in the fields and factories," while building the railroads and transforming "the American land." The song is another example of the ways in which Springsteen so adeptly juxtaposes the dream of America with its reality and, although a bonus track, it bookends effectively with the satirical "We Take Care of Our Own" at the beginning of the album. In its *Bruce Springsteen Collector's Edition* (2022), *Rolling Stone* listed "American Land" as number ninety-nine among the artist's top 100 songs.

High Hopes (Alamy) [performance photo]

HIGH HOPES

Released in January 2014, *High Hopes* comprised cover versions, outtakes, and repurposed tracks from previous Springsteen albums. Coproduced with Ron Aniello (along with Brendan O'Brien on selected tracks), *High Hopes* proved to be an enormous commercial and critical success, while also featuring new band members in guitarist Tom Morello and saxophonist Jake Clemons.

When it came to *High Hopes*'s origins, Springsteen recalled that "when I'm on tour, I'll often carry with me a collection of my unfinished music. I'll bring a few unfinished projects along that I'll pop on in the wee, wee hours after the show and listen to. I'm looking to see if there's something there whispering in my ear. I still had a nice set of songs from my production work with Brendan and night after night, they'd call to me, looking for a home. This coincided with Tom Morello's joining the band and suggesting we dust off 'High Hopes,' a song by L.A. group the Havalinas that we'd covered in the nineties."

In short order, the E Street Band took a stab at performing the song that would become the LP's title track. "As we gathered in Australia at our first rehearsal for the *Wrecking Ball* tour's resumption," said Springsteen, "I had an arrangement that I thought might work. This was going to be Tom's first stint subbing for Steve, who was busy with his acting commitments, so I wanted him to be able to put his imprint on the show. He did that. The arrangement caught fire live and we decided to cut it in a Sydney studio along with a favorite song of mine by the Australian group the Saints, 'Just Like Fire Would.' With the inclusion of these songs and studio recordings we made of 'American Skin' and 'The Ghost of Tom Joad,' a real album began to take shape. I then recorded Tom onto some of our Brendan O'Brien tracks and things really began to spark. Tom proved to be a fabulous and fascinating substitute for Steve, melding into the band seamlessly while greatly increasing our sonic palette" (Springsteen, *Born to Run*, 2016).

High Hopes is also notable for its inclusion of "American Skin (41 Shots)," a powerful response to the killing of Amadou Diallo, an unarmed African immigrant who was shot by the police in New York City in 1999. The song features a haunting melody and powerful lyrics that speak to the ongoing struggle for racial justice in America. Springsteen's latest album concluded with "Dream Baby Dream," a song that had been originally recorded in 1979 by electro-punk band Suicide. For Springsteen, the unabashed sentimentality and optimism of "Dream Baby Dream" made for a perfect conclusion to an album devoted to reveling in justice and ferreting out the good that exists at humanity's heart.

HISTORICAL CONTEXT

As was the case with the *Seeger Sessions*, Bruce Springsteen's 2014 album *High Hopes* has a historical context that extends to well before the date of its release. In fact, given the eclectic material and assorted provenances of the songs that appear on the album, one might say that it is a work without a specific historical context, or at least a readily identifiable one. Of course, like all works of art or literature, by virtue of its release into a specific time and place it becomes part of its time, whatever the sources of inspiration or origin of the material included on it. Springsteen put the album together while on his *Wrecking Ball* tour and, also like the *Seeger Sessions*, he seems to have done so more out of a desire to have some fun, do some covers of songs he liked, and revisit some of his earlier material, including unreleased songs from *The Rising* sessions and new versions of "The Ghost of Tom Joad" and "American Skin (41 Shots)." The album received mixed reviews and is generally not thought of particularly highly by Springsteen fans, although David Fricke in his review in *Rolling Stone* praised it for its "rock-soul dynamite and finely drawn pathos bound by familiar, urgent themes (national crisis, private struggle, the daily striving for more perfect union) and the certain-victor's force in Springsteen's singing." Even in his newer material on the album, Springsteen revisited earlier concerns; prompted by a visit to the Vietnam War Memorial in Washington, DC, in "The Wall," Springsteen remembers the young men from his old stomping grounds who died in Vietnam.

As for the more immediate context surrounding the release of the album, things had not changed appreciably in the country since the release of *Wrecking Ball* almost two years earlier. The economy showed some further signs of recovery, with unemployment dropping to its lowest levels since 2009. However, most people who lost their jobs during the recession did not return to them, but rather had to find work in lower-paying and temporary positions. With the United States, having withdrawn combat troops from Iraq in 2011, there was talk of a total withdrawal from Afghanistan, though we now know that would not take place until 2021. Barack Obama had won reelection in November 2012, but his administration had become mired in congressional gridlock, with only the controversial passage of his health care program, known (usually derisively) as "Obamacare," to show as a major legislative achievement.

Closer to home, the latest scandal exposing political corruption involved New Jersey governor Chris Christie, a huge Springsteen fan, whose aides had ordered lane closures on the George Washington Bridge in September 2013 in an effort to exact revenge on a political opponent. Springsteen denounced Christie and lampooned him in a parody of "Born to Run" on *The Tonight Show Starring Jimmy Fallon*. People joked about Christie possibly shutting down the Tunnel of Love in response, in reference to Springsteen's 1987 release. In short, even though on *High Hopes* Springsteen did not comment on its times in the same way he had on *Wrecking Ball*, the themes and the material on the album were still relevant—they just failed to have the impact or gain the attention that some of his earlier releases did.

PRODUCTION

Released on January 14, 2014, Columbia Records

Produced by Bruce Springsteen, Brendan O'Brien, and Ron Aniello

Engineered by Ross Petersen, Toby Scott, and Nick DiDia

Mixed by Bob Clearmountain at Mix This!, Mix LA, Henson Recording Studios, and Southern Tracks

Mixing Assistant: Brandon Duncan

Mastered by Bob Ludwig at Gateway Mastering

Recorded at Thrill Hill Studios, March to June 2013

PERSONNEL

Bruce Springsteen: vocals, electric and acoustic guitars, percussion, organ, mandolin, synthesizers, vibraphone, piano, banjo, harmonium, drums

Tawatha Agee: backing vocals

Ron Aniello: bass, synthesizer, acoustic guitar, drum loop, percussion, synthesizer, Farfisa organ, vibraphone, accordion

Sam Bardfeld: violin

Roy Bittan: piano, organ

Everett Bradley: percussion, backing vocals

Clarence Clemons: tenor saxophone

Jake Clemons: tenor saxophone

Barry Danielian: trumpet

Danny Federici: organ

Keith Fluitt: backing vocals

Josh Freese: drums

Clark Gayton: trombone

Charles Giordano: organ, accordion

Stan Harrison: saxophone

John James: backing vocals

Jeff Kievit: piccolo trumpet

Curtis King Jr.: backing vocals

Nils Lofgren: electric guitar, pedal steel guitar, mandolin, backing vocals

Ed Manion: saxophone

Cindy Mizelle: backing vocals

Michelle Moore: backing vocals

Tom Morello: guitar, backing vocals

Curt Ramm: trumpet, cornet

Patti Scialfa: backing vocals

Evan Springsteen: backing vocals

Jessica Springsteen: backing vocals

Sam Springsteen: backing vocals

Garry Tallent: electric bass

Al Thornton: backing vocals

Scott Tibbs: horn orchestration

Soozie Tyrell: backing vocals, violin

Cillian Vallely: uilleann pipes, high and low whistle

Steven Van Zandt: guitar, backing vocals

Max Weinberg: drums, percussion

Brenda White-King: backing vocals

The Magic String Section: Eddie Horst (string arrangements, conductor); Justin Bruns, Jay Christy, Sheela Iyengar, John Meisner, William Pu, Christopher Pulgram, Olga Shpitko, and Kenn Wagner (violins); Amy Chang, Tania Maxwell Clements, and Lachlan McBane (violas); Karen Freer, Charae Krueger, and Daniel Laufer (cellos)

New York String Section: Rob Mathes (arranger and conductor); Lisa Kim (concertmaster); Quan Ge, Hyunju Lee, Jessica Lee, Ann Lehman, Joanna Maurer, Suzanne Ornstein, Annaliesa Place, David Southorn, Jeanine Wynton, and Sharon Yamada (violins); Maurycy Banaszek, Désirée Elsevier, Shmuel Katz, and Robert Rinehart (violas); Maria Kitsopoulos, Alan Stepansky, and Ru Pei Yeh (cellos)

COVER ART AND PACKAGING

Design: Michelle Holme

Photography: Danny Clinch, assisted by Edward Smith and Nyra Lang

TRACK LISTING

All songs by Bruce Springsteen, except where indicated.

1. "High Hopes" (Tim Scott McConnell)
2. "Harry's Place"
3. "American Skin (41 Shots)"
4. "Just Like Fire Would" (Chris Bailey)
5. "Down in the Hole"
6. "Heaven's Wall"
7. "Frankie Fell in Love"
8. "This Is Your Sword"
9. "Hunter of Invisible Game"
10. "The Ghost of Tom Joad"
11. "The Wall"
12. "Dream Baby Dream" (Martin Rev and Alan Vega)

UNRELEASED OUTTAKES

"American Beauty": released on *American Beauty* EP (2014)

"Hey Blue Eyes": released on *American Beauty* EP (2014)

"Hurry Up Sundown": released on *American Beauty* EP (2014)

"Mary Mary": released on *American Beauty* EP (2014)

CONTEMPORARY REVIEWS

Ian Gittins (*Virgin Media Music*, January 13, 2014): "Inevitably, being Springsteen, there are highlights. 'The Wall' is a rambunctious tribute to his childhood hero, Walter Cichon, the singer in 1960s New Jersey bar band the Motifs who was lost in action in Vietnam; the righteous 'American Skin (41 Shots)' was originally written in reaction to the 1999 shooting of immigrant Amadou Diallo by New York cops, and is now re-dedicated to Trayvon Martin. Rage Against the Machine's Tom Morello appears throughout and duets on a reworking of Springsteen's classic protest song 'The Ghost of Tom Joad', while covers range from a throbbing roustabout through Australian punks the Saints' 'Just Like Fire Would' to a visceral take on Suicide's drone anthem, 'Dream Baby Dream.' Nevertheless, this album may be one for hardcore fans more than floating voters.

David Fricke (*Rolling Stone*, January 6, 2014): "Bruce Springsteen's 18th studio album is a portrait of the artist at the top of his 21st-century game: rock-soul dynamite and finely drawn pathos bound by familiar, urgent themes (national crisis, private struggle, the daily striving for more perfect union) and the certain-victor's force in Springsteen's singing. *High Hopes* is also a deep look back over Springsteen's past decade, his best onstage and record since the first, with a keen eye turned forward. The cumulative effect of this mass of old, borrowed, blue and renewed—covers, recent outtakes and redefining takes on two classics—is retrospect with a cutting edge, running like one of the singer's epic look-ma-no-set-list gigs: full of surprises, all with a reason for being there. Much of *High Hopes* comes from the what-was-he-thinking shelf: unreleased songs cut for albums going back to 2002's *The Rising*, revived with freshening parts. It's hard to see how 'Frankie Fell in Love,' a frat-rock riot, and the letter from rock bottom 'Down in the Hole' ('My Hometown' with less light) ever got the

chop. But Springsteen effectively recasts this material with the folk-soul-gospel-army might of his current E Street Big Band. The background-vocal choir puts a literal finishing touch on the warrior-hymn charge of 'Heaven's Wall.' In the gangsters' convention 'Harry's Place,' recent E Street recruit Tom Morello fires chain-saw bursts of guitar across meaty peals of sax originally laid down by the late Clarence Clemons. And that's Danny Federici, who died in 2008, playing organ on 'The Wall,' a requiem for one of Springsteen's Jersey-bar-band mentors, underscoring the singer's belief in the unbroken chains running through his band."

PROMOTION

On January 14, 2014, NBC devoted the entire episode of *Late Night with Jimmy Fallon* to Springsteen's new LP. Springsteen and the E Street Band performed "High Hopes," "Heaven's Wall," and "Just Like Fire Would." Springsteen and Fallon also performed a skit in which they mocked Governor Chris Christie for the scandal associated with George Washington Bridge lane closure scandal. The skit included a song parody titled "Governor Christie Traffic Jam" and performed to the tune of "Born to Run."

On January 12, 2014, the CBS television series *The Good Wife* featured excerpts from three *High Hopes* songs: the title track, "Hunter of Invisible Game," and "The Ghost of Tom Joad." The crossover initiative marked an unusual instance in Springsteen's career, with CBS hoping to draw Baby Boomers to *The Good Wife* and Springsteen seeking greater exposure for his latest LP.

The *High Hopes* tour spanned from January through May 2014, consisting of thirty-four concerts and earning $65 million in receipts.

CHART ACTION

Billboard 200: number one.

Released on January 14, 2014, *High Hopes* debuted at number one on February 1, unseating the soundtrack for *Frozen* from the top spot.

High Hopes spent eighteen weeks on the *Billboard* charts.

COMMENTS FROM SPRINGSTEEN AND HIS CIRCLE

Springsteen: "This is music I always felt needed to be released. From the gangsters of 'Harry's Place,' the ill-prepared roomies on 'Frankie Fell in Love' (shades of Steve and I bumming together in our Asbury Park apartment), the travelers in the wasteland of 'Hunter of Invisible Game,' to the soldier and his visiting friend in 'The Wall,' I felt they all deserved a home and a hearing" (*High Hopes* liner notes).

Ron Aniello: "Bruce and I were working tirelessly, though communications was a huge obstacle between us when he was on tour. But the day before he flew to Australia, he came to Los Angeles. We were doing mixes, and he was posing for the pictures, too. He was working his ass off, just working his ass off. I've never seen someone his age work like that. He put in a 15-hour day in the studio" (*Rolling Stone*, December 30, 2013).

SONG ANALYSES

"High Hopes"
Bruce Springsteen: vocals, guitar, percussion, vibraphone
Ron Aniello: drum loops
Roy Bittan: piano
Everett Bradley: percussion, backing vocals
Clark Gayton: trombone

Charles Giordano: accordion
Stan Harrison: saxophone
Curtis King Jr.: backing vocals
Nils Lofgren: guitar
Ed Manion: saxophone
Cindy Mizelle: backing vocals
Michelle Moore: backing vocals
Tom Morello: guitar
Curt Ramm: trumpet
Patti Scialfa: backing vocals
Garry Tallent: bass
Soozie Tyrell: backing vocals
Max Weinberg: drums

One of three cover songs on the album, "High Hopes" was written by Tim Scott McConnell for his 1987 album *The High Lonesome Sound*. It is not surprising that its lyric would resonate with Springsteen, with the singer poised between the disappointments of the real world and the hope for a better future for himself and his children, a common theme for Springsteen. The song also has the same kind of spiritual resonances found in much of Springsteen's work. It operates as a kind of prayer: "Give me help, give me strength, give a soul a night of fearless sleep."

At the same time, the singer wants to know the cost of having the kind of life he hopes to live. "Don't you know these days you pay for everything," a sentiment that resonated as much in 2014 as it had in the late 1980s, in the waning years of the Reagan administration. In that way, the title of the album could relate to the "high hopes" that accompanied the election of Barack Obama to the US presidency in 2008—"hope" was a key word used during his campaign—and the disappointment even many of his supporters felt by the midpoint of his second term.

CHART ACTION
Billboard Hot 100: did not chart. The song registered a number-fifteen showing on the magazine's Adult Alternative Songs chart.

"High Hopes" was released on November 25, 2013. The number-one song that week was Lorde's "Royals."

"Harry's Place"

Bruce Springsteen: vocals, guitar
Roy Bittan: piano
Clarence Clemons: tenor saxophone
Nils Lofgren: guitar
Tom Morello: guitar
Garry Tallent: bass
Max Weinberg: drums
The Magic String Section: Eddie Horst (string arrangements, conductor); Justin Bruns, Jay Christy, Sheela Iyengar, John Meisner, William Pu, Christopher Pulgram, Olga Shpitko, and Kenn Wagner (violins); Amy Chang, Tania Maxwell Clements, and Lachlan McBane (violas); Karen Freer, Charae Krueger, and Daniel Laufer (cellos)

This disconsolate song about the endemic problem of drug addiction suggests that the true wielders of power are those who control the supply of what so many desperate people crave and need, even to the point where the leaders of church and state look the other way, if they are not directly involved in illicit drugs and backstreet crime. "Mayor Connor's on the couch, Father McGowan's at the bar, Chief Horton's at the door checkin' who the f-ck you are." At the same time that he deploys these specific names, and refers to "Harry" as the one who owns the streets and makes the rules, Springsteen also makes clear that the problem is social and systematic, and that even "if he didn't exist it'd all go down just the same." The song also suggests that an individual's drug problem—"the one little weakness you allow yourself"—has particular roots and causes unique to that person, but that the totality of all of those people who feel that way fuels the "blood and money spit [that] shines Harry's crown"; in other words, fuels the drug trade that causes the death and destruction of so many people's lives.

"American Skin (41 Shots)"

Bruce Springsteen: vocals, guitar, percussion
Ron Aniello: bass, synthesizer, guitar, drum loop, percussion, organ, vibraphone
Roy Bittan: piano
Jake Clemons: tenor saxophone
Barry Danielian: trumpet
Clark Gayton: trombone
Charles Giordano: organ
Stan Harrison: saxophone
Curtis King Jr.: backing vocals
Nils Lofgren: backing vocals
Ed Manion: saxophone
Cindy Mizelle: backing vocals
Tom Morello: guitar, backing vocals
Curt Ramm: trumpet
Patti Scialfa: backing vocals
Scott Tibbs: horn orchestration
Soozie Tyrell: backing vocals
Steven Van Zandt: guitar, backing vocals
Max Weinberg: drums

Springsteen wrote this song in the aftermath the violent shooting death by police of a black immigrant from Guinea named Amadou Diallo in New York City on February 4, 1999. The fact that Springsteen included it on this album speaks to the fact that he did not consider the problem of race and the targeting of African Americans by police a thing of the past in 2014, anticipating the growing Black Lives Matter movement that culminated in the nationwide protests against the murder of African American George Floyd by a Minneapolis police officer on May 25, 2020. Springsteen originally took a lot of heat for this song, but here he reminded his listeners of a tragic death that resulted when police officers mistakenly thought Diallo was reaching for a gun instead of the wallet he actually sought to retrieve—a death that many people might have otherwise forgotten. The political climate was different in 2014 and the song had perhaps lost some of its initial shock value, but it fit on an album that largely details the disappointments and shattered hopes of many people who yearned for a better and fairer America that was still very much a work in progress and in some ways seemed to be in regression.

"Just Like Fire Would"
Bruce Springsteen: vocals, guitar
Ron Aniello: 12-string guitar
Roy Bittan: piano
Everett Bradley: percussion, backing vocals
Jake Clemons: saxophone
Barry Danielian: trumpet
Clark Gayton: trombone
Charles Giordano: organ
Stan Harrison: saxophone
Jeff Kievit: piccolo trumpet
Curtis King Jr.: backing vocals
Nils Lofgren: guitar
Ed Manion: saxophone
Cindy Mizelle: backing vocals
Michelle Moore: backing vocals
Tom Morello: guitar
Curt Ramm: trumpet
Patti Scialfa: backing vocals
Garry Tallent: bass
Steven Van Zandt: backing vocals
Max Weinberg: drums
New York String Section: Rob Mathes (arranger and conductor); Lisa Kim (concertmaster); Quan Ge, Hyunju Lee, Jessica Lee, Ann Lehman, Joanna Maurer, Suzanne Ornstein, Annaliesa Place, David Southorn, Jeanine Wynton, and Sharon Yamada (violins), Maurycy Banaszek, Désirée Elsevier, Shmuel Katz, and Robert Rinehart (violas), Maria Kitsopoulos, Alan Stepansky, and Ru Pei Yeh (cellos)

The second of three cover songs on the album, "Just like Fire Would" was written by Chris J. Bailey in 1986 for his Australian alternative rock band, the Saints. The lyric could have resonated with Springsteen as a performer obsessed with working hard to please his audience and redeem himself through the splendor and

ecstasy of his live performances. "I go to work and I earn my pay Lord," the singer claims, "The sweat it falls to the ground." This could be a perfect description of the lengthy and passionate concerts given by Springsteen and the E Street Band. But, like similar songs dealing with life on the road as a rock star, such as Bob Seger's "Turn the Page" or Jackson Browne's "The Load Out," Bailey here captures the loneliness of the motel room and the feelings of displacement and ennui that come with the downtime involved in moving from town to town. The lines, "I drank the wine that they left on the table [because] I knew the morning was too far," conclude the first and last (repeated) verse of the song. In the third verse the singer refers to the "500 miles I have gone today / Tomorrow's 500 more." The title refers to the singer burning up and, perhaps, burning out.

"Down in the Hole"
Bruce Springsteen: vocals, guitar, banjo
Clarence Clemons: tenor saxophone
Danny Federici: organ
Patti Scialfa: backing vocals
Evan Springsteen: backing vocals
Jessica Springsteen: backing vocals
Sam Springsteen: backing vocals
Garry Tallent: bass
Soozie Tyrell: violin
Max Weinberg: drums

With "Down in the Hole," Springsteen returns to the theme of depression, although in this song it does have a specific cause, presumably a broken romance, although the lyric could refer to the loss of any friend or loved one through death, separation, or absence. The song begins, "Sun comes up every morning, but it ain't no friend," which immediately sets the tone for the rest of the song. Throughout the lyric, the singer struggles through his day-to-day existence, but cannot seem to escape the metaphorical hole in which he finds himself. It is commonly said that the first thing to do when you find yourself in a hole is to stop digging, but here instead of trying to escape the hole he is in, the singer insists that he is going to keep on digging "until I get you back." Originally an outtake recorded during *The Rising Sessions* in 2002, the song is another example of one that might have arisen out of a specific situation but whose lyric is in fact timeless and deals with a universal situation.

"Heaven's Wall"
Bruce Springsteen: vocals, guitar, bass, percussion loop, organ, synthesizers
Tawatha Agee: backing vocals
Ron Aniello: percussion loops, synthesizer, Farfisa organ
Sam Bardfeld: violin
Everett Bradley: percussion
Keith Fluitt: backing vocals
John James: backing vocals
Curtis King Jr.: backing vocals
Cindy Mizelle: backing vocals
Tom Morello: guitar
Patti Scialfa: backing vocals
Garry Tallent: bass
Al Thornton: backing vocals
Soozie Tyrell: backing vocals
Max Weinberg: drums
Brenda White-King: backing vocals
New York String Section: Rob Mathes (arranger and conductor); Lisa Kim (concertmaster); Quan Ge, Hyunju Lee, Jessica Lee, Ann Lehman, Joanna Maurer, Suzanne Ornstein, Annaliesa Place, David Southorn, Jeanine Wynton, and Sharon Yamada (violins); Maurycy Banaszek, Désirée Elsevier, Shmuel Katz, and Robert Rinehart (violas); Maria Kitsopoulos, Alan Stepansky, and Ru Pei Yeh (cellos)

"Heaven's Wall" offers another Springsteen song with strong biblical references from the perspective of people from the Bible who hungered for entry into the Promised Land, which can and often does serve as a metaphor for heaven itself. "Heaven's Wall" is what separates those waiting for entry, which in this song are the Jews as God's chosen people, designated here as "men of Gideon," "men of Saul," and "all sons of Abraham." The song has a gospel-like chorus exhorting its listeners to "raise your hand" (repeated multiple times) "and together we'll walk into Canaan land."

"Heaven's Wall" draws on the example of Jonah as a reminder that God is watching over us and begins with the New Testament example of the "woman waiting at the well," referring to the story in the Gospel of John about Jesus's conversation with a Samaritan woman in which he revealed himself as the Jewish messiah and told her things about herself that truly amazed and convinced her. Her subsequent testimony to the encounter is summarized in the song in the lines "She said he'll heal the blind, raise the dead, cure the sickness out of you." For all of Springsteen's ambivalence about his Catholic upbringing, he never hesitated to draw on it or the Bible as inspirations for his songs and this is one of the most obvious examples of that.

"Frankie Fell in Love"
Bruce Springsteen: vocals, guitar, percussion, organ, mandolin
Ron Aniello: bass, guitar
Sam Bardfeld: violin
Roy Bittan: piano
Steven Van Zandt: backing vocals
Max Weinberg: drums

Even though the character of "Frankie" in the song is clearly a woman, speculation about the identity has centered on Obediah "Obie" Dziedzic, whom Springsteen had known since the mid-1960s and who worked for him in several capacities, including as his personal chef, over the years before Dziedzic's death in 2017. This could explain the line in the song that "she ain't gonna be cookin' for the likes of us." Springsteen himself described the vibe of the song as intended to recall his early days hanging out with Steven Van Zandt in Asbury Park. The most interesting lines in the song posit Shakespeare and Einstein having a beer together, with Shakespeare explaining to Einstein that love is not a mathematical equation, "it's one and one makes three, That's why it's poetry." The song also carries the message that if Frankie fell in love, then anyone can; "Yea it's gonna happen to you," the singer affirms.

"This Is Your Sword"

Bruce Springsteen: vocals, guitar, synthesizers, piano, banjo, mandolin
Ron Aniello: bass, synthesizer, guitar
Sam Bardfeld: violin
Roy Bittan: piano, organ
Josh Freese: drums
Patti Scialfa: backing vocals
Soozie Tyrell: backing vocals
Cillian Vallely: uilleann pipes, high and low whistle
Steven Van Zandt: backing vocals

In "This Is Your Sword," Springsteen offers encouragement to his listeners to stay strong and not give in to despair, no matter how dark the times. He bequeaths them a metaphorical sword, the sword of love, the sword or righteousness, "The sword of our fathers with lessons hard taught." Although the song has biblical overtones, its references are vaguer than those, for example, in "Heaven's Wall." Springsteen holds out hope that "the age of miracles will come along," that better times lie ahead, that good will triumph over evil. In the

meantime, he exhorts us to "give all the love that you have in your soul" and the power of love will become the sword that shields and protects you from the despair and cynicism to which this world can so easily lead.

"Hunter of Invisible Game"

Bruce Springsteen: vocals, guitar
Tom Morello: guitar
Garry Tallent: bass
Soozie Tyrell: violin
Max Weinberg: drums
The Magic String Section: Eddie Horst (string arrangement, conductor); Justin Bruns, Jay Christy, Sheela Iyengar, John Meisner, William Pu, Christopher Pulgram, Olga Shpitko, and Kenn Wagner (violins); Amy Chang, Tania Maxwell Clements, and Lachlan McBane (violas); Karen Freer, Charae Krueger, and Daniel Laufer (cellos)

"Hunter of Invisible Game" presents yet another example of how the meaning of Springsteen's songs deepens when considered in juxtaposition to the songs that come before and after them on his albums. Following "This is Your Sword," this song reinforces the message that we must keep faith and arm ourselves with love in the face of even the most cataclysmic events that are always lurking to rock or even destroy our world. The first verse makes direct reference to building an ark like the one Noah built in the book of Genesis, right down to the "gopher wood and pitch" the Bible says he used to construct it.

The second verse refers to "empty cities and burnin' plains, perhaps a reference to the destruction of Sodom and Gomorrah, also from the book of Genesis. The third verse seems to refer to the threat of the apocalypse, with reference to "the beast" (a common pseudonym for the Antichrist), as the singer travels "through the bone yard rattle and black smoke." And yet, he concludes in the third and fourth verses that "strength is vanity and time is illusion," and all that really matters is love, both sexually and spiritually. In the here and now, "Your skin touches mine, what else to explain." Then, "When the hour of deliverance comes to us all . . . There's a kingdom of love waiting to be reclaimed." Just as the sword of the previous song is a symbol of the power of love, so the game the singer hunts in this song is invisible and is vanquished through love rather than action or violence.

"The Ghost of Tom Joad"
Bruce Springsteen: lead vocals, guitar
Ron Aniello: bass, synthesizer
Roy Bittan: piano
Charles Giordano: accordion
Nils Lofgren: pedal steel guitar, mandolin
Tom Morello: lead vocals, guitar
Soozie Tyrell: violin
Max Weinberg: drums

Springsteen likely included the previously released "The Ghost of Tom Joad" on *High Hopes* to reaffirm that its message remained relevant two decades after its original release. Lines such as "Wherever there's a cop beatin' a guy / Wherever a hungry new born baby cries," certainly applied in the 2010s as much as they had in the 1990s. Perhaps Springsteen included the song here to amplify the inclusion on the album of "American Skin (41 Shots)," another song written in the 1990s. The version on this album is different, too; Springsteen sounds even angrier and more passionate than in the somewhat restrained yet soulful version included on the earlier album. The song has aged well, and it will probably continue to do so as the human condition is likely to remain somewhat static for the near future.

"The Wall"
Bruce Springsteen: vocals, guitar, drums
Ron Aniello: synthesizer, accordion
Roy Bittan: piano
Danny Federici: organ
Nils Lofgren: guitar
Curt Ramm: cornet
Patti Scialfa: backing vocals
Garry Tallent: bass
Max Weinberg: percussion

In the liner notes for the album, Springsteen credits fellow singer-songwriter Joe Grushecky for the idea and title of this song, which concerns the Vietnam War Memorial in Washington, DC. "The Wall" honors all of the men and women who fought and died in Vietnam, but it also personalizes Springsteen's own experience watching people whom he knew leave for Southeast Asia. "I remember you in your Marine uniform, laughin' / Laughin' at your ship out party," he writes in the first verse. That verse concludes with the line, "I read Robert McNamara says he's sorry," a reference to the former secretary of defense's book *In Retrospect: The Tragedy and Lessons of Vietnam*, which became a bestseller in 1995.

The rest of the song deals with a visit to the stone black wall with the names of all the soldiers who died in Vietnam engraved on it, an annual ritual that the singer reproaches himself for missing last year in which he would leave cigarettes and a bottle of beer by the name of his friend Walter Cichon, who goes unnamed in the song. Of course, the lack of a specific name helps to universalize the song for its listeners, a song that ends with a bitter reproach of a government and its leaders who sacrificed so many lives: "Apology and forgiveness / Got no place here at all / Here at the wall."

"Dream Baby Dream"

Bruce Springsteen: vocals, guitar, synthesizers, piano, mandolin, harmonium
Ron Aniello: percussion loops, bass, synthesizer, guitar
Roy Bittan: piano
Barry Danielian: trumpet
Clark Gayton: trombone
Stan Harrison: saxophone
Ed Manion: saxophone
Tom Morello: guitar
Curt Ramm: trumpet

The album concludes with the third cover song, this one a ballad written in 1979 by Martin Rev and Alan Vega and released by their electro-punk band, Suicide. Springsteen wrote in the liner notes for the album that the songs here represented "music I always felt needed to be released." Yet for such an eclectic collection of songs written at various points in Springsteen's career, the album contains a surprising coherence that must have resulted from his usual meticulous and painstaking thought about which songs to include on the album and in which order they should appear. The album appropriately enough ends with "Dream Baby Dream," a song that leaves the listener with a feeling of tranquility and peace, and a simple lyric that repeats the message of many of Springsteen's own songs, including some that appear on this album: keep on dreaming, open your heart, and try to find happiness amid the tears that life invariably brings.

WESTERN STARS

With the release of his nineteenth studio album *Western Stars* in June 2019, Bruce Springsteen elevated the trajectory of his magisterial career yet again. A great American storyteller in the vein of Woody Guthrie and Bob Dylan, Springsteen dares to be earnest in an age of mind-numbing cynicism.

During the album's production, Springsteen playfully described the sound of *Western Stars* as "Grand Canyon music." As with the national park's cavernous, awe-inspiring immensity, *Western Stars* accentuates Springsteen's character-driven narratives with the cinematic power of honest-to-goodness orchestration. But in truth, *Western Stars* has far less in common with classical music, with Springsteen eschewing such ornate, highbrow sounds for the grand sweep and lush arrangements of Southern California pop in the early 1970s.

As musical palettes go, drawing on the heyday of the singer-songwriter era proves to be a deft choice for this album. With its powerful orchestral backdrop, *Western Stars* is mindful of Glen Campbell's classic collaborations with Jimmy Webb on such hit songs as "Galveston" and "Wichita Lineman," among others.

A musical and lyrical tour de force, *Western Stars* offers one of Springsteen's most coherent and carefully plotted LPs.

Coproduced by Springsteen and Ron Aniello, *Western Stars* offers a powerful, sobering narrative about life in these United States. By the end of the LP, Springsteen has succeeded in bridging the wide-eyed optimism of his earlier self to the universalizing experiences of his everyman American characters. Featuring standout performance from a host of musicians—including wife Patti Scialfa, Jon Brion, David Sancious, and Soozie Tyrell—the album was brilliantly mixed by Tom Elmhurst, who imbues Springsteen's narrative settings with expansive vistas of emotional power and grace at every turn.

For many listeners, *Western Stars* may understandably sound and feel like a much-needed nostalgia trip to a simpler time and place in comparison with our conflicted present. But for Springsteen, evoking a 1970s ambience is not merely an act of genre experimentation, but rather, the setting for communicating even greater truths about the highpoints and heartbreaks of human experience.

HISTORICAL CONTEXT

Despite his strong local roots in New Jersey, Springsteen has long had a fascination with the American West, both the green valleys and urban landscapes of California and the unsparing and vast expanses of the desert. On *Western Stars*, his nineteenth studio album, released on June 14, 2019, he uses the West as a backdrop for a new set of stories he wants to tell about characters who have much in common with those he introduced on his early albums, despite a shift in locale.

At a time when the United States was embroiled in a culture war over the meaning of American history and was approaching another critical election between the controversial and divisive incumbent Donald J. Trump and a yet-to-be chosen Democratic challenger, Springsteen looked West and to the past in yet another effort to define symbolically if not literally what it meant to live in America in the twenty-first century. Approaching seventy, Springsteen seemed to have the most in common with Senator Bernie Sanders, the Vermont liberal and presidential candidate eight years his senior, who remained committed to basic causes of economic justice and racial equality while largely abstaining from the culture wars that seemed increasingly unbridgeable. On *Western Stars*, for all of the ways in which it differs from his previous albums, he did not depart from the trajectory his material had taken over the years, including returning to the plight and disillusionment of the returning war veteran in "Tucson Train."

By 2019, Springsteen himself had become a legendary American figure, even performing a one-man Broadway show to sold-out audiences, in which he reflected on and revisited his own past, career, and musical legacy. But *Western Stars*, with its lush pop orchestral arrangements, soulful vocal performances, and lyrics that combine effective storytelling with philosophical insights and wisdom that comes with age, indicated that his career was far from over. Springsteen elaborated on many of these reflections in monologues he included in the beautiful and moving film he made to accompany the album. His use of the West as a metaphor shines through on songs such as "Chasin' Wild Horses," which refers to the desire to pursue an elusive and out-of-reach dream instead of living up to one's responsibilities and dealing with the more prosaic realities that bound our life but offer fulfillment if we seek our happiness within them.

But Springsteen's fascination with the West also had its roots in the California sound of so many of the pop-rock groups he listened to as a teenager: the Beach Boys, the Doors, Buffalo Springfield, the Byrds, and even the pop standards written by Burt Bacharach that appeared so often on the Top Forty in the 1960s and early 1970s. The album, therefore, despite its uniqueness in the Springsteen canon, actually reflects a combination of past musical influences, echoes of his own personal history, and his usual concern with characters and stories that reflect important aspects of the American experience.

PRODUCTION

Released on June 14, 2019, Columbia Records
Produced by Ron Aniello and Bruce Springsteen
Engineered by Ron Aniello and Toby Scott
Recording Assistants: Rob Lebret and Ross Petersen
Mixed by Tom Elmhirst at Electric Lady Studios
Mixing assistant: Joe Visciano
Mastered by Bob Ludwig at Gateway Mastering
Recorded at Thrill Hill Studio, 2018–2019

PERSONNEL

Bruce Springsteen: vocals, acoustic guitar, glockenspiel, synth strings, banjo, percussion, electric guitar, Hammond B3 organ, piano, orchestral samples, celeste, organ solo, 12-string guitar, mellotron
Ron Aniello: upright bass, piano, electric guitar, percussion, vibraphone, bass, synth strings, orchestral samples, acoustic guitar, drums, Hammond B3 organ, celeste, loops, synth, background vocals
Alden Banta: bassoon
Jon Brion: electric guitar, Moog synthesizer, drums, celeste, Farfisa organ, timpani
Lenny Castro: conga, shaker, tambourine
Matt Chamberlain: drums
Barry Danielian: trumpet
Rachel Drehmann: French horn
Clark Gayton: trombone
Charles Giordano: piano, accordion
Curtis King Jr.: backing vocals
Matthew Koma: backing vocals
Rob Lebret: electric guitar, baritone guitar
Greg Leisz: pedal steel guitar
Dan Levine: trombone
Ed Manion: saxophone
Cindy Mizelle: backing vocals
Michelle Moore: backing vocals
Marc Muller: lap and pedal steel guitars
Gunnar Olsen: drums
Charles Pillow: oboe
Curt Ramm: trumpet, flugelhorn
Marty Rifkin: pedal steel guitar
Matt Rollings: piano
David Sancious: piano, Hammond B3 organ
Patti Scialfa: backing vocals
Toby Scott: loop, programming
Andrew Sterman: flute
Leelanee Sterrett: French horn
Soozie Tyrell: violin, backing vocals
Luis Villalobos: violin
The Avatar Strings: Rob Mathes (string arrangement, conductor); Lisa Kim, Hyunju Lee, Elizabeth Lim-Dutton, Joanna Maurer, Suzanne Ornstein, Annaliesa Place, Emily Popham, Sharon Yamada, and Jungsun Yoo (violins); Désirée Elsevier, Vivek Kamath, and Robert Rinehart (violas); Alan Stepansky and Nathan Vickery (cellos)

Stone Hill Strings: Scott Tibbs (string arrangement, conductor); Lisa Kim, Hyunju Lee, and Joanna Maurer (violins); Shmuel Katz and Rebecca Young (violas); Alan Stepansky (cello)

COVER ART AND PACKAGING

Design: Michelle Holme
Photography: Kalle Gustafsson (cover) and Danny Clinch

TRACK LISTING

All songs composed by Bruce Springsteen.

1. "Hitch Hikin'"
2. "The Wayfarer"
3. "Tucson Train"
4. "Western Stars"
5. "Sleepy Joe's Café"
6. "Drive Fast (The Stuntman)"
7. "Chasin' Wild Horses"
8. "Sundown"
9. "Somewhere North of Nashville"
10. "Stones"
11. "There Goes My Miracle"
12. "Hello Sunshine"
13. "Moonlight Motel"

CONTEMPORARY REVIEWS

Will Hermes (*Rolling Stone*, May 30, 2019): "A number of the songs here straddle the classic and the cliché, as country songs often do, though they're not country, exactly. Taken individually, they can also seem thin. As the singer himself cops at one point, 'Same old cliché, a wanderer on his way.' But framed by the album's larger themes, they hit home, deepened by a seasoned actor's self-awareness. *Western Stars* shows Springsteen pulling back the curtain on his craft in much the same way *Springsteen on Broadway* did. In fact, in its elliptical narratives, it might have the makings of a good musical itself."

Sam Sodomsky (*Pitchfork*, June 14, 2009): "The voices in *Western Stars* are old and restless, lost and wandering. On the title track, Bruce Springsteen sings from the perspective of an actor who once worked with John Wayne but now mostly does commercials—credit cards, Viagra. Elsewhere, we meet a stuntman whose body has been destroyed by the job, a lonely widower idling in his old parking spot, and a failed country songwriter wondering if any of the sacrifices he made in his youth were worth it. Sung in a defeated growl, this latter track is among the shortest, starkest things that Springsteen has ever recorded: an acknowledgment of how quickly a song—and life—can pass by. That song is called 'Somewhere North of Nashville,' and it's an outlier on Springsteen's 19th studio album, both geographically and musically. On the rest of the record, Springsteen, with producer Ron Aniello, aims to conjure the golden expanse of the American West, with sweeping orchestral accompaniments unlike anything in his catalog. Springsteen albums are usually grand affairs, but he's never made one that sounds so vast and luxurious throughout. Paired with the down-and-out characters who haunt its mountains and canyons, the purposefully anachronistic arrangements—recalling jukeboxes, FM radios, sepia-toned montages, faded memories—carry an elegiac tone. It's been a long time since popular music sounded like this, and it ties these characters to an era as much as a place."

Kenneth Womack (*Salon*, June 14, 2019): "The album's song cycle kicks into gear—and without preamble, no less—with 'Hitch Hikin',' the story of a free-wheeling wanderer living out his dreams and curiosities on the Southwest's wind-swept highways. For the narrator, it's a decidedly simpler time, a place where 'Maps don't do much for me, friend / I follow the weather and the wind.' By the time that 'The Wayfarer' roars to life, the lonely realities and inherent dangers of being an unchecked rambler have begun to fracture the sunny optimism of Springsteen's narrator. 'Same sad story, love and glory, going 'round and 'round / Some old cliché, a wanderer on his way, slippin' from town to town.' . . . Western Stars' forward momentum continues unabated with "Tucson Train," the moment when Springsteen's wayfarer gives way to the tensions and anxiousness of ill-timed love. But with the title track and "Sleepy Joe's Café," the narrator regains his youthful whimsy, if only briefly, under the big sky of the Southwest, where he dances the night away at a folksy road-side bar. . . . Brimming with regret and felled by his own ill temper, Springsteen's narrator hits rock bottom—quite literally—with 'Stones.' While listeners have already likened Western Stars to the sounds of such classic 1970s artists as Glen Campbell, Gordon Lightfoot, and Harry Nilsson, 'Stones' evokes the bold orchestral power of Aaron Copland. The song's plaintive brass introduction effects a fitting background for the narrator's heartrending realization that his romantic life has become riddled by the lies and betrayal of his lover's easy duplicity. By the advent of 'There Goes My Miracle,' the narrator can only wail at the awful measure of his loneliness and his loss. In so doing, Springsteen sets up two of his finest closing numbers in 'Hello Sunshine' and 'Moonlight Motel,' tales that communicate the gravity of encroaching adulthood as effectively as just about any composition in his incredible songbook."

PROMOTION

With Springsteen devoting his efforts to an accompanying film production, Western Stars marked the first album for which he hadn't undertaken a tour since 1982's Nebraska. Released on October 25, 2019, the Western Stars concert film was codirected by Springsteen and Thom Zimny. The documentary concludes with Springsteen's cover version of Glen Campbell's 1975 chart-topper "Rhinestone Cowboy."

CHART ACTION

Billboard Top Pop Albums: number two.

Released on June 14, 2019, Western Stars debuted at number two, its peak position, on June 29. The number-one album that week was Madonna's Madame X. The album also notched a number-one showing on the magazine's Top Rock Albums chart.

The album spent four weeks on the Billboard charts.

COMMENTS FROM SPRINGSTEEN AND HIS CIRCLE

Springsteen: "I wrote most of [Western Stars] before Wrecking Ball, and I stopped making that record to make Wrecking Ball, and then I went back to it. So it's been awhile since I've written, but that's not unusual. That's occurred plenty of other times in my working life. It's the record I wrote before Wrecking Ball but could not finish, and in attempting to finish it, I wrote 'Wrecking Ball.' So the roots of the record go back quite a ways. Sometimes you have to wait for these puzzles to sort themselves out, and it can take years. I mean, I have a record that I've been working on that's 20 years old. That's just the way the process is working at the moment" (*Rolling Stone*, October 5, 2016).

Springsteen, reflecting on the "trilogy" of his memoirs, his Broadway residency, and *Western Stars*: "I think probably coming up on 70 had something to do with it and just being at a certain point in your life and your work life where you felt prepared to sort of summarize the trip you've been on for quite a while. It all happened as an accident. Obviously, the timing was right, and it was the kind of work I was ready and anxious to do. But all those three things, I'm very proud of all those three things. I think they're three of the best things I've ever done" (*Asbury Park Press*, October 21, 2019).

MISCELLANEOUS

Recorded at Stone Hill Farm in Colts Neck, New Jersey, the soundtrack album for the *Western Stars* concert documentary was released on October 25, 2019, notching a number-141 showing on the *Billboard* Hot 200 charts.

SONG ANALYSES

"Hitch Hikin'"

Bruce Springsteen: vocals, acoustic guitar, glockenspiel, synth strings, banjo, percussion, electric guitar, Hammond B3 organ, piano, orchestral samples, celeste, organ solo, 12-string guitar, mellotron
Ron Aniello: upright bass, piano, electric guitar, percussion, vibraphone, bass, synth strings, orchestral samples, acoustic guitar, drums, Hammond B3 organ, celeste, loops, synth, background vocals
The Avatar Strings: Rob Mathes (string arrangement, conductor); Lisa Kim, Hyunju Lee, Elizabeth Lim-Dutton, Joanna Maurer, Suzanne Ornstein, Annaliesa Place, Emily Popham, Sharon

Yamada, and Jungsun Yoo (violins); Désirée Elsevier, Vivek Kamath, and Robert Rinehart (violas); Alan Stepansky and Nathan Vickery (cellos)

Springsteen kickstarts *Western Stars* into being with "Hitch Hikin'," the story of a simple, wistful life unfolding on the roadside. With the warm swell of the orchestra as his musical backdrop, there is a sense of majesty inherent in the music as he ponders his carefree workaday world on the road. Springsteen recalled in the mid-1960s, "I'd hitchhiked the 20 miles from Freehold to Manasquan and back almost every day. I'd ridden with concerned moms, drunk drivers, truckers, street racers eager to show off what they had under the hood, traveling businessmen, and only one middle-aged salesman who was a little too interested in me. I'd hopped in with guys who had souped-up sound systems with echo chambers connected to their AM radios, 'in-car' 45 record players set on springs under the dash near the shifter. Every sort of rube, redneck, responsible citizen, and hell-raiser the Jersey Shore had to offer, I rode with 'em. I loved hitchhiking and meeting people. I miss it today" (Springsteen, *Born to Run*, 2016).

"The Wayfarer"

Bruce Springsteen: vocals, acoustic guitar, glockenspiel, synth strings, banjo, percussion, electric guitar, Hammond B3 organ, piano, orchestral samples, celeste, organ solo, 12-string guitar, mellotron
Ron Aniello: upright bass, piano, electric guitar, percussion, vibraphone, bass, synth strings, orchestral samples, acoustic guitar, drums, Hammond B3 organ, celeste, loops, synth, background vocals
Matt Chamberlain: drums
Rachel Drehmann: French horn
Curt Ramm: trumpet, flugelhorn
David Sancious: piano
Patti Scialfa: backing vocals
Leelanee Sterrett: French horn

Soozie Tyrell: backing vocals
Stone Hill Strings: Scott Tibbs (string arrangement, conductor); Lisa Kim, Hyunju Lee, and Joanna Maurer (violins); Shmuel Katz and Rebecca Young (violas); Alan Stepansky (cello)

Springsteen's debt to Glen Campbell's "Wichita Lineman" in particular and the work of Jimmy Webb in general is especially evident on "The Wayfarer," the taut second track on *Western Stars*. With a sense of musical tension playing out in the background, Springsteen's narrator considers his rootless place in the world. As with the character in "Hitch Hikin'," he treasures his nomadic existence. But that's where the similarities end. "The Wayfarer" may be pursuing an itinerant life, but that's not to say that he isn't suffering from the earthly ties that bind: "It's the same sad story, love and glory going 'round and 'round / It's the same old cliché, a wanderer on his way, slipping from town to town."

"Tucson Train"

Bruce Springsteen: vocals, acoustic guitar, glockenspiel, synth strings, banjo, percussion, electric guitar, Hammond B3 organ, piano, orchestral samples, celeste, organ solo, 12-string guitar, mellotron
Ron Aniello: upright bass, piano, electric guitar, percussion, vibraphone, bass, synth strings, orchestral samples, acoustic guitar, drums, Hammond B3 organ, celeste, loops, synth, background vocals
Alden Banta: bassoon
Barry Danielian: trumpet
Rachel Drehmann: French horn
Dan Levine: trombone
Gunnar Olsen: drums
Charles Pillow: oboe
Curt Ramm: trumpet
Matt Rollings: piano
Toby Scott: loop, programming
Andrew Sterman: flute
Leelanee Sterrett: French horn
Stone Hill Strings: Scott Tibbs (string arrangement, conductor); Lisa Kim, Hyunju Lee, and Joanna

Maurer (violins); Shmuel Katz and Rebecca Young (violas); Alan Stepansky (cello)

In the *Western Stars* documentary, Springsteen admits to the dark heart that lives at the core of "Tucson Train," a song about coming to terms with one's past and seeking a form of redemption in this life before it's too late. "How do you change yourself?" he asked in the concert film. "I've spent my 10,000 hours (and then some) learning my musical craft, but I've spent a lot more time than that, some 35 years, trying to learn how to let go of the destructive parts of my character. They did not go easily into that good night. For a long time, if I loved you and if I felt a deep attachment to you, I would hurt you if I could. It was a sin, and I still have days when I struggle with it. But I've gotten better. Through the love of my family, my good friends, I've learned how to love. And to be compassionate with those close to me, and to try and live with some small honor. 'Tucson Train' is about a guy who's trying to follow his better angels, working in the sun for a new start. He's trying to change."

CHART ACTION
Billboard Hot 100: did not chart. The song notched a number-forty-nine showing on the magazine's Hot Rock and Alternative Songs chart.

"Tucson Train" was released on May 30, 2019. The number-one song that week was Ed Sheeran and Justin Bieber's "I Don't Care."

"Western Stars"

Bruce Springsteen: vocals, acoustic guitar, glockenspiel, synth strings, banjo, percussion, electric guitar, Hammond B3 organ, piano, orchestral samples, celeste, organ solo, 12-string guitar, mellotron
Ron Aniello: upright bass, piano, electric guitar, percussion, vibraphone, bass, synth strings, orchestral samples, acoustic guitar, drums,

Hammond B3 organ, celeste, loops, synth, background vocals
Alden Banta: bassoon
Jon Brion: electric guitar, Moog synthesizer
Lenny Castro: conga, tambourine
Matt Chamberlain: drums
Barry Danielian: trumpet
Rachel Drehmann: French horn
Curtis King Jr.: backing vocals
Rob Lebret: electric guitar, baritone guitar
Dan Levine: trombone
Cindy Mizelle: backing vocals
Michelle Moore: backing vocals
Marc Muller: lap steel guitar
Charles Pillow: oboe
Curt Ramm: trumpet
Matt Rollings: piano
Andrew Sterman: flute
Leelanee Sterrett: French horn
Stone Hill Strings: Scott Tibbs (string arrangement, conductor); Lisa Kim, Hyunju Lee, and Joanna Maurer (violins); Shmuel Katz and Rebecca Young (violas); Alan Stepansky (cello)

Western Stars' title track offers a love letter to the Southwest, as well as to its composer's longtime love for Western cinema, stories about wayward, hard-luck cases coming to grips with the sins inherent in their often-irredeemable pasts. In "Western Stars," his narrator takes the guise of a fading actor still hoping to retain his vigor and his relevance even as the ground shifts beneath his feet. Brimming with nostalgia and a glint of loss, "Western Stars" finds the narrator attempting to find his footing in the present; but even still, true to his character to the end, he can't resist sharing anecdotes about his glory days: "Once I was shot by John Wayne, yeah it was towards the end / That one scene's bought me a thousand drinks, set me up and I'll tell it for you, friend." In its *Bruce Springsteen Collector's Edition* (2022), *Rolling Stone* listed "Western Stars" as number sixty-nine among the artist's top 100 songs.

"Sleepy Joe's Café"

Bruce Springsteen: vocals, acoustic guitar, glockenspiel, synth strings, banjo, percussion, electric guitar, Hammond B3 organ, piano, orchestral samples, celeste, organ solo, 12-string guitar, mellotron
Ron Aniello: upright bass, piano, electric guitar, percussion, vibraphone, bass, synth strings, orchestral samples, acoustic guitar, drums, Hammond B3 organ, celeste, loops, synth, background vocals
Jon Brion: Farfisa organ, Moog synthesizer
Lenny Castro: conga, shaker
Barry Danielian: trumpet
Clark Gayton: trombone
Charles Giordano: accordion
Ed Manion: saxophone
Gunnar Olsen: drums
Curt Ramm: trumpet

With its ironic title, "Sleepy Joe's Café" traces the story of a rowdy biker bar. The song's release sent a number of Southern Californians in search of the watering hole that Springsteen depicts in the tune, with folks identifying Joe Suarez's long-defunct joint on Cajon Boulevard (Route 66, no less) near San Bernardino. As with so many of the album's lush Southwestern landscapes, "Sleepy Joe's Café" highlights the transient nature of human existence—with all of the Sturm und Drang of its inevitable dramas—against an unforgiving environment that will one day reclaim the land.

"Drive Fast (The Stuntman)"

Bruce Springsteen: vocals, acoustic guitar, glockenspiel, synth strings, banjo, percussion, electric guitar, Hammond B3 organ, piano, orchestral samples, celeste, organ solo, 12-string guitar, mellotron
Ron Aniello: upright bass, piano, electric guitar, percussion, vibraphone, bass, synth strings, orchestral samples, acoustic guitar, drums, Hammond B3 organ, celeste, loops, synth, background vocals
Marc Muller: pedal steel guitar

Gunnar Olsen: drums
David Sancious: Hammond B3 organ
Luis Villalobos: violin
Stone Hill Strings: Scott Tibbs (string arrangement, conductor); Lisa Kim, Hyunju Lee, and Joanna Maurer (violins); Shmuel Katz and Rebecca Young (violas); Alan Stepansky (cello)

In the *Western Stars* documentary, Springsteen remarked that "in 'Drive Fast,' I had that metaphor of the stuntman (which is always a metaphor of risk) and this idea that we all have our broken pieces. What frightens and what exhilarates and inspires us are often very close together. Those feelings are the essence of what drives us to risk, in life and in love." "Drive Fast" shrewdly juxtaposes the inherent difficulties of the stuntman's work with the challenge of fomenting and sustaining human relationships.

But ultimately, we're all like the stuntman, bravely trying to forge a path for ourselves and gathering plenty of bumps and bruises along the journey. "Everybody's broken in some way—physically, emotionally, spiritually," Springsteen continued. "In this life, nobody gets away unhurt. I wrote a song about a guy not just finding the fearlessness to do his job, but the fearlessness to risk being with somebody that you love. We're always trying to find somebody whose broken pieces fit with our broken pieces, and something whole emerges."

"Chasin' Wild Horses"

Bruce Springsteen: vocals, acoustic guitar, glockenspiel, synth strings, banjo, percussion, electric guitar, Hammond B3 organ, piano, orchestral samples, celeste, organ solo, 12-string guitar, mellotron
Ron Aniello: upright bass, piano, electric guitar, percussion, vibraphone, bass, synth strings, orchestral samples, acoustic guitar, drums, Hammond B3 organ, celeste, loops, synth, background vocals
Barry Danielian: trumpet

Rachel Drehmann: French horn
Marc Muller: pedal steel guitar
Leelanee Sterrett: French horn
The Avatar Strings: Rob Mathes (string arrangement, conductor); Lisa Kim, Hyunju Lee, Elizabeth Lim-Dutton, Joanna Maurer, Suzanne Ornstein, Annaliesa Place, Emily Popham, Sharon Yamada, and Jungsun Yoo (violins); Désirée Elsevier, Vivek Kamath, and Robert Rinehart (violas); Alan Stepansky and Nathan Vickery (cellos)

The notion of wild horses has long been one of popular music's favorite metaphors (take the song by the Rolling Stones, for example). In "Chasin' Wild Horses," Springsteen's narrator reflects on the arduousness of living when you come to realize an existence without hope, a mindset in which the world holds out nothing new on your horizon. For the song's narrator, emotional pain emerges when he recognizes that there aren't any more wild horses coming to drag him away toward life's next great adventure.

"Sundown"

Bruce Springsteen: vocals, acoustic guitar, glockenspiel, synth strings, banjo, percussion, electric guitar, Hammond B3 organ, piano, orchestral samples, celeste, organ solo, 12-string guitar, mellotron
Ron Aniello: upright bass, piano, electric guitar, percussion, vibraphone, bass, synth strings, orchestral samples, acoustic guitar, drums, Hammond B3 organ, celeste, loops, synth, background vocals
Barry Danielian: trumpet
Clark Gayton: trombone
Gunnar Olsen: drums
Curt Ramm: trumpet
Matt Rollings: piano
Patti Scialfa: backing vocals
Soozie Tyrell: backing vocals
The Avatar Strings: Rob Mathes (string arrangement, conductor); Lisa Kim, Hyunju Lee, Elizabeth Lim-Dutton, Joanna Maurer, Suzanne

Ornstein, Annaliesa Place, Emily Popham, Sharon Yamada, and Jungsun Yoo (violins); Désirée Elsevier, Vivek Kamath, and Robert Rinehart (violas); Alan Stepansky and Nathan Vickery (cellos)

In its title as well as its execution, "Sundown" reveals Springsteen's clear influence from Canadian singer-songwriter Gordon Lightfoot, who scored a raft of 1970s-era hits in such tunes as "If You Could Read My Mind," "Carefree Highway," "Rainy Day People," "The Wreck of the Edmund Fitzgerald," and, yes, "Sundown." In Springsteen's composition, Sundown is both geographical place and twilight time. "Just wishing you were here with me in Sundown," Springsteen sings, "Sundown ain't the kind of place you want to be on your own." Without his beloved by his side, the narrator drifts "from bar to bar here in lonely town," where he is forced to watch carefree lovers passing the time in cafés, while "all I've got's trouble on my mind." In many ways, "Sundown" offers a callback of sorts to the music of *Nebraska* and *The Ghost of Tom Joad*—songs where Springsteen's restless narrators are untethered to the people who keep them grounded and teeter on the verge of crossing ethical lines.

"Somewhere North of Nashville"

Bruce Springsteen: vocals, acoustic guitar, glockenspiel, synth strings, banjo, percussion, electric guitar, Hammond B3 organ, piano, orchestral samples, celeste, organ solo, 12-string guitar, mellotron

Ron Aniello: upright bass, piano, electric guitar, percussion, vibraphone, bass, synth strings, orchestral samples, acoustic guitar, drums, Hammond B3 organ, celeste, loops, synth, background vocals

Charles Giordano: piano

Marty Rifkin: pedal steel guitar

Patti Scialfa: backing vocals

Soozie Tyrell: violin, backing vocals

"I wrote this song quickly at the kitchen table one morning," Springsteen remarked about the composition of "Somewhere North of Nashville," adding that "it's just about being lost on the highway of life. Lost is something I'm good at writing about." In the song, Springsteen's narrator seems reflective, even upbeat about the reality of his situation: "All I've got's this melody and time to kill." But as he explained in the *Western Stars* documentary, "Somewhere North of Nashville" is also about the nature of pain and depression, particularly the ways in which we seem, at times, to drift toward such emotions. "Sometimes you've been too beat up or haven't healed enough of the fear out of you to know a good thing when you've found it," he observed. "Sometimes you just gravitate to the pain. It's what you're used to. It's how you recognize yourself. It feels like home. It feels more familiar to you than love. So that's where you go. You don't know how to hold on to love, but you know how to hold on to hurt."

"Stones"

Bruce Springsteen: vocals, acoustic guitar, glockenspiel, synth strings, banjo, percussion, electric guitar, Hammond B3 organ, piano, orchestral samples, celeste, organ solo, 12-string guitar, mellotron

Ron Aniello: upright bass, piano, electric guitar, percussion, vibraphone, bass, synth strings, orchestral samples, acoustic guitar, drums, Hammond B3 organ, celeste, loops, synth, background vocals

Jon Brion: timpani

Rachel Drehmann: French horn

Gunnar Olsen: drums

Leelanee Sterrett: French horn

Luis Villalobos: violin

The Avatar Strings: Rob Mathes (string arrangement, conductor); Lisa Kim, Hyunju Lee, Elizabeth Lim-Dutton, Joanna Maurer, Suzanne Ornstein, Annaliesa Place, Emily Popham, Sharon Yamada, and Jungsun Yoo (violins); Désirée

Elsevier, Vivek Kamath, and Robert Rinehart (violas); Alan Stepansky and Nathan Vickery (cellos)

With "Stones," Springsteen explores the insidious nature of building one's life on a foundation of untruths. Like the heavy weight of stones, they drag you down into an abyss. "Lies," Springsteen remarked in the *Western Stars* documentary, "they will devour everything you have and everything you will ever have. Faith, hope, trust—all those things that are hard to come by. That's what grows your garden of love. Lies will try to make a fool out of all those things. But without them, all you have is stones."

"There Goes My Miracle"

Bruce Springsteen: vocals, acoustic guitar, glockenspiel, synth strings, banjo, percussion, electric guitar, Hammond B3 organ, piano, orchestral samples, celeste, organ solo, 12-string guitar, mellotron
Ron Aniello: upright bass, piano, electric guitar, percussion, vibraphone, bass, synth strings, orchestral samples, acoustic guitar, drums, Hammond B3 organ, celeste, loops, synth, background vocals
Jon Brion: Moog synthesizer, timpani
Lenny Castro: tambourine, shaker
Barry Danielian: trumpet
Clark Gayton: trombone
Matthew Koma: backing vocals
Michelle Moore: backing vocals
Gunnar Olsen: drums
Curt Ramm: trumpet
Patti Scialfa: backing vocals
Stone Hill Strings: Scott Tibbs (string arrangement, conductor); Lisa Kim, Hyunju Lee, and Joanna Maurer (violins); Shmuel Katz and Rebecca Young (viola); Alan Stepansky (cello)

Influenced by English R&B sensation Amy Winehouse, "There Goes My Miracle" finds Springsteen delivering one of his most soaring, heartfelt vocals. Performed against the orchestral warmth of the Stone Hill Strings,

"There Goes My Miracle" offers a hopeful ballad arrayed against the less sanguine songs that comprise *Western Stars*. As with so many of the album's compositions, the narrator's optimism is tempered by an overarching nostalgia, a belief that perhaps life's finest moments have already passed him by.

"Hello Sunshine"

Bruce Springsteen: vocals, acoustic guitar, glockenspiel, synth strings, banjo, percussion, electric guitar, Hammond B3 organ, piano, orchestral samples, celeste, organ solo, 12-string guitar, mellotron
Ron Aniello: upright bass, piano, electric guitar, percussion, vibraphone, bass, synth strings, orchestral samples, acoustic guitar, drums, Hammond B3 organ, celeste, loops, synth, background vocals
Matt Chamberlain: drums
Marc Muller: pedal steel guitar
The Avatar Strings: Rob Mathes (string arrangement, conductor); Lisa Kim, Hyunju Lee, Elizabeth Lim-Dutton, Joanna Maurer, Suzanne Ornstein, Annaliesa Place, Emily Popham, Sharon Yamada, and Jungsun Yoo (violins); Désirée Elsevier, Vivek Kamath, and Robert Rinehart (violas); Alan Stepansky and Nathan Vickery (cellos)

As the album's first single, "Hello Sunshine" evokes the lush musical landscapes of the singer-songwriter era with a nod to Harry Nilsson's "Everybody's Talkin'." In contrast with *Western Stars*' early songs such as "Hitch Hikin'" and "The Wayfarer," the narrator in "Hello Sunshine" registers welcome relief for the calm that life has afforded him. Folksy cheer is no longer part of his emotional repertoire; instead, the narrator seems thankful for the privilege of living another day, of having "had enough of heartbreak and pain."

CHART ACTION

Billboard Hot 100: did not chart. The song notched a number-sixteen showing on the magazine's Hot Rock and Alternative Songs chart.

"Hello Sunshine" was released on April 26, 2019. The number-one song that week was Lil Nas X's "Old Town Road" (featuring Billy Ray Cyrus).

"Moonlight Motel"

Bruce Springsteen: vocals, acoustic guitar, glockenspiel, synth strings, banjo, percussion, electric guitar, Hammond B3 organ, piano, orchestral samples, celeste, organ solo, 12-string guitar, mellotron

Ron Aniello: upright bass, piano, electric guitar, percussion, vibraphone, bass, synth strings, orchestral samples, acoustic guitar, drums, Hammond B3 organ, celeste, loops, synth, background vocals

Jon Brion: drums, celeste
Greg Leisz: pedal steel guitar
Matt Rollings: piano

Springsteen concludes *Western Stars* in unforgettable style. A song about the twilight of our experience, about the vexing nature of nostalgia, "Moonlight Motel" brings the song cycle that began with the sunny optimism of "Hitch Hikin'" to an uncertain close. "There's a place on a blank stretch of road," Springsteen sings, "Where nobody travels and nobody goes." With "Moonlight Motel," the composer undercuts the carefree cheerfulness of "Hitch Hikin'" with a reflective melancholy about the realities inherent in growing up and growing older.

LETTER TO YOU

Released in 2020, *Letter to You* was Springsteen's twentieth studio album, as well as the first LP to feature the E Street Band since *High Hopes* in 2014. With its overarching themes associated with regret, aging, and death, *Letter to You* enjoyed rave reviews in the international press, registering top-ten status in the United States and abroad. Springsteen imagined the LP as being a direct conversation with his listeners. Pointedly, the album was released in the midst of the COVID-19 pandemic, forestalling the opportunity for Springsteen and the E Street Band to undertake a world tour in support of *Letter to You.*

The album was recorded across four days in November 2019 at Springsteen's Stone Hill Studios in Colts Neck, New Jersey. Springsteen had been originally inspired to compose the lion's share of the songs after the death of George Theiss, Springsteen's pre-fame bandmate from the Castiles. The composer supplemented the new songs with three works that had been written prior to the release of his debut LP in 1973, *Greetings from Asbury Park, N.J.*: "If I Was the

Priest," "Janey Needs a Shooter," and "Song for Orphans." Cover versions of "If I Was the Priest" and "Janey Needs a Shooter" had previously been released by Allan Clarke and Warren Zevon, respectively.

Letter to You holds the distinction of being the only album in which Springsteen and the E Street Band recorded every instrument and vocal live, with only a handful of superimpositions involving guitar solos and handclaps. As with *Western Stars*, Ron Aniello served as coproducer with Springsteen, with Aniello, Rob Lebret, Ross Petersen, and Toby Scott handling engineering and postproduction duties.

Given that touring to promote the album was out of the question, Springsteen publicized the album via the debut video releases of the lead single, "Letter to You," and "Ghosts," as well as with Apple Music's *Letter to You Radio*, a bespoke channel that featured Springsteen interviews with musicians such as Brandon Flowers, Dave Grohl, and Eddie Vedder, and political commentators such as Jon Stewart, among other guests. Directed by Thom Zimny, a documentary about the making of *Letter to You* was released by Apple TV in October 2020. Springsteen and the E Street Band performed "Ghosts" and "I'll See You in My Dreams" on the December 12, 2020, episode of *Saturday Night Live*. The appearance marked the band's first performance on *SNL* since 2016, although bassist Garry Tallent and violinist Soozie Tyrell opted out because of COVID-19 travel issues. Bassist Jack Daly from the Disciples of Soul sat in for Tallent.

HISTORICAL CONTEXT

Just a year after releasing *Western Stars* as both a film and an album, Springsteen duplicated the feat with *Letter to You*, which, like his Broadway show, saw the mature, mellowing rocker looking more backward than forward. Obviously in a thoughtful mood, more concerned with his own mortality than with the unfolding political and cultural crises confronting the country, on *Letter to You* Springsteen clearly yearned to revisit his past as a way of continuing to make sense out of his own life and times. Partly inspired by the death of his old bandmate George Theiss, leaving Springsteen the only surviving member of his teenage band, the Castiles, he clearly felt more than a pang of sorrow for how much time had passed and how many friends he had lost.

Despite (or perhaps because of) the personal nature of the material and his reunion with the E Street Band for the first album since *High Hopes* in 2014, one cannot help but think the album also carried with it a positive message when it was released on October 23, just days before the November 2020 election that would do so much to decide the future of the nation, even if the response to the result threatened the very fabric of American democracy. Of course, the United States, along with the rest of the world, also found itself in the midst of a pandemic caused by the spread of the novel coronavirus that had changed the daily patterns of everyday life. It seemed like half the country questioned the very nature of reality, whether regarding the legitimacy of the 2020 election, the scientific evidence connected to climate change, or the existence of the coronavirus itself, despite President Donald J. Trump's own bout with it at the time of the release of *Letter to You*.

Nineteen years earlier, as the horror of the 9/11 attacks stunned the nation, a passing motorist on Ocean Boulevard in Monmouth County recognized Springsteen while he was on his way to pick up his children from school and yelled at him, "Bruce, we need you." He responded, of course, with *The Rising* and, as we have seen in our discussion of several albums that followed, he remained actively engaged with the political issues that confronted the nation in the ensuing decade. Arguably, the country needed Springsteen just as much if not more in the multiple crises that confronted America as it entered the third decade of the twenty-first century. But perhaps the divisions in the country had become too deep and irreconcilable for even as popular and venerated a figure as Springsteen to help heal.

President Trump had repeatedly flouted the law, managed to get himself impeached not once but twice, refused to say during a nationally televised debate with his rival Joe Biden whether he would accept the results of the 2020 election (ultimately, he would not), and would go on to inspire an insurrection on January 6, 2021, that attempted to prevent the peaceful transition of power in the nation's capital. Yet Trump retained a tremendous amount of support from many people who continued to believe his unsubstantiated allegations about election fraud, long after even many of his closest allies and every court in which the vote was challenged had declared that no such fraud existed. In such circumstances, can Springsteen be blamed for turning nostalgic about the past, even going so far as to include several songs on the album that date from his earliest days as a songwriter?

PRODUCTION

Produced by Ron Aniello and Bruce Springsteen
Engineered by Aniello, assisted by Brandon Duncan, Rob Lebret, Ross Petersen, and Toby Scott
Mixed by Bob Clearmountain
Mastered by Bob Ludwig at Gateway Mastering

Recorded at Thrill Hill Recording, Colts Neck, New Jersey, November 2019

PERSONNEL

Bruce Springsteen: vocals, electric and acoustic guitars, harmonica
Roy Bittan: piano, backing vocals
Jake Clemons: tenor saxophone
Charles Giordano: organ, backing vocals
Nils Lofgren: guitar, backing vocals
Patti Scialfa: backing vocals
Garry Tallent: bass, backing vocals
Steven Van Zandt: guitar, backing vocals
Max Weinberg: drums, backing vocals

COVER ART AND PACKAGING

Design: Michelle Holme
Photography: Danny Clinch

TRACK LISTING

All songs composed by Bruce Springsteen.

1. "One Minute You're Here"
2. "Letter to You"
3. "Burnin' Train"
4. "Janey Needs a Shooter"
5. "Last Man Standing"
6. "The Power of Prayer"
7. "House of a Thousand Guitars"
8. "Rainmaker"
9. "If I Was the Priest"
10. "Ghosts"
11. "Song to Orphans"
12. "I'll See You in My Dreams"

CONTEMPORARY REVIEWS

Kory Grow (*Rolling Stone*, October 15, 2020): "Over the past half a century, Springsteen has played down-on-their-luck working men, wide-eyed youngsters growing up too quickly, local-circuit rockers who can only dream of playing stadiums, Cadillac ranchers tearin' up the highway for cheap kicks, and on and on in his songs. Although he was playing roles in his songs, the same sense of hope for the future and desire to live a simpler life have connected his characters since the beginning, and those threads have only become more apparent as time has gone on. Now on his 20th album, *Letter to You* and at age 71, Springsteen seems to be making sense of all of his brilliant disguises for himself. The sentimentality that pulses through *Letter to You* feels more authentic and personal than the fictional stories he dreamt up in his early work or even his recent dives into nostalgia, like his *Magic* album. He recorded the album in just five days, live in the studio with the E Street Band. Together, they sound comfortable rescaling the Phil Spector-inspired Wall of Sound they built in the Seventies with glockenspiels, saxophone expositions, and thousands of guitars. When Springsteen sings about glory days, this time, they're his own glory days."

Kenneth Womack (*Salon*, October 23, 2020): "With *Letter to You*, Bruce Springsteen provides fans with a powerful meditation on humanity's transient, ephemeral nature and the inevitability of our own mortality. . . . One of Springsteen's most inspired choices on *Letter to You* was the inclusion of a trio of his earliest songs, "If I Was the Priest," "Janey Needs a Shooter," and "Song for Orphans." Likely composed in the days before he had a record contract—and certainly prior to the production of his debut album *Greetings from Asbury Park, N.J.* (1973)—these tunes are mindful of Springsteen's nascent days as a composer, when he often worked with a rhyming dictionary by

his side. With the E Street Band roaring into life behind these songs, Springsteen's early compositions act like a time-capsule. The early compositions, especially "Janey Needs a Shooter," brim with the youthful energy and character sketches of songs like "Blinded by the Light" and "Jungleland." At the same time, recording the songs nearly 50 years after their original inspiration finds Springsteen lending the nuance and sagacity of his age to the flights of fancy that he imagined during his early twenties. . . . *Letters to You* offers a cautionary tale about the importance of living in the here and now, of turning a blind eye to the world's con artists and embracing our better angels instead."

PROMOTION

Due to the COVID-19 pandemic, *Letter to You* marked the second consecutive album for which Springsteen hadn't undertaken a tour since 1982's *Nebraska*.

In lieu of a concert tour, Springsteen promoted the album via a partnership with Apple Music titled *Letter to You Radio* in which the musician interviewed a host of personalities, including comedian Jon Stewart and fellow artists Brandon Flowers, Dave Grohl, and Eddie Vedder.

On December 12, 2020, Springsteen and the E Street Band performed "Ghosts" and "I'll See You in My Dreams" on NBC's *Saturday Night Live*.

CHART ACTION

Billboard 200: number two.

Released on October 23, 2020, *Letter to You* debuted at number two, the album's peak position, on November 7. The number-one album that week was Luke Combs's *What You Get*.

Letter to You spent nine weeks on the *Billboard* charts.

COMMENTS FROM SPRINGSTEEN AND HIS CIRCLE

Springsteen: "You have to capture a little piece of the divine. And it can come in many, many forms. But whenever I really have written something that I felt has some quality to it, there's always that little piece of 'I'm not exactly sure where that came from. I know how I got here or how I got there." He added that " I've spent about seven years without writing anything for the band. I couldn't write anything for the band. And I said, 'Well, of course—you'll never be able to do that again!' And it's a trick every time you do it, you know? But it's a trick that, because of that fact that you can't explain, cannot be self-consciously duplicated. It has to come to you in inspiration" (*Variety*, May 5, 2019).

Springsteen: "It's the only album where it's the entire band playing at one time, with all the vocals and everything completely live. The record is the first record that I've made where the subject is the music itself. . . . It's about popular music. It's about being in a rock band, over the course of time. And it's also a direct conversation between me and my fans, at a level that I think they've come to expect over the years" (*New York Times*, October 18, 2020).

MISCELLANEOUS

For the album cover's photo session, Danny Clinch met Springsteen in Central Park on a blustery winter day. The cover shot depicts Springsteen at the park's West 72nd entrance, mere feet away from the Dakota apartment building where John Lennon was murdered in December 1980.

SONG ANALYSES

"One Minute You're Here"
Bruce Springsteen: vocals, guitar, harmonica
Roy Bittan: piano, backing vocals
Charles Giordano: organ, backing vocals
Nils Lofgren: guitar, backing vocals
Patti Scialfa: backing vocals
Garry Tallent: bass, backing vocals
Steven Van Zandt: guitar, backing vocals
Max Weinberg: drums, backing vocals

On the surface, this song would seem to require little analysis beyond its title and the line that follows, "Next minute you're gone." Clarence Clemons died in 2011, and the track clearly shows Springsteen attempting to come to terms with that and his own mortality early in his eighth decade on earth, a theme that is repeated throughout the album. But introducing the song in the documentary *Letter to You*, Springsteen relates how common and frequent were his encounters with death as a young child through the many wakes and funerals he attended with his family. So he uses another image from his childhood—of the train that passed through Freehold, where he and his friends would lay their pennies on the track for the iron horse to flatten. Now he sees the train as a metaphor for death approaching all too quickly. The song also refers to summer singing "its last song," and the singer feeling alone but also confident he is "coming home," another metaphor for death he repeats later on the album in "Ghosts."

"Letter to You"
Bruce Springsteen: vocals, guitar, harmonica
Roy Bittan: piano, backing vocals

Charles Giordano: organ, backing vocals
Nils Lofgren: guitar, backing vocals
Patti Scialfa: backing vocals
Garry Tallent: bass, backing vocals
Steven Van Zandt: guitar, backing vocals
Max Weinberg: drums, backing vocals

In addition to evoking the Beatles' "All My Loving," the title track reaffirms Springsteen's religious commitment to his music and the higher purpose he believes it serves for himself and his audience. For Springsteen, his music acts as a form of prayer, an act of devotion, singing here that he has "dug deep" in his soul to find the words to send in this song, which doubles as his letter to his listeners, individually and collectively. As always, he recognizes the contrast between "happiness and pain," "sunshine and rain," which form the experience of all our lives. In fact, "Letter to You" not only refers to this specific song but is a metaphor for the totality of Springsteen's music in which he has shared with his fans and listeners "all that I've found true."

CHART ACTION

Billboard Hot 100: did not chart. The song registered a number-thirty-four showing on the Hot Rock and Alternative Songs chart, number twenty-eight on the Rock Airplay chart, and number one on the Alternative Songs chart.

"Letter to You" was released on September 10, 2020. The number-one song that week was BTS's "Dynamite."

"Burnin' Train"

Bruce Springsteen: vocals, guitar, harmonica
Roy Bittan: piano, backing vocals
Charles Giordano: organ, backing vocals
Nils Lofgren: guitar, backing vocals
Patti Scialfa: backing vocals
Garry Tallent: bass, backing vocals
Steven Van Zandt: guitar, backing vocals
Max Weinberg: drums, backing vocals

This is another song that refers to trains, a significant motif in Springsteen's later work. Springsteen combines here his train metaphor with his frequent use of the verb "to burn," by which he means "to set on fire metaphorically," as in, "to fill with the holy spirit," or perhaps sometimes just the spirit of rock and roll. Like many songs on this album, this one also deals with death, as he addresses someone, God presumably, to "shake me from this mortal cage" and "take me on your burnin' train." Instead of light and darkness, here the contrast is between the holy water in which the singer bathes at the beginning of the song, and fire, as he rises up in flames after whispering his "black prayers." It is another song that accepts the inevitability of death, almost welcoming it, in a rock song that could double as part of a spiritual revival.

"Janey Needs a Shooter"

Bruce Springsteen: vocals, guitar, harmonica
Roy Bittan: piano, backing vocals
Charles Giordano: organ, backing vocals
Nils Lofgren: guitar, backing vocals
Patti Scialfa: backing vocals
Garry Tallent: bass, backing vocals
Steven Van Zandt: guitar, backing vocals
Max Weinberg: drums, backing vocals

In the late 1970s, Springsteen cowrote a song with Warren Zevon called "Jeannie Needs a Shooter" that appeared on Zevon's 1980 album *Bad Luck Streak in Dancing School*. The song was about a girl the singer wants to make his, but her father was a sheriff opposed to the match who ended up shooting the singer when he tried to get the girl to run away with him. In this version, not only has Springsteen changed the name of the girl in the song, but he has substantially revised the lyrics, actually moving away from the pseudo-Western theme of the original lyrics. Instead of the sheriff being the girl's father, in this version a doctor, a priest, and a cop are looking after her. But the doctor and the priest make inappropriate advances and she's afraid of the cop, the very sound of whose siren makes her skin turn pale. As in so many songs, from "Rosalita" to "Thunder Road" and "Born to Run," to "I Wanna Marry You," and "Man's Job," Springsteen offers himself up as the one the girl really needs: "So I held her real close, she was more a saint than a ghost / And told her I so long had been prepared for her." In other words, "the shooter" that Janey needs is the singer himself, "a man who knows her style."

"Last Man Standing"
Bruce Springsteen: vocals, guitar, harmonica
Roy Bittan: piano, backing vocals
Jake Clemons: saxophone
Charles Giordano: organ, backing vocals
Nils Lofgren: guitar, backing vocals
Patti Scialfa: backing vocals
Garry Tallent: bass, backing vocals
Steven Van Zandt: guitar, backing vocals
Max Weinberg: drums, backing vocals

This is another song that sees Springsteen reflecting on his past, a time when he was "out of school and out of work," wearing "thrift store jeans and flannel shirt." As in many of the other songs on this album, Springsteen approaches the past from the perspective of the present, in this case the title referencing his realization that with the death of George Theiss he is the last surviving member of his teenage band, the Castiles. As such, we encounter the usual blend of temporal and secular images, the lights at the Legion Hall signifying the end of the band's last set of the evening, after which you would "pack your guitar and have one last beer," while in the same song asking the "Rock of ages" to lift him up. Springsteen frequently contrasts light and darkness, good and evil, hope and despair throughout his work. Here it is left implied that the end of the last set signified by the lights coming on contrasts with the darkness that will descend with the last set of a musician's life, after which any light must come from a higher realm.

"The Power of Prayer"
Bruce Springsteen: vocals, guitar, harmonica
Roy Bittan: piano, backing vocals
Jake Clemons: saxophone
Charles Giordano: organ, backing vocals
Nils Lofgren: guitar, backing vocals
Patti Scialfa: backing vocals
Garry Tallent: bass, backing vocals
Steven Van Zandt: guitar, backing vocals
Max Weinberg: drums, backing vocals

With Jake Clemons in full bloom on the tenor saxophone, "The Power of Prayer" seems a direct sequel to "Last Man Standing," which perhaps reflects the extent to which Springsteen continues to think carefully about the ordering of songs on his albums to convey a particular message, if not to tell a story. In the film on the making of the album, Springsteen identifies the power of prayer with the power of pop and the notion that the sacred exists in the ordinary events of everyday life. In this song, he contrasts the apparent meaninglessness that many find in a world that seems "a fixed game without any rules," with us sitting at "empty tables on a ship of fools." The power of prayer comes in with those special moments that give us glimpses into something transcendent, which for Springsteen in particular lies in the popular music he listened to in his younger years. It seems highly significant that the one popular song he mentions is "This Magic Moment," since magic moments are exactly when one experiences the power of prayer, those special moments of grace that make life worth living. "This Magic Moment" also stands in for the pop music that has a unique ability to bless us with so many of those "magic moments."

"House of a Thousand Guitars"

Bruce Springsteen: vocals, guitar, harmonica
Roy Bittan: piano, backing vocals
Jake Clemons: saxophone
Charles Giordano: organ, backing vocals
Nils Lofgren: guitar, backing vocals
Patti Scialfa: backing vocals
Garry Tallent: bass, backing vocals
Steven Van Zandt: guitar, backing vocals
Max Weinberg: drums, backing vocals

"House of a Thousand Guitars" is another reference to Springsteen's musical journey and to all of the musicians he has listened to and played with along the long road of his career that have left him to "tally [his] wounds "and count the scars." Like "Land of Hope and Dreams," it is also a call for "all good souls from near and far" to join him, in this case in the house of a thousand guitars rather than on a train bound for glory. Springsteen's affirmation in the song that "It's All Right" contains echoes of the Beatles' 1968 song "Revolution," also written at a time of deep political turmoil and division within the country. While this is a less overtly political statement than John Lennon was making at the height of the Vietnam War, it is still an affirmation of the healing power of music, which will continue long after the current political climate has changed because in the house of a thousand guitars "the music never ends" and is always there to sustain us, even as we near death or make our way through our darkest times.

"Rainmaker"

Bruce Springsteen: vocals, guitar, harmonica
Roy Bittan: piano, backing vocals
Charles Giordano: organ, backing vocals
Nils Lofgren: guitar, backing vocals
Patti Scialfa: backing vocals
Garry Tallent: bass, backing vocals
Steven Van Zandt: guitar, backing vocals
Max Weinberg: drums, backing vocals

Dating back to 2003, "Rainmaker" offers a cautionary tale about an "American charlatan." In the song, Springsteen relies on American Western and biblical imagery, both familiar themes in many of his compositions. The topic and message of the song seem clear enough: when people go through difficult and desperate times they often resort to extraordinary measures or look for someone else to provide the answers or solutions to their problems. A "rainmaker" in popular parlance refers to someone who makes money for other people, though the literal origins of the term refer to certain individuals in some cultures with the power to end a drought. The message here is that such people are actually charlatans, con men who offer "faith for hire" and "will take everything you have."

The chorus continues, "Sometimes folks need to believe in something so bad . . . they'll hire a rainmaker." A more specific interpretation, in light of the political context of the time in which the album appeared, might be that sometimes people will elect a politician who promises big things, but is really concerned more for what you can do for him than what he can do for you. The words "Brother patriot, come forth and lay it down / Your blood brother for king and crown" actually seem to anticipate the events that transpired on January 6, 2021, but those events might have been predicted from the relationship between a certain "rainmaker" and his followers in the years leading up to them and to this song, one of Springsteen's most overtly political creations.

"If I Was the Priest"

Bruce Springsteen: vocals, guitar, harmonica
Roy Bittan: piano, backing vocals
Charles Giordano: organ, backing vocals
Nils Lofgren: guitar, backing vocals
Patti Scialfa: backing vocals

Garry Tallent: bass, backing vocals
Steven Van Zandt: guitar, backing vocals
Max Weinberg: drums, backing vocals

"If I Was the Priest" is one of Springsteen's early songs that he revived for this album, its inclusion fitting because in many ways *Letter to You* looks back at the entire span of Springsteen's life and career. What is so interesting about this song is the way in which it so seamlessly incorporates two of the singer-songwriter's favorite subjects: religion and the American West. "Now if Jesus was a sheriff and I were a priest," the chorus begins, while elsewhere in the song, "The Virgin Mary runs the Holy Grail Saloon" and the Holy Ghost "runs the burlesque show."

In short, "If I Was the Priest" not only blurs the boundaries between the sacred and the profane, it frequently reverses the roles so that the sacred is found in everyday life and heaven is like the Wild West in its corruption filled with outlaws, not having been the same since "big bad Bobby came to town." Meanwhile, the singer has scabs on his knees "from kneeling way too long," a line that dovetails with "The Power of Prayer," the power that comes not from kneeling but from making and listening to music and enjoying the mundane as if it were indeed what was really sacred.

"Ghosts"

Bruce Springsteen: vocals, guitar, harmonica
Roy Bittan: piano, backing vocals
Jake Clemons: saxophone
Charles Giordano: organ, backing vocals
Nils Lofgren: guitar, backing vocals
Patti Scialfa: backing vocals
Garry Tallent: bass, backing vocals
Steven Van Zandt: guitar, backing vocals
Max Weinberg: drums, backing vocals

This song continues the theme of the album concerning mortality, blended with the contrasting spirit of affirming life and all the varied experiences it has to offer us. In the documentary film on the making of the album, Springsteen says that "'Ghosts' is about the beauty and joy of being in a band and the pain of losing one another to illness and time." But the song does not refer to ghosts as simply the spiritual presence of those who have left but as the ways in which their spirit specifically lives on through the music. According to Springsteen, the E Street Band itself was a spiritual entity that "resides in our collective soul powered by the heart."

"Ghosts" is filled with images from Springsteen's musical past, an affirmation that he is still alive and "can feel the blood shiver in my bones" combined with a promise that he is "coming home," a metaphor for his own eventual death. In the meantime, though, he sings that he will "turn up the volume and feel the spirit" until he meets his spiritual brothers and sisters "on the other side." In its *Bruce Springsteen Collector's Edition* (2022), *Rolling Stone* listed "Ghosts" as number eighty-four among the artist's top 100 songs.

CHART ACTION
Billboard Hot 100: did not chart. The song registered a number-five showing on the magazine's Rock Digital Song Sales chart.

"Ghosts" was released on September 24, 2020. The number-one song that week was BTS's "Dynamite."

"Song to Orphans"

Bruce Springsteen: vocals, guitar, harmonica
Roy Bittan: piano, backing vocals
Charles Giordano: organ, backing vocals
Nils Lofgren: guitar, backing vocals
Patti Scialfa: backing vocals
Garry Tallent: bass, backing vocals
Steven Van Zandt: guitar, backing vocals
Max Weinberg: drums, backing vocals

This is another song that Springsteen resurrected from his youth, one of his earliest; in the documentary, Springsteen confesses that his "songs from 1972 are and remain a mystery to me." Yet it seems to fit perfectly as the penultimate song on this album. In 1972, Springsteen was still struggling to find himself even though he also seemed to have a deep reservoir of hope and self-confidence that carried him through the travails of his youth, which included his parents moving to California, leaving Springsteen with a sense of abandonment at the same time that his decision to stay in New Jersey brought him a measure of freedom and independence. "A Song for Orphans," then, was a song that Springsteen wrote for himself, as well as all of those who, like him, felt alone, providing encouragement from the example of someone who took responsibility for his life and rose above challenging circumstances.

"I'll See You in My Dreams"
Bruce Springsteen: vocals, guitar, harmonica
Roy Bittan: piano, backing vocals
Charles Giordano: organ, backing vocals
Nils Lofgren: guitar, backing vocals
Patti Scialfa: backing vocals
Garry Tallent: bass, backing vocals

Steven Van Zandt: guitar, backing vocals
Max Weinberg: drums, backing vocals

The album represents partially a lament for the friends and loved ones that Springsteen had lost, particularly Danny Federici, Clarence Clemons, and George Theiss, along with many others. It is also an affirmation that he believes that they and their music still live, alongside the hope that we do live on in some spiritual form after death; as he sings, "Death is not the end." Springsteen himself described this song as "very basic," with the simple message that he has not and will not forget those who have enriched his life in so many ways. In short, his message to his lost friends and former bandmates is that I will not forget you, we will meet again someday, and in the meantime, "I'll see you in my dreams."

CHART ACTION
Billboard Hot 100: did not chart. The song registered a number-twenty-one showing on the magazine's Rock Digital Song Sales chart.

"I'll See You in My Dreams" was released on March 3, 2021. The number-one song that week was Olivia Rodrigo's "Drivers License."

Only the Strong Survive (Shutterstock) [performance photo]

ONLY THE STRONG SURVIVE

Released in November 2022, *Only the Strong Survive* marks Springsteen's twenty-first studio album, as well as his second LP devoted entirely to cover versions since *We Shall Overcome: The Seeger Sessions* (2006). Coproduced by Springsteen and Ron Aniello, who provided much of the supporting instrumentation outside of Springsteen's guitar and piano parts, *Only the Strong Survive* features a pair of duets with the legendary Sam Moore of Sam and Dave fame. With the exception of his first two albums and *The Ghost of Tom Joad* (1995), which notched

a number eleven showing on the US charts, *Only the Strong Survive* was Springsteen's eighteenth top ten LP release.

Much of *Only the Strong Survive*'s sensory impact can be credited to the album's atmospherics. A collection of carefully selected cover versions, the LP *sounds* like the music and textures from the heyday of soul and rhythm and blues. That's not to suggest that the album feels dated—far from it. Rather, Springsteen and his coproducer's careful attention to sonic detail establishes a soulful ambience that draws listeners in from the snare shot that kicks the title-track into being. The two establish a musical thread that drapes itself across the rest of the album—indeed, right on through to the final cut, "Someday We'll Be Together."

Only the Strong Survive is an album that benefits from repeated listenings, with Springsteen's cover versions taking on greater nuance with each new pass. He recently remarked that making the LP marked his effort to "do justice" to "the great American songbook of the '60s and '70s." With *Only the Strong Survive*, he demonstrates his artistic debt to his American R&B and soul roots. But it proves to be more than that: by producing an album's worth of top-flight cover versions, Springsteen pays powerful homage to the songwriters and musicians who paved the way for his own vaunted place among their number.

HISTORICAL CONTEXT

The historical context for this 2022 album really belongs more to the 1960s, when most of these soul and rhythm and blues songs were first released by their original artists, than to the 2020s when Bruce Springsteen decided to cover them. If *Letter to You* paid tribute to the friends and former bandmates that Springsteen had lost, as well as to his fans to some degree, *Only the Strong Survive* pays tribute to the popular music of his youth that he loved and whose many influences he imbibed and that influenced so much of his own career as a rock musician. He does so here by not departing too much from the initial arrangements, even though his own distinctive voice and passion for the songs make them distinguishable as covers rather than as exact replicas of the originals.

The title of the album could relate to a story he told Howard Stern in a 2022 interview, in which he talked about being at the Rock and Roll Hall of Fame finding himself next to Mick Jagger and George Harrison and reflecting on the odds of his being the one standing there between these two rock icons out of all the millions of kids who picked up a guitar in the 1960s and decided to learn to play in imitation of Elvis Presley or the Beatles. In his interview with Stern, Springsteen recognized that the odds of anyone making a single record, of having a hit, of making more than one record, became increasingly longer, while the odds of someone having the type of career he himself has had were almost infinitesimal. "Only the Strong Survive," indeed.

To the extent that one can relate this album to the specific chronological context of 2022, beyond Springsteen's simple desire to revisit the music of his youth, one might find it on two covers in particular that appear early on the album. The first is a song written in 2001 by Dobie Gray, perhaps best known for his 1973 hit "Drift Away," a classic song about the desire to get lost in the music of a talented rock and roll performer and escape from the troubles of one's life and times. Here Springsteen covers Gray's song "Soul Days," which itself is a tribute to soul singers from the 1960s, including Wilson Pickett, Joe Tex, Sam and Dave, Ray Charles, Aretha Franklin, Sam Cooke, Arthur Conley, and Edwin Starr. The song is about the desire to escape to "another time and place."

Meanwhile, "Nightshift" was a 1985 hit by the Commodores, written by Dennis Lambert, Franne Golde, and Walter Orange. It is a tribute to Marvin Gaye and Jackie Wilson and a remembrance of their "soulful noise" and the hope that, long after they were lost to us, somewhere they are still making their beautiful sounds "on the nightshift." Perhaps amid the culture wars, political upheaval, threats to American democracy, the COVID-19 pandemic, and a struggling economy, Springsteen sought to remember what now seemed like a golden age of music, even if the times that produced it were no less turbulent than the period in which this album was released.

PRODUCTION

Released on November 11, 2022, Columbia Records
Produced by Ron Aniello with Bruce Springsteen
Engineered by Rob Lebret and Ron Aniello
Mixed by Rob Lebret with Ron Aniello at Thrill Hill Recording
Mastered by Bob Ludwig at Gateway Mastering
Recorded at Thrill Hill Recording, Colts Neck, New Jersey, 2020 to 2022

PERSONNEL

Bruce Springsteen: vocals, electric and acoustic guitars, piano
Ron Aniello: drums, electric bass, guitar, piano, Farfisa organ, glockenspiel, percussion, backing vocals, vibes, timpani, chimes, drums
Dennis Collins: backing vocals
Barry Danielian: trumpet
Clark Gayton: trombone
Bill Holloman: tenor saxophone
Curtis King Jr.: backing vocals
Rob Lebret: guitar
Lisa Lowell: backing vocals
Ed Manion: baritone saxophone
Michelle Moore: backing vocals
Sam Moore: harmony vocals
Curt Ramm: trumpet
Fonzi Thornton: backing vocals
Tom Timko: baritone saxophone

Soozie Tyrell: backing vocals
Strings: Rob Mathes (arranger and conductor); Lisa Kim (concertmaster); Kristi Helberg, Dasol Jeong, Kuan Cheng Lu, Joanna Maurer, Suzanne Ornstein, Su Hyun Park, Annaliesa Place, Sein Ryu, and Sharon Yamada (violins); Danielle Farina, Devin Moore, and Rebecca Young (violas); Patrick Jee, Clarice Jensen, and Sophie Shao (cellos)

COVER ART AND PACKAGING

Design: Michelle Holme and Meghan Foley
Photography: Danny Clinch, except the *Night Shift Portrait*, by Rob DeMartin

TRACK LISTING

1. "Only the Strong Survive" (Jerry Butler, Kenny Gamble, and Leon Huff)
2. "Soul Days" (Jonnie Barnett)
3. "Nightshift   " (Walter Orange, Dennis Lambert, and Franne Golde)
4. "Do I Love You (Indeed I Do)" (Frank Wilson)
5. "The Sun Ain't Gonna Shine Anymore" (Bob Crewe and Bob Gaudio)
6. "Turn Back the Hands of Time" (Jack Daniels and Bonnie Thompson)
7. "When She Was My Girl" (Larry Gottlieb and Marc Blatte)
8. "Hey, Western Union Man" (Butler, Gamble, and Huff)
9. "I Wish It Would Rain" (Norman Whitfield, Barrett Strong, and Rodger Penzabene)
10. "Don't Play That Song" (Ahmet Ertegun and Betty Nelson)
11. "Any Other Way" (William Bell)
12. "I Forgot to Be Your Lover" (Bell and Booker T. Jones)
13. "7 Rooms of Gloom" (Brian Holland, Lamont Dozier, and Eddie Holland)

14. "What Becomes of the Brokenhearted" (William Weatherspoon, Paul Riser, and James Dean)
15. "Someday We'll Be Together" (Johnny Bristol, Jackey Beavers, and Harvey Fuqua)

CONTEMPORARY REVIEWS

Jonathan Bernstein (*Rolling Stone*, November 4, 2022): "*Only the Strong Survive* is a product of backyard-studio sessions during lockdown, with longtime producer Ron Aniello playing every non-brass and string instrument. Adding to the album's retro-soul pastiche are Aniello's occasionally thin arrangements (see his take on Chuck Jackson's 'Any Other Way') that recall the forgotten latter-day LPs where soul greats like Sam and Dave and Percy Sledge released sterile rerecordings of their greatest hits. But even if the arrangements occasionally feel static in their mimicry, Springsteen's voice shines and sparkles. Listen to how his phrasing draws out the meditative nostalgia of Dobie Gray's 'Soul Days,' or the way he deploys falsetto as a narrative device on the Temptations' 'I Wish It Would Rain.' Springsteen has long sung (and written in) a soul voice, but until now, that voice has usually been relegated to side projects (an outtake like 'Back in Your Arms' or a song written for someone else, like Clarence Clemons' 'Savin' Up'). Here, he uses that voice to inhabit many roles: crate-digger (Frankie Wilson's 'Do I Love You'), forgive-me repenter (William Bell's 'I Forgot to Be Your Lover'), elder memorializer (the Commodores' 'Nightshift'), blue-eyed interloper (Jerry Butler's title track), and canon redefiner (to this Jersey native, Frankie Valli's 'The Sun Ain't Gonna Shine Anymore' is just as soul as Stax). Then there's the moment halfway through, on the Aretha/Ben E. King classic 'Don't Play That Song,' when Springsteen strays off-script: 'I remember those summer nights down by the shore,' he ad-libs in spoken word before the final chorus. 'As the band played, with you in my arms, and we moved across that floor.' It's part James Brown showmanship, part boardwalk reverie, part camp. And if it sounds like something he might have done with one of his own songs onstage way back when, that's his whole point. He's finding a different way to fold his story into American music's living history."

Kenneth Womack (*Salon*, November 11, 2022): "There's a lot to be admired in *Only the Strong Survive*, Bruce Springsteen's 21st studio album. But I find myself enjoying it in dramatically different ways than, say, his 1970s-era masterworks *Born to Run* and *Darkness on the Edge of Town*. Those records stirred our intellect and our emotions via the excitement of the artist's storytelling and attendant musical drama. With *Only the Strong Survive*, Springsteen succeeds, simply put, by elevating our senses through the pure power of song. Springsteen's vocals . . . feel right at home in the grooves of the cover versions that he has selected. With *Only the Strong Survive*, he's in fine fettle as a singer, affording homage to the music and an era that have clearly existed at the heart of his life's inspiration. At times, the album makes for a dizzying array of standout vocal performances, as Springsteen reels off unforgettable takes of such 1960s classics as 'Hey, Western Union Man,' 'Don't Play That Song,' and '7 Rooms of Gloom.' As incredible as those numbers prove to be, Springsteen shifts into yet another gear altogether for 'What Becomes of the Brokenhearted,' Jimmy Ruffin's Motown hit. In a career filled with awe-inspiring musical highs, his vocal interpretation of 'What Becomes of the Brokenhearted' makes for one of his finest performances, brimming with drama and foreboding."

PROMOTION

During the week of November 14, 2022, Springsteen made four appearances on the *Tonight Show Starring Jimmy Fallon* in support of *Only the Strong Survive*. He also appeared on Fallon's Thanksgiving special on November 24.

In February 2023, Springsteen and the E Street Band embarked on a ninety-show, eleven-month tour across North America and Europe, marking Springsteen's first concert performances since the summer 2017 tour in support of *The River*.

CHART ACTION

Billboard 200: number three.

Released on November 11, 2022, *Only the Strong Survive* debuted at number eight, the album's peak position, on November 26. The number-one album that week was Taylor Swift's *Midnights*.

Only the Strong Survive spent four weeks on the *Billboard* charts.

COMMENTS FROM SPRINGSTEEN AND HIS CIRCLE

Springsteen: "In my memoirs, I made a little confession saying that I didn't consider myself a great singer. But once I started this project, after listening to some of the stuff we recorded, I thought, 'my voice is great! I'm 73-years-old, and I'm kicking ass. I'm a vigorous old man!'" (*Billboard*, September 29, 2022).

MISCELLANEOUS

On December 16, 2021, news outlets report that Springsteen had sold his entire back catalog to Sony Music Group for some $500 million.

SONG ANALYSES

"Only the Strong Survive"
Bruce Springsteen: vocals
Ron Aniello: drums, bass, percussion, guitar, vibes, piano, organ
Barry Danielian: trumpet
Clark Gayton: trombone
Bill Holloman: tenor saxophone
Lisa Lowell: backing vocals
Ed Manion: baritone saxophone
Curt Ramm: trumpet
Tom Timko: baritone saxophone
Soozie Tyrell: backing vocals
Strings: Rob Mathes (arranger and conductor); Lisa Kim (concertmaster); Kristi Helberg, Dasol Jeong, Kuan Cheng Lu, Joanna Maurer, Suzanne Ornstein, Su Hyun Park, Annaliesa Place, Sein Ryu, and Sharon Yamada (violins); Danielle Farina, Devin Moore, and Rebecca Young (violas); Patrick Jee, Clarice Jensen, and Sophie Shao (cellos)

Soul icon Jerry Butler, known as the "Ice Man," included this classic, cowritten with Kenneth Gamble and Leon Huff, on his 1968 album *The Ice Man Cometh*. The song is written retrospectively from the perspective of an adult male remembering the advice his mother gave to him as an emotionally distraught youth on the loss of his first love. But the song could just as easily have been interpreted as a cautionary tale for Black youths in America at a time of race riots, the backlash against the civil rights movement, and the assassination of Martin Luther King Jr. The singer's mother warns him, "There's gonna be a whole lot of trouble in your life." In fact, the whole song could be taken as a metaphor for the struggles of Black Americans and the hope the 1960s had inspired that a better world was coming.

The words of the mother in the song are not merely that "only the strong survive," but that "there's always gonna be a better day," if only you refuse to give up and hold on to hope. The song follows a familiar pattern of a son or daughter echoing back to the next generation the advice received from their parents, as, for example, in Smokey Robinson's 1960 single "Shop Around" (cowritten with Berry Gordy) or Clarence Carter's 1970 hit "Patches" (written by Ron Dunbar and General Johnson). This song took on special resonance in the bleak days of November 1968 (the same month Richard Nixon was elected president) and in the lingering period of the COVID-19 pandemic and the troubled world of the early 2020s, when Springsteen released this cover. The song has another meaning, though, that becomes clear as the album progresses that has to do with the theme of lost love to which the song refers directly.

"Soul Days"

Bruce Springsteen: vocals, guitar
Ron Aniello: drums, bass, percussion, guitar, piano, organ
Barry Danielian: trumpet
Clark Gayton: trombone
Bill Holloman: tenor saxophone
Ed Manion: baritone saxophone
Sam Moore: harmony and second vocals
Curt Ramm: trumpet
Tom Timko: baritone saxophone

Unlike most of the other songs on the album, this was a fairly obscure song written by Jonathan Barnett Kaye, a.k.a. Jonnie Barnett, a minor singer-songwriter who died in 2002. Dobie Gray recorded the original version of the song in 2000. It perfectly encapsulates the purpose of this album, opening with the singer waking up and the sunshine taking him "back to emotions from another time and place." It expresses the near universal feeling of many baby boomers who remember the music of the era as much as they do the actual events of their lives, which they often frame against

the music associated with those images. In the song, the singer recaptures the feeling of a lost youth, emulating the swagger of James Dean, "Thinking I was still nineteen." He takes a trip down a back country road to a barbecue shack by the river with a jukebox that still plays those old songs that spoke to his heart's desire. The song is about the past, but it is set in an eternal present in which the songs of soul icons like Sam Cooke, Aretha Franklin, and Ray Charles will live forever. The song appropriately ends with a reference to Edwin Starr, whose song "War" Springsteen has frequently performed in concert and which was included in his 1986 live boxed set of him and the E Street Band.

"Nightshift"

Bruce Springsteen: vocals
Ron Aniello: drums, bass, percussion, guitar, piano, organ, keyboards
Dennis Collins: backing vocals
Barry Danielian: trumpet
Clark Gayton: trombone
Bill Holloman: tenor saxophone
Curtis King Jr.: backing vocals
Ed Manion: baritone saxophone
Curt Ramm: trumpet
Fonzi Thornton: backing vocals
Tom Timko: baritone saxophone

Another retrospective song, "Nightshift" was a 1985 hit for the Commodores, their first following the departure of Lionel Richie from the group to pursue what turned out to be a stellar solo career. The song, written by Dennis Lambert, Franne Golde, and Walter Orange, wistfully recalls the careers of two soul icons, who, perhaps significantly, are not among the eight artists referenced in "Soul Days." We don't know if Springsteen intentionally included this song for that reason, but Marvin Gaye and Jackie Wilson certainly represent significant figures in the pantheon of soul artists from the

1960s. They both died in 1984, the year before the Commodores released "Nightshift."

In a long and varied career, Marvin Gaye, who was murdered by his father in the midst of a family dispute, had been as well known for such socially conscious songs as "Mercy Mercy Me" and "What's Going On?" as for such Motown classics as "I Heard It through the Grapevine" and his love duets with Tammi Terrell. Jackie Wilson died of pneumonia in obscurity, despite his career as a flamboyant and charismatic performer with a string of hits in the late 1950s and 1960s, five of which reached the top spot on the US R&B chart. Springsteen's cover of "Soul Days" and "Nightshift" both speak to the purpose of the album as a whole and in a sense serve as an introduction to the songs that follow.

CHART ACTION

Billboard Hot 100: did not chart.

"Nightshift" was released on October 14, 2022. The number-one song that week was Steve Lacy's "Bad Habit."

"Do I Love You (Indeed I Do)"

Bruce Springsteen: vocals
Ron Aniello: drums, bass, percussion, guitar, piano, organ, vibes, glockenspiel
Barry Danielian: trumpet
Clark Gayton: trombone
Bill Holloman: tenor saxophone
Lisa Lowell: backing vocals
Ed Manion: baritone saxophone
Michelle Moore: backing vocals
Curt Ramm: trumpet
Tom Timko: baritone saxophone
Soozie Tyrell: backing vocals
Strings: Rob Mathes (arranger and conductor); Lisa Kim (concertmaster); Kristi Helberg, Dasol Jeong, Kuan Cheng Lu, Joanna Maurer, Suzanne Ornstein, Su Hyun Park, Annaliesa Place, Sein Ryu, and Sharon Yamada (violins); Danielle Farina, Devin Moore, and Rebecca Young (violas); Patrick Jee, Clarice Jensen, and Sophie Shao (cellos)

This 1965 Motown hit for Frank Wilson is perhaps not one of the best-known songs on the album, but it fits Springsteen's range perfectly and could be interpreted in the context of this album as an affirmation of his love for the soul classics of the era of Springsteen's teenage years. The song has a strong upbeat tempo with short verses sung with the utmost enthusiasm alternating with the titular question "Do I Love You?" sung by a backup female chorus. Here, as in Ray Charles's famous song "Hit the Road Jack," the title of the song is never actually sung by the lead singer. Instead, he lets the chorus ask the question before he answers back, "Indeed I Do."

The song offers a simple promise of eternal love and fidelity, the singer's devotion encapsulated in the altering of the traditional nighttime prayer taught to many children, "Now I lay me down to sleep / I pray the Lord *your* soul to keep" (italics ours). As Springsteen made clear on his previous album, *Letter to You*, by this point in his career love had become to him something more universal and general. It is not unreasonable to think that the promise here is not just to a romantic partner, but to something larger—the musical tradition of which he was a part, and perhaps his fans, too. But the song also serves as an introduction and contrast to those that follow.

CHART ACTION

Billboard Hot 100: did not chart.

"Do I Love You (Indeed I Do)" was released on September 29, 2022. The number-one song that week was Harry Styles's "As It Was."

"The Sun Ain't Gonna Shine (Anymore)"

Bruce Springsteen: vocals, keyboards
Ron Aniello: drums, bass, percussion, guitar, piano, keyboards, backing vocals

Barry Danielian: trumpet
Clark Gayton: trombone
Bill Holloman: tenor saxophone
Ed Manion: baritone saxophone
Curt Ramm: trumpet
Tom Timko: baritone saxophone
Strings: Rob Mathes (arranger and conductor);
  Lisa Kim (concertmaster); Kristi Helberg, Dasol
  Jeong, Kuan Cheng Lu, Joanna Maurer, Suzanne
  Ornstein, Su Hyun Park, Annaliesa Place, Sein
  Ryu, and Sharon Yamada (violins); Danielle
  Farina, Devin Moore, and Rebecca Young
  (violas); Patrick Jee, Clarice Jensen, and Sophie
  Shao (cellos)

Of course, Springsteen had come to know the feeling of loss and pain that comes with living and loving, including periods of depression when he must have truly felt the emotions expressed in this song, written by Bob Gaudio, which was a hit for the Walker Brothers in 1966. The song begins with the singer addressing the listener with a general description of how it feels to live without love. The song speaks to loneliness as "the cloak you wear" and describes the feeling as "a deep shade of blue that is always there." When one experiences loss through the end of a relationship, a broken friendship, physical separation, or the death of a loved one, it can color every aspect of one's daily existence. The song is descriptive of that feeling that "the sun ain't gonna shine anymore" and "the moon ain't gonna rise in the sky." It is only midway through that the singer indicates that he is addressing his girl directly, singing "Girl, I need you / I can't go on." After these lines the singer sings the chorus twice, followed by the titular refrain sung a half dozen times to end the song. It does not end with hope or offer any consolation, just the affirmation of the feeling that life, in any meaningful sense of the word at least, feels like it is over.

"Turn Back the Hands of Time"

Bruce Springsteen: vocals, lead guitar
Ron Aniello: drums, bass, percussion, guitar, piano,
  organ, vibes
Barry Danielian: trumpet
Clark Gayton: trombone
Bill Holloman: tenor saxophone
Lisa Lowell: backing vocals
Ed Manion: baritone saxophone
Michelle Moore: backing vocals
Curt Ramm: trumpet
Tom Timko: baritone saxophone
Soozie Tyrell: backing vocals
Strings: Rob Mathes (arranger and conductor);
  Lisa Kim (concertmaster); Kristi Helberg, Dasol
  Jeong, Kuan Cheng Lu, Joanna Maurer, Suzanne
  Ornstein, Su Hyun Park, Annaliesa Place, Sein
  Ryu, and Sharon Yamada (violins); Danielle
  Farina, Devin Moore, and Rebecca Young
  (violas); Patrick Jee, Clarice Jensen, and Sophie
  Shao (cellos)

It is here that the positioning of the songs on the album really begins to take on the feeling of a narrative structure. We are told from the outset of the album that "only the strong survive," preparing us for some trouble that might lie ahead. Then Springsteen takes us back in time to remind us of the great soul and R&B artists of the 1960s, who had so much to tell us and still speak to us of universal human emotions and experiences. The story then begins, unsurprisingly, with a love song that emphasizes just how much the main character in this story is devoted to his lover, answering the question "Do I Love You?" emphatically with "Indeed I Do." Then we encounter the initial breakup, in which the singer now feels like without his love his life is over and "The Sun Ain't Gonna Shine Anymore." Then after that initial shock, we get this song, with the singer having time to reflect on what went wrong and wishing he could "Turn Back the Hands of Time."

The song, a hit for Tyrone Davis in 1972, co-written by Bonnie Thompson and Jack Daniels, expresses sentiments similar to those in the previous song but it has a more joyful, hopeful sound with a stronger tempo and even some excitement in the voice of the singer. That excitement is attributable to the fact that in the song the singer is no longer living in the present moment but alternating between a past in which, if he could revisit it, he knows exactly what he would do, and "leaving would be the last thing on my mind,' and a future in which he asks his girl for "just one more try," returning to the promise made in "Do I Love You (Indeed I Do)" that "I'd be yours alone until the day I die and we'd have a love so divine." The title of the song, of course, indicates that this is not possible because everyone knows that we cannot "turn back the hands of time," as universal a wish as that might be.

CHART ACTION
Billboard Hot 100: did not chart.

"Turn Back the Hands of Time" was released on November 11, 2022. The number-one song that week was Nikki Minaj's "Super Freaky Girl."

"When She Was My Girl"
Bruce Springsteen: vocals, piano
Ron Aniello: drums, bass, percussion, guitar, piano, organ, glockenspiel, keyboards
Dennis Collins: backing vocals
Barry Danielian: trumpet
Clark Gayton: trombone
Bill Holloman: tenor saxophone
Curtis King Jr.: backing vocals
Ed Manion: baritone saxophone
Curt Ramm: trumpet
Fonzi Thornton: backing vocals
Tom Timko: baritone saxophone
Strings: Rob Mathes (arranger and conductor); Lisa Kim (concertmaster); Kristi Helberg, Dasol Jeong, Kuan Cheng Lu, Joanna Maurer, Suzanne Ornstein, Su Hyun Park, Annaliesa Place, Sein Ryu, and Sharon Yamada (violins); Danielle Farina, Devin Moore, and Rebecca Young (violas); Patrick Jee, Clarice Jensen, and Sophie Shao (cellos)

This song, and indeed most of the rest of the songs on the album as we will see, continues with the theme of lost love and in a way each song represents one of the five stages of grief identified by Elisabeth Kübler-Ross and David Kessler, though not in the order they postulated. Kübler-Ross and Kessler identified the five stages of grief as: denial, anger, bargaining, depression, and acceptance. But Springsteen, like any good psychologist, knows that life and emotions do not always conform to such neat patterns—we advance, regress, advance, and regress again. Using these categories, the first trilogy of the soul story Springsteen seems to be telling on the album moves from depression ("The Sun Ain't Gonna Shine Anymore") to bargaining ("If I Could Turn Back the Hands of Time") to acceptance ("When She Was My Girl)."

As we will see, the remaining songs revisit various emotions before returning to a more hopeful note at the end of the album. This song, released by the Four Tops in 1981 and cowritten by Larry Gottlieb and Marc Blatte, has a pleasant melody that is offset in this cover by the plaintive, aching sound of Springsteen's voice. Here the singer is not happy about the loss of his girl by any means and still resorts to thinking back to how good things were when they were together in contrast to how bad things are now. But he acknowledges acceptance of the fact that she is no longer his girl, while seeming to rejoice that he at least still possesses the pleasant memories of when she was.

"Hey, Western Union Man"

Bruce Springsteen: vocals
Ron Aniello: drums, bass, percussion, guitar, piano, organ, vibes, keyboards
Dennis Collins: backing vocals
Barry Danielian: trumpet
Clark Gayton: trombone
Bill Holloman: tenor saxophone
Curtis King Jr.: backing vocals
Rob Lebret: guitar
Ed Manion: baritone saxophone
Curt Ramm: trumpet
Fonzi Thornton: backing vocals
Tom Timko: baritone saxophone
Strings: Rob Mathes (arranger and conductor); Lisa Kim (concertmaster); Kristi Helberg, Dasol Jeong, Kuan Cheng Lu, Joanna Maurer, Suzanne Ornstein, Su Hyun Park, Annaliesa Place, Sein Ryu, and Sharon Yamada (violins); Danielle Farina, Devin Moore, and Rebecca Young (violas); Patrick Jee, Clarice Jensen, and Sophie Shao (cellos)

"Hey, Western Union Man" was a 1968 single by soul icon Jerry Butler, which he cowrote with Kenny Gamble and Leon Huff. In an age before email, voicemail, text messages, Federal Express, or Venmo, if you wanted to get a message, gift, or money transfer to someone quickly, one possibility would be to go downtown or the location of your nearest Western Union station and have them wire a message via telegram or wire money directly to an individual or to a business that would deliver the gift. Somewhat in the spirit of "Please Mr. Postman," the 1961 hit by the Marvelettes, later covered by the Beatles, the singer here pleads with an objective third party to come to the rescue of his broken heart.

Whereas the singer of "Please Mr. Postman" pleads to have a letter delivered, the singer of "Hey, Western Union Man," urges him to "hurry up, send a telegram," because he is in so much misery and cannot reach his lover on the phone. While you're at it, the singer pleads, "Send a box of candy too and maybe some flowers." The song, like "Please Mr. Postman," is not meant to be taken literally, of course, but is just a way for the singer to express the frustration of not hearing from or being able to contact the object of his romantic love and the sense of panic that comes with the realization that the relationship is probably over.

"I Wish It Would Rain"

Bruce Springsteen: vocals
Ron Aniello: drums, bass, percussion, guitar, piano, vibes
Dennis Collins: backing vocals
Barry Danielian: trumpet
Clark Gayton: trombone
Bill Holloman: tenor saxophone
Curtis King Jr.: backing vocals
Ed Manion: baritone saxophone
Curt Ramm: trumpet
Fonzi Thornton: backing vocals
Tom Timko: baritone saxophone
Strings: Rob Mathes (arranger and conductor); Lisa Kim (concertmaster); Kristi Helberg, Dasol Jeong, Kuan Cheng Lu, Joanna Maurer, Suzanne Ornstein, Su Hyun Park, Annaliesa Place, Sein Ryu, and Sharon Yamada (violins); Danielle Farina, Devin Moore, and Rebecca Young (violas); Patrick Jee, Clarice Jensen, and Sophie Shao (cellos)

Here Springsteen reprises the 1967 hit by the famous Motown group the Temptations, written by Barrett Strong, Norman Whitfield, and Roger Penzabene. Sometimes one has to wait until well into a song, or even until the end to discern its true or full meaning or message. In this case, the opening line of the song, preceded by a beautiful instrumental intro on the piano, sets the tone for the rest of the song. The first three words—"Sunshine, blue skies"—by themselves would evoke a completely different meaning if not sung in a soulful, pleading, somber key. However, if there were any doubt that these words meant something different to the singer than they would if spoken or sung normally, that is immediately removed when the singer follows with the injunction for them to "please go away." The singer is in no mood for sunshine or blue skies and if we are wondering why, we don't have to wait long because he immediately tells us, "My girl has found another, and gone astray."

In the remainder of the song, the singer elaborates on his feelings, expressed with heartfelt and sincere emotion throughout, serving one main purpose—to explain to his listener to whom he realizes "it might sound strange" that he wishes it would rain. There is often a parallel in popular music between raindrops and teardrops, both connoting sadness. In this song, one could also interpret the need to explain why the singer longs for rain as symbolizing his need to shed tears for, after all, he acknowledges, "Everybody knows that a man ain't supposed to cry," just as, unless we are farmers or in an areas suffering from drought, people generally prefer sunshine to rain, unlike our singer here.

"Don't Play That Song"

Bruce Springsteen: vocals, guitar
Ron Aniello: drums, bass, percussion, guitar, piano, organ, keyboards
Dennis Collins: backing vocals
Barry Danielian: trumpet
Clark Gayton: trombone
Bill Holloman: tenor saxophone
Curtis King Jr.: backing vocals
Ed Manion: baritone saxophone
Curt Ramm: trumpet
Fonzi Thornton: backing vocals
Tom Timko: baritone saxophone
Strings: Rob Mathes (arranger and conductor); Lisa Kim (concertmaster); Kristi Helberg, Dasol Jeong, Kuan Cheng Lu, Joanna Maurer, Suzanne Ornstein, Su Hyun Park, Annaliesa Place, Sein Ryu, and Sharon Yamada (violins); Danielle Farina,

Devin Moore, and Rebecca Young (violas); Patrick Jee, Clarice Jensen, and Sophie Shao (cellos)

So many soul and R&B songs deal with the troubles and pain that come from relationships that are either on the rocks or have recently ended. That is especially the case with most of the songs that appear on this album, especially after the first few tracks, which start the album on a more positive, upbeat note, accompanied by a bit of nostalgia. But starting with track 5, "The Sun Ain't Gonna Shine (Anymore)," the album takes on a more melancholy air, even though songs like "Turn Back the Hands of Time" and "When She Was My Girl" have a pop, upbeat sensibility to the music, if not the lyrics. While this is definitely not true of "I Wish It Would Rain," the contrast between music that sounds at least somewhat joyful and lyrics that belie the accompaniment applies especially in "Don't Play That Song," a song written by Ahmet Ertegun and Betty Nelson recorded by Ben E. King, of "Stand by Me" fame, in 1962.

Springsteen's version is louder and played with more enthusiasm than the original, which has a sadder, more plaintive air about it. Springsteen even opens the song with the spoken injunction, "Yeah, come on, let's get the band on," before launching into an inspired and passionate rendition. Unlike "I Wish It Would Rain," here the opening words convey exactly what they mean, that is, there is a particular song the singer does not wish to hear. We need to find out why he doesn't want to hear the song, but we can hazard a pretty good guess, which in this case would turn out to be correct, that it is because "it fills my heart with pain," even if at the same time "it brings back sweet memories." We can surmise that the reason Springsteen performs the song in a playful, lighthearted way is because of the way he feels about the song and the music, which makes him happy because here it is the song that "brings back sweet memories" without the accompanying pain that the song itself was originally meant to convey.

CHART ACTION
Billboard Hot 100: did not chart.

"Don't Play That Song" was released on October 28, 2022. The number-one song that week was Sam Smith and Kim Petras's "Unholy."

"Any Other Way"
Bruce Springsteen: vocals, guitar
Ron Aniello: drums, bass, guitar, piano, organ, keyboards
Barry Danielian: trumpet
Clark Gayton: trombone
Bill Holloman: tenor saxophone
Ed Manion: baritone saxophone
Curt Ramm: trumpet
Tom Timko: baritone saxophone

This forgotten and highly underrated gem by soul singer and songwriter William Bell appeared on the Stax record label in 1962. Springsteen did a great service on this album in not only including major hits by artists who remain well known but by reviving some great songs that even Baby Boomers might not be familiar with or remember. This song definitely falls into the great category, both musically and lyrically. The lyric is constructed beautifully, with the true meaning of the song implied but not certain in the opening verse but actually tucked into a single line that appears in about the middle of the song. The song opens with the singer approached by a friend of his ex, whom he suspects of wanting to find out how he is doing so they can report back to his former partner. He tells this "friend" that he is on to them and that they can report back that he is "doing great" and he wouldn't have it "any other way."

We suspect that the singer is lying, although the tone of the music and the expression in his voice do not presume the possibility that he is actually happier without someone who, for all we know, was deeply unpleasant. In the second verse, he denies the rumors that he has a broken heart and once again affirms that in truth, he wouldn't have it "any other way." It is in the third verse that he tells the friend that they had better leave, then expresses the same sentiment with some urgency, "I think you should go right now, or you might see a grown man cry." Like the singer of "I Wish It Would Rain," he knows that in the cultural ethos of the early 1960s, this is not something men are supposed to do. And, of course, he would not cry if he were being truthful throughout the rest of the song. Yet, even after this confession, he makes sure to tell the friend that they should still say, when asked, that he would not have it "any other way." Springsteen sings this song more in the spirit of the original than he did on "Don't Play That Song," though that was the exception rather than the rule on this album.

"I Forgot to Be Your Lover"
Bruce Springsteen: vocals
Ron Aniello: drums, bass, guitar, piano, glockenspiel, organ, keyboards
Barry Danielian: trumpet
Clark Gayton: trombone
Bill Holloman: tenor saxophone
Ed Manion: baritone saxophone
Sam Moore: harmony vocals
Curt Ramm: trumpet
Tom Timko: baritone saxophone
Strings: Rob Mathes (arranger and conductor); Lisa Kim (concertmaster); Kristi Helberg, Dasol Jeong, Kuan Cheng Lu, Joanna Maurer, Suzanne Ornstein, Su Hyun Park, Annaliesa Place, Sein Ryu, and Sharon Yamada (violins); Danielle Farina, Devin Moore, and Rebecca Young (violas); Patrick Jee, Clarice Jensen, and Sophie Shao (cellos)

Another song released by William Bell on the Stax label, this one in 1969, was cowritten by Bell and Booker T. Jones, the leader of the famed 1960s group Booker T and the MGs. The simple, straightforward, and familiar message of this song is an apology for taking one's lover or spouse for granted and focusing more on work and not enough on the relationship, followed by a promise to do better in the future. This song has fewer nuances than some of the other songs on the album, but what it lacks in lyrical creativity or poetic gymnastics is more than made up for by the soulful and heartfelt way in which the words and meaning of the song are expressed, both by Bell in the original and by Springsteen in this faithful cover version.

"7 Rooms of Gloom"

Bruce Springsteen: vocals
Ron Aniello: drums, bass, guitar, piano, Farfisa organ, vibraphone, organ
Dennis Collins: backing vocals
Barry Danielian: trumpet
Clark Gayton: trombone
Bill Holloman: tenor saxophone
Curtis King Jr.: backing vocals
Ed Manion: baritone saxophone
Curt Ramm: trumpet
Fonzi Thornton: backing vocals
Tom Timko: baritone saxophone

This 1967 song by the Four Tops was written by the renowned songwriting team of Brian Holland, Eddie Holland, and Lamont Dozier, who composed many of the familiar hits that emanated from Motown in its heyday in the 1960s. This song was an interesting choice for the album because it is not one of their better-known songs, nor was it one of the bigger hits for the group that recorded it. It is also harder to argue that it is an underrated or forgotten classic, but it does represent the subgenre known as "psychedelic soul," and perhaps Springsteen

wanted to include at least one song that fell into that category. Or perhaps he simply likes the song. None of this is to imply that it is any way a bad song. It engages the listener immediately with the singer almost shouting, "I see a house, a house of stone," while background singers foreshadow the rest of the song by singing simultaneously "Seven rooms, filled with gloom." The lead vocals are more spoken than sung as the singer acknowledges the expected reason why the house is filled with gloom; it is "a lonely house, 'cause now you're gone." In fact, the song suggests, it is not only not a home anymore, it is not even a house, or at least he cannot think of it that way. To him, it is just "7 rooms of gloom." The rest of the song is a plea for the absent lover to return and the inability of the singer to do anything meaningful until that happens. He spends his time watching the clock and has even painted all the windows black. All he wants to know, is "when are you coming back," a question repeated three times at the end of the song.

"What Becomes of the Brokenhearted?"

Bruce Springsteen: vocals
Ron Aniello: drums, bass, percussion, guitar, piano, vibes, timpani, chimes, organ
Dennis Collins: backing vocals
Barry Danielian: trumpet
Clark Gayton: trombone
Bill Holloman: tenor saxophone
Curtis King Jr.: backing vocals
Ed Manion: baritone saxophone
Curt Ramm: trumpet
Fonzi Thornton: backing vocals
Tom Timko: baritone saxophone
Strings: Rob Mathes (arranger and conductor); Lisa Kim (concertmaster); Kristi Helberg, Dasol Jeong, Kuan Cheng Lu, Joanna Maurer, Suzanne Ornstein, Su Hyun Park, Annaliesa Place, Sein Ryu, and Sharon Yamada (violins); Danielle Farina, Devin Moore, and Rebecca Young (violas); Patrick Jee, Clarice Jensen, and Sophie Shao (cellos)

It is interesting that even on this album of covers, there is a structure to the story the songs collectively tell that suggests why each song is placed where it is on the album. The title song that opens the album foreshadows the rest of the album in a way; because so many of the songs deal with pain and heartache, the opening song and the album are appropriately titled "Only the Strong Survive." Then we get a kind of introduction to the purpose of the album through the transcendently nostalgic songs "Soul Days" and "Night Shift." In track 4, we find a song proclaiming the singer's love for his partner in "Do I Love You (Indeed I Do)." Then we have a series of songs that deal with relationships that are either in the process of ending or have ended, a sequence that ends with "7 Rooms of Gloom," which concludes with the singer wanting to know when his love is coming back.

Since we can surmise that the answer, in most of these songs, is probably "never," it makes sense that the sequence from tracks 5 through 13 would be followed by a song asking the question, "What becomes of the broken-hearted?" This is another from 1967, this one written by James Dean, Paul Riser, and William Weatherspoon and which became the biggest hit for Jimmy Ruffin. Of course, the song never really answers the question, but regardless, the singer vows to never give up on love, to never stop searching for someone who will love him, confidently affirming "I'm gonna find my way," a phrase repeated half a dozen times at the end of the song. The note of hope on which this song ends leads then perfectly into the next, which, taken in isolation, seemed a strange one for Springsteen to cover but which has a double meaning that ties the whole album together.

"Someday We'll Be Together"

Bruce Springsteen: vocals
Ron Aniello: drums, bass, percussion, guitar, piano, organ, keyboards
Barry Danielian: trumpet
Clark Gayton: trombone
Bill Holloman: tenor saxophone
Curtis King Jr.: backing vocals
Lisa Lowell: backing vocals
Ed Manion: baritone saxophone
Curt Ramm: trumpet
Tom Timko: baritone saxophone
Soozie Tyrell: backing vocals
Strings: Rob Mathes (arranger and conductor); Lisa Kim (concertmaster); Kristi Helberg, Dasol Jeong, Kuan Cheng Lu, Joanna Maurer, Suzanne Ornstein, Su Hyun Park, Annaliesa Place, Sein Ryu, and Sharon Yamada (violins); Danielle Farina, Devin Moore, and Rebecca Young (violas); Patrick Jee, Clarice Jensen, and Sophie Shao (cellos)

Springsteen ends the album with this appropriate finale, a 1969 hit for Diana Ross and the Supremes written by Harvey Fuqua, Jackey Beavers, and Johnny Bristol. The first of the two meanings we mentioned above refers to the title line of the song, which could refer to a couple in a romantic relationship, as most of the songs on this album do, and thus it ends as a fitting and hopeful conclusion to an album that includes so many breakup songs. It follows logically the end of "What Becomes of the Brokenhearted?" and its affirmation that the singer will "find a way" to find love in the future even if it is lacking in the present. But the song could also refer to the breakup of a group, a common feature of the rock and pop music scene in the late 1960s and 1970s, which included the breakup of such iconic acts as the duo Simon and Garfunkel, the Fab Four known as the Beatles, and the trio that produced this, their last hit together, Diana Ross and the Supremes, originally known simply as the Supremes.

In the case of Springsteen, the second meaning most likely refers to the loss of previous band members such as Danny Federici and Clarence Clemons, as well as former bandmates, friends, and associates that so influenced his previous studio album, *Letter to You*. "Someday We'll Be Together" then is actually another breakup song, in which the singer admits their mistakes and laments that they have caused their relationship to fail, but both musically and lyrically it sounds more hopeful than melancholic, even though at one point the singer says that all they want to do is "cry, cry, cry." The song ends, as does "7 Rooms of Gloom," with the singer wishing for the lover to return, but this time the singer sounds much more confident that a happy reunion will ensue, at least at some point in the future.

Discography

This discography is based on Springsteen's US release history.

STUDIO ALBUMS

Greetings from Asbury Park, N.J. (Columbia, 1973)

The Wild, the Innocent and the E Street Shuffle (Columbia, 1973)

Born to Run (Columbia, 1975)

Darkness on the Edge of Town (Columbia, 1978)

The River (Columbia, 1980)

Nebraska (Columbia, 1982)

Born in the U.S.A. (Columbia, 1984)

Tunnel of Love (Columbia, 1987)

Human Touch (Columbia, 1992)

Lucky Town (Columbia, 1992)

The Ghost of Tom Joad (Columbia, 1995)

The Rising (Columbia, 2002)

Devils & Dust (Columbia, 2005)

We Shall Overcome: The Seeger Sessions (Columbia, 2006)

Magic (Columbia, 2007)

Working on a Dream (Columbia, 2009)

Wrecking Ball (Columbia, 2012)

High Hopes (Columbia, 2014)

Western Stars (Columbia, 2019)

Letter to You (Columbia, 2020)

Only the Strong Survive (Columbia, 2022)

SINGLES

"Blinded by the Light" b/w "The Angel" (Columbia, 1973)

"Spirit in the Night" b/w "For You" (Columbia, 1973)

"Born to Run" b/w "Meeting across the River" (Columbia, 1975)

"Tenth Avenue Freeze-Out" b/w "She's the One" (Columbia, 1975)

"Prove It All Night" b/w "Factory" (Columbia, 1978)

"Badlands" b/w "Streets of Fire" (Columbia, 1978)

"Hungry Heart" b/w "Held Up without a Gun" (Columbia, 1980)

"Fade Away" b/w "Be True" (Columbia, 1981)

"Dancing in the Dark" b/w "Pink Cadillac" (Columbia, 1984)

"Cover Me" b/w "Jersey Girl (live)" (Columbia, 1984)

"Born in the USA" b/w "Shut out the Light" (Columbia, 1984)

"I'm on Fire" b/w "Johnny Bye Bye" (Columbia, 1985)

"Glory Days" b/w "Stand on It" (Columbia, 1985)

"I'm Goin' Down" b/w "Janey, Don't Lose Your Heart" (Columbia, 1985)

"My Hometown" b/w "Santa Claus Is Comin' to Town (live)" (Columbia, 1985)

"War" b/w "Merry Christmas Baby" (Columbia, 1986)

"Fire" b/w "Incident on 57th Street (live)" (Columbia, 1987)

"Brilliant Disguise" b/w "Lucky Man" (Columbia, 1987)

"Tunnel of Love" b/w "Two for the Road" (Columbia, 1987)

"One Step Up" b/w "Roulette" (Columbia, 1988)

"Human Touch" b/w "Souls of the Departed" (Columbia, 1992)

"Better Days" b/w "Tougher Than the Rest (live)" (Columbia, 1992)

"57 Channels (and Nothin' On)," b/w "Part Man, Part Monkey" (Columbia, 1992)

"Streets of Philadelphia" b/w "If I Should Fall Behind" (Columbia, 1994)

"Murder Incorporated" (Columbia, 1995)

"Secret Garden" b/w "Thunder Road (live)" (Columbia, 1995)

"The Rising" b/w "Land of Hope and Dreams" (Columbia, 2002)

"Lonesome Day" (Columbia, 2002)

"Waitin' on a Sunny Day" (Columbia, 2003)

"Devils & Dust" (Columbia, 2005)

"All the Way Home" (Columbia, 2005)
"Radio Nowhere" (Columbia, 2007)
"Girls in Their Summer Clothes" (Columbia, 2008)
"My Lucky Day" (Columbia, 2008)
"Working on a Dream" (Columbia, 2008)
"The Wrestler" (Columbia, 2008)
"We Take Care of Our Own" (Columbia, 2012)
"Death to My Hometown" (Columbia, 2012)
"High Hopes" (Columbia, 2013)
"Hello Sunshine" (Columbia, 2019)
"Tucson Train" (Columbia, 2019)
"Letter to You" (Columbia, 2020)
"Ghosts" (Columbia, 2020)
"I'll See You in My Dreams" (Columbia, 2021)
"Do I Love You (Indeed I Do)" (Columbia, 2022)
"Nightshift" (Columbia, 2022)
"Don't Play That Song" (Columbia, 2022)
"Turn Back the Hands of Time" (Columbia, 2022)

LIVE ALBUMS

Live/1975–85 (Columbia, 1986)
In Concert/MTV Plugged (Columbia, 1993)
Live in New York City (Columbia, 2001)
Hammersmith Odeon London '75 (Columbia, 2006)

Live in Dublin (Columbia, 2007)
Live Archive Releases series (Columbia, 2014 to present)
Springsteen on Broadway (Columbia, 2018)
The Legendary 1979 No Nukes Concerts (Columbia, 2021)

COMPILATIONS AND RETROSPECTIVES

Greatest Hits (Columbia, 1995)
Tracks (Columbia, 1998)
18 Tracks (Columbia, 1999)
The Essential Bruce Springsteen (Columbia, 2008)
Greatest Hits (Columbia, 2009)
The Promise (Columbia, 2010)
The Ties that Bind (Columbia, 2015)
Chapter and Verse (Columbia, 2016)
Best of Bruce Springsteen (Columbia, 2024)

SOUNDTRACKS

Blinded by the Light: Original Motion Picture Soundtrack (Columbia, 2019)
Western Stars: Songs from the Film (Columbia, 2019)

Bibliography and Sources for Further Reading

Beviglia, Jim. *Counting Down Bruce Springsteen: His 100 Finest Songs*. Lanham, MD: Rowman and Littlefield, 2014.

Bruce Springsteen Collector's Edition. New York: Rolling Stone, 2022.

Burke, David. *Heart of Darkness: Bruce Springsteen's Nebraska*. London: Cherry Red, 2011.

Carlin, Peter Ames. *Bruce*. New York: Simon and Schuster, 2012.

Clemons, Clarence, and John Deo. *Big Man: Real Life and Tall Tales*. New York: Grand Central, 2009.

Cohen, Jonathan, and June Skinner Sawyers, eds. *Long Walk Home: Reflections on Bruce Springsteen*. New Brunswick: Rutgers University Press, 2019.

Cologne-Brookes, Gavin. *American Lonesome: The Work of Bruce Springsteen*. Baton Rouge: Louisiana State University Press, 2018.

Cross, Charles R. *Backstreets: Springsteen—The Man and His Music*. New York: Harmony, 1989.

Cullen, Jim. *Born in the U.S.A.: Bruce Springsteen and the American Tradition*. Middletown, CT: Wesleyan University Press, 2005.

Dolan, Marc. *Bruce Springsteen and the Promise of Rock 'n' Roll*. New York: Norton, 2012.

Eliot, Marc, with Mike Appel. *Down Thunder Road: The Making of Bruce Springsteen*. New York: Simon and Schuster, 1992.

Goldstein, Stan. *Rock 'n' Roll Tour of the Jersey Shore*. 4th ed. Self-published, NJ Rock Map, NJ, 2014.

Goodman, Fred. *The Mansion on the Hill: Dylan, Young, Geffen, Springsteen, and the Head-On Collision of Rock and Commerce*. New York: Vintage, 1998.

Guterman, Jimmy. *Runaway American Dream: Listening to Bruce Springsteen*. Cambridge, MA: Da Capo, 2005.

Harde, Roxanne, and Irwin Streight, editors. *Reading the Boss: Interdisciplinary Approaches to the Works of Bruce Springsteen*. Lanham, MD: Lexington, 2010.

Hiatt, Brian. *Bruce Springsteen: The Stories behind the Songs*. New York: Abrams, 2019.

Himes, Geoffrey. *33⅓: Born in the USA*. New York: Continuum, 2005.

Humphries, Patrick. *Bruce Springsteen*. London: Omnibus, 1996.

Kaye, Jessica, and Richard Brewer, eds. *Meeting across the River: Stories Inspired by the Haunting Song by Bruce Springsteen*. New York: Bloomsbury, 2005.

Kirkpatrick, Rob. *Magic in the Night: The Words and Music of Bruce Springsteen*. New York: St. Martin's, 2009.

Luerrsen, John D. *Springsteen FAQ: All That's Left to Know about the Boss*. New York: Backbeat, 2012.

MacLeod, Dewar. *Making the Scene in the Garden State; Popular Music in New Jersey from Edison to Springsteen and Beyond*. New Brunswick: Rutgers University Press, 2020.

Madden, Caroline. *Springsteen as Soundtrack: The Sound of the Boss in Film and Television*. Jefferson, NC: McFarland, 2020.

Mangione, Lorraine, and Donna Luff. *Mary Climbs In: The Journeys of Bruce Springsteen's Women Fans*. New Brunswick: Rutgers University Press, 2023.

Marsh, Dave. *Born to Run: The Bruce Springsteen Story*. New York: Doubleday, 1981.

———. *Two Hearts: The Definitive Biography, 1972–2003*. New York Routledge, 2004.

Massaro, John. *Shades of Springsteen: Politics, Love, Sports, and Masculinity*. New Brunswick: Rutgers University Press, 2021.

Masur, Louis P. *Runaway Dream: Born to Run and Bruce Springsteen's American Vision*. New York: Bloomsbury, 2009.

Monroe, Marty. *Springsteen: Back in the USA*. Wauwatosa, WI: Robus, 1984.

Neer, Richard. *FM: The Rise and Fall of Rock Radio*. New York: Random House, 2001.

Phillips, Christopher and Louis P. Masur, eds. *Talk about a Dream: The Essential Interviews of Bruce Springsteen*. New York: Bloomsbury, 2013.

Randall, Linda. *Finding Grace in the Concert Hall: Community and Meaning among Springsteen Fans*. Grove, IL: Waveland, 2011.

Sandford, Christopher. *Springsteen: Point Blank*. New York: Little, Brown, 1999.

Santelli, Robert. *Greetings from E Street: The Story of Bruce Springsteen and the E Street Band*. San Francisco: Chronicle, 2006.

——. *This Land Is Your Land: Woody Guthrie and the Journey of an American Folksong*. Philadelphia, PA: Running Press, 2012.

Sawyers, June Skinner, ed. *Racing in the Street: A Bruce Springsteen Reader*. New York: Penguin, 2004.

——. *Tougher than the Rest: 100 Best Bruce Springsteen Songs*. London: Omnibus, 2008.

Smith, Larry David. *Bob Dylan, Bruce Springsteen, and American Song*. Westport, CT: Praeger, 2002.

Springsteen, Bruce. *Born to Run*. New York: Simon and Schuster, 2016.

——. *Songs*. New York: William Morrow, 1998. Rev. ed., New York: HarperCollins, 2003.

——. *VH1 Storytellers*. DVD, 2005.

St. John, Allen. "Bruce Springsteen's Favorite Guitar: The Story Behind One-of-a-Kind Fender." *Rolling Stone*, October 16, 2016.

Sweeting, Adam. *Springsteen: Visions of America*. London: Horborn, 1985.

White, Ryan. *Springsteen: Album by Album*. New York: Sterling, 2014.

Wolff, William I., ed. *Bruce Springsteen and Popular Music*. New York: Routledge, 2018.

Womack, Kenneth, and Eileen Chapman, eds. "Darkness on the Edge of Town: Hard Truths in Hard Rock Settings." Special issue, *Interdisciplinary Literary Studies* 21, no.1 (2019).

Womack, Kenneth, Jerry Zolten, and Mark Bernard, eds. *Bruce Springsteen, Cultural Studies, and the Runaway American Dream*. London: Routledge, 2012.

Yadin-Israel, Azzan. *The Grace of God and the Grace of Man: The Theologies of Bruce Springsteen*. Halifax: Lingua, 2016.

Zimny, Thom, dir. *The Promise: The Making of Darkness on the Edge of Town*. Sony, 2010.

——. *Wings for Wheels: The Making of Born to Run*. Sony, 2005.

INTERNET RESOURCES

BruceBase. Comprehensive website devoted to Springsteen's life and times. brucebase.wikidot.com.

Bruce Springsteen's Lyrics. Detailed compendium of Springsteen's lyrics. https://www.springsteenlyrics.com.

"Current Holdings." Bibliography of primary and secondary materials associated with the study of Springsteen and his circle. brucespringsteenspecialcollection.monmouth.edu/current-holdings/.

Acknowledgments

An undertaking of this nature and scope depends upon the generosity of a vast number of friends and colleagues, who have included Steven Bachrach, John Christopher, Chris DeRosa, Mike Farragher, Furg, Dave Golland, Susan Goulding, J. P. Hanly, Pamela Scott Johnson, Jon Landau, Pat Leahy, Nancy Mezey, Nicole Michael, Mike Plodwick, Joe Rapolla, Joe Riccardello, David Tripold, Rich Veit, Kurt Wagner, George Wurzbach, and Azzan Yadin-Israel. The efforts of our colleagues at the Bruce Springsteen Archives and Center for American Music, especially Bob Santelli, Eileen Chapman, Syd Whalley, Jeri Houseworth, and Melissa Ziobro are especially valued. We are particularly grateful for the enthusiasm and vision provided Peter Mickulas, our editor at Rutgers University Press, as well as the meticulous work done by production editor Vincent Nordhaus and undergraduate assistant Laura Lassen. We appreciate the efforts of the editorial team, especially Angela Piliouras and Michael Durnin.

We humbly thank the students in our undergraduate Bruce Springsteen seminars at Monmouth University for being a constant fount of inspiration. James Brodowski merits special mention for his research on the geographical locations in Springsteen's work, as does graduate research assistant Jennifer Rivera for providing vital editorial expertise. This book would not have been possible without the determination and expertise of Carlee Migliorisi, who worked tirelessly on behalf of this project. Her efforts were supported by a Creativity and Research Grant from Monmouth University.

As always, we are indebted to our wives, Jeanine and Millie, for sharing our journeys down the Tunnel of Love.

Index of Songs

About the Authors

KENNETH WOMACK, professor of English and popular music at Monmouth University, New Jersey, is one of the world's foremost writers and thinkers about the Beatles. In addition to such titles as *Long and Winding Roads: The Evolving Artistry of the Beatles* (2007), the *Cambridge Companion to the Beatles* (2009), and *The Beatles Encyclopedia: Everything Fab Four* (2014), he is the author of a two-volume biography devoted to the life and work of Beatles producer George Martin, including *Maximum Volume* (2017) and *Sound Pictures* (2018). His latest Beatles-related books include *Solid State: The Story of Abbey Road and the End of the Beatles* (2019), *John Lennon 1980: The Last Days in the Life* (2020), and *Living the Beatles Legend: The Untold Story of Mal Evans* (2023). Womack serves as the Music Culture critic for *Salon*, for which he hosts the *Everything Fab Four* podcast.

KENNETH L. CAMPBELL is a professor of History at Monmouth University, where he teaches courses on the Beatles and Bruce Springsteen, in addition to a variety of undergraduate and graduate courses in British, Irish, and European history. He is a past recipient of Monmouth University's Distinguished Teacher Award. He has written and edited a number of books on various topics, including *The Beatles and the 1960s: Reception, Revolution, and Social Change* and *American Popular Culture and the Beatles*. He is currently working on a book titled *Unveiling the Global Sixties: Social Movements, Cultural Change and International Revolution*.